THE GRIEF OF INFLUENCE

The Grief of Influence

Sylvia Plath and Ted Hughes

HEATHER CLARK

OXFORD
UNIVERSITY PRESS

SOUTH HUNTINGTON
PUBLIC LIBRARY
HUNTINGTON STATION, NY 11746

811.54
Plath
C

OXFORD
UNIVERSITY PRESS

Great Clarendon Street, Oxford OX2 6DP

Oxford University Press is a department of the University of Oxford.
It furthers the University's objective of excellence in research, scholarship,
and education by publishing worldwide in

Oxford New York

Auckland Cape Town Dar es Salaam Hong Kong Karachi
Kuala Lumpur Madrid Melbourne Mexico City Nairobi
New Delhi Shanghai Taipei Toronto

With offices in

Argentina Austria Brazil Chile Czech Republic France Greece
Guatemala Hungary Italy Japan Poland Portugal Singapore
South Korea Switzerland Thailand Turkey Ukraine Vietnam

Oxford is a registered trade mark of Oxford University Press
in the UK and in certain other countries

Published in the United States
by Oxford University Press Inc., New York

© Heather Clark 2011

The moral rights of the author have been asserted
Database right Oxford University Press (maker)

First published 2011

All rights reserved. No part of this publication may be reproduced,
stored in a retrieval system, or transmitted, in any form or by any means,
without the prior permission in writing of Oxford University Press,
or as expressly permitted by law, or under terms agreed with the appropriate
reprographics rights organization. Enquiries concerning reproduction
outside the scope of the above should be sent to the Rights Department,
Oxford University Press, at the address above

You must not circulate this book in any other binding or cover
and you must impose the same condition on any acquirer

British Library Cataloguing in Publication Data

Data available

Library of Congress Cataloging in Publication Data

Library of Congress Control Number: 2010936872

Typeset by SPI Publisher Services, Pondicherry, India
Printed in Great Britain
on acid-free paper by
MPG Books Group, Bodmin and King's Lynn

ISBN 978–0–19–955819–3

1 3 5 7 9 10 8 6 4 2

In Memoriam
Emily Clark Holcomb

Let love
Be the light that shows again
The blossom to the root.

—Eavan Boland, "Tree of Life"

Contents

List of Abbreviations

CPH	*Collected Poems of Ted Hughes*
CPP	*Collected Poems of Sylvia Plath*
JP	*Johnny Panic and the Bible of Dreams*
L	*Letters of Ted Hughes*
WP	*Winter Pollen: Occasional Prose*
J	*Journals of Sylvia Plath, 1950-1962,* ed. Karen Kukil
LH	*Letters Home*
Emory	Manuscript, Archives, and Rare Book Library, Emory University
Lilly	Lilly Library, Indiana University
Smith	Mortimer Rare Book Room, Smith College

Acknowledgments

First and foremost, I thank the US National Endowment for the Humanities for a year-long research fellowship that enabled me to work solely on this book. Others who provided invaluable help along the way include Steve Enniss and Kathy Shoemaker at Emory University's MARBL, Karen Kukil at Smith College's Rare Book Room, and the librarians at the Lilly Library, the British Library, and the Huntington Library. Thanks to Marlboro College and Emory University for research grants that helped fund my trips to Ted Hughes's and Sylvia Plath's archives; I am also grateful to the Huntington for providing an ideal place to write during my NEH fellowship year. Thanks also to Marlboro College's Dean of Faculty, Felicity Ratté, for allowing me to take a pre-tenure leave to work on this book, and for offering me support after my daughter, Isabel, was born; to my colleagues at Marlboro, particularly Catherine O'Callaghan and Gloria Biamonte, who have indulged my interest in Plath and Hughes over the years; Tim Kendall for his insightful suggestions regarding the manuscript; Jon Stallworthy for his continual support and encouragement; Andrew McNeillie at Oxford University Press for commissioning the project; Jacqueline Baker for her help in the final stages; and the Plath and Hughes Estates for allowing me to quote generously from published and unpublished material. As always, my most heartfelt thanks goes to my husband, Nathan Holcomb.

Brooklyn, New York   H.C.
January 2010

Introduction

In January of 1961, Ted Hughes and Sylvia Plath were interviewed by BBC commentator Owen Leeming about their marriage and their poetry in a radio broadcast entitled "Two of a Kind: Poets in Partnership." Plath and Hughes must have guessed that Leeming would question them about their influence on each other's poetry, yet when he did so, both seemed caught off guard. When he asked whether there was anything in their collections "to" or "about" each other apart from the dedications, Plath responded with an unusually muddled answer—one that revealed her deep anxiety and ambivalence about the very nature of poetic "partnership" itself:

Well I think that all the poems that we wrote to each other and about each other were really before our marriage, and then something happened, I don't know what it was, I hope it was all to the good, but we began to be able to, well, somehow free ourselves for other subjects and I think the dedications, at least as far as mine goes, I feel that I'd never be writing as I am, and as much as I am, without Ted's understanding and cooperation, really.

(Hughes and Plath: 1961)

Plath here dismisses those poems she and Hughes wrote to each other before their marriage as somehow less substantial than the work that came later, presumably after they were able to "free" themselves and their poems from each other's influence. She is vague about how they were able to attain this freedom ("something happened, I don't know what"), and not entirely certain that it was for the best ("I hope it was all to the good"). When she says that her success is due to Hughes, she seems to contradict her earlier claim that the marriage was poetically liberating; she rushes in to credit Hughes's influence the moment she declares herself free of it.

The two poets continued to send contradictory messages about their collaborative relationship throughout the interview. Hughes says that he and Plath have "a single, shared mind," "a telepathic union" that is "a source of a great deal" in his poetry, but then emphasizes that when they "happen" to write about the same subject, they always approach it differently. Plath says Hughes inspired her to become more interested in nature, but becomes defensive when Leeming remarks that she and Hughes write about nature in similar ways. Clearly uncomfortable with this observation, she says "this was true of our poems before we ever knew each other" and reiterates that their work is "really quite, quite different."

The fact that both Plath and Hughes at turns embrace and reject each other's influence should come as no surprise, for both were wary of being, in Plath's words, "made by" the other (*J* 401).[1] Following the poets' lead, Plath and Hughes critics also offer conflicting views on the extent to which the poets influenced one another. Margaret Dickie Uroff, author of the only previous full-length study of poetic influence between Plath and Hughes, insists that their poems should be read "as parts of a continuing debate about the nature of the universe, in which Plath's reservations and Hughes's assertions play against each other" (12). Uroff sees Plath's "interest in psychological states and extreme human experiences" as similar to Hughes's "concern with the non-human cosmos" (13), and argues that they influenced each other in equal measure, albeit at different stages of their poetic development. Yet Uroff's claims have been largely ignored by other Plath scholars who have questioned Hughes's editorial decisions concerning Plath's posthumous publications—particularly his decisions to rearrange Plath's *Ariel* manuscript and burn her last journal, his labeling of her pre-Cambridge work juvenilia, and his insistence that her "real self" appeared only in the *Ariel* poems.[2] Hughes critics, angered by these claims and determined to defend Hughes, tend to dismiss Plath's influence upon his work.

Missing from these scholars' discussions is a thorough analysis of the ways in which Plath and Hughes looted each other's poems. Of course, many studies of Plath and Hughes have argued that each influenced the other; indeed, mutual influence is by now taken for granted. Susan Van Dyne, for example, has written that "Plath's dialogue with Hughes's poems is always competitive and her strategy revisionary" (1993: 40), while Diane Middlebrook has commented upon "the call-and-response manner of their productive collusion" (2003: 191). Yet such claims are rarely substantiated with close intertextual analysis. For example, few critics, apart from Uroff, have examined the frequent allusions to *The Hawk in the Rain* and *Lupercal* in *Ariel*.[3] Plath's separation from Hughes has long been discussed as a factor in the creation of *Ariel*, yet when we consider how often Plath incorporates Hughesian motifs in these poems, we might begin to reconsider to what extent she had truly succeeded in breaking away from his influence. Although her ability to refute, resist, problematize, and interrogate many of Hughes's poetic motifs resulted in innovation rather than mere imita-tion, the idea that Plath's late poems "freed" her from Hughes needs to be

---

[1] Plath wrote, "We are amazingly compatible. But I must be myself—make myself & not let myself be made by him" (*J* 401).

[2] These critics include Marjorie Perloff, Susan Van Dyne, Jacqueline Rose, and Lynda Bundtzen.

[3] Middlebrook briefly addresses Hughes's influence in *Her Husband*, insisting that *Ariel* was "aimed at Hughes" (218). She recognizes that Plath's original *Ariel* manuscript contained forty-one poems, the same number in Hughes's *Lupercal*, and posits that the word "Ariel" was an echo of "Lupercal" (218). See also Paul Bentley's " 'Hitler's Familiar Spirits': Negative Dialectics in Sylvia Plath's 'Daddy' and Ted Hughes's 'Hawk Roosting,' " *Critical Survey* 12.3 (2000): 27–38.

qualified. While several Plath scholars have recently looked at the dialogue between Hughes's *Birthday Letters* and Plath's poems, the connections in Hughes's earlier work, particularly *Crow*, are still generally ignored.

This reluctance to acknowledge mutual influence may be due to the fact that many Plath scholars regard Hughes with hostility and are uncomfortable with the idea that he may have influenced Plath's remarkable late poems. For example, Van Dyne, a feminist critic, has claimed, "Plath's fondest fiction about her relationship with Hughes was that it was a mutually beneficial collaboration" (1993: 19). At the other end of the critical spectrum, Hughes scholar Keith Sagar has written, "His was the stronger, surer poetic voice, and the immediate effect [on Plath] was of ventriloquism" (qtd. in Brain 2001: 91).[4] Hughes, in fact, anticipated the difficulties involved in studying mutual influence between himself and Plath. When in 1987 Lucas Myers sent him a draft of a memoir about their early years at Cambridge, in which he discussed Plath's and Hughes's poetic dialogue, Hughes asked Myers to remove the entire section:

No doubt Sylvia & I plundered each other merrily—but if you say it, in my words—God, what new theses of accusation, what Job-loads of righteous wrath! If you say that, our generous readers will multiply it by ten. Your balancing statement, that she profited a little from me, will be reduced to one tenth. That's the biological 1st law of human malice in action. It's no good for me to say I designed prototypes, which she put into full Germanic production—though there's truth in it. I would never be believed. But to say I stole from her—that would be an instant religion of verification, & my wretched undated efforts would reveal the new gospel, under compulsion. (*L* 536)

To suggest that Plath borrowed from Hughes or that Hughes borrowed from Plath, however, does not diminish their individual achievements; on the contrary, reading these poets side by side (indeed, they often wrote back to back) reveals that the two engaged in a long and intense dialogue fueled by both rivalry and grief. Yet such an interpretation of the couple's literary relationship remains controversial, for what Uroff argued in 1979 is still by and large true today: "the critical effort to get behind these legends and assess the poems has tended to regard the two writers as figures isolated from each other, responsive only to the inner compulsions of their independent spirits" (vii).[5] As Sarah Churchwell more recently put it, "critical gamesmanship does not allow for the private

---

[4] As Tracy Brain has written, "Hughes, the reasoning seems to go, cannot be good if she is not bad. One cannot help suspect, reading Keith Sagar's work, that Plath simply cannot do anything right" (2003: 177).

[5] The exception to this trend is Diane Middlebrook's *Her Husband*, which many critics agreed was the most balanced biographical portrait of the two writers to date. See, for example, the following reviews of *Her Husband*: Christina Nehring, "Domesticated Goddess," *Atlantic Monthly* (April 2004): 120–6; Jeffery Meyers, "Terminator: The Legacy of Ted Hughes," *Virginia Quarterly Review* 80.2 (Spring 2004): 219–32; Sarah Churchwell, "Love at the Barre," *Times Literary Supplement* (17 December 2004); Richard Whittington-Egan, "Ted Hughes and Sylvia Plath—A Marriage Examined," *Contemporary Review* 286.1669 (February 2005): 117–19.

possibility that both Plath and Hughes abandoned each other at various times in their lives and with tragic effect, but that their public (published) writings do not abandon each other" (1998: 108).

This critical gamesmanship has a volatile history. Jacqueline Rose has convincingly argued that "Plath has generated a form of 'psychotic' criticism" (14), not only among her hostile critics but also among mentors such as Al Alvarez and Robert Lowell.[6] She claims that such critics have treated Plath, in the words of Stephen Spender, as a "priestess cultivating her hysteria" (17), and has shown that "No writer more than Plath has been more clearly hystericised by the worst of a male literary tradition" (28). But if Plath has been bruised by the male literary tradition, Hughes has fared no better at the hands of feminist critics, who tend to see him as the embodiment of a violent, even fascist imagination. Indeed, critics who refuse to treat Plath as "a clinical case" (Rose 16) and instead find in her poetry a narrative of liberation can be quite harsh in their writings about Ted Hughes.[7] Steven Axelrod, for example, claimed that Hughes "unconsciously sought to keep [Plath] weak, subordinate, distant, and injured" (182–3), that he had a "hidden agenda for his wife" (154), that she willingly adopted the poetic identity he bestowed upon her (154), and that she "was strongly attracted to Hughes as a sort of dominator—one who could overmatch her in wildness and thereby domesticate her" (191). Bundtzen called Plath's relationship with Hughes "masochistic" (2001: 23), Sandra Gilbert and Susan Gubar referred to him as an "antagonist" (1994: 3.302), Sarah Churchwell called him "tyrannical" (1998: 117), while Perloff angrily criticized his editorial stewardship of Plath's work. The most infamous attack on Hughes came from the radical feminist poet Robin Morgan, who famously accused him of "murdering" Plath in her poem "The Arraignment." As Nathalie Anderson has written, "This for many quite ordinary, unimaginative, non-vindictive people, is the accepted wisdom: Hughes kills. Hughes is inimical—no, downright dangerous to women" (91). In a sense, these critics have embraced Plath's bitter late reading of Hughes (Hughes as "vampire" or "man in black"), just as critics hostile to Plath have amplified the more troubling notions of Hughes's late reading of Plath (Plath as hysteric, oracular high priestess, or Electra). Such positions help explain why there have been so few studies of mutual influence between Plath and Hughes: in a sense, the critics are replicating the same rivalry that existed between the poets themselves.

Anyone who has read Sylvia Plath's unsettling journals knows that she was an extraordinarily competitive woman who constantly compared herself to roommates, boyfriends, co-workers, doctors, professors, and—especially—other female writers. As she candidly confessed in 1959, "I want the world's praise, money & love, and am furious with anyone, especially with anyone I know or has

---

[6] Christina Britzolakis writes that for these critics, "madness and suicide became the telos and ultimate meaning of Plath's career" (2).

[7] These critics include Susan Van Dyne, Steven Axelrod, and Marjorie Perloff.

Plath's anxieties about collaboration surfaced again in 1961 during the BBC "Poets in Partnership" interview, when Owen Leeming noted similarities in the couple's work. When Plath protested that their poems were "quite, quite different," Leeming responded:

I don't think they're as different as all that. I think your—the type of contortion, the way that the line rides over into the next, for instance, the sort of technical trick of vigor—the way you use syntax, words. Also, you both have a concern, I think, with the animal creation, not that other poets don't, and also with a type of rural landscape and the way you use it is very similar I think.

Plath was quick to retort:

this was true in our poems really before we even knew each other or met each other. And in that sense we would probably be alike—if we are at all alike—whether we had even encountered each other and so I don't think that this is a result of our meeting, this is something that went on before. I mean, we were writing for ten years before we ever heard of each other.... And the kind of toughness and knottiness that we admire, both of us, I think is, again, something we've always... always admired. And perhaps that's why we met in the first place [laughs] because we both felt that we had similar interests.   (Plath and Hughes: 1961)

While Plath is clearly uncomfortable addressing the subject of influence—she does not want to present herself as Hughes's disciple, nor suggest that he is hers—her explanation cannot be reduced to mere defensive posturing, for she is correct when she says that both she and Hughes shared similar aesthetic leanings before their relationship began. Yet these similarities were a source of deep anxiety for both. It would be Plath's and Hughes's fate to downplay *and* emphasize their shared poetic preoccupations, as they did throughout the "Poets in Partnership" interview. On the one hand they were careful to present a united, anti-Movement front and to campaign on the BBC and elsewhere for a new direction in British poetry. On the other, they needed to prove to themselves and each other that they possessed full ownership of their respective voices. This was a precarious balancing act that both would find increasingly difficult to sustain.

Harold Bloom has defined the push-pull relationship between living and dead poets as "the paradox of the precursor's implicit charge to the ephebe": " 'Be me but not me' " (1973: 70). In Plath's and Hughes's case, each directed this charge toward the other, a fact that differentiates their relationship from Bloom's hierarchy of dead precursor over living ephebe. Ultimately, it was in both Plath's and Hughes's interest to distinguish one's work from the other's; this is part of the reason critics have discerned more differences than similarities between the two. And of course, critics now seek to protect each poet's turf from the other's as much as the poets did when they were alive. Yet it is a mistake to ignore the "similar interests" that Plath says she shared with Hughes. As Plath told her mother, she and Hughes were "alone, really alone... among young modern poets"—few shared their commitment to "the great subjects of life: love, death, war."[18]

Their interest in those "great subjects" had roots in the work of Schopenhauer, Nietzsche, and especially Lawrence, who influenced Plath's and Hughes's thinking about individualism, creativity, and the will. These thinkers' metaphors of violence, which they used to elucidate the struggle of the animal or the individual for dominance, had a powerful grip upon the young poets determined to exert their own artistic wills. Their influences partially account for Plath's and Hughes's repeated explorations of competition, struggle, and war in their poetry, as well as for why both were determined to expose what they believed to be the weak, fraudulent nature of Movement verse. Their shared interests and influences also help explain Plath's and Hughes's attraction, and why each came to see the other as an embodiment of an aesthetic as much as a real person—"chapters in a mythology" (1966: 81), as Hughes once put it. For Plath, Hughes was part Heathcliff, part Oliver Mellors, and part *übermensch*. As she wrote in her journal in April 1956, "in my mind I am ripped to bits by the words he welds and wields... let him run, reap, rip—and glory in the temporary sun of his ruthless force" (567; 570); Hughes's poems and person were "strong and blasting like a high wind in steel girders" (*J* 212). For Hughes, Plath was an American Connie Chatterley, trapped by her stifling bourgeois upbringing and longing to tap into her "blood-consciousness." He encouraged Plath to release and harness her violent energy, as he recalled in "The Minotaur," a *Birthday Letters* poem that recounts the day Plath smashed his writing table in a fit of jealousy:

> "Marvellous!" I shouted, "Go on,
> Smash it into kindling.
> That's the stuff you're keeping out of your poems!"
> And later, considered and calmer,
>
> "Get that shoulder under your stanzas
> And we'll be away."   (*CPH* 1120)

Such encouragement exemplified Hughes's preference for a "strong," masculine aesthetic. But Plath had already embraced such an aesthetic before she met Hughes, for, like him, she had been profoundly influenced by D. H. Lawrence.

Plath and Hughes had each fallen under Lawrence's sway as adolescents in the 1950s, when his reputation was at its height (Feinstein 76). According to Diane Middlebrook, Hughes told Al Alvarez that he was "besotted with" Lawrence (2003: 141), who provided an aesthetic and erotic reference point for the two lovers. As Middlebrook notes, Plath's and Hughes's common, Lawrentian vocabulary underlay their first meeting:

---

[18] Sylvia Plath to Aurelia Plath, March 18, 1957, Lilly.

Hughes had read Lawrence avidly in his teens, and Lawrence's notorious celebration of "blood consciousness" appears undisguised in this poem ["Law in the Country of Cats"] that Plath picked out to memorize. Plath had read the same books, and had undergone a similar literary infatuation with Lawrence—she couldn't miss the allusion. . . . When he kissed her, when she bit him, they were acting out a scene of primitive impulsiveness that would have been at home in one of Lawrence's novels. (2003: 4–5)

Lawrence's work embodied values that both poets sought to live by: like him, they felt society sought to sunder the imaginative and physical inner self from the respectable but repressed outer self. While Hughes was more confident than Plath about his ability to live without money, friends, or even a fixed abode, she too was determined to devote her life to her art, even if this meant following the Lawrences and the Joyces to "exile" on the Continent. Like Lawrence, the couple came to see teaching as an unsuitable alternative to writing full time, and gave up comfortable careers in academia in order to perfect their craft. Their determination to direct all of their energy into writing shows the extent to which they had assimilated, early on, Lawrentian and Nietzschean ideas about the importance of the individual will struggling to pursue its own course.

Plath's and Hughes's reading of Lawrence exposed them to Lawrence's main philosophical influences, Schopenhauer and Nietzsche.[19] Nietzsche's conception of the striving will, which he believed was central to man's vitality, shaped a number of Lawrentian characters: the philosopher's pronouncement in *Thus Spoke Zarathustra* that "to *will* this way which man has walked blindly, and to affirm it, and no longer to sneak away from it like the sick and decaying" (144) defines, for example, the mindset of Gerald Crich in *Women in Love*, one of Plath's favorite novels. Crich, in his position as the head of the local coal mining industry, is a living manifestation of Nietzsche's will to power:

The sufferings and feelings of individuals did not matter in the least. They were mere conditions, like the weather. What mattered was the pure instrumentality of the individual. As a man as of a knife: does it cut well? Nothing else mattered. . . . The will of man was the determining factor. Man was the archgod of earth. His mind was obedient to serve his will. Man's will was the absolute, the only absolute. (246)

While Schopenhauer's understanding of the will was more pessimistic than Nietzsche's (and, subsequently, Lawrence's), his "gladiatorial view of existence" and emphasis on life as never-ending "conflict, cruelty and suffering" (Milton 6) also profoundly influenced Lawrence.

Perhaps the most important lesson Lawrence took from Schopenhauer and Nietzsche was skepticism toward rationalism, which both philosophers believed had

---

[19] Lawrence's friend Jessie Chambers remembered him reading and discussing Nietzsche during his first year at the University of Nottingham in 1907–8: "I began to hear about the 'Will to Power', and perceived that he had come upon something new and engrossing." She felt that "the Lawrence who came out of College at the end of two years was a different man from the Lawrence who entered" on account of his serious engagement with Nietzsche and Schopenhauer (qtd. in Milton 3).

severed man from his primal instincts. (Freud and Jung, also important influences on Plath's and Hughes's thinking, shared this view.) Schopenhauer had declared that "with the appearance of reason, this certainty and infallibility of the will's manifestations . . . are almost entirely lost. Instinct withdraws altogether; deliberation, now supposed to take the place of everything, begets . . . irresolution and uncertainty" (*World* 1: 151–2; Eddins 98). Nietzsche echoed this idea in *On the Genealogy of Morals* when he wrote that "the greatest and most disastrous of maladies, of which humanity has not to this day been cured" was "his sickness of himself, brought on by the violent severance from his animal past . . . by his declaration of war against the old instincts that had hitherto been the foundation of his power, his joy, and his awesomeness" (153). Lawrence sought to prove the philosophers' view that rationalism had cut man off from his deepest unconscious instincts. As Rupert Birkin tells Ursula and Hermione in *Women in Love*, "You've got to lapse out before you can know what sensual reality is, lapse into unknowingness, and give up your volition. You've got to do it. You've got to learn not-to-be, before you can come into being" (42).[20] For Lawrence, as for Nietzsche, the need to accept and cultivate the apocalyptic, Dionysian instinct was the key to living fully, creatively, and in synchronicity with one's true desires. It was an ideal that appealed intensely to Plath and Hughes.

"POSITIVE VIOLENCE": HUGHES, LAWRENCE, AND SCHOPENHAUER

Hughes began reading Lawrence "at an impressionable age" (Faas 1980: 203); as he told Ekbert Faas, "Lawrence I read entire in my teens . . . except for all but a few of the poems. His writings coloured a whole period of my life" (1980: 202).[21] From Lawrence Hughes learned, as Elaine Feinstein notes, a "rich awareness of the physical world"; he "confirmed Ted's respect for primitive instinct as a means of preserving his own inner being" (18). Lawrence's influence is particularly pronounced in Hughes's early work: "Wind" invokes elements of Lawrence's "Discord in Childhood," while Lawrence's animal poems are a clear influence on *The Hawk in the Rain* and *Lupercal*. Hughes's "Pike," for instance, alludes heavily to Lawrence's "Fish." In Lawrence's poem, the speaker silently observes the wild, primeval creature:

> A slim young pike, with smart fins
> And grey-striped suit, a young cub of a pike
> Slouching along away below, half out of sight,
> Like a lout on an obscure pavement . . .

---

[20] Even though Lawrence would eventually quarrel with Nietzsche in *Aaron's Rod*, his incorporation *and* rejection of Nietzschean motifs does not nullify Nietzsche's influence on his work. As John Burt Foster writes, "Lawrence has an uncommon need to present the philosopher as a rival if he must hide his role as a model with such deceptive mystifications" (182).

[21] Faas's ellipses.

Aha, there's somebody in the know!

But watching closer
That motionless deadly motion,
That unnatural barrel body, that long ghoul nose, . . .
I left off hailing him.

I had made a mistake, I didn't know him,
This grey, monotonous soul in the water,
This intense individual in shadow,
Fish-alive.

I didn't know his God,
I didn't know his God.   (1986: 146–7)[22]

"That motionless deadly motion" brings to mind Schopenhauerian ideas about nature in static conflict, but the poem is more Nietzschean in its celebration of the "intense individual" life of the "Fish-alive." Presumably, the fish's god is not man's, but pre-Christian and primordial. Lawrence may be attempting to wrest the symbol of the fish from its association with Christianity and instead link it with the instinctive unconscious, or "the will," that lies below the surface.

Likewise, in "Pike," Hughes's speaker stands apart from the pike, carefully observing:

Pike too immense to stir, so immense and old
That past nightfall I dared not cast

But silently cast and fished
With the hair frozen on my head
For what might move, for what eye might move.
The still splashes on the dark pond,

Owls hushing the floating woods
Frail on my ear against the dream
Darkness beneath night's darkness had freed,
That rose slowly towards me, watching.   (*CPH* 85–6)

Like Lawrence, Hughes suggests a barrier between his outer self and his inner "depths." Yet by acknowledging the pike's strangeness, his speaker, like Lawrence's, comes closer to an understanding of his own buried instinctual life—"Darkness beneath night's darkness." Hughes and Lawrence both intimate that what lies "half out of sight"—the intuitive instincts from which modern man has been severed—may most illuminate the way forward. (Hughes included a copy of "Pike" along with Lawrence's *The Rainbow* and *Lady Chatterley's Lover* in an August 1958 letter to his brother Gerald, in which he exhorted him to read Lawrence's short stories.)[23]

---

[22] Lawrence's ellipses.
[23] Ted Hughes to Gerald Hughes, August 1958, MSS 854, Emory. Hughes also included "Thrushes," "Relic," and "Crow Hill" in this letter.

Similar moments of connection between man and animal appear in Hughes's "The Hawk in the Rain," "The Horses," "View of a Pig," "The Bull Moses," and "Bullfrog," to give only a sampling. Lawrence's "Glory," with its assumptions about what Hughes would later term the divine law of nature, was an obvious influence on some of Hughes's best early poems, such as "The Hawk in the Rain," "Hawk Roosting," and "The Jaguar":

> Most of his time, the tiger pads and slouches in a burning peace.
> And the small hawk high up turns round on the slow pivot of peace.
> Peace comes from behind the sun, with the peregrine falcon, and the owl.
> Yet all of these drink blood.   (1986: 198)

C. J. Rawson has pointed out that "The Hawk in the Rain" also owes some of its imagery to a passage in Lawrence's *The Rainbow*. Where Hughes's speaker says, "I drown in the drumming ploughland, I drag up | Heel after heel from the swallowing of the earth's mouth, | From clay that clutches my each step to the ankle | With the habit of the dogged grave" (*CPH* 19), Lawrence had written that the Brangwens felt "the pulse and body of the soil, that opened to their furrow for the grain, and became smooth and supple after their ploughing, and clung to their feet with a weight that pulled like desire" (qtd. in Rawson 1965: 80). This passage, of course, also brings to mind imagery from Plath's "Ariel."

Hughes and Lawrence shared ideological as well as aesthetic affinities. Perhaps through Lawrence, Hughes became interested in both Schopenhauer and Nietzsche, though he credited the former as the more important philosophical influence in a 1970 interview with Faas, saying, "The only philosophy I have ever really read was Schopenhauer. He impressed me all right. You see very well where Nietzsche got his Dionysus. It was a genuine vision of something on its way back to the surface. The rough beast in Yeats' poems" (1980: 205). He told Myers he was immersed in Schopenhauer in 1957, and later discussed the philosopher's influence in a letter to the *Spectator* regarding *Crow* in 1971.[24]

Dwight Eddins has argued that what impressed Hughes most about Schopenhauer's philosophy was his understanding of nature. Eddins reminds us that in *The World as Will and Idea*, Schopenhauer wrote of "the observable life of animals" in terms that recall Hughes's own *Weltanschauung*:

We see only momentary gratification, fleeting pleasure conditioned by wants, much and long suffering, constant struggle, *bellum omnium*, everything a hunter and everything hunted, pressure, want, need and anxiety, shrieking and howling, and this goes on in *saecula seculorum*.   (*World* 2: 254; Eddins 94)

Eddins notes that "The Hawk in the Rain," "Pike," "Hawk Roosting," "Mayday on Holderness," "Still Life," "Sugar Loaf," "Pibroch," "Poor Birds,"

---

[24] Ted Hughes to Lucas Myers, spring 1957, MSS 865, Emory; March 5, 1971, Box 114, MSS 644, Emory.

"A Sparrow Hawk," and "Macaw" all reveal Schopenhauer's influence, and concludes, "it is hard to locate a point in Hughes's development where his profound affinity with Schopenhauer is not evident, and where it does not illuminate a poetry that explores more intrepidly than any other the nightmare of ravening cosmic energies" (108). Robin Peel, in turn, links Hughes's Schopenhauerian vision with his unease with modernity; from *The Hawk in the Rain* to *Wodwo*, Peel reads Hughes's "hatred for what he saw as the superficial distractions of twentieth-century modernity. . . . If the positive power of nature is to triumph over the cold, deadening forces in the world, thrushes have to be 'terrifying' stabbers . . . hawks omnipotent, jaguars menacing and pikes killers" (2006: 164; 166).

But Hughes did not interpret nature's cycle of endless competitive struggle as pessimistically as Schopenhauer. In a 1963 review of Philip O'Connor's *Vagrancy* he instead exhibited a Nietzschean admiration of competition:

is the spirit of competition picked up with such difficulty, and so against nature? . . . is it true that competition is as thoroughly evil in fact as it is in his imagination? When non-competition is enforced, what sort of genetic torpor ensues, and worse? (*WP* 37)

Although Hughes would become increasingly uncomfortable with the epithet "poet of violence," he was in fact partly responsible for this characterization, for he had admitted early on in his career that violence was a sustaining interest. When the Poetry Book Society chose *The Hawk in the Rain* as one of its top choices for 1957, Hughes famously wrote in its bulletin, "After thinking the poems over I have decided to say this. What excites my imagination is the war between vitality and death, and my poems may be said to celebrate the exploits of the warriors of either side" (1957: 1). He went on to use words such as "battleground," "combatant," and "uproar" to describe his composition process. Hughes was staking out his poetic territory, attempting to distinguish his verse from that of the Movement poets, who, having been through the Second World War, viewed Hughes's interest in "the war between vitality and death" as a near-endorsement of the fascist aesthetic. As Hughes told Faas, "Where I conjured up a jaguar, they smelt a stormtrooper. Where I saw elementals and forces of Nature they saw motorcyclists with machine guns on the handlebars" (1980: 201). Still, Hughes did not protest when Robin Skelton of the *Manchester Guardian*, in a review of *The Hawk in the Rain*, noted his "masculine vigour," or when W. S. Merwin, in the *New York Times Book Review*, praised his "capacity for incaution," or when Alvarez drew attention to his "anti-poetical toughness," "belligerent ugliness," and "heroical, misanthropic swagger" in the *Observer*. Nor did he complain when John Press, in the *Sunday Times*, compared his words to "a hard, relentless assault-weapon." Later, Hughes would protest when reviewers focused on violence in *Crow*, but these early reviews pleased him. He frequently quoted them in letters to his siblings and friends, while Plath carefully saved each cutting in a scrapbook.

Given Hughes's early self-identification as a poet of violence, it is not surprising that critics began to focus on this aspect of his work. Edwin Muir, in his influential 1957 *New Statesman* review of *The Hawk in the Rain*, wrote that Hughes's "images have an admirable violence," while A. E. Dyson expounded upon Hughes's fascination with power in a 1959 article for the *Critical Quarterly*:

> For Ted Hughes, power and violence go together: his own dark gods are makers of the tiger, not the lamb. He is fascinated by violence of all kinds, in love and in hatred, in the jungle and in the arena, in battle, murder and sudden death. Violence, for him, is the occasion not for reflection, but for *being*. (220)

By the early sixties, the morality of Hughes's "violence" was frequently debated in the pages of magazines, academic journals, and anthologies, just as Plath's would be after the posthumous publication of *Ariel*. Much of the debate would eventually center upon Hughes's "Hawk Roosting," first published in 1959. Critics debated whether the poet and/or speaker idealized the "bloodthirsty" hawk (Rawson 1966: 129), which Hughes later characterized as "a fascist" or "some horrible totalitarian genocidal dictator," "Hitler's familiar spirit" (Faas 1980: 199).[25] The morality of Plath's use of violence and fascist imagery in *Ariel* would later inspire similar, and equally heated, critical debate.

Al Alvarez's introduction to his 1962 anthology *The New Poetry*, entitled, "Beyond the Gentility Principle," laid much of the groundwork for this debate.[26] The anthology itself was a response to Robert Conquest's 1956 *New Lines*, which helped to launch the Movement poets.[27] Alvarez's book sought to challenge Movement "gentility"; he noted that the Movement poets' occupations included librarian, civil servant, and university professor, and that their verse could best be described as "academic-administrative ... polite, knowledgeable, efficient" (23). Like Hughes and Plath, Alvarez was a devotee of Lawrence, whom he called the only English writer who had faced "the more uncompromising forces at work in our time" (26). He advocated, again like Hughes and Plath, for a new poetry which would acknowledge that postwar life had been

---

[25] In a 1963 article in *Stand*, Jon Silkin defended the poem, arguing that Hughes implicitly criticized the violence the hawk embodied (7); J. D. Hainsworth concurred in *English*, writing that "the reader is not expected to agree" with the hawk (227). Yet C. J. Rawson responded in 1965 that "Everybody knows Ted Hughes's subject is violence.... The violence is pervasive" (77). While Rawson admired Hughes's "conciseness" (78), he was nevertheless troubled by his "attitudinizing brutalism" (83), his "masculine ethos" (87), and his contempt for "the man-made, the civilized" (91). Rawson's article prompted a heated rebuttal from Hainsworth, who correctly pointed out that Hughes sometimes wrote poems "against violence," and insisted that "Hawk Roosting" was an "anti-violence poem" (1965: 357).

[26] Hughes was included in the 1962 edition, Plath in the revised 1966 edition.

[27] Hughes was, surprisingly, featured in Conquest's anthology as well as Alvarez's.

influenced profoundly by forces which have nothing to do with gentility, decency or politeness. Theologians would call these forces evil, psychologists, perhaps, libido. Either way, they are the forces of disintegration which destroy the old standards of civilization. Their public faces are those of two world wars, of the concentration camps, of genocide, and the threat of nuclear war. (26)[28]

To emphasize his point, Alvarez compared Hughes's "The Horses" to Philip Larkin's "At Grass," a poem about retired racehorses, and concluded that Hughes's poem was superior: "Unlike Larkin's, Hughes's horses have a violent, impending presence" (31). Alvarez also emphasized the Lawrence–Hughes lineage when he noted with admiration that "The Horses" was most likely influenced by "the strange, savage horses which terrorize Ursula Brangwen at the end of *The Rainbow*" (31). (When Hughes and Alvarez eventually fell out over Alvarez's memoir of Plath's last days in *The Savage God*, Hughes wrote to him, "I'm absolutely amazed to see you joining that mob. Imagine what Lawrence would have said about it" [*L* 324].) Hughes's prominence within Alvarez's anthology—he had more poems featured than any other poet—helped to solidify his reputation as a 'poet of violence' and ensured his work would become the subject of intense moral scrutiny, just as Plath's would be.

In 1970, Faas finally asked Hughes outright about the label that had come to define his poetic identity: "Critics have often described your poetry as the 'poetry of violence.' . . . How does such poetry relate to our customary social and humanitarian values and to what degree can it be considered a criticism of those values?" (1980: 197). Hughes responded by expressing resentment towards those "huge numbers of people in England" with their "total ignorance" of poetry—he used his aunt as an example—who found his verse "horrible and violent":

In a sense, critics who find my poetry violent are in her world, and they are safeguarding her way of life. So to define their use of the word violence any further, you have to work out just why her way of life should find the behaviour of a hawk "horrible" or any reference to violent death "disgusting," just as she finds any reference to extreme vehemence of life "frightening somehow." It's a futile quarrel really. (197)

A year later, when Faas again asked him about his use of violence, he was more defensive. He explained that his aim was to expose the "divine law" (*WP* 259) at work in animals and artists and to show that this law had been corrupted by man,

---

[28] *The New Poetry* inspired a follow-up anthology from Conquest in 1963, *New Lines II*, in which he berated Alvarez's aesthetic judgment in his introduction. Conquest wrote that "there are those who treat verse as no more than a means of whipping up their emotions—(and increasingly, these days, not even as an aphrodisiac but rather as what one might call an areac, a drug for arousing feelings of violence). Some justify this on the grounds that verse should match the age. It is maintained, rather dubiously yet at least arguably, that our present situation is the most extreme, the most appalling that has ever existed. But even granting this, there is no reason whatever to draw from it the conclusion commonly seen, that poetry should 'reflect' it, or 'cope with' it by itself falling into violence and disproportion" (xxiii).

who no longer understood the "positive" (*WP* 255) aspects of violence.[29] In Hughes's eyes, animals possessed a more acute sense of actual purpose than deskbound modern man.

Hughes's understanding of "positive violence" (*WP* 255) was clearly influenced by Nietzsche, whom he read in 1958 while in America, as well as by Blake, Lawrence, Yeats, and even Plath.[30] As Hughes told Faas, "One can use the word [violence] to describe a passion, a cavorting horse, or a dancer, and be perfectly well understood to mean something positive and exciting admiration" (*WP* 253–4). He asserted that positive violence is "a life-bringing assertion of sacred law which demolishes, in some abrupt way, a force that oppressed and *violated* it" (254).[31] Hughes went on to echo both Nietzsche and Lawrence when he said that "the strong, positive mode of violence ought to concern us more than the strong negative, since behind it presses the revelation of all that enables human beings to experience—with mystical clarity and certainty—what we call truth, reality, beauty, redemption and the kind of fundamental love that is at least equal to the fundamental evil" (*WP* 255). "Thrushes," Hughes said, was "an attempt to bring one aspect of that strong, specific, positive violence into focus" (255). He lamented the fact that critics had rushed to label the predators in his poems "negative," since he considered them to be "strongly positive" (256), metaphors of "the operation of divine law" in nature (259). In response, he mocked the notion of "humanitarian" (259) values, which he believed had prevented humans from facing "our extraordinary readiness to exploit, oppress, torture and kill our own kind" (256). Hughes rested his defense by situating himself as one in a line of poets who glorified the strength of the "rough beast," the primal energy that animates the life force:

does it make any sense whatsoever to say that in these poems—Blake, Yeats, or Popa were "celebrating violence"? Or does it make more sense to say: "these sacred animals emerged into the field of vision of these poets, charged with special glamour, 'terrible beauty' and force, and the poets simply felt compelled to make an image of what they saw—at the same time trying to impose some form of ethical control on it". In this sense, such poems simply bear witness. And I would have thought, any culture that would prefer to be without poetry of this kind—one would prefer to be without. (266)

---

[29] This interview originally appeared in the *London Magazine* in January 1971. Hughes later expanded upon his answers to Faas's questions regarding violence and included the new version, titled "Poetry and Violence," in *Winter Pollen*.

[30] Ted Hughes to Olwyn Hughes, summer 1958, MSS 980, Emory. A drawing of Nietzsche's astrological chart (next to a drawing of Virginia Woolf's) appears on the back of a letter Hughes wrote to Olwyn during the early summer of 1956 (MSS 980, Emory).

[31] For Nietzsche, in *On the Genealogy of Morals*, it is "the priests"—symbols of all moral arbiters—who have vilified this "positive" violence: "There is from the first something *unhealthy* in such priestly aristocracies and in the habits ruling in them which turn them away from action. . . . For with the priests everything becomes more dangerous, not only cures and remedies, but also arrogance, revenge, acuteness, profligacy, love, lust to rule, virtue" (2000: 468–9).

Hughes understood why his poems might be interpreted as glorifying violence, yet he insisted they did not: "If the Hawk and the Pike kill, they kill within the law and their killing is a sacrament" (262). He later defended *Crow* along similar lines in one of his notebooks: "That he explodes is positive. It is not an image of 'violence' but an image of breakthrough. . . . That he pushes to the point where he is annihilated means that now nothing remains for him but what has exploded him—his inner link with his creator, a thing of spiritfire."[32]

Feminist critics would nevertheless remain skeptical of Hughes's intentions. Rose, for example, criticized poems like "Hawk Roosting" and "Thrushes" as verse that appeared "complicit with what it condemns," work in which Hughes "seems to venerate or even idealise the same spirit of masculine identity as the celebration and completion of itself" (156). Such accusations echo common criticisms of Nietzsche and Lawrence. They also echo later criticisms of Plath's "Daddy" and "Lady Lazarus," which have been condemned for venerating the fascist mindset.[33] The similar questioning of Plath's and Hughes's moral stances should come as little surprise, given their mutual interest in the Nietzschean motifs of strength, dominance, and "positive violence."

Although Hughes's fascination with violence had initially attracted Plath, by 1962, in the wake of his adultery, she was eager to renounce the aesthetic preoccupations she had once passionately shared with him. Yet she would have been surprised to hear, in the mid-fifties, that she would ever adopt such a position.

WRITING THE BLOOD-JET: PLATH, NIETZSCHE, AND LAWRENCE

It is a critical commonplace to portray Plath in the 1950s as Hughes's protégé. Steven Axelrod writes that during this time Plath "wrote in a Hughesian style on Hughesian themes" and "adopted Hughes's favorite writers as her own (Blake, Hopkins, Lawrence, Thomas)" (195). Peter Davison remarks that during the early months of their courtship, Plath "began to learn what Ted Hughes had to teach her as a poet—a great deal, to be sure, but some of the results could be almost ventriloquial" (161–2). Christina Britzolakis notes that "Lawrentian themes of sexuality, violence, and power struggle are central to Plath's creative dialogue with Ted Hughes. . . . Her desire to produce 'the strongest female paean yet for the creative forces of nature' (*LH* 277) announces a conversion to a Dionysian aesthetic, which is explicitly connected with his influence" (79). Faas writes that Plath "became the disciple" of Hughes, and that "the major impact on her poetic

---

[32] Ted Hughes, unidentified fragment regarding *Crow*, Box 115, MSS 644, Emory.
[33] See Chapter 6 for a detailed discussion of the hostile criticism that has been launched against "Daddy" and "Lady Lazarus."

development derived from the psychic powers of her 'hypnotizing husband'"
(1980: 41); he also claims that Hughes was responsible for "freeing her imagin-
ation" (1983: 110). Yet Plath was not a mere "disciple" of Hughes. Rather, she saw
themes in his work—war, violence, anger, the competitive drive, the battle between
real and false selves—that appealed to her own burgeoning aesthetic.

Robin Peel has argued that Plath would have received a broader philosophical
and political education in America than Hughes would have in England, since
British students specialized at the age of sixteen. Yet he rightly notes that Plath's
philosophical interests have been relatively ignored: Sandra Glibert and Susan
Gubar, for example, have written that Plath "did not have an explicitly political
imagination" (1994: 3.297). Too little attention has been paid to the fact that
Plath was significantly influenced by Nietzsche, whom she read in high school
and college. Peel notes that Plath's mother first gave her a copy of *Thus Spoke
Zarathustra* for Christmas in 1949, and that she later re-read it in 1954 while
writing her dissertation on Dostoyevsky. That year, she also studied *Zarathustra*
in a European history class; her copy, which she called "our bible of individu-
alism at present" in a class paper, is heavily annotated.[34] A paper she wrote for
this class, "The Age of Anxiety and the Escape from Freedom," gives a good
sense of her interest in Nietzsche at this time. Although the paper was ostensibly
about Erich Fromm's *Escape from Freedom,* Plath continually brought her
argument back to Nietzsche. In the beginning of the paper, she wrote that she
had read *Zarathustra* "which was not on the reading list but which I devoured
because I have become intensely enamoured of his poetic lightning flashes of
insight." She continued:

My mind has sneezed itself (to use a Nietzschean verb!) into new and more difficult
awarenesses. And it wants to climb still higher, out of the womblike security of compla-
cent collective values into the realm of the strong, individualistic winds: "for rather will I
have noise and thunders and tempest blasts, than this discreet, doubting cat-repose."

(*Zarathustra*, 182)

Later, speaking of Auden's "September 1939" she wrote:

This verse, I think, contains the kernel of our modern problem. The insecure individual
"clings to the average." (How Nietzsche scorned and shouted against this: "That . . . is
mediocrity, though it be called moderation. . . . Ye ever become smaller, ye small people!
Ye crumble away, ye comfortable ones! Ye will yet perish. By your many small virtues, by
your many small omissions, and by your many small submissions! Too tender, too
yielding, so is your soil! But for a tree to become great, it seeketh to twine hard roots
around hard rocks!"   (*Zarathustra*, 188–89)[35]

---

[34] The class was History 38b, with Mrs. Koffka. Peel writes that it was "a history of thought
which looked at such topics as Romanticism, Conservatism, and Liberalism, and examined the ideas
of Carlyle, Nietzsche, Socialism, Marx, Engels, and the key thinkers of nineteenth century liberal-
ism" (2004: 64).
[35] Plath's ellipses.

Plath called Auden's drinkers in the bar "pathetic weaklings," and ended her paper by again invoking Nietzsche:

before we close, a word about our enchanting poetic polemicist, Nietzsche. (Zarathustra is our bible of individualism at present!) One aspect needed on the road to genuine freedom is accentuated by Nietzsche as it is not in Fromm (who offers more of a diagnosis than a prognosis)—and that is suffering!

Man wants to "alleviate suffering", in the words of Fromm, but if he is to achieve the fullest measure of his individual potential, according to Nietzsche, he must not only accept suffering (Nietzsche abhors effeminate Christian humility) but seek it! And we agree heartily here: tempting as it is to avoid pain, the strong individual must perceive that "pain is also a joy, curse is also a blessing, night is also a sun . . ."

For us, this eloquent paradox expresses the full, honest, courageous acceptance of freedom and all its implications: an affirmation of the value of evil as well as good, discord as well as harmony, hardship as well as comfort, and pain as well as pleasure. Like Zarathustra, we cry for the rich, complex, sturdy individual who evolves by a dynamic dialectic of struggle and surmounting, resolving antitheses into larger, more comprehensive syntheses (which themselves become new theses for conflict)—and rising to higher statures and perspectives through conflict and suffering.

Our favorite Nietzschean epigraph will close this paper: "One must still have chaos in one, to give birth to a dancing star!" (Zarathustra, 363)[36]

Note Plath's emphasis on struggle and conflict here, two ideas which would propel her later dialogue with Hughes.

In a paper written for her Russian class on Dostoevsky in March of 1954, Plath again introduced Nietzsche, beginning the paper with an epigraph from *Zarathustra*: "For there is a salt which uniteth good with evil; and even the evilest is worthy, as spicing." Later in the paper, she wrote, "Zarathustra proclaims the gospel of the will: 'yea something invulnerable, unburiable is with me, something that would rend rocks asunder: it is called my will.' Since God is dead, the prophet asserts it is: 'better to set up destiny in one's own account, better to be a fool, better to be god oneself.'"[37] Here Plath indulges her youthful interest in what Hughes would later call "positive violence" (*WP* 255). Plath's experiments with Nietzschean ideas in her journal and early poetry reveal that she recognized him as an enabling literary and philosophical model: "Doomsday," "Insolent Storm Strikes at the Skull," "Temper of Time," and "Song for a Revolutionary Love" all exhibit the influence of Nietzsche, as well as Yeats. Plath's uncollected 1955 poem, "Notes on Zarathustra's Prologue," shows that at Smith she had already begun to incorporate Nietzsche's philosophy into her art:

[36] Sylvia Plath, "The Age of Anxiety and the Escape from Freedom," May 1954. Written for History 38b with Mrs. Koffka. Plath MSS II, Box 13, Lilly.

[37] Sylvia Plath, "The Devil's Advocate," March 24, 1954. Written for Russian 35b with Mr. Gibian. Plath MSS II, Box 13, Lilly.

> Look to the lightning for tongues of pain
> Steep are the stairs to the Superman
>
> Go flay the frail sheep in the flock
> And strip the shroud from coward's back
>
> Till the womb of chaos sprouts with fire
> And hatches Nietzsche's dancing star.[38]

As a young New England woman, Plath had been thoroughly, if informally, immersed in Emerson's philosophy of self-reliance.[39] Yet by the time she entered college, she was ready for a new perspective that resonated with her own growing sense of her talent and calling.[40] Nietzsche was an appealingly subversive philosophical alternate. Up until the fifties, Nietzsche was viewed in the United States as a "prophet of the Third Reich," labeled "half a Nazi" in a 1941 study by Harvard historian Crane Brinton (Gay xi). It was not until Walter Kaufmann's *Nietzsche: Philosopher, Psychologist, Antichrist* (1950) that the academy began to reassess Nietzsche.[41] Still, Plath's embrace of Nietzsche in the early fifties was a radical act in "a period which exalted the most oppressive ideal of reason and stability," as one reviewer of *The Bell Jar* put it (Harris 108).

Nietzsche's melding of puritanism and romanticism—what Michael Tanner has called "the paradox of Nietzsche's extreme fastidiousness consorting with the will to deny nothing" (101)—would have appealed to Plath who, as Britzolakis notes, enacted her own Yeatsian dialogue of self and soul in her journals.[42] This is the woman who declared, "O what a poet I will flay myself into," and later, in 1958, "I am, at bottom, simple, credulous, feminine and loving to be mastered, cared for—but I will kill with my mind, my ice-eye, anyone who is weak, false, sickly in soul" (qtd. in Peel 2004: 103). Emerson's Unitarian-approved version of individualism must have seemed tepid when set beside Nietzsche's Will to Power. After all, Plath frequently called herself "The girl who wanted to be God" (*LH* 40).[43] Importantly, she associated Nietzsche with her Teutonic father, while she may have associated Emerson with her gratingly cheerful mother. In Plath's autobiographical story "Among the Bumbleees," for example, Alice grows up worshipping her "proud and arrogant" (*JP* 266) father who is closely identified

---

[38] Sylvia Plath, "Notes on Zarathustra's Prologue," Plath MSS II, Box 8, Folder 1, Lilly.

[39] See Tim Kendall's *Sylvia Plath: A Critical Study* for a full discussion of Emerson's influence on Plath.

[40] In April 1953, the year before she studied Nietzsche in her history class, *Harper's* magazine bought three of her poems.

[41] Kaufmann exposed the machinations of Nietzsche's anti-Semitic sister Elisabeth, who manipulated Nietzsche's legacy so that he appeared to espouse beliefs central to Nazism.

[42] Britzolakis writes that the *Journals'* "rhetoric of soul-searching and self-exhortation resembles nothing so much as puritan spiritual autobiography" (15).

[43] In her journal, Plath wrote, "I will be a little god in my small way" (22); "Frustrated? Yes. Why? Because it is impossible for me to be God—or the universal woman-and-man" (*J* 45).

with Nietzsche, and dismissing her mother, who is aligned with feminine passivity and submission.[44]

Nietzsche's ideas about self-affirmation, or 'self-becoming,' dovetailed with Plath's.[45] In her journals, Plath frequently called herself "strong and assertive" (106), and longed to give voice to the "masculine" elements within herself. "I am jealous of men," she wrote in 1951. "I envy the man his physical freedom to lead a double life—his career, and his sexual and family life" (*J* 98). These admissions did not accord with the image of the demure, self-effacing model of fifties femininity, and Plath knew it. She records her anxiety in her early poem "Family Reunion," in which the speaker steels herself to play the part her family deems proper:

> Like a diver on a lofty spar of land
> Atop the flight of stairs I stand.
> A whirlpool leers at me,
> Absorbent as a sponge;
> I cast off my identity
> And make the fatal plunge.   (*CPP* 301)

Although Nietzsche has been criticized as a misogynist, he nevertheless offered Plath an ideological foundation that validated her own desire for autonomy and opened up possibilities of liberation from the tyranny of gender. In Eisenhower's America, Plath was not expected to pursue her own career; subordination was the only option available to her if she wished to marry, which she did.[46] Yet Nietzsche thought subordination was a surrender to the enervating Judeo-Christian doctrine of humility and submission. Plath, too, vowed not to surrender. In the same journal entry in which she wrote, "I do not love anybody except myself," she swore to live a life determined by her own standards and goals. She would hatch her escape

in the exercise of a phase of life inviolate and separate from that of my future mate.... I am not only jealous; I am vain and proud. I will not submit to having my life fingered by my husband, enclosed in the larger circle of his activity, and nourished vicariously by tales of his actual exploits. I must have a legitimate field of my own, apart from his, which he must respect.   (98–9)[47]

[44] Britzolakis speculates that Plath's disdain for her mother's overbearing solicitousness, and, hence, identification with her father's fearlessness and arrogance, was partly a result of the "matrophobic popular Freudianism of the 1950s" (26) evident in Philip Wylie's bestselling *Generation of Vipers*, which blamed overprotective mothers for emasculating their children. (In "Among the Bumblebees," Alice's mother exhibits the insidious 'Momism' Wylie scourged by continually coddling Alice's sickly younger brother.) If so, then Plath would have had even more reason to adopt Nietzsche's preference for stoicism over pity, strength over weakness, and pride over humility.

[45] I will discuss Plath's later rejection of Nietzsche in Chapter 6.

[46] As Adlai Stevenson told Plath's graduating class at Smith, the best way to assume a role in the wider world was, paradoxically, to stay put: "This assignment for you, as wives and mothers, you can do in the living room with a baby in your lap or in the kitchen with a can opener in your hand.... I think there is much you can do about our crisis in the humble role of housewife. I could wish you no better vocation than that" (qtd. in Friedan 61).

[47] Yet, perhaps on account of her Emersonian upbringing, Plath was conflicted about her feeling of superiority, and often worried that she was selfish. In September 1951 she wrote "I feed myself on

Hughes, for his part, insisted in a private letter that Plath was " 'Laurentian', not woman's lib."[48] This was indeed the case, but perhaps only because her life and death preceded the modern feminist movement. In November 1952, Plath poignantly expressed in her journal what Betty Friedan later called "the problem that has no name":

Why did Virginia Woolf commit suicide? Or Sara Teasdale—or the other brilliant women—neurotic? Was their writing sublimation (oh horrible word) of deep, basic desires? If only I knew. If only I knew how high I could set my goals, my requirements for my life! I am in the position of a blind girl playing with a slide-ruler of values.... Will I be a secretary—a self-rationalizing, uninspired housewife, secretly jealous of my husband's ability to grow intellectually & professionally while I am impeded—will I submerge my embarrassing desires & aspirations, refuse to face myself, and go either mad or become neurotic?... Whom can I talk to? Get advice from? No one.   (151)

In the age before *The Feminine Mystique*, Nietzsche's philosophy of individualism and self-actualization offered Plath an alternative source of inspiration and affirmation. As Nietzsche wrote in *Thus Spoke Zarathustra*, "The creation of freedom for oneself and a sacred 'No' even to duty—for that, my brothers, the lion is needed. To assume the right to new values—that is the most terrifying assumption for a reverent spirit that would bear much" (139).[49]

Plath also absorbed Nietzschean concepts of individualism through Lawrence. Though Lawrence thought that female emancipation had resulted in "a tyranny of women" in which "man is submissive to the demands of woman" (1936: 196), he nevertheless created heroines who challenged the cultural constructs that prevented them from engaging equally with men.[50] As Susan Weisser wrote of *Lady Chatterley's Lover*, "It is the woman who is most repressed and dehumanized, and so it is the heroine who must free herself, from being a wife into the more true and alive relation of lover... certainly a radical (and modern) view" (xxx–xxxi). Thus Lawrence affirmed Plath's own "modern" view of women's equality.

By 1956, Plath had already read most of Lawrence's novels. Years before she met Hughes, she explored ideas and themes that critics generally ascribe to Hughes's influence—or Lawrence's influence via Hughes—in her journal. She was particularly inspired by Lawrence's depictions of nature as the embodiment of the vital, Dionysian, life-affirming force that had the power to renew modern, mechanized man. During the summer of 1951, for example, she wrote rhapsodically about a moment

---

the food of pride. I cultivate physical appearance—Pride. I long to excel—to specialize in one field, one section of a field, no matter how minute, as long as I can be an authority there. Pride, ambition—what mean, selfish words!" (*J* 100).

[48] Ted Hughes to Aurelia Plath, January 1975, MSS 644, Emory.

[49] Although critics have focused on the biblical allusions in "Ariel," Plath's identification with "God's lioness" in that poem may also allude to Nietzsche's philosophy of autonomy.

[50] Britzolakis notes that Lawrence, in *Studies in Classic American Literature*, one of Plath's "sacred texts" (169), wrote that " 'woman out of bounds is a devil' " and "looked forward to a time when she would 'choose to experience the great submission' " (170).

of Lawrentian communion with nature (alluding to a scene from *Women in Love*) while she was living on the North Shore of Massachusetts:[51]

Lying on my stomach on the flat warm rock, I let my arm hang over the side, and my hand caressed the rounded contours of the sun-hot stone.... Burning through the material of my bathing suit, the great heat radiated through my body, and my breasts ached against the hard flat stone.... Stretching out on the rock, body taut, then relaxed, on the altar, I felt that I was being raped deliciously by the sun, filled full of heat from the impersonal and colossal god of nature. Warm and perverse was the body of my love under me, and the feeling of his carved flesh was like no other—not soft, not malleable, not wet with sweat, but dry, hard, smooth, clean and pure. High, bonewhite, I had been washed by the sea, cleansed, baptised, purified, and dried clean and crisp by the sun.... An orgiastic sacrifice on the altar of rock and sun, and I arose shining from the centuries of love, clean and satiated from the consuming fire of his casual and timeless desire. (*J* 74)

Critics sometimes suggest that Hughes single-handedly introduced Plath to nature (Plath herself demurely suggests as much in her letters), yet the above entry shows she had already developed a passionate, indeed erotic, attitude toward nature—especially the sea—during her childhood and adolescence. In her early poems about Hughes, Plath would portray her speakers as Lawrentian nature goddesses, yet it is clear from this entry that she had imagined herself in this role before she met her husband.

Plath also assimilated Lawrence's notion that, as Rupert Birkin put it, man and woman could exist in "mystic conjunction" (164) without sacrificing themselves to the other's ambitions or desires. This idea appealed to the young female artist trying to imagine a future in which writing and marriage would not be mutually exclusive. As she wrote in her journal in May 1952:

Never will there be a circle, signifying me and my operations, confined solely to home, other womenfolk, and community service, enclosed in the larger worldly circle of my mate.... No, rather, there will be two over-lapping circles, with a certain strong riveted center of common ground, but *both* with separate arcs jutting out in the world. A balanced tension; adaptable to circumstances, in which there is an elasticity of pull, tension, yet firm unity. Two stars, polarized...in moments of communication that is

---

[51] Plath is alluding to a scene in *Women in Love* in which Rupert Birkin, after being struck by Hermione, retreats to the woods, strips naked, and fantasizes about a quasi-sexual union with nature:

He took off all his clothes, and sat down naked among the primroses, moving his feet softly among the primroses, his legs, his knees, his arms right up to the arm-pits, lying down and letting them touch his belly, his breasts. It was such a fine, cool, subtle touch all over him, he seemed to saturate himself with their contact.... To lie down and roll in the sticky, cool young hyacinths, to lie on one's belly and cover one's back with handfuls of fine wet grass, soft as breath, soft and more delicate and more beautiful than the touch of any woman; and then to sting one's thigh against the living dark bristles of the fir-boughs; and then to feel the light whip of the hazel on one's shoulders, stinging, and then to clasp the silvery birch-trunk against one's breast, its smoothness, its hardness, its vital knots and ridges—this was good, this was all very good, very satisfying.... This was his place, his marriage place. The world was extraneous. (113–14)

complete . . . almost fusing onto one. . . . I do not believe . . . that artistic creativity can best be indulged in masterful singleness rather than in marital cooperation. I think that a workable union should heighten the potentialities in *both* individuals.   (*J* 105–7)

Plath was clearly moved by the scene in *Women in Love* where Birkin tells Ursula that love is "not meeting and mingling" but "an equilibrium, a pure balance of two single beings:—as the stars balance each other" (160); and later, "he wanted a further conjunction, where man had being and woman had being, two pure beings, each constituting the freedom of the other, balancing each other like two poles of one force, like two angels, or two demons" (219). As John Burt Foster notes, such analogies "reenact" Nietzsche's "drama of Apollo and Dionysus" (181), and in these scenes Lawrence "echoes star imagery from key passages of *Thus Spoke Zarathustra*" (200).

Plath again drew on Nietzsche and Lawrence in another journal entry, dated May 15, 1952, which, as Middlebrook has noted (2003: 41), rehearses the language of Lawrentian eroticism:

I could feel the inevitable magnetic polar forces in us, and the tidal blood beat loud, Loud, roaring in my ears, slowing and rhythmic. . . . To lie with him, to lie with him, burning forgetful in the delicious animal fire. Locked first upright, thighs ground together, shuddering, mouth to mouth, breast to breast, legs enmeshed, then lying full together, with the good heavy weight of body upon body, arching, undulating, blind, growing together, force fighting force: to kill? To drive into burning dark of oblivion? To lose identity? . . . And giving up to the corrosive black whirlpool of mutual necessary destruction.—Once there is the first kiss, then the cycle becomes inevitable. Training, conditioning, make a hunger burn in breasts and secrete fluid in vagina, driving blindly for destruction. What is it but destruction? Some mystic desire to beat to sensual annihilation—to snuff out one's identity on the identity of the other—a mingling and mangling of identities? A death of one? Or both? A devouring and subordination? No, no. A polarization rather—a balance of two integrities, changing, electrically, one with the other, yet with centers of coolness, like stars. (And D. H. Lawrence did have something after all—).   (104–5)[52]

Here, sex is not decorous but lustful, primitive, and animalistic, while love is a predatory battle ("force fighting force") that threatens to annihilate identity. Although Plath ultimately rejects this idea, her list of questions shows she is nevertheless fascinated by it. This passage, while overwritten, comes close to the spirit of the Ariel voice with its "drive into burning dark of oblivion" (*J* 105); it

---

[52] This passage also alludes to Lawrence's *Fantasia of the Unconscious*, where he elaborates upon the metaphor of the star: "One is one, but one is not all alone. There are other stars buzzing in the centre of their own isolation. . . . I am I, but also you are you, and we are in sad need of a theory of human relativity. We need it much more than the universe does." Plath used the phrase "I am I" several times in her early journals (34; 45; 62) to reinforce her sense of singularity, as when she writes, "I am I now. . . . I: how firm a letter; how reassuring the three strokes: one vertical, proud and assertive, and then the two short horizontal lines in quick, smug succession. The pen scratches on the paper . . . I . . . I . . . I . . . I . . . I . . . I" (*J* 34).

shows that while Hughes may have influenced the development of the Ariel voice, he did not deliver it into being.[53]

Plath would also have been intrigued by Lawrence's representations of female violence against male lovers.[54] Several times in *Women in Love*, women are overcome by the desire to hurt their male lovers. Early on, for example, Hermione attempts to kill Birkin with a lapis lazuli paperweight. As she brings the weapon down on his head, the narrator reports, "She must smash it, it must be smashed before her ecstasy was consummated, fulfilled for ever" (111). Hermione's rationale for attempting the murder might have struck a nerve with Plath, given her frequent expressions of anxiety in her journal about being dominated by a male partner:

And then she realised that his presence was the wall, his presence was destroying her. Unless she could break out, she must die most fearfully, walled up in horror. And he was the wall. She must break down the wall—she must break him down before her, the awful obstruction of him who obstructed her life to the last. It must be done, or she must perish most horribly.   (Lawrence 110–11)

Later, Gudrun enacts a similar performance with Gerald, who has made the mistake of assuming a "domineering" smile. After striking him, "she felt in her soul an unconquerable desire for deep violence against him. She shut off the fear and dismay that filled her conscious mind. She wanted to do as she did, she was not going to be afraid" (185). When Gerald recovers, he looks at Gudrun, astonished, and utters, "'You have struck the first blow.'... 'And I shall strike the last,' she retorted involuntarily, with confident assurance. He was silent, he did not contradict her" (186).[55]

Such scenes probably inspired Plath to experiment with violent representations of erotic love in her early poetry; later, they may even have helped inspire the dangerous women of "Daddy," "Purdah," and "Lady Lazarus." Indeed, Nietzschean conceptions of the aggressive sexual partner color her journal entries as early as 1953: "How do I like men?... Giant, superman: mental and physical" (171); "I need a strong mate: I do not want to accidentally crush and subdue him like a steamroller...I must find a strong potential powerful mate who can counter my vibrant dynamic self: sexual and intellectual" (173); "let's face it, I am in danger of wanting my personal absolute to be a demigod of a man.... I want a romantic nonexistant [*sic*] hero" (182).

[53] As Peel writes, "It is not true to say that Plath discovers a completely 'new' language when she comes to write the *Ariel* poems; certain elements of the imaginative rhetoric of that productive period in England can be found in the archaeology of the earlier writing" (2002: 98).

[54] Plath sometimes glorified violence, like Nietzsche, as when she admitted in her journal, "in my head I know it is too simple to wish for war, for open battle but one cannot help but wish for those situations that make us heroic, living to the hilt of our total resources" (195).

[55] These instances of female violence against men reflect Lawrence's understanding of Nietzsche's contempt for submission and his advocacy of self-determination through action. For a detailed account of Nietzsche's influence on *Women in Love*, see Foster's *Heirs to Dionysus*, 185–229.

Moments of erotic struggle in Lawrence's "Love on the Farm" and "Rabbit Snared in the Night" likely influenced several poems Plath wrote both before and after she met Hughes. In Lawrence's "Love on the Farm," a woman describes her erotic encounter with a man who has just killed a rabbit:

> ... he raises up my face to him
> And caresses my mouth with his fingers, which still smell grim
> Of the rabbit's fur! God, I am caught in a snare!
> I know not what fine wire is round my throat,
> I only know I let him finger there
> My pulse of life, letting him nose like a stoat
> Who sniffs with joy before he drinks the blood:
> And down his mouth comes to my mouth, and down
> His dark bright eyes descend like a fiery hood
> Upon my mind: his mouth meets mine, and a flood
> Of sweet fire sweeps across me, so I drown
> Within him, die, and find death good.   (1986: 29)

In "Rabbit Snared in the Night," Lawrence again uses motifs of hunter and hunted as a metaphor for sex—as Plath will when she writes of her lust for Hughes in "Pursuit":

> Twas not *I* that wished it,
> that my fingers should turn into these flames
> avid and terrible
> that they are at this moment.
>
> It must have been *your* inbreathing, gaping desire
> that drew this red gush in me;
> I must be reciprocating *your* vacuous, hideous passion.
>
> It must be the want in you
> that has drawn this terrible draught of white fire
> up my veins as up a chimney.
>
> It must be you who desire
> this intermingling of the black and monstrous fingers of Moloch
> in the blood-jets of your throat.   (69)

While the role of these two Lawrence poems in the poets' later dialogue has been well documented, their influence on Plath's early work (pre-1956) has been overlooked.[56] Lawrence's violent language likely influenced, for example, Plath's "Sonnet: To Eva," which Hughes placed in the juvenilia section of Plath's *Collected Poems*:

---

[56] Perloff and Middlebrook have pointed out that both "Love on the Farm" and "Rabbit Snared in the Night" would become important referents later on in Plath's and Hughes's dialogue, when Plath would paint Hughes as a sadistic hunter in "The Rabbit Catcher." (Hughes would rewrite his own version of "The Rabbit Catcher" in *Birthday Letters*.)

> All right, let's say you could take a skull and break it
> The way you'd crack a clock; you'd crush the bone
> Between steel palms of inclination, take it,
> Observing the wreck of metal and rare stone.   (*CPP* 304)

Plath goes on to compare the broken skull to a broken woman, "her loves and stratagems | Betrayed." Or consider the violent language in Plath's "I Have Found the Perfect World" (1948), written when she was sixteen:

> When you pretended to praise me, I used to feel the primitive desire to kill you.
> I wanted to claw at your face until the blood ran down in wet red drops.
> I wanted to tear your hair out in rough handfuls.
> I wanted to beat your head against the ground until your skull was smashed to
> fragments.
> I wanted to do all this and more, while I laughed a mad vicious laughter.[57]

The language echoes that of the Lawrence poems quoted above, or even Hughes's in "Law in the Country of Cats," a poem that refutes " 'universal brotherhood,' | 'Love of humanity and each fellow-man' ":

> There will be that moment's horrible pause
> As each looks into the gulf in the eye of the other,
> Then a flash of violent incredible action,
> Then one man letting his brains gently to the gutter,
> And one man bursting into the police station
> Crying: "Let Justice be done. I did it, I."   (*CPH* 41)

Although Rose claims that Plath, in the famous description of her first meeting with Hughes, "requests admission to . . . the law of the country of the cats" (124)—that is, the world of violence—"I Have Found the Perfect World" and "Sonnet: To Eva" suggest that Plath had acquainted herself with this world through Lawrence long beforehand.

Lawrentian motifs also appear in "Item: Stolen, One Suitcase," written while Plath was a student at Smith. Here, the female speaker finds her male lover's cruelty seductive:

> Perilously silent, as I rave
> about my bankrupt home in hock
> which even this sweet weekend cannot save,
> you sit, severe; sarcastic as a clock,
> you ask if I am done, then give
>
> a savage slap across my mouth. "No dress,"
> you blaze, "shall hide the bruises of

---

[57] Sylvia Plath, "I Have Found the Perfect World," Box 7a, Plath MSS II, Lilly.

> my hands." Scalding through a fine, fierce kiss,
>   tears fall: I walk the city with my love,
>   naked, proud, and penniless.[58]

"Harlequin Love Song," also written while Plath was at Smith, likewise describes desire for a lover who will "Rage or ravish, bruise me black."[59] Both poems indulge in Lawrentian fantasies of erotic struggle. Plath would later cast "Gerald," the Hughes figure in *Falcon Yard*, as a lover who left her "black and blue." These early poems show that Plath's typecasting of Hughes conformed to much earlier representations of male lovers as cruel and violent.

Later, at Cambridge, Plath experienced a more complex and sustained encounter with Lawrence. Her tutor F. R. Leavis was one of Lawrence's most influential admirers; she, in turn, admired Leavis, calling him "magnificent" (*LH* 186). She also studied Lawrence with Dorothea Krook, her favorite tutor, in the months before she met Hughes. In an essay on Lawrence, Plath made it clear that she "approved" of his Nietzscheanism, writing, "The implication is that spontaneous hate is infinitely better than faked love" (qtd. in Peel 2004: 62). She was deeply moved by Lawrence's *The Man Who Died*, a novel that became for her a treasure trove of themes and imagery. She called it an "incredible fable" (*J* 229), and recorded the effect as Krook read from it aloud: "felt chilled, as in last paragraph of 'The Dead', as if angel had hauled me by the hair in a shiver of gooseflesh. . . . All seemed shudderingly relevant; I read in a good deal; I have lived much of this. It matters. Finished Lawrence before supper" (*J* 229). Plath starred and heavily underlined the following passage, which must have resonated with her desire, as the speaker of "Daddy" later put it, to "get back" to her dead father:

It was Isis Bereaved; Isis in Search. The goddess, in painted marble, lifted her face and strode, one thigh forward through the frail fluting of her robe, in the anguish of bereavement and of search. She was looking for the fragments of the dead Osiris, dead and scattered asunder, dead, torn apart, and thrown in fragments over the wide world. And she must find his hands and his feet, his heart, his thighs, his head, his belly, she must gather him together and fold her arms round the re-assembled body till it became warm again, and roused to life, and could embrace her, and could fecundate her womb. And the strange rapture and anguish of the search went on through the years. . . . And through the years she found him bit by bit, heart and head and limbs and body. And yet she had not found the last reality, the final clue to him, that alone could bring him really back to her.

(Lawrence 1931; 1950: 86)

Two days after reading *The Man Who Died*, Plath recorded her previous night's dream: "Then I was in my black coat and beret: Isis bereaved, Isis in search,

---

[58] Sylvia Plath, "Item: Stolen, One Suitcase," ibid.
[59] Sylvia Plath, "Harlequin Love Song," ibid.

walking a dark barren street" (*J* 234). These passages show that before she met Hughes, Plath had already imagined herself a shaman on a journey to the underworld, someone who would endure a symbolic death in order to make whole that which she had lost.

Of course, Plath's reverence for Lawrence intensified after she met Hughes in 1956. In February of 1957, she wrote a paper on Lawrence titled "D. H. Lawrence: The Tree of Knowledge Versus the Tree of Life," in which she displayed her extensive knowledge of Lawrence's work.[60] The paper suggests that she had begun to read Lawrence through the lenses of Hughes and Graves. According to Lawrence, Plath wrote:

Science has robbed the sun and moon of magic, leaving a spotted ball of gasses and a dead crater-pocked world in place of gold god and silver queen: a poor trade. Worse, men and women no longer live by intuition, but by ideas. The chittering dictums of the head and the will block out the spontaneous voices of the blood and the impulse . . . today, since we live from the head, instead of the "spontaneous centers",

> We have beastly benevolence, and foul good will,
> And stinking charity, and poisonous ideals.
>
> <u>Fantasia</u>, 129

. . . Deprived of the rhythm of savage song, the meaning of the animal yell, we exist for the mechanical screak of steel on steel. . . . What's to be done? . . . Well, we can destroy our mirrors, microscopes and telescopes. We can kneel in a grove "thronging with greenness" and pray for feeling to flow. We must not nudge, urge, thrust our Ideas about feeling on ourselves. But simply to wait. For the resurgence of the sun. For the resurgence of love.

We must get back "in touch."[61]

She also praised Connie Chatterley, writing that she "identifies herself with life. She chooses the spontaneous, intuitive expression of her own woman's nature. And becomes linked again with the creative rhythms of the universe."[62]

In a paper on Blake and Lawrence, written about three weeks later, she emphasized that

Both men were prophets. . . . both take a vehement, eloquent stand against all the forces in the world which would constrict the spontaneous actions of the whole man. . . . Lawrence, like Blake, fights constriction and deadness in its many protean forms. Both refuse to accept authority imposed on man from the outside: by Church, State, or strict moral code. Lawrence . . . like Blake, deplores the short work the scientists and rationalists have made of the luminous mysteries of the universe: of the sun and moon.[63]

---

[60] In this paper she cited passages from *Lady Chatterley's Lover, Fantasia of the Unconscious, The Plumed Serpent, The Man Who Died,* and *The Woman Who Rode Away.*

[61] Sylvia Plath, "D. H. Lawrence: The Tree of Knowledge Versus the Tree of Life," February 18, 1957, Plath MSS II, Box 13, Lilly.

[62] Ibid.

[63] Sylvia Plath, "Blake and Lawrence: A Brief Comparison and Contrast," March 14, 1957, Plath MSS II, Box 13, Lilly.

Plath went on to compare Lawrence's views to Zarathustra's. Hughes's contempt for science probably influenced Plath's reading of Lawrence in both papers, but each recalls themes she had already touched upon in her Smith essays.

CONJURING ADAM

In his portrait of Connie Chatterley and Oliver Mellors, Lawrence offered Plath a literary couple that spoke to her almost as much as Brontë's Cathy and Heathcliff. In February 1958, she re-read Lawrence's novels and lingered on parallels between his fictional lovers and herself and Hughes:

Today, from coffee till tea time at six, I read in "Lady Chatterley's Lover", drawn back again with the joy of a woman living with her own game-keeper, and "Women in Love" & "Sons & Lovers". Love, love: why do I feel I would have known & loved Lawrence— how many women must feel this & be wrong! I opened *The Rainbow* which I have never read & was sucked into the concluding Ursula & Skrebensky episode & sank back, breath knocked out of me, as I read of their London hotel, their Paris trip, their riverside loving while Ursula studied at college. This is the stuff of my life—my life, different, but no less brilliant & splendid, and the flow of my story will take me beyond this in my way— arrogant? I felt mystically that if I read Woolf, read Lawrence—(these two, why?—their vision, so different, is so like mine)—I can be itched and kindled at a great work: burgeoning, fat with texture & substance of life: this my call, my work.   (*J* 337)

It is likely Lawrence (and Nietzsche) had inspired Plath to look for a Heathcliffian partner—someone who, like Mellors in *Lady Chatterley's Lover*, would "match" her strength, even treat her with disdain.[64] There can be little doubt that Plath saw Hughes through such a Lawrentian lens. Plath's earliest descriptions of Hughes cast him as Adam, a Lawrentian hero or Nietzschean superman. In her letters to her mother she wrote that he was "the strongest man in the world...a large, hulking, healthy Adam...with a voice like the thunder of God" (*LH* 233), "violent," "tall, hulking," "a breaker of things and people," "a blast of Jove's lightning," someone whose "least gesture is like a derrick."[65] She later wrote to Lucas Myers that *The Hawk in the Rain* was a book "at which to stare awestruck, read in wild reverence, and built [*sic*] a great rock altar for in the middle of wild islands."[66]

The earliest poetic example of this Lawrentian typecasting occurs in Plath's "Pursuit," which she wrote on February 27, 1956, two days after she met Hughes. She was supposed to write a paper on Racine, but instead devoted her

[64] Middlebrook writes that Lawrence became "Plath's authority on the subject of finding an enabling partner, because he affirmed the idea that a great love was utterly recognizable.... Plath's copy of *Women in Love* is heavily, heavily underlined, marking the trail of her quest for the exact way to understand a true and authentic relationship between the sexes" (2003: 42).

[65] Sylvia Plath to Aurelia Plath, April 19, 1956, Lilly.

[66] Sylvia Plath to Lucas Myers, March 7, 1957, MSS 865, Emory.

afternoon to the poem, which, in her words, was about "the dark forces of lust" (*J* 214). "It is not bad," she wrote in her journal. "It is dedicated to Ted Hughes" (214). But no such dedication appears in the poem itself, only an epigraph from Racine's *Phèdre*: "*Dans le fond des forêts votre image me suit.*" (It is worth remembering that Connie Chatterley, flushed with excitement after an encounter with Mellors, asks her husband to read her Racine before bed.) Plath described the poem in greater detail to her mother, writing, with Yeatsian flourish, that it was "a symbol of the terrible beauty of death . . . death, here, includes the concept of love" (*LH* 222).

As Margaret Uroff has observed, the poem shows "how completely [Plath and Hughes] shared a predatory concept of passion" (70). While Plath seems to answer back to Hughes's "The Jaguar" in "Pursuit," she also alludes to his "Law in the Country of Cats" when she writes, "Insatiate, he ransacks the land | Condemned by our ancestral fault, | Crying: blood, let blood be spilt" (*CPP* 22). It is as if she is paraphrasing Hughes's "I did it, I." She also incorporates motifs from Lawrence's "Love on the Farm," "Snap-Dragon," and "Rabbit Snared in the Night"; her panther is like the rabbit hunter who "sniffs with joy before he drinks the blood" (1986: 29). Like those poems, "Pursuit" glorifies the violent dance between the male hunter and the female hunted. Yet it is more than merely an example of the "Bluebeard meets abjection" phenomenon that Rose sees as an essential part of the Plath–Hughes dialogue. On the surface, the poem seems like a fantasy of domination, even rape. The hunted female knows she is in dangerous territory; even as she runs from the slathering panther, she admits "His voice waylays me, spells a trance." She is "Appalled by secret want" and attempts to "shut my doors on that dark guilt" (*CPP* 23). Yet the second line of the poem suggests a less submissive speaker: "One day I'll have my death of him." The syntax seems intentionally ambiguous here: it is the hunted, not the hunter, who is in control of when and where her death will occur. This is a pattern we will encounter frequently in Plath's poems, particularly those influenced by, or in some sense about, Hughes. Although Plath often presents her speakers as submissive or naïve, closer analysis shows that they are in fact competing or debating with Hughes, and that they are often more violent than Hughes's animal predators.

Hughes's defense of his use of "positive violence" would have resonated with Plath's understanding of her predatory panther in "Pursuit": when Hughes called Blake's Tyger the "embodiment of divine life-energy" (*WP* 263), he may have remembered that Plath had declared her own panther a variant of that same Tyger. As she told her mother, the panther was "a symbol of the terrible beauty of death, and the paradox that the more intensely one lives, the more one burns and consumes oneself" (*LH* 222). Like Hughes, Plath cited Yeats's concept of "terrible beauty" to elucidate her own "rough beast." As we will see in Chapter 5, poems such as "The Shrike" and "Soliloquy of the Solipsist" show that Plath, like Hughes, sought to expose the beauty of the "divine law" in her early work; she may have even intensified Hughes's own interest in this theme, though she is rarely given credit for doing so. As Uroff notes, "it would be several years before Hughes himself would write of an animal as ravenous as her panther. His early jaguar was caged, and not until *Lupercal* (1960) did Hughes release his animals from their bars" (70).

Like "Pursuit," several pages from Plath's fragmentary "Venus in the Seventh"—likely an early draft of *Falcon Yard*, her lost novel—provide a revealing fictional representation of the couple in the early stages of their courtship. The first few pages recount the escapades of Jess Greenwood, an American Cambridge student and poet, as she travels through Munich and Venice during her Easter vacation. These pages are based on Plath's journey to the Continent during the spring of 1956, shortly after she had met Hughes. Jess's former beau, Winthrop, accompanies her, but his solicitous presence is a constant source of annoyance. She looks forward to her reunion with her British lover, clearly based on Hughes, back in London. Jess's language echoes Lawrence's in *Women in Love*. "The newness of Gerald caught at her. She knew nothing much. But he was hard, and cruel. And if she could take it without whimpering... then she might take life, after a fashion.... Just feel, stride along with him, until he bashed her head in and went off with the next."[67] When Jess returns to London, she sticks her carefully coiffed head out the window of the taxi on her way to Rugby Street. "She would look wild, but what did she care. The recklessness came banging up in her: stronger and fiercer than she had ever known it."

Plath's first description of Ian (formerly Gerald) as a dark outsider recalls Heathcliff: "Ian hulked there, in his black sweater, with the collar up, unshaven. He stepped back to let her in.... And his voice. UnBritish. Refugee Pole rather, mixed with something of Dylan Thomas: rich and mellow-noted. Half sung." He directs her upstairs to meet a friend, Jim, whose presence Jess immediately resents. "She just wanted Ian: very simply. She could swim in him: that incredible violent presence of his: leashed. Too much man for this island. The only man on it. He didn't think: he was." Later, Ian tells her of his dreams of white leopards and foxes, while Jess talks about her "black dreams... Nightmares, all dark and sultry with the air yellow as sulphur." They discuss their first night together before Jess left for Europe. Both hint at violent passion:

> "If you hadn't come back, I would have come to Cambridge to find you again. To make up for that last time..."
> She shivered, holding herself up against him, their toes touching. "Oh," she laughed ruefully. "It was terrible, that. I went to Paris all scarred. Black and blue..."
> "But you liked it?"
> "Yes."
> "I was furious with myself. I don't know what happened to me..."[68]

---

[67] Sylvia Plath, "Venus in the Seventh," Box 140, MSS 644, Emory.
[68] Plath's ellipses.

Inevitably, they begin reciting poetry. Jess recites her "Conversation Among the Ruins"—the title of an actual poem by Plath which Hughes later placed at the beginning of her *Collected Poems*. She tells Ian she has dedicated it to him. This poem is a strange choice, as it foretells the lovers' doom: "the play turned tragic." After listening, he remarks, "You like one-syllabled words, don't you? Squab, patch, crack. Violent." Jess answers, "Yes, I guess I do. I hate 'ation' words. They're so abstract. I like words to sound what they say: bang crash. Not mince along in iambic pentameters." Importantly, it is Jess, rather than her male lover, who stakes her claim to violent language; it is clear from this passage that she does not co-opt her lover's words. Rather, *he* remarks upon *her* preference for words that "sound what they say: bang, crash." Plath suggests that Jess did not learn this violent language from Ian; on the contrary, she presents the couple as lovers drawn together by a shared aesthetic.

Plath's early representation of Hughes in "Pursuit" and "Venus in the Seventh" is fictionalized—she is responding to elements of violence in his poetry rather than in his person. Critics would later complain at length about Hughes's refusal to separate Plath's "body" from the body of her poems and his tendency to claim that Plath's poems were an outward performance of her inner drama. But Plath too saw her husband as the embodiment of his writing, and was just as guilty of failing to delineate between the life of the writer and the story of the work. If Hughes represents Plath as damaged and passive, Plath sees Hughes as damaging and aggressive. Hughes was cast as Bluebeard after only the briefest of auditions.[69] Yet Hughes, too, revered Lawrence, and one gets the sense, in his early letters to Plath, that he did not mind playing Oliver Mellors to her Lady Chatterley. In a letter to Plath in October 1956, for example, he wrote of being stopped by a police car on an evening walk to Hebden Bridge: "They checked me over as if I were some wild man.... The fact is, I'm unrecognisable and look like a strange beast unless you're with me.... I was just stepping up into the fish and chip shop ... when two little girls ran out with their arms full of wrapped fish and chips, when they saw me one let out a scream" (*L* 58). Three years later, they were still playing their respective parts. In 1959, Hughes wrote to Olwyn that he and Plath had dressed up for a New Year's Eve party: "Sylvia as Red Riding Hood, me as the Wolf."[70]

The themes of competition, erotic struggle, and violence at the heart of "Pursuit" would become touchstones in the couples' poetic dialogue. Although Plath would eventually disavow the ideas of Nietzsche and Lawrence in her late work, their doctrines of willful self-actualization gave her the necessary "strength" to challenge Hughes's aesthetic and to compete with him as an

---

[69] Stephen Ennis has noted that the deposit of Hughes's papers at Emory has given way to a more complex understanding of the poet: "With the passing of each year the shrillest accusations leveled at Hughes have grown a little fainter, and from our present vantage point, Robin Morgan's charge that Hughes murdered Plath seems a dated period piece" (66).

[70] Ted Hughes to Olwyn Hughes, January 1959, MSS 980, Emory.

equal. Thus, even as she mocked Hughes's Nietzschean masculine sublime in *Ariel,* she could not help but invoke it in her own quest for self-becoming. The influences she shared with Hughes would continue to shape her work even after they separated—and that work would, in turn, shape Hughes's later work. The Lawrentian theatrics both performed the night they met revealed the extent to which each had already forged an aesthetic identity around "positive violence." Yet these affinities, which initially inspired trust, would eventually lead to suspicion. Plath's and Hughes's shared interest in Nietzschean and Lawrentian concepts of self-actualization helps account for why their "collaboration" would unravel after only seven years of marriage: to champion the other was to deny the self. Neither was wholly prepared for such self-denial, despite the facade of mutual support. While Plath frequently assumed the traditional female role of the "abject" partner—typing Hughes's manuscripts, performing his poetic exercises, reading what he instructed—many of her early poems and short stories reveal that she was undermining this position through her art. Hughes, too, took Plath's threat to his hermetic poetic selfhood seriously; his early writings are filled with femme fatales and motifs of struggle and competition. As we will see, both poets were deeply worried about the other's perceived attempts at "remaking." Ironically, the philosophy of willful self-assertion that had initially brought the poets together would play a large role in driving them apart.

2

Secret Anxieties

For several decades now, critics have taken for granted the idea that Ted Hughes was, in Harold Bloom's terms, the "strong" poet in the Plath–Hughes partnership. Janet Malcolm, for example, has written that Plath "looks up to him, and she seeks help from him in filling the 'huge, sad hole' of her inadequacy" (89). John Beer claims that Plath had "a desperate urge to anchor herself against someone who could offer the stability of a firm point of reference" (172), while Erica Wagner writes that Plath felt Hughes was "superior" (22). Diane Middlebrook similarly notes that Plath's "sense of security...rested on a belief in his superiority to her" (2003: 186).[1] Of course, there is reason for this assumption. Hughes, after all, was more firmly rooted in an English literary tradition from which Plath, on account of her gender and nationality, felt estranged; he also received far more literary accolades than Plath during the years of their marriage. Plath herself frequently cast Hughes as her teacher and caregiver.[2]

Yet epistolary evidence undermines the view that Hughes was confident of his superiority over Plath, and that he attempted to sabotage Plath's writing in order to tame her into a submissive housewife. While Plath at times did feel such a threat from Hughes, early letters from Hughes to friends, family, and Plath herself suggest that he took his wife's vocation seriously; that he believed in her talent; and that he understood Plath's genius well before it was obvious to anyone else. As he told the *Paris Review* in 1995, "Once I got to know her and read her poems, I saw straight off that she was a genius of some kind" (77). While Hughes did make sexist comments to Plath in some of his letters—telling her, for example, that her verse never went " 'soft' like other women's" (*L* 82)—those comments need to be read in their historical context. As Sandra Gilbert and Susan Gubar remind us, Plath belonged to only the second generation of women poets to achieve public success in their lifetimes; one must remember "how new Plath's historical situation was" (1994: 3.271). This "situation" was a reality to which Hughes, as well as Plath, had to adjust. If Plath veered between "scholarly

---

[1] Middlebrook also writes that Plath believed "that while she is immensely strong, too strong for most men to take, Hughes is stronger.... She *gains* power in connecting to Hughes; he *has* power, no matter what" (2003: 42–3).

[2] Malcolm writes, "we cannot fail to notice a common denominator in the two visions of Hughes: he is a brilliant, kindly, lovable teacher or he is a stupid, smug, hateful one, but in both cases he is the *teacher* and she the pupil" (88–9). Rose, too, notes this tendency (128).

admiration of an often misogynistic male modernist tradition and secret anxiety about that tradition" (Gilbert and Gubar, 1994: 3.270), then Hughes too may have veered between admiration for the woman poet and anxiety about how to negotiate her emerging "tradition." Unlike a number of Plath's male critics, Hughes *was* receptive to Plath's "female" genius, even if also unsettled by it.[3] Ironically, Hughes's firm belief in Plath may have caused him to feel as hampered by domesticity as she did, and equally afraid of becoming the abject or displaced partner. Indeed, there is ample evidence in the couple's poems, correspondence, and prose that *both* thought of themselves as "strong, authentic poets" (Bloom 1973: 30) in danger of being "remade" by the other.

"MARRIAGE IS MY MEDIUM"

In 1962, after Plath began work on *Ariel*, she famously linked her newfound creative energy to her independence from Hughes, claiming, "domesticity had choked me" (*LH* 466). Even if this were true, it would be a mistake to assume that Hughes had "silenced" Plath from the early years of their marriage. While Plath sometimes hinted that she felt Hughes caused her writing blocks, he never actively prevented her from writing. On the contrary, he encouraged her to try to break through her blocks by setting up exercises—later to be interpreted, by Plath, as orders—and by acting as a springboard for poetic themes and short story plots. (It is worth noting that Hughes set exercises for male poets, too; in 1971 he sent a list of 15 ideas for poetic exercises to the Irish poet Richard Murphy [*L* 314].) In fact, during the early years of the marriage, there was as much mutual support and collaboration as there was suspicion. Hughes, in his letters to Plath, her mother Aurelia, and his brother Gerald, comes across as a sensitive, supportive husband who cared deeply about his wife's career. There is no evidence in these letters that Hughes belittled Plath's ambitions. Instead, the letters from Hughes to Plath, written during October 1956 when the newlyweds were living apart, are filled with praise and encouragement, even good-natured envy. Hughes told Plath she would be "famous" (*L* 49), that she would "spell-bind" America's editors (*L* 56), that she was a brilliant writer and student who would undoubtedly get a first on her Cambridge exams, and that her poems were becoming ever tighter. He also provided moral support when Plath was feeling intimidated or inferior. When she wrote to him of her encounters with arrogant male poets at Cambridge that autumn, he told her not to worry, since she was by far the better poet—in fact, he assured her that she was the only *real* poet in the entire university. When she complained about her rejections from the *New Yorker*, he lambasted the quality of the magazine's poems and exhorted her not to change her style to fit theirs. To do so, he wrote, would kill not only her spirit,

---

[3] These critics include Irving Howe, Hugh Kenner, and Harold Bloom.

but also her talent. Instead, he urged her to pursue her own course, saying that none of the great writers pandied to anyone else's style—least of all a magazine's. If only she could find the confidence to write how and what she wanted, he suggested, she would become a great poet: "Just write it off, in your own way" (*L* 66). To others, too, Hughes boasted of Plath's triumphs. In April 1957 he wrote to Aurelia and Warren Plath that Plath's poetry manuscript (what would eventually become *The Colossus*) was outstandingly accomplished, and that each poem reinforced the next. She had avoided all the pitfalls of the amateur—in particular, writing poems whose styles were so different as to upset the unity of the collection—and had proven herself on her own terms.[4]

Hughes's letters during this time reveal a working partnership. In a letter to his brother Gerald in 1956, he wrote that "As a result of her influence I have written continually and every day better since I met her. She is a very fine critic of my work, and abuses just those parts of it that I daren't confess to myself are unworthy" (*L* 46–7). A year later, in 1957, Hughes told Gerald that he and Plath constantly worked together to improve each other's poems. No one, he said, understood his mind better than she did: "Marriage is my medium. Also my luck thrives on it, and my productions. You have no idea what a happy life Sylvia and I lead. . . . We work and walk about, and repair each other's writings. She is one of the best critics I ever met and understands my imagination perfectly, and I think I understand hers. It's amazing how we strike sparks" (*L* 97). Plath's letters home during this time are filled with similar sentiments; she wrote constantly to her mother, brother, and Olive Prouty that she and Hughes worked well together and that the partnership stimulated her creativity. In one early letter, for example, she wrote, "both of us are so fluent with writing and ideas, and criticize each other's output every day, stimulating each other and exchanging ideas."[5]

There were several instances of collaboration. Hughes trusted Plath's judgment enough to help him choose the final poems for *The Hawk in the Rain*.[6] When the Faber proofs of the book arrived in May 1957, Plath told her mother that she "limited" Hughes's revisions, and implied that if not for her restraining hand he "he would rewrite a poem to eternity" (*LH* 313). These proofs suggest that Hughes may have accepted Plath's edits (if these edits, in her handwriting, were in fact her suggestions) to "Griefs for Dead Soldiers" and "The Ancient Heroes and the Bomber Pilot." Plath helped Hughes with many short story and drama plots; in one letter he apologized for stealing her material,[7] while elsewhere he wrote that she supplied the "exercise" which inspired his short story "Snow."[8] Letters also reveal that Plath suggested major revisions to Hughes's

---

[4] Ted Hughes to Aurelia and Warren Plath, April 1957, Lilly.
[5] Sylvia Plath to Aurelia Plath, August 10, 1956, Lilly.
[6] Ted Hughes, "Notes on Published Works," March 1992, Box 115, MSS 644, Emory.
[7] Ted Hughes to Sylvia Plath, October 16, 1956, Lilly. Hughes wrote "I'm sorry to steal your own material" in reference to a plotline involving a couple at a party in Cambridge.
[8] Ted Hughes, "Notes on Published Works," March 1992, Box 115, MSS 644, Emory.

children's book, *How the Whale Became* (originally entitled *How the Donkey Became*), some of which he accepted.[9] He wrote to his sister Olwyn from Spain that he was excited the fables passed muster with Plath, whom he called "as fine a literary critic as I have met" (*L* 46).

Hughes, too, encouraged Plath in certain aesthetic directions. He advised her to read poetry out loud as she walked in time to the meter (*L* 50–1), a method that may have influenced her composition of several *Ariel* poems. And he spent considerable time commenting upon Plath's poems in his letters, a practice that shows he took her writing seriously. His suggestions for revision were always minor; he usually picked two or three words he disagreed with, and gave a long and thorough explanation as to why another choice would be better. He was always complimentary, and sometimes amazed. When Plath published a batch of poems in *Poetry*, for example, Hughes's showered her with praise: "Now you are set. I never read six poems of anyone all together in *Poetry*. It means the wonderful thing. It will spellbind every Editor in America. It will also be a standing bottomless battery to charge what you write from now on, because you are almost certain to sell nearly everything you write now. . . . Joy Joy" (*L* 56). Plath recorded Hughes's considered reaction to one of her short stories in a letter to her mother:

Well, he took me on a long evening walk, listened to me talk the whole plot out, showed me what I'd vaguely felt I should change about the end. Last night he read all 30 pages of it, word for word, unerringly pointing out awkwardness here or an unnecessary paragraph there. He is proud of the story, thinks it's exciting and valid.   (*LH* 301)

This is not a portrait of a master teacher speaking down to his acolyte, but rather one writer offering his perspective, for what it is worth, to another. When we remember the bewilderment of Thomas Wentworth Higginson upon receiving Emily Dickinson's verse, or John Ruskin's dismissal of Christina Rossetti's manuscript, Hughes's support of a woman poet's work stands out as exceptional.

Hughes also introduced Plath to the war poetry of Wilfred Owen and Keith Douglas (Hughes, in fact, was largely responsible for resurrecting Douglas's reputation in the 1960s).[10] Olwyn Hughes gives a vivid account of Plath and Hughes reading Douglas together at her parents' house in Yorkshire in 1956:

Ted and Sylvia spent most of a beautiful summer day there, laying on a rug in the field beyond the low garden wall, engrossed in Keith Douglas's *Collected Poems* of 1951. Two poets communing with a precursor whose work had many affinities with their own . . . I always saw this as an image of Sylvia and Ted's central shared allegiance to poetry. In his introduction to the Douglas selection (Faber, 1964), Ted lists the qualities he sees in Douglas, and it could well be an appraisal of the direction of Ted's own work. Douglas's

    [9] Sylvia Plath to Aurelia Plath, October 16, 1956, Lilly; Ted Hughes to Sylvia Plath, October 17, 1956, Lilly.
    [10] Hughes told Douglas's mother he discovered her son's writing in an anthology, and then "procured a copy of his Collection, with great difficulty, from an American book dealer" (qtd. in Pearsall 526).

skills and the presentiment of his death that haunted him must have deeply affected Sylvia. Douglas's poem THE SEA BIRD, with its dazzling flight and doom, mirrors her inmost fears and her own soaring achievement and end.[11]

Hughes was so impressed by Douglas that he delivered a short program on the BBC about him in 1962, and then, at Faber's request, edited and introduced a collection of Douglas's poetry.[12] Hughes was initially drawn to Douglas's work on account of his father's service in the Great War, but the abiding interest was based on more than historical affinity: he likely found in Douglas's verse an antidote to what he perceived as the Movement's timidity. In his Faber introduction, he made clear that what Cornelia Pearsall called Douglas's "masculine postures" and "muscular poetics" (529) appealed to him: he praised Douglas's "extremely forceful" language, his "razor energy," and his "feat of great strength" (1964: ix).[13] By reintroducing Douglas back into the English canon, Hughes was promoting his own aesthetic; his comments regarding Douglas's poetic preoccupations were also true of his own: "In a sense, war was his ideal subject: the burning away of all human pretensions in the ray cast by death" (1964: xi).

Both Cornelia Pearsall and Tim Kendall have persuasively documented Douglas's influence on Hughes, yet they say less about his influence on Plath, who also embraced Douglas.[14] After Hughes's BBC broadcast, she wrote to her mother, "Both of us mourn this poet immensely and feel he would have been like a lovely big brother to us. His death is really a terrible blow and we are trying to resurrect his image and poems" (*LH* 456). Plath surely would have been affected by what Pearsall has called Douglas's "skeletal poetics." Consider, for example, Douglas's "Simplify Me When I'm Dead":

> Remember me when I am dead
> and simplify me when I'm dead.
>
> As the processes of earth
> strip off the colour and the skin
> take the brown hair and blue eye
>
> and leave me simpler than at birth
> when hairless I came howling in
> as the moon came in the cold sky.   (21)

The theme of rebirth, as well as the chilly moon imagery, must have appealed to Plath. Likewise, Douglas's "Bête Noire," which tells of an insidious, internal

---

[11] Olwyn Hughes, "Notes on Correspondence [with Ted Hughes]," n.d., MSS 980, Emory.

[12] He also wrote an essay on Douglas for the *Listener* in June 1962 and another for *Critical Inquiry* in the spring of 1963.

[13] In his 1987 introduction to Douglas's work, Hughes again praised his "masculine movement, a nimble, predatory attack, hard-edged" and his "tensile strength" (qtd. in Pearsall 531; 529).

[14] See Tim Kendall's "Fighting Back over the Same Ground: Ted Hughes and War" and Cornelia Pearsall's "The War Remains of Keith Douglas and Ted Hughes" for extended discussions of Douglas's influence on Hughes.

double, brings to mind Plath's use of the same trope in poems such as "In Plaster":

> This is my particular monster. I know him;
> he walks about inside me: I'm his house
> and his landlord. . . .
>
> .   .   .   .   .   .
>
> The Beast is a jailer
> allows me out on parole
> brings me back by telepathy
> is inside my mind
> breaks into my conversation with his own words,
> speaking out of my mouth
> can overthrow me in a moment
> writes what I write, or edits it (censors it) . . .   (31–2)

While other male poets of the period may have assumed, condescendingly, that a female peer would not be interested in—or able to understand—the masculine verse of a war poet, Hughes felt no such reluctance in sharing Douglas's verse with Plath. His desire to introduce Plath to Douglas's poems shows that he assumed, on account of their shared aesthetic, that she would feel a similar kinship. The couple's reading of Douglas was another example of the kind of literary collaboration which benefited both poets during the early years of the marriage.

"WIVED, RINGED AND ROOFED"

These letters and instances of collaboration suggest what Hughes himself has always insisted: that he took Plath's poetic talent seriously—so seriously, in fact, that he may have felt threatened by her ambition, worried that his own writing would suffer in the hothouse atmosphere of a rivalrous marriage. As he told Drue Heinz in 1995, "Our telepathy was intrusive" (77). Hughes's unpublished explication of Plath's "The Munich Mannequins" suggests that he really did believe his wife could steal his ideas through what he called "clairvoyant divination": he suggests that in this poem, Plath had invoked the figure of Assia Wevill through the "demon queen" Nehamah, "whose amusement was to masquerade as a human beauty, seduce a husband, and direct the consequences." Because Plath was not aware of the figure of Nehamah, he assumed she must have found the figure in his mind. "She had great reason, last resource reason, in other words, to use a little telepathic power, of which she had an abundance, and pick his brains for an image that would awaken him. . . . Since the cultural fossil figure of Nehamah lay in her husband's brain, it cannot be counted out."[15] If Hughes believed Plath was capable of literally reading his mind, he would

[15] Ted Hughes, "Notes on Sylvia Plath's 'Munich Mannequins' and 'Totem'," Box 115, MSS 644, Emory.

have had all the more reason to view her as a threat to his poetic autonomy. Indeed, in a letter to Plath's mother after her suicide, he spoke about the "strangling quality of our closeness" (*L* 218).

Middlebrook has written that Hughes was "an authoritative and a close, even jealous, witness" to Plath's poetic development ("Stevens" 2006: 50). Middlebrook's tentative and qualifying "even" illustrates the hesitancy with which Plath and Hughes critics broach the subject of Hughes's jealousy. Hughes, however, was not immune to the threat of Plath's own crossover into his poetic territory. While Hughes encouraged Plath's ambition, he may have also felt increasing anxiety about that ambition and its potentially emasculating effect. The observations of psychologist Jean Miller suggest that such a reaction would not have been unusual:

when women begin to move out of their restricted place, they threaten men in a very profound sense with the need to reintegrate many of the essentials of human development—the essentials that women have been carrying for the total society. Those things have been warded off and become doubly fearful because they look as if they will entrap men in "emotions," weakness, sexuality, vulnerability, helplessness, the need for care, and other unsolved areas. (120)

According to Joan Riviere, women who take up masculine roles "exaggerate" their femininity in order to appear less threatening to men. Yet this strategy does not always work, for exaggerated femininity becomes a construct "behind which man suspects some hidden danger" (43). Whether or not Hughes suspected that Plath's eagerness to take on the role of the model fifties housewife was a way for her to minimize her literary "threat," many of his poems betray suspicion towards women, especially those who flaunt their femininity.

Several potential BBC radio play plots, which Hughes sent to Plath during the autumn of 1956, suggest he was anxious about the nature of a marriage in which husband and wife both sought to become great writers. Interestingly, many of these plots concerned marriages that self-destruct on account of jealousy. One, for example, revolves around a woman trapped in an abusive marriage who tries to poison herself but, on second thought, decides to poison her husband instead.[16] Another plot tells of a husband who flies into a jealous rage after finding his wife with another man,[17] while still another tells the story of a woman living alone in the countryside who harbors, and eventually falls in love with, an outlaw who has murdered his wife (*L* 67–8). One plot is uncannily prophetic: in it a newly married couple decides to move to the country in order to find solitude and escape the adulterous temptations of the city (*L* 54–5). Soon, however, they grow tired of the country and decide to start an inn. Before long, their city friends

[16] Ted Hughes to Sylvia Plath, October 5, 1956, Lilly. This plot was omitted from the published *Letters*.

[17] Ted Hughes to Sylvia Plath, October 8, 1956, Lilly. This plot was omitted from the published *Letters*.

flock to the inn, and both husband and wife are tempted by their old lovers. In the end, the couple buys a cottage closer to the city so that they will no longer feel so isolated. Was this plot a kind of warning, both to himself and Plath, of the potential dangers that awaited such a relationship as theirs? Besides being prophetic—how could Hughes have known that he and his wife would move to Devon, that their city friends would later descend upon them and wreak havoc upon their marriage?—the plot may have been a way to suggest to Plath what Hughes could never have said himself: that lovers who depended solely upon one another, who did not allow others into their world, would soon find that world stifling rather than liberating. The other plots, in which unhappy couples are unhinged by jealousy, further suggest that Hughes may have already been skeptical of monogamy. Indeed, a 1986 letter from Hughes to his son Nicholas hints at the claustrophobia he experienced during the early years of the marriage, when he and Plath were living in America:

We made hardly any friends, no close ones, and neither of us ever did anything the other didn't want wholeheartedly to do.... Since the only thing we both wanted to do was write, our lives disappeared into the blank page.... Why didn't I explore America then? I wanted to. I knew it was there. Ten years later we could have done it, because by then we would have learned, maybe, that one person cannot live within another's magic circle, as an enchanted prisoner. (*L* 512)[18]

Hughes's anxieties may have been provoked by Plath's campaign, during the late fifties, to "remake" her husband into the kind of mate she could proudly present to her middle-class friends and family in America. While Plath was deeply attracted to Hughes's Heathcliffian persona, she must have realized that her mother would be less impressed. Plath's letters to her family in the mid-fifties suggest that Hughes was a work in progress; in April 1956, about two months after meeting him, she wrote to her mother and brother of her plans to pacify him, to "teach him care...gentleness," to "make him kind," and of her "faith and work and fighting to re-make him daily according to his best potential."[19] It seems that by late May of 1956 this "remaking" was complete: "I have saved him to be the best man he can be. As he says himself, in two more years he would have grown to be a hard, knotty nut to crack, bitter & cynical, and destructive. Now he is responding, re-forming."[20] Two months later Plath again reported on Hughes's progress to her mother: "I have worked hard & given my all to bring him to his proper self."[21] She hoped that they would "become truly one person in the world's eyes."[22]

---

[18] Hughes's memory is slightly faulty—Leonard Baskin, whom the couple met at Smith, surely counts as a close friend.

[19] Sylvia Plath to Aurelia and Warren Plath, April 19, 1956, Lilly; April 23, 1956, Lilly; May 6, 1956, Lilly.

[20] Sylvia Plath to Aurelia Plath, May 26, 1956, Lilly.

[21] Sylvia Plath to Aurelia Plath, August 10, 1956, Lilly. That same month she wrote to her brother Warren, "I could make him kind, I think, and a little more caring of other people" (April 23, 1956, Lilly).

[22] Sylvia Plath to Aurelia Plath, May 26, 1956, Lilly.

This "remaking" began with Hughes's physical appearance; Plath noted in letters home that he was a "Big unruly Huckleberry Finn" who "hadn't even a suit of clothes."[23] Although this was part of his charm at the beginning of the relationship, by 1958 it had become a source of annoyance: "Shut eyes to dirty hair, ragged nails," she wrote in her journal (420). She took it upon herself to intervene. In 1959 she wrote to her mother of her pleasure at seeing her husband well dressed for once:

did I tell you that along with Ted's charcoal gray suit I have made him get a lovely brown-and-black tweed jacket...which he wore to London last weekend and looked handsome as a Duke. He could do with another, though. I'd postpone shirts till America, when I can take proper care of them; I'll try to get him a bathrobe; what he needs very badly is a kind of leather shaving kit....He also needs luggage...he needs just about everything.[24]

Hughes was a literary celebrity by this point, and Plath wanted him to look preened and professional. Note, however, that she says she "made" Hughes purchase the new clothes, as if she were dressing him against his will.

Plath felt that in America, she would free Hughes from the "sick small insular inbred land" that had caused him to go "wild."[25] She told her brother that her "secret campaign is to make Ted <u>love</u> America" and wrote her mother that Hughes would "change if he gets somewhere the land is big enough, free enough for his colossal gestures."[26] Yet Hughes, predictably, felt ill at ease in suburban America; it was he, after all, who, according to Seamus Heaney, "recalled English poetry in the fifties from a too suburban aversion of the attention from the elemental" (1983: 17). When he first arrived at Plath's home in Wellesley, Massachusetts, in June 1957, he expressed his unease with the life he felt Plath was leading him toward. He soon wrote to his brother Gerald that he wanted to sleep on the floor "just to keep in contact with a world that isn't quite so glazed as this one"; in the same letter he compared American life to "an officially entered numbered trap in the rat-race" (*L* 103). Later that autumn he experienced a debilitating writing block, telling Lucas Myers, "I have never known it so hard to write" (*L* 110). Elaine Feinstein notes that during this time he urged Myers "to compose, behave and fornicate" for him since he was now "'wived, ringed and roofed'" (79). That March, Plath quoted Hughes in her journal as saying "I want to get clear of this life: trapped" (Feinstein 81), while two months later he complained to his brother that American culture was "anti-mental, anti-solitary-study, anti-thinking for yourself."[27] Hughes made a

---

[23] Sylvia Plath to Aurelia Plath, May 4, 1956, Lilly.
[24] Sylvia Plath to Aurelia Plath, October 16, 1956, Lilly.
[25] Sylvia Plath to Aurelia Plath, April 19, 1956, Lilly.
[26] Sylvia Plath to Warren Plath, February 28, 1957, Lilly; Sylvia Plath to Aurelia Plath, April 19, 1956, Lilly.
[27] Ted Hughes to Gerald Hughes, May 1958, MSS 854, Emory.

telling remark in a Christmas card to Myers in 1957 that hints at the marital tension surrounding the prospect of staying in America. When Plath asked Myers when he was coming back to America, Hughes wrote underneath, "She doesn't mean 'will you ever come home,' she means 'will we ever get back to Europe.' Our hope."[28] These early letters from America show that as much as Hughes complied with Plath's wishes, he resented the toll the move took upon his writing life. He probably feared the fate laid out in Robert Graves's *The White Goddess*: "the woman whom he took to be a Muse, or who was a Muse, turns into a domestic woman and would have him turn similarly into a domestic man" (449). (Indeed, he admitted to Olwyn that he was "living on Sylvia's money entirely, and [had] been doing so for some time" during his honeymoon in Spain.[29])

Perhaps Plath's most successful act of remaking—one that later caused resentment on Hughes's part—was her insistence that he stop shooting. As Hughes told Jack Brown in 1998, he "stopped shooting" in 1956. "It was S.P. who transformed me actually—in one flash." Hughes went on to say that when he stopped shooting,

I lost a whole faculty of vision & awareness. Before then, whatever landscape I looked into, I saw every living thing—every tiniest trace. It never occurred to me, what I had lost, till about 15 years ago a friend down here invited me on a farmer's shoot . . . he shoved a gun into my hands. My heart began to pound and instantly, I realised, I could see absolutely everything—just as when I was a boy. I had a clairvoyant, dream sort of day, shot my pheasants, then gave back the gun. Instantly—the vision went, the old, marvelous alertness simply went. (*L* 705)

Hughes links Plath's demand for him to stop shooting to his loss of a dream-like—perhaps even poetic—vision. Considering the extent to which Hughes's early poetic identity was bound up with the metaphor of the hunt, Plath's demand must have been a source of frustration. Even forty years later, his sense of regret is palpable.

"THE MAELSTROM DARK OF THE OTHER"

Writing about war was perhaps a way for Hughes to 'protect' himself from Plath's efforts to remake or suburbanize him. Of course, Hughes was inspired to write about war for other reasons—his father was a survivor of Gallipoli, and many men from his region had died in the First World War. Several poems of war in *The Hawk in the Rain* lament the loss of the legions of young Yorkshiremen who had died on the battlefields of Flanders; from a young age, Hughes felt

---

[28] Ted Hughes and Sylvia Plath to Lucas Myers, Christmas 1957, MSS 865, Emory.
[29] Ted Hughes to Olwyn Hughes, summer 1956, MSS 980, Emory.

that "the whole region is in mourning for the first world war" (qtd. in Kendall 2005: 87).[30] Yet the battle between the sexes also played a part in Hughes's desire to write about war. Indeed, many love poems in Hughes's early work rely heavily on war imagery, and suggest that his attraction to the theme during the late fifties and early sixties was influenced not only by the work of Wilfred Owen and Keith Douglas, but also by Plath's rivalrous "threat."

In Hughes's work, love is frequently viewed as a competition, a game that ends in mutual obliteration. "Incompatibilities," for example, exhibits anxiety toward a powerful female rival/lover while alluding to the war poetry of Wilfred Owen. Although the poem suggests an intense sexual encounter, the speaker appears uncomfortable with the surrender of self such an encounter entails. He notes that just as desire "welds hot | Iron of their separates to one," it also "Cold-chisels two selfs single" (*CPH* 28). The moment of orgasm is construed ambiguously:

> Each, each second, lonelier and further
> Falling alone through the endless
> Without-world of the other, though both here
> Twist so close they choke their cries. (28)

The language here echoes that of "Bawdry Embraced" (dedicated to Plath), in which two lovers merge into a single self in a moment of fiery transcendence. In both poems, that moment is described in the language of loss. Although the "fall" to the core of another is exhilarating, it is also marked by a descent into loneliness. And the characterization of "the endless | Without-world of the other" suggests terror as much as it does freedom. The image of the couple choking each other's cries carries similar ambiguity. Hughes uses pararhymes that belie a reassuring completion, and point to the eerie underworld of Owen's "Strange Meeting," in which a fallen soldier recognizes his double in the ghost of the enemy he has killed. The imagery of impersonal, mechanized violence, the suggestion of choking lovers and "blackouts of impassables" bring the literary tropes of the Great War to mind. Hughes's penultimate stanza enacts the gruesome ritual of going over the top as much as it does romantic fusion:

> Each body still straining to follow down
> The maelstrom dark of the other, their limbs flail
> Flesh and beat upon
> The inane everywhere of its obstacle (28)

---

[30] As Kendall notes, Hughes became alternately obsessed with, then repulsed by, his own "'permanent preoccupation' with the Great War" (2005: 87). Although Hughes has often been read as a nature poet, Kendall shows that his interest in war was equally important in determining the shape of his work. "Writing about the natural world," Kendall writes, "he therefore appears less a war poet manqué than a war poet by other means. . . . Inescapably influenced by the Great War, his language goes over the top even when his subjects do not" (88).

Hughes again uses Great War imagery in "Two Phases," in which the speaker regrets going willingly into love's captivity. Although he would once do anything for his lover,

> Now, stripped to the skin,
> Can scarcely keep alive,
> Sweats his stint out,
> No better than a blind mole
> That burrows for its lot
> Of the flaming moon and sun
> Down some black hole.   (*CPH* 30–1)

The lover is here compared to a Great War soldier, initially naïve and eager to beat the Hun, now mournfully completing his "stint" in the trenches alongside the vermin. That these love poems should also suggest the terror and despair of trench warfare reveals, perhaps, Hughes's skepticism toward the myth of romantic love. Hughes would later use the imagery of the Great War in reference to his relationship with Plath in a letter to Herbert Lomas in 1998. Writing about his decision to publish *Birthday Letters*, he spoke of "the big logjam holding back any inside story of my first wife's death" that "had gagged my whole life, arrested me, essentially, right back there at that point. Like those First World War survivors who never climbed entirely out of the trench" (*L* 731).

"Two Wise Generals" may likewise have served as a cautionary tale about the dangers of surrendering: in the poem, two generals meet, divide the disputed territory between them, and vow to end their war. After successfully negotiating the cease-fire, they return to their respective armies only to discover that both have been "massacred" in their sleep (*CPH* 47). We do not know who is responsible for massacring both armies, nor is this detail important. Hughes suggests there will always be forces that wreak havoc on our best intentions—undercurrents of violence, hatred, and jealousy that threaten our fragile equilibrium. Each general would have been better off protecting his own ground, rather than meeting the other halfway. Despite the fact that the two generals "drank, joked, waxed wise" (47), as they sealed the treaty, their desires for peace and prosperity were violently smashed. "Fair Choice," in which Hughes blasts the concept of modern equality, explores a similar idea. "Before choice's fairness | Humanized both," he writes, "barbarously you might | Have made beast-death of the one a sacrifice | To the god-head of the other, and buried its right | Before it opened eyes to be emulous" (*CPH* 31). But in the tyranny of fairness, both twins will be reared with disastrous consequences: one will become "An Abel to the other's bloody Cain" (32). Our mistake, Hughes suggests, is deceiving ourselves about our own humanity in the face of struggle, for we are too bloodthirsty to extol the virtues of fairness. Hughes believed humans were inherently incapable of selflessness; that below the facade of decency "moves our extraordinary readiness to exploit, oppress, torture and kill our own kind" (qtd. in Kendall 2005: 95). His belief that nothing in the human or natural world was fair may have influenced his perception of Plath's ambition as a threat to the marriage's stability and his own writing life.

The Wound, a surreal drama written in 1961 and broadcast on BBC radio in early 1962, also brings together the imagery of love and war. As the protagonist, Ripley, lies unconscious on the battlefield, suffering from a head wound, he dreams he and his sergeant are seduced and harmed by a group of young women in a chateau. At the end of the play, Ripley promises to marry one of the women, even though it is clear to the reader that this is a bad decision. Ripley says, "I'll marry you. I swear by these boots, by the two holes in my head, entrance and exit, that I'll put my whole body in your bank and you can let me out to myself on an annuity. Will you marry me, though? I'm forgetting, aren't I? That should come first. Will you marry me?"[31] (As Tracy Brain has noted, these lines bring Plath's "The Applicant" to mind.) Submission in marriage here functions as a metaphor for death, the ultimate emasculating force. But before Ripley "surrenders," he is found and rescued by comrades from another platoon; significantly, male soldiers rescue him from the embrace of Lady Death. Although, as we will see in Chapter 6, *The Wound* is a subtle exposition of man's culpability in the exploitation of women, it also registers fears of emasculation—fears Plath will later exploit in her own "war poems."

DANGEROUS WOMEN

Many critics date Hughes's obsession with femme fatales to his first encounter with Graves's *The White Goddess*, which his grammar school English teacher, John Fisher, gave him in 1951 when he went up to Cambridge. *The White Goddess* would become almost talismanic for Hughes; in 1967, he wrote to Graves thanking him for the book, saying it had become "the chief holy book of my poetic conscience" (*L* 273). However, he told Nick Gammage in 1995 that he had always been fascinated by mythology, even before he read Graves: "in particular, I suppose, what really interested me were those supernatural women. Especially the underworld women" (*L* 679). Indeed, Hughes had already integrated the idea of the demon lover into poems such as "Song" and "Initiation" during the late forties, before he read Graves. In the Keatsian "Song," the object of the speaker's love takes on various forms in nature, such as moon, cloud, and sea; she torments by refusing to appear human by his side, and by her insistence upon her own omnipotence. "Initiation" incorporates Gravesian motifs in its celebratory evocation of sex, dance, ritual, and madness. The demon lovers "Fling out and stamp, hair whirling, eyes, mad jerk | Of glazed crazed faces... ||

---

[31] Ted Hughes, "The Wound," BBC script (ts), MSS 644, Emory.

They know the helplessness of insanity" (*CPH* 7). These early poems show that Hughes was predisposed to share Graves's interest in resurrecting poetry's ancient, primal, and mystical function.

The White Goddess soon became "a cult book at Cambridge" (Middlebrook 30) after Graves gave a series of lectures denouncing several modernist poets. Hughes told Gammage in 1995 that he "soaked the book up" during his three years at university, and recalled his "slight resentment to find him taking possession of what I considered to be my secret patch" (*L* 679). Hughes saw his Cambridge friends as Gravesian devotees of the Goddess—keepers of a lost wisdom that patriarchal capitalism (or, as Graves put it, the "usurping Father-god" (476)) had tried to suppress. Graves believed that the source of the poet's inspiration was a seductive but ultimately dangerous muse, the White Goddess, and that poetry was "magically potent in the ancient sense" (17). As he explained:

The poet is in love with the White Goddess, with Truth: his heart breaks with longing and love for her. She is the Flower-goddess Olwen or Blodeuwedd; but she is also Blodeuwedd the Owl, lamp-eyed, hooting dismally, with her foul nest in the hollow of a dead tree, or Circe the pitiless falcon, or Lamia with her flickering tongue, or the snarling chopped Sow-goddess, or the mare-headed Rhiannon who feeds on raw flesh. *Odi atque amo*: "to be in love with" is also to hate. (448)

Graves thought that all authentic poets were acolytes to this cruel muse, and that the more one gave in service to the White Goddess, the larger the literary return. Poems were, in effect, offerings, though true devotion required complete sacrifice:

she will gladly give him her love, but only at one price: his life. She will exact her payment punctually and bloodily .... No poet can hope to understand the nature of poetry unless he has had a vision of the Naked King crucified to the lopped oak, and watched the dancers, red-eyed from the acrid smoke of the sacrificial fires, stamping out the measure of the dance, their bodies bent uncouthly forward, with a monotonous chant of: "Kill! kill! kill!" and "Blood! blood! blood!" (447–8)

Themes of sacrifice, martyrdom, and primitive ritual all accord with the Romantic understanding of the poet's religious function. The White Goddess appealed to Hughes for other reasons, however. Not only was she a poetic muse and a symbol of ancient, anti-patriarchal religion, but she was also a nature deity. As Graves wrote, "The Goddess is no townswoman: she is the Lady of the Wild Things, haunting the wooded hill-tops" (481).

Graves instructed that "By ancient tradition, the White Goddess becomes one with her human representative—a priestess, a prophetess, a queen-mother. No Muse-poet grows conscious of the Muse except by experience of a woman in whom the Goddess is to some degree resident" (490). Plath was destined to become, for Hughes, the human embodiment of the White Goddess—a role she was happy to play for some time, but which she eventually saw as both reductive and repressive.[32] (According to Lucas Myers, he and Hughes were in the process of "rereading" the book when Plath came into their lives (Middlebrook 2003: 31)). Graves reminded his readers that love for a woman should not "blind the poet to the cruel side of woman's nature" (491). After reading Graves, Hughes may have understood his fascination with dangerous woman as proof that he was a true poet—or, as Graves put it, a "the real, perpetually obsessed Muse-poet" (490). Thus Hughes did not see his use of the femme fatale as reductive or sexist; on the contrary, she was testament to his devotion to the Goddess and his rejection of a rationalist, patriarchal society. "Apollonian" poets did not look to the Muse for inspiration, and, in Hughes's and Graves's estimation, their poetry suffered for this lack of reverence. Graves's influence on Plath, too, should not be underestimated— Hughes told Gammage it had "a big effect" on Plath "when I got her into it" (*L* 679). In a July 1957 journal entry, Plath contemplates inventing a heroine for her novel who is "a bitch: she is the white goddess. Make her a statement of the generation. Which is you" (289). As we will later see, Plath would eventually parody the White Goddess, and her previous identification with that figure, in *Ariel.*

Manifestations of this "cruel" Goddess feature in Hughes's early poem, "The Women with Such High Heels She Looked Dangerous," originally published in the Spring 1955 issue of *Delta.* Here, woman is a deceptive seductress bent upon the destruction of her male lover:

> You would say the way she was painted was for the war-path,
> And sure all sorts of corners stack her dead.
> The way she comes at a man gives him no chances
> To smile be suave and complicate a truce
> And retire undefeated if disgraced.
> When her blood beats its drum nobody dances.
>
> Men become wolves, but a wolf has become a woman.
> The light in her eyes slants hard and blue as hail.
> And when the sun gets at her it is as if
> A windy blue plume of fire from the earth raged upright,
> Smelling of sulphur, the contaminations of the damned,
> The refined fragile cosmetic of the dead.
>
> She clings at your guarding arm as a grass-wisp weakly,
> And her eyes are timid as a hare's,
> And her mouth merry as a robin on your finger.
> O she is slick and silver as a whiting
> To coax your delight as far as the dark, and there, friend, there
> Darkness is the scabbard of her knife.   (*CPH* 11)

Hughes uses animal imagery to convey both the woman's feigned innocence and her danger: she is variously described as wolf, hare, robin, and fish.

---

[32] In her journal, Plath talks about modeling one of her heroines on the White Goddess (289), and looking to Graves's book for potential names for their unborn children (377).

(The Goddess, after all, is a nature deity.) The metaphorical drumming suggests a primitive otherness, and even brings to mind scenes from Conrad's *Heart of Darkness*. Here, woman is "the horror."[33]

Anxieties of emasculation surface often in Hughes's early poems: as Margaret Uroff notes, "[Plath's] presence is everywhere felt in Hughes's elevation of women to predatory status equal with men.... From 'Billet-Doux' on ... the women are no longer passive victims or tamed hawks or frigid virgins; instead, they are equal partners, or occasionally superiors" (52–3).[34] Hughes may have been disturbed by the fact that within days of their meeting, Plath had already cast him, in "Pursuit," "as a violent sexual predator, the relationship doomed to end in her death" (Roberts 2003: 163). He may also have been alarmed by Plath's weird syntax in the second line of that poem: "One day I'll have my death of him" (*CPP* 22). The line identifies the hunter as the predator but in fact yields active control to the hunted. In several early poems, it is as if Hughes is already revising Plath's depiction of him in "Pursuit": "Bawdry Embraced," "The Drowned Woman," "Fallgrief's Girlfriends," "The Hag," "Billet-Doux," "A Modest Proposal," "Macaw and Little Miss," "The Martyrdom of Bishop Farrar," "Witches," and "Cleopatra to the Asp" all display anxiety over a powerful (female) rival, and frame this anxiety through struggle.

In Hughes's first poem to Plath, which he addressed to the American Express office in Rome on April 9, 1956 (it is not clear whether he sent the poem), he casts her as she had cast him in "Pursuit"—as the hunter whose "shot" wounds the hunted. The lover, and love itself, is construed as dangerous, predatory:

> Ridiculous to call it love.
> Even so, fearfully I did sound
> Your absence, as one shot down feels to the wound,
> Knowing himself alive
>
> Only by what most frightens, the suddenly
> Anxious and kneeling sky, clouds, trees,
> The headlong instant that halts, stares, comes close
> With an incredulous ghastly eye.
>
> That man struck looks up:
> A bird, gathering the world in its throat—one note
> About to be heard—, stands, beak agape:
> What ghostly hands his hearing strains to it!
>
> One cry—then death, all into darkness.
> Hands here were as inadequate,—
> Wherever you haunt earth, you are shaped and bright
> As the true ghost of my loss   (*L* 38)

---

[33] I will discuss Plath's revision of Hughes's femme fatales, and this poem in particular, in Chapter 6.

[34] See also Nathalie Anderson's "Ted Hughes and the Challenge of Gender" in *The Challenge of Ted Hughes*.

The poem's speaker is frightened by the lover, whose offer of love is "ghastly." Like a true femme fatale, the lover "haunts" him, and he associates her with his "loss." The poem shows that Hughes, like Plath, was constructing a violent image of his partner from the earliest days of the courtship.

Hughes's early "A Modest Proposal," from *The Hawk in the Rain*, also provides a counterpoint to Plath's "Pursuit." Here, the speaker envisions himself and his lover as competing predators:

> There is no better way to know us
> Than as two wolves, come separately to a wood.
> Now neither's able to sleep—even at a distance
> Distracted by the soft competing pulse
> Of the other; nor able to hunt—at every step
> Looking backwards and sideways, warying to listen
> For the other's slavering rush. Neither can make die
> The painful burning of the coal in its heart
> Till the other's body and the whole wood is its own.
> Then it might sob contentment toward the moon.   (*CPH* 27)

The "wood" is associated with the "midnight moment's forest" where poetic inspiration occurs in "The Thought-Fox"; the wolves, too, bring that poem's fox and its metaphor of creativity to mind. Indeed, the burning coal in the heart of both creatures echoes Shelley's famous image of poetic inspiration, suggesting that this may be a poem about two poets competing for the muse's attention. The competition is tinged with eroticism, not unlike the kind Plath depicted in "Pursuit": the "soft competing pulse" and "the other's slavering rush" suggest the imagery of orgasm, while "the painful burning of the coal" calls up sexual longing, which will only fade when "the other's body" is conquered. The poem may seek to "creatively correct" "Pursuit," in which Plath had already framed the relationship as a competition, and implicitly asks, Who will outrun whom? Who will obliterate the other? Hughes's allusion to Swift's satirical work further emphasizes the competitors' cannibalistic impulse. They will never know the sense of unity and collaboration that the hounds and their master exhibit at the poem's end as all return from a successful hunt. The wolves can only watch, dreaming of their own "mad final satisfaction" in the obliteration of the other, while the hounds "Leap like one, making delighted sounds" (28). The poem's opening stanza, with its invocation of a perverse symbiosis, suggests that Hughes may have been voicing anxieties about his relationship with Plath. As his letters to Gerald reveal, Hughes feared marriage would prove confining, and that his poetry, as a result, would become suburbanized, divested of all traces of the primitive. Hughes recognizes the tragic nature of rivalry in the last line, in which the victor will "sob contentment toward the moon" (27).

"The Martyrdom of Bishop Farrar" deals with the threat of a femme fatale—this time out of real life—whose male victim ultimately manages to defeat her.[35] The poem recounts the story of Nicholas Farrar's death at the stake by fire, ordered by Bloody Mary—here characterized as a demonic, almost supernatural figure who is able to summon her flames "from Hell" (*CPH* 48). Hughes quotes Farrar before his death as saying, "If I flinch from the pain of the burning, believe not the doctrine that I have preached" (48); thus, Farrar summons up the requisite strength to die without revealing his agony to his parishioners:

> . . . the fire that struck here, come from Hell even,
> Kindled little heavens in his words
> As he fed his body to the flame alive.
> Words which, before they will be dumbly spared,
> Will burn their body and be tongued with fire
> Make paltry folly of flesh and this world's air.   (49)

Ultimately, "Out of his mouth, fire like a glory broke, | And smoke burned his sermons into the skies" (49). We might read in "The Martyrdom of Bishop Farrar" a narrative of sexual competition in which the female attempts to silence the male voice, while the male, who refuses to submit, emerges victorious. Farrar's fate resonated with Hughes for moral reasons, but there was a personal connection as well. Hughes was a descendant of Farrar's (his mother's maiden name was Farrar), a fact that suggests his interest in Farrar was more than elegiac. Hughes constructs an alignment between himself and Farrar that reinforces the sense of kinship and continuity between martyred bishop and martyred poet. As Scigaj writes, Hughes is "identifying both a personal and a national inheritance" (45). The poem also exhibits anxiety about female power. Here, the women's commanding, authorial voice is subsumed by the dying man's last words. It is Farrar's "words" that are literally "at stake" here; though he may be silenced through death, his voice will live on through others. Plath will later revise this poem in "Lady Lazarus," in which the tortured, martyred woman defies male authority. Indeed, "The Martyrdom of Bishop Farrar" foreshadows the later struggle between Plath and Hughes to have the "last word" in both *Ariel* and *Birthday Letters*.

Competition of any kind rarely ends peacefully in Hughes's poetic schema. Kendall observes that Hughes's nature poems are really war poems in disguise; we might also think of his war poems as marriage poems in disguise. While not all of Hughes's poems about violence speak to his rivalry with Plath, this theme has been insufficiently explored. As we have seen, Hughes worried that underneath her Lawrentian exterior, his wife wanted the same things Aurelia Plath expected from her son-in-law: financial security and professional stability. He was concerned that by giving in to these demands, he would sever his link with the primal

---

[35] Keith Sagar notes that this poem was hailed as both the best and worst poem in the book by different reviewers (1975: 34).

instincts that compelled him to write poetry; he was all too aware of Graves's warning that one cannot serve Goddess and wife at the same time (456). Beyond his fears of suburban remaking, however, lurked what was perhaps a greater, secret anxiety: that Plath really was—or had the potential to be—the better poet. Thus his later separation from Plath in the autumn of 1962 may have been necessitated by the need for a poetic as well as personal break. At the time, he wrote to W. S. and Dido Merwin that he was developing a "new method of navigation" as a result of leaving Plath, and taking up the "simple life": "I'm finding it much easier to write." He also told them Plath was "much better off now—it's thrown her onto her better self."[36] By then Hughes may have suspected that the Goddess could bestow her favor on his wife just as easily as she could bestow it on him. Well before the combative poems of *Ariel* and *Birthday Letters*, both battled for her gift.

[36] Ted Hughes to Dido and W. S. Merwin, late 1962, MSS 866, Emory.

3

The Other Two

During the mid-fifties, Sylvia Plath constantly stressed that her husband's company was all she desired, and that he was the only man she could have married. "I feel that all my life, all my pain and work has been for this one thing," she wrote to her mother in May 1956. "All the blood spilt, the words written, the people loved, have been a work to fit me for loving Ted" (*LH* 248). For Plath, Hughes was all-knowing: "Ted is right, infallibly, when he criticizes my poems" (*J* 359); "Ted's faith: don't expect: just write, listen to self, scribble" (304); "Ted will be proud of me, which is what I want. He doesn't care about the flashy success, but about me and my writing" (296); "The main problem is breaking open rich, real subjects to myself & forgetting there is any audience but me & Ted" (293). She gushed to her mother that she and Hughes had established an ideal working relationship: "such lovely hours together.... We read, discuss poems we discover, talk, analyze—we continually fascinate each other... our writing is founded in the inspiration of the other."[1]

While there was much truth in Plath's statements of joy and creative productivity in 1956–7, the undercurrents of anger in her stories and poems of doubling from this period suggest she was beginning to question the ideal of a mutually productive poetic partnership. Letters from the spring of 1956 show that, despite what seem like cries of abjection in her poems and journal, she longed to match Hughes's physical and literary "strength":

I am a match: I feel a growing strength, I do not merely idolize, I see right into the core of him, and he knows it, and knows that I am strong enough, and can make him grow.[2]

I am the first one, I think, who is as strong in herself... as he is, who can see the lack of care in him, and be independent: this gives me a kind of balance of power.... never have two people, too strong for most in one dose, lived so powerfully & creatively![3]

... there are only the two of us who are whole and strong enough to be a match, one for the other.[4]

I am strong in myself and in love with the only man in he world who is my match.

(*LH* 240)

[1] Sylvia Plath to Aurelia Plath, October 8, 1956, Lilly.
[2] Sylvia Plath to Aurelia Plath, April 19, 1956, Lilly.
[3] Sylvia Plath to Warren Plath, April 23, 1956, Lilly.
[4] Sylvia Plath to Aurelia Plath, April 29, 1956, Lilly.

I am learning and mastering new words each day, and drunker than Dylan, harder than Hopkins, younger than Yeats in my saying. Ted reads in his strong voice; is my best critic, as I am his. (*LH* 243)

I have new power by pouring all my love and care in one direction to someone strong enough to take me in my fullest joy. (It is interesting to know that most Cambridge boys preferred me when I was sick with sinus and they could take care of me, because that was the only time they were stronger.) (*LH* 250)

These letters suggest that Plath's pose as prey to Hughes's predator was at least partly disingenuous: it was she, after all, who would tame this force of nature, this "breaker of things and people."[5] (As Plath wrote in an early, unpublished poem "Song of Eve," written while at Smith, "to each leaf and flower I gave a name | that put Adam's vocabulary to shame."[6]) When she tells her mother that the day *Harper's* accepted *The Hawk in the Rain* was also "the anniversary of that fatal party where I met Ted" (*LH* 297), one wonders to what extent she was already aware of the painful rivalry that would burden her marriage in the coming years. Although she insisted she was "more happy than if it was my book published," and that there was "no question of rivalry, but only mutual joy and a sense of us doubling our prize-winning and creative output" (*LH* 297), Plath treated such "doubling" more ambivalently in her poems and short stories during the early years of her marriage. Many works from the late fifties portray dueling couples who experience the same kind of competitive tension that haunted Plath and Hughes as Hughes's work steadily gained recognition and Plath lingered in his shadow. By creating fictional doubles of herself and her husband, Plath was able both to address and to contain her own misgivings about the creative partnership. For, like the heroine of *Falcon Yard*, Plath felt herself a "voyager, no Penelope."[7]

While critics have documented Plath's later hostility toward Hughes, they have generally assumed that it took several years for her to confront the more troubling aspects of the "collaboration."[8] There is little critical commentary about Plath's (or Hughes's) anxiety of influence as it manifested itself during the early years of the marriage. Despite Plath's statement to a *Mademoiselle* journalist in early 1959 that "Most of the problems of being married to another poet turn out to be advantages" (Robins 1959: 32), Plath had already admitted in 1958 that she felt stirrings of "The famed & fatal jealousy of professionals" (*J* 421). She knew that Faber's acceptance letter for *The Hawk in the Rain* had contained a personal message from T. S. Eliot congratulating Hughes on his achievement; later, along with the rest of London, she would have seen in the *Sunday Times* the now-famous photograph of Hughes standing alongside Eliot, Stephen Spender,

---

[5] Sylvia Plath to Aurelia Plath, April 19, 1956, Lilly.
[6] "Song of Eve," Box 7a, Plath MSS II, Lilly.
[7] Sylvia Plath, notes on *Falcon Yard*, Box 139, MSS 644, Emory.
[8] See, for example, Lynda Bundzten's *The Other Ariel*, Steven Axelrod's *Sylvia Plath: The Wound and the Cure of Words*, Susan Van Dyne's *Revising Life*, and Christina Britzolakis's *Sylvia Plath and the Theatre of Mourning*.

W. H. Auden, and Louis MacNeice at a Faber and Faber cocktail party.[9] The photo, reproduced in several newspapers, gave the impression that Hughes had been canonized by the elder statesmen of British letters. Plath, meanwhile, continued to struggle for recognition.

Plath's misgivings about the relationship (her numerous assertions of marital bliss notwithstanding) began as early as her honeymoon, in the summer of 1956. From this time on, complaints about Hughes's role in her writing life, though often veiled, began to appear with greater frequency in her journals. Already in March 1957 she spoke of the marriage's potential danger when she confided to her journal, "I get quite appalled when I realize my whole being... has grown and interwound so completely with Ted's that if anything were to happen to him, I do not see how I could live. I would either go mad, or kill myself" (274). By the late fifties, Plath expressed serious doubts about her collaborative relationship with her "genius" (*J* 420) husband. In the summer of 1958, she began to blame Hughes for her prolonged bouts of writer's block:

My danger, partly, I think, is becoming too dependent on Ted. He is didactic, fanatic.... It is as if I were sucked into a tempting but disastrous whirlpool. Between us there are no barriers—it is rather as if neither of us—or especially myself—had any skin, or one skin between us & kept bumping into and abrading each other. I enjoy it when Ted is off for a bit. I can build up my own inner life, my own thoughts, without his continuous "What are you thinking? What are you going to do now?" which makes me promptly and recalcitrantly stop thinking and doing. We are amazingly compatible. But I must be myself—make myself & not let myself be made by him. He gives orders—mutually exclusive: read ballads an hour, read Shakespeare an hour, read history an hour, think an hour & then "you read nothing in hour-bits, read things straight through".   (*J* 401)

Plath presents a conflicted portrayal of her life with Hughes: they are "amazingly compatible," yet he "gives orders." She is "too dependent" on him, yet she blames him for this dependence; she is Odysseus forging ahead, while he is Charybdis, sucking her into his "disastrous whirlpool." He pushes her to read and write more, yet out of stubbornness she rebels and writes nothing. She admits to feeling threatened by his success, his "fanatic" demands, even his presence. She knows that her very identity is at stake, and recognizes the need to "make myself & not let myself be made by him."

Plath plays here with the dual meanings of the word "made"—both to force and to create. Hughes not only makes her read certain things, makes her "stop thinking and doing," but threatens to make (or remake) *her*. Because, as Plath writes, there are no barriers between them, she feels herself morphing into Hughes; at times, she says, it feels as if they share a single skin. These misgivings persisted: two months later she wrote, "I must be happy first in my own work and struggle to that end, so my life does not hang on Ted's.... Do we, vampire-like, feed on each other?" (*J* 421). She worried, "I am too ingrown—as if I no longer

⁹ See Philip Day, "A Pride of Poets," *Sunday Times* (June 26, 1960).

knew how to talk to anyone but Ted" (*J* 422) and later reaffirmed her need to be "sure I'm myself and not him" (*J* 451). Her position crystallized over the coming months: "Dangerous to be so close to Ted day in day out. I have no life separate from his, am likely to become a mere accessory" (*J* 524). As Ted ascended, she became a mute admirer: "No criticism or nagging. Shut eyes to dirty hair, ragged nails. He is a genius. I his wife" (*J* 420). Yet such statements seem loaded with irony. Even at the height of Hughes's success, Plath still yearned to "match" her "force" against his.

During the late fifties, Plath developed two strategies of resistance against remaking: she would keep her work to herself, and spend more time alone. As she wrote in her journal, "Must work & get out of paralysis—write & show him nothing. . . . A wall, sound-proof, must mount between us. Strangers in our study, lovers in bed" (421). She returned to these thoughts again and again in her subsequent entries: "How to develop my independence? Not tell him everything" (445); "Must try poems. DO NOT SHOW ANY TO TED" (467); "Didn't show him the bull one: a small victory" (467); "Tell T nothing" (484); "I must work for independence" (518); "How many couples could stand to be so together? The minute we get to London I must strike out on my own" (525). Plath's repeated insistence on not showing Hughes her poetry suggests that his evaluation of her work had begun to threaten her own. And indeed, she never let him know she was working on the novel that would become *The Bell Jar*.[10] As the following poems and stories of doubling suggest, it was not long before the man who had inspired Plath to believe in a marriage of true minds would become her rival.

FACING OFF

In the summer of 1956, Plath and Hughes honeymooned in Benidorm, Spain, a small coastal fishing village still undiscovered by tourists. They intended to spend that summer as they did all of their free time: writing productively. Although the honeymoon began happily enough (apart from a disagreeable stay with the Widow Mangada), Plath and Hughes soon experienced what was probably their first major argument. After a long period of silence, the two took a walk in the moonlight. As Plath noted in her journal, nothing seemed to help:

No sleep, smothering. Sitting in nightgown and sweater in the dining room staring into the full moon, talking to the full moon, with wrongness growing and filling the house like a man-eating plant. The need to go out. It is very quiet. Perhaps he is asleep. Or dead. How to know how long there is before death. The fish may be poisoned, and the poison working. And two sit apart in wrongness. . . . Two silent strangers. (*J* 250–1)

---

[10] Ted Hughes told Nick Gammage in 1993 that he was unaware of the novel while Plath was writing it (*L* 644).

This was the first time Plath had written about her relationship with Hughes in anything other than celebratory terms; indeed, her language foreshadows the flat, resigned tone of later poems like "Sheep in Fog," "Edge," and "Words."

She followed this somber entry with an autobiographical vignette about two honeymooners, entitled "Marcia and Tom," one of several works in which Plath explored themes of marital unhappiness, anger, and rivalry through doubles of herself and Hughes. In the story, the honeymooners travel to Spain by train and amuse themselves drinking wine with two Spanish soldiers—an experience clearly based on an actual event that Hughes recounted in a letter to Olwyn from Benidorm that summer.[11] Soon, however, Marcia begins to grow restless and despondent:

> Leaning out of the train window, she let the wind dry the perspiration and grime on her face, wondering if she might be condemned by some sophisticated heavenly order to wander through eternity in this present limbo - - - always dirty, hot, fatigued, longing only for a distant paradise of cold showers and clean sheets. By twilight, she was sheathed in a protective coat of numbness. (*J* 252–3)

The train journey setting of this vignette is significant; as Tim Kendall and Al Strangeways have noted, trains in Plath's work are "often sinister" (Kendall 2001: 176).[12] Marcia seems to feel that she is heading toward some kind of loss, perhaps of "personal will," when she describes herself succumbing to numbness. Significantly, this transformation begins after Tom takes Marcia's hand. The sudden image of a "turreted palace" (*J* 253), which appears as the train rounds a bend, smacks of irony. Plath may be questioning the happily-ever-after attitude that has taken Marcia (and herself) this far. The fact that Plath wrote this story after the despondent journal entry quoted above suggests that she was beginning to feel, as she wrote in "Metaphors," that she had "Boarded the train there's no getting off" (*CPP* 116).

Once Plath and Hughes had settled comfortably at 59 Tomas Ortunio in Benidorm, they spent their mornings writing at opposite ends of a large dining room table—a configuration that, to Plath, came to resemble a face-off. She addressed the situation in a vignette she called "Mr. and Mrs. Ted Hughes' Writing Table," a title which, given that Plath kept her maiden name, suggests an ironic treatment of the collaborative literary partnership. In this vignette, Plath makes clear that the table, and hence the act of writing itself, belongs more to Hughes than it does to her. Hughes's section reads:

---

[11] Hughes described reaching the Spanish border by train and "passing round a leather wine-bottle and squirting wine into my throat, and communicating with a compartment full of 'obreros' via my tiny Spanish dictionary." Ted Hughes to Olwyn Hughes, summer 1956, MSS 980, Emory.

[12] Kendall writes that in "Daddy," "Getting There," "Metaphors," "Sheep in Fog," and "Totem," trains suggest death or danger (2001: 176), while Strangeways notes that train rides speak of "mechanized society, involvement in which may lead to loss of personal will, as the passenger is carried along, a mere observer, toward both physical and spiritual death" (qtd. in Kendall 2001: 176).

At the head of the table, Ted sat in a squarely built grandfather chair with wicker back and seat; his realm was a welter of sheets of typing paper and ragged cardboard-covered notebooks; the sheets of scrap paper, scrawled across with his assertive blue-inked script, rounded, upright, flaired, were backs of reports on books, plays and movies written while at Pinewood studios; typed and re-written versions of poems, bordered with drawings of mice, ferrets and polar bears, spread out across his half of the table. A bottle of blue ink, perpetually open, rested on a stack of paper. Crumpled balls of used paper lay here and there, to be thrown into the large wooden crate placed for that purpose in the doorway. All papers and notebooks on this half of the table were tossed at angles, kitty-corner and impromptu.   (*J* 259)

Plath's description of her half, however, is very different:

The other half of the table, coming into my premises, was piled with tediously neat stacks of books and papers, all laid prim and four-squared to the table corners: A large blue-paper-covered notebook, much thinned, from which typing paper was cut, topped by a ragged brown covered Thesaurus, formed the inner row of books. . . . Along the edge of the table, from left to right, were . . . an open Cassell's French dictionary on which also opened an underlined copy of *Le Rouge et Le Noire* in a yellow-bound ragged-edged paper-back edition, a bottle of jet black ink, scrupulously screwed shut, a small sketch book of rag paper atop Ted's anthology of Spanish poems, and a white plastic sunglasses case sewn over with a decorative strewing of tiny white and figured shells, a few green and pink sequins, a plastic green starfish and rounded, gleaming oval shell.   (259)

Every detail concerning Hughes's half of the table suggests that he is the more serious, prolific writer at work. He is the one who sits "At the head," surrounded by "his realm" of books and papers, "typed and re-written versions of poems" and essays. His bottle of ink is "perpetually open," while "Crumpled balls of used paper lay here and there." Everything on this half of the table, Plath tells us, is disorganized, "impromptu"—a description that suggests Hughes's writing is the work of an inspired mind straining at the bit.

Plath's half of the table is the opposite of Hughes's in almost every way. Whereas Hughes is surrounded by his own poems and essays, there is no work of Plath's on the table. She uses a thesaurus, while Hughes presumably has no need for one. Unlike Hughes's open ink bottle, hers is "scrupulously screwed shut." There are no "crumpled balls of used paper" on her half, nor other evidence of prolonged effort. Instead, all is "tediously neat" and "prim." Because Plath often complained, before *Ariel*, that her poems were too neat, too strictly formal, that she was trapped inside a "glass caul" (*J* 470), such adjectives have a pejorative ring. They are also gendered: "prim" suggests an oppressive femininity, as in "prim and proper." Reading between the lines, one finds anger, mockery, and self-contempt in Plath's description of her half of the table, which is clearly written "against" Hughes's: what he is, she is not. Hughes sits at the head, but Plath seems strangely disembodied. We do not even know if she is seated at the table at all, for no sentences begin, "I sit." By omitting her physical presence from the description, she strengthens the idea that the writing table (and writing itself) is Hughes's domain. Indeed, Plath seems more pleased with her delicately embroidered sunglass case than any poems she may have written. Yet what appears to be an expression of low self-esteem may instead be a bitterly self-conscious mockery (and perhaps indictment) of the subordinate "place" of the woman writer. Despite Plath's exclamations of marital bliss in her letters home, "Mr. and Mrs. Ted Hughes's Writing Table" shows that she was aware of the partnership's potential to inhibit her writing from the earliest days of her marriage.

Plath returned to the image of the writing table again in "The Other Two," written in 1958–9 but set during the summer in Benidorm. Read in light of "Mr. and Mrs. Hughes's Writing Table," the poem speaks to creative tension as much as it does a lovers' quarrel. In the poem, the speaker feels haunted by a pair of Keatsian lovers she sees in the wood of the "baronial" dining room table, doomed to simmer in anger for eternity:

> He lifts an arm to bring her close, but she
> Shies from his touch: his is an iron mood.
> Seeing her freeze, he turns his face away.
> They poise and grieve as in some old tragedy.   (*CPP* 68)

This ghostly couple follows the real lovers, invading their dreams, until

> ... we seemed the lighter—
> Ourselves the haunters, and they, flesh and blood;
> As if, above love's ruinage, we were
> The heaven those two dreamed of, in despair.   (69)

Here Plath uses the idea of the double to express the same anxieties about her relationship with Hughes that she had tentatively explored in "Mr. and Mrs. Hughes's Writing Table." The fact that the real-life couple seems, inadvertently, to switch places with the wounded lovers to become "the haunters" suggests that, despite their current happiness, they are no strangers to "love's ruinage" (69). Furthermore, it is no accident that the spectral doubles emerge out of the writing table: "the other two" do not only represent, as Diane Middlebrook writes, "a psychological portrait of the disorienting inner shift that rises ... when one or the other partner suddenly turns opaque" (2003: 93), but also Plath's exploration of the undercurrents of her rivalry with Hughes.

"THE WISHING BOX"

In October 1956, after the couple returned from Spain, the BBC hired Hughes to read a selection of Yeats's poems on the Third Program. An ecstatic Plath wrote to her mother, "MY HUSBAND IS A GENIUS AND WILL READ YEATS ON THE BBC!" (*LH* 276). To Plath, the BBC's acceptance of Hughes's recording intensified her sense of a mystical connection between

Yeats and her husband. Yet, when she wrote that she and Hughes would become "a team better than Mr. and Mrs. Yeats" (*LH* 280), did she realize the inherent hierarchy such a comparison entailed? Or, as Sandra Gilbert and Susan Gubar put it, "if Plath and Hughes were to become 'Mr. and Mrs. Yeats,' would Plath have to be *Mrs.* Yeats, the entranced transmitter of 'metaphors for poetry' to her genius husband?" (1994: 3.278). This question cuts to the heart of a dilemma Plath explored in her powerful portrait of rivalry within marriage, "The Wishing Box."

This short story, written in 1957 during the first year of Plath's marriage, portrays a pair of newlyweds, Agnes and Harold, who are engaged in a kind of creative competition that serves as a metaphor for Plath's and Hughes's poetic rivalry.[13] Each morning, Harold relays his vivid dreams to Agnes, the story's narrator, who listens with envy and bitterness. Agnes cannot match the radiance of her husband's dreams, which she calls "meticulous works of art" (*JP* 49). While Harold tells her of evenings spent in the company of poets such as William Blake, Robert Frost, and William Carlos Williams, Agnes simply "smoldered in silence" (48), unable to recall anything equally vibrant or important from her own dreams. She feels "perpetually exiled" (49) from Harold's dream-world, and incapable of conjuring one of her own. When Agnes confesses to Harold that her dreams are dull and mundane, he directs her in an imaginative exercise. But his efforts only make matters worse; soon Agnes is relying on sherry, the cinema, and television to distract herself from her imaginative void. The story ends absurdly and pathetically, with Agnes dressed in an emerald evening gown, dead on the sofa, an empty pillbox by her side.

Gilbert and Gubar note that "The Wishing Box" was written at a time when Plath was confiding to her journal that Hughes was a better poet than she. The story, as they see it, "dramatizes a profound battle within the young poet-wife's psyche, revealing both a traditional female anxiety that she *could* not compete with the élan of the male imagination, and a deep Ladies Home Journal conviction that she *should* not. Better death than the expression of (female) desire, the story seems to say" (1994: 3.281). Jacqueline Rose links Harold's dreams to a high, sanctified (male) literary culture, Agnes's with low, melodramatic (female) popular culture. Although Plath herself links popular culture to Agnes's demise in the story, Rose sees it, rather than high culture, as the force which "releases the woman's imagination from the killing objectivity of the world. . . . Popular culture kills, but it also saves" (181–2). Janet Malcolm understands "The Wishing Box" as Plath's "coded message" that "a woman's life can be poisoned, and even ultimately destroyed, by her feelings of inadequacy in the face of a man's superior achievements" (87).

---

[13] Tracy Brain has pointed out that the story is indebted to Virginia Woolf's "The Legacy" (2001: 145).

Yet the code in "The Wishing Box" is almost too easy to crack. Although Harold is an accountant in the story rather than a writer, Plath makes sure that the reader identifies him with Hughes by mentioning that Harold dreams of a red fox who gives him "a bottle of permanent black Quink" (*JP* 51), an obvious allusion to Hughes's "The Thought-Fox." Plath also tells us that Harold dreams of a gigantic pike and muses about idyllic days fishing with his cousin Albert, a stand-in for Hughes's brother Gerald. Nor is Plath subtle about the similarities between herself and Agnes—Agnes, once a fan of Superman, has now married a man with whom she finds herself locked in creative competition. And of course Plath, like Agnes, had also attempted suicide rather than face "an intolerable prospect of wakeful, visionless days and nights stretching unbroken ahead of her, her mind condemned to perfect vacancy, without a single image of its own" (54). (Years later, Hughes would write in "The God," one of the *Birthday Letters* poems, "Your heart, mid-Sahara, raged | In its emptiness. | Your dreams were empty" (*CPH* 1163).)

Given its obvious connections between art and life, one is tempted to read "The Wishing Box" not only as a "critique of marriage," as Tracy Brain claims (2001: 145), but as an admission of Plath's resentment towards Hughes and an expression of her deep frustration with her own writing as it flounders in the face of a "superior" male talent. But if the story is such an admission, why would Plath have published it in *Granta*, the Cambridge literary magazine, in 1957? Surely Plath realized that Hughes, as well as their literary friends at Cambridge, would have recognized the main characters in "The Wishing Box"; given her relentless pursuit of perfection and her need to present an unblemished front to the social milieu in which she moved, it is unlikely that at this stage of her marriage she would have chosen to lash out against her husband so publicly.

Instead, Plath may have intended the story to be read as parody, something Gilbert and Gubar hint at when they call it an "ironic tale of female powerlessness" (1994: 3.280). It is important to note that the story is set in America, and that Plath means to satirize crude American materialism. Though Rose argues that popular culture serves a positive function in the story in that it "releases" (181) Agnes, that same culture is the cause of Agnes's undoing. Instead of turning to poetry or art, Agnes races through "novels, women's magazines, newspapers, and even the anecdotes in her *Joy of Cooking*; she read travel brochures, home appliance circulars, the *Sears Roebuck Catalogue*, the instructions on soap-flake boxes, the blurbs on the back of record-jackets" (*JP* 53). Agnes's reading material descends down a scale of cultural worth—she begins with novels, moves down to catalogues, then, finally, to simple directions. Soon she finds that she can no longer engage with words at all, and so she turns to images; her visits to the cinema and afternoons in front of the television coincide with her downward spiral into alcoholism and death. The further Agnes moves from high culture, the closer she moves to total breakdown.

Was Plath expressing her anger at a society that equated woman's art with low culture and male art with high, or was she commenting, in the manner of F. R. Leavis, upon the dangers of following the siren song of popular culture? Plath hints at the latter by the story's end, a moment of high parody where we find our heroine dead on the sofa, "dressed in her favourite princess-style emerald taffeta evening gown, pale and lovely as a blown lily," her lips set in a "secret smile of triumph" as if she were waltzing with Superman (55). As Malcolm notes, "the story ends ludicrously" (87)—so ludicrously, in fact, that it is hard to believe Plath was not chuckling as she wrote it. There is no triumph in Agnes's suicide; she has become a character out of a soap opera. To be sure, there is a sinister edge to this parody, for there can be little doubt that Harold is partly to blame for Agnes's breakdown, which begins directly after Harold says, "Every day, just practice imagining different things like I've taught you" (53). In *Poetry in the Making*, Hughes similarly instructs, "Imagine what you are writing about. See it and live it. Do not think it up laboriously, as if you were working out mental arithmetic. Just look at it, touch it, smell it, listen to it, turn yourself into it" (qtd. in Sagar 2000: 58). And we know that Hughes did indeed hypnotize Plath, as he told Olwyn in 1957: "I practise hypnotising Sylvia, and am gradually getting better. I can now remove slight pains, relax her so completely that after five minutes she feels to have had a night's sleep,—and soon I shall move onto other things, such as make her write poems and stories, then to write them down without difficulty."[14] But it is all too easy, in hindsight, to equate Plath completely with Agnes, for in 1957 she was still intent on forging an equal creative partnership, and, in the process, resisting her husband's perceived attempts at remaking. Plath put more distance between herself and Agnes than she did between Hughes and Harold. Agnes is not Plath, but rather the woman she vowed not to become: a depressed housewife who lets her husband bully her imagination into submission, who turns away from poetry to clothing catalogues, television, and sherry for solace, and who finally succumbs to her own self-loathing in an act of suicide. "The Wishing Box" is a lesson in the perils of submitting to the low expectations of female culture: Agnes conforms exactly to the stereotype of the 1950s housewife, incapable of engaging in any complex way with serious literature, or, for that matter, in an intellectual discussion with her own husband. Agnes must be the subject of parody—must be pathetic rather than heroic—in order for Plath to assume a superior distance. The couple in "The Wishing Box" is not unlike the ghostly couple in "The Other Two": both are doubles of Plath and Hughes in whom the issue of competition within marriage is addressed and contained.

[14] Ted Hughes to Olwyn Hughes, n.d., 1957, MSS 980, Emory.

"DAY OF SUCCESS"

Despite Plath's effort to mock Agnes, there is little doubt that she feared assuming such a role herself. In her short story, "Day of Success" (written, Hughes estimated, in 1960 but not published until sixteen years later), Plath again explored her anxieties about creative partnership through a set of doubles. Like Plath and Hughes at one time, Jacob and Ellen live in London with their young daughter, whom Ellen cares for while her husband writes in a neighbor's flat. An important producer has recently accepted Jacob's play, and he is currently on the cusp of fame—a fact that both excites and concerns Ellen, who is worried she will lose her husband to another woman once he joins London's literary elite. Unlike Plath, Ellen harbors no professional or literary ambitions herself; Plath portrays her as an ordinary housewife whose main goal is to keep her family together: "*Please don't let it change*, she begged of whatever fates might be listening. *Let the three of us stay happy as this forever*" (*JP* 185). Yet Plath prompts us to wonder whether Ellen is truly happy. Not only does she spend her days alone with a baby while her husband retreats to his own private study, she must pinch pennies to keep the household afloat. Ellen is the model fifties mother: self-effacing and self-sacrificing, as Plath emphasizes in the story's first paragraph. The effort to present a portrait of domestic tranquility is almost parodic: Ellen makes her way to the bedroom "with an armload of freshly folded nappies" as she contemplates "the delicate rose-patterned wallpapers, the forest-green cord drapes she'd hemmed by hand while waiting for the baby to come, the old-fashioned four-poster ... and, in the corner, the pale pink crib holding sound asleep six-month old Jill, the centre of it all" (185). Plath continues to emphasize Ellen's maternal qualities throughout the story as if to establish her moral superiority over the "career women" Ellen fears will seduce her husband. For example, when Jacob offers to take her out to an expensive dinner in Soho, she declines, saying the money would be better spent on a pram. She refuses to go to the hairdresser's, instead wearing her hair in unfashionable braids; nor does she feel free to douse herself with the French perfume Jacob has given her. "*I'm homespun, obsolete as last year's hemline*" (191), she says. Plath aligns Ellen with Agnes when Ellen admits to her friend Nancy that she has no imagination; the same friend also observes that Ellen has "no self confidence" (195). But Ellen distinguishes herself from Agnes when she recognizes that, in her role as angel in the house, she has become a drudge. Self-effacement slowly gives way to self-awareness.

This newfound self-awareness, however, is not prompted by desire for autonomy but jealousy of another woman. Ellen is worried that Denise Kay, the assistant of a high-powered television producer and "real career girl" (195), will seduce Jacob. She imagines them together at rehearsals, "author and producer collaborating on the birth of something wonderful, uniquely theirs" (185). This is a significant detail, given that Plath frequently framed her relationship with Hughes in similar metaphorical terms in her letters home. Plath may be suggesting that Ellen ought to be envious of Denise Kay for professional, rather than sexual, reasons. Although Plath may have felt superior in her poetic ambition to women like Denise, she also worried, at times, that she was "obsolete" like Ellen—that she had squandered her elite education and a career in academia to spend her days at home folding nappies. When Plath was pregnant with Nicholas, she admitted as much in her journal: "This is the need I have, in my 30th year - - - to unclutch the sticky loving fingers of babies & treat myself to myself.... To purge myself of sour milk, ruinous nappies, bits of lint and the loving slovenliness of motherhood" (632). Yet just when Ellen finally decides to treat herself by taking a bath, changing her hairstyle, dressing up, and using the last of the French perfume, Plath abruptly changes course. We soon learn that Ellen's efforts to focus on herself are not inspired by a new sense of self-worth, but rather anxiety that she is not feminine *enough*—that in mastering her role as asexual mother she has neglected her role as sexy wife. She must appear as fashionable as a "career girl" while still retaining her motherly demeanor. (Plath is careful to note that after her dressing "ritual," Ellen immediately berates herself for forgetting the baby and spends the next hour tending exclusively to Jill.)

When Jacob comes home, his patriarchal tone perfectly matches Ellen's demure guise: "Now that's what I like to see. . . . Wife and daughter waiting by the fireside to welcome the lord of the house" (*JP* 197). After Jacob compliments her appearance, Ellen senses victory: "Jacob obviously saw her as the wife and mother type, and she couldn't be better pleased" (197). Plath implies that Ellen has beaten Denise Kay; rather than confront Jacob honestly about her fears, she resorts to what her friend Nancy calls "little feminine tricks" (194). Her performance pays off when Jacob admits he was unimpressed with Denise Kay's ambition. "That Denise Kay," he says, "is a career woman with a mind of her own—a regular diesel engine. Catch me crossing her path! Why, she's so highpowered she even fueled up on the martini she'd ordered for me when I told her I never touch the stuff on weekdays" (198). The story ends happily as Jacob reveals he has bought a cottage in the country with the hefty advance for his play. When Nancy calls to give Ellen the name of her hairdresser, Ellen says she no longer needs a haircut since "Braids are back in style this season, love—the latest thing for the country wife!" (198). The story's ending squares perfectly with *Ladies' Home Journal* values: country triumphs over city, motherhood over career, sobriety and thrift over indulgence, self-sacrifice and submission over ambition and autonomy.

Does Plath stand behind Ellen as she defeats the "highpowered" Denise Kay, or does she suggest, through subtle, subversive hints, that Ellen's victory was hollow? Anne Stevenson believes Plath treats Ellen without irony:

Sylvia's attitude *was* naïve; she really *did* imagine that any "real" man would find it a drag to come home to diapers and cod liver oil instead of the Japanese silks and French perfume of the story. . . . in her heart Sylvia was afraid the editors of *Mademoiselle* and *Seventeen* had got it right, and that, given a glamorous enough rival, she would lose her husband, the chief prop of her precarious happiness. (205–6)

To be sure, Plath did fear losing Hughes. In February 1961, she was racked by jealousy after Hughes returned late from a lunch with a BBC Schools producer, Moira Doolan. Unlike Ellen, however, Plath did not prepare for battle by loosening her braids and slipping into silk; rather, she famously ripped Hughes's manuscripts and his prized edition of Shakespeare to shreds. Stevenson and others have used this incident as an illustration of Plath's "irrational and uncontrollable rage" (206), perhaps insinuating that she should have behaved in a more lady-like (or Ellen-like) fashion. However, the fact that Plath refused to stifle her anger when she felt the real threat of a "Denise Kay" suggests that she may have regarded Ellen's retaliatory strategy as ridiculous and slightly tragic. As we have seen, Plath's journals reveal that she felt hampered and shortchanged by notions of fifties femininity, that she was well aware of double standards, and that she was envious of men's freedom. Stevenson is quite wrong to insist that Plath was just as "naïve" as Ellen.

Plath possessed a shrewd understanding of the magazine market and knew that if "Day of Success" was to be published, Ellen needed to reflect conservative values. As Betty Friedan noted in *The Feminine Mystique*, women's magazine fiction in the late fifties treated ambitious women as femme fatales who threatened the orderly, secure world of the housewife:

The new feminine morality story is the exorcising of the forbidden career dream, the heroine's victory over Mephistopheles: the devil, first in the form of a career woman, who threatens to take away the heroine's husband or child, and finally, the devil inside the heroine herself, the dream of independence, the discontent of spirit, and even the feeling of a separate identity that must be exorcised to win or keep the love of husband and child.   (46)

Plath knew that her story could not have ended with Ellen triumphantly destroying Jacob's manuscript in a fit of rage. But in light of her reaction to Doolan's phone call, it is possible to read "Day of Success" ironically, even parodically. (Even the story's title smacks of irony.) As Britzolakis has observed, Plath's irony in "The Wishing Box" and "Day of Success" functions on an even deeper level, since she is parodying the hierarchical marriage dynamic through the kind of stories that Hughes considered beneath him:

"Low" or "slick" forms of writing are often represented, in *Letters Home*, and the *Journals*, as a solution to the conflict between the vocations of professional authorship and domesticity, allowing Plath a professional identity in her own right within the marriage partnership without bringing her writings into collision with those of her "genius" husband. However, the secondary status to which the Oedipal marriage plot assigns the woman's writing wrankles, and nowhere more so than in the very stories which she often represents as her "own corner" (*LH* 249).   (29)[15]

---

[15] In a draft of the introduction to *Johnny Panic and the Bible of Dreams*, Hughes wrote that Plath's "dogged, year-in, year-out effort to write conventional fiction ... was a persistent refusal of her genius." Ted Hughes, draft introduction to *Johnny Panic and the Bible of Dreams*, Box 112, MSS 644, Emory.

Britzolakis's assessment of the complexity of Plath's parodic impulse further undermines Stevenson's assumption that Plath "really *did* imagine" that Ellen's actions were commendable. Given that Plath had spent several afternoons in Boston's Ritz Bar drinking martinis with Anne Sexton and George Starbuck after Robert Lowell's poetry classes, she may have secretly approved of Denise Kay's refusal to let a martini go to waste. She may also have envied Denise's luck: as Nancy tells Ellen, Denise "always manages to land a man with complications, so she never ends up drying dishes or wiping a baby's nose" (*JP* 195). Ellen's guilt over her own anger—she feels "profoundly ashamed of herself" for her jealousy and calls herself "small-minded and spiteful" (188)—probably did not accurately reflect the attitude of a writer who had admitted "I have a violence in me that is hot as death-blood." And while Plath frequently embraced the role of a no-nonsense homemaker to her mother and Hughes, her journals suggest she pined for American kitchens, fancy clothes, and rich food. Plath's refusal to buy items second-hand suggests the distance between herself and the happy-to-hem Ellen, while her desire to wrest herself of babies and housework, which she confided to her journal, hints that Denise may be the true heroine of "Day of Success."

"THE FIFTY-NINTH BEAR"

Plath addressed her marital rivalry in starker, less ambiguous terms in "The Fifty-Ninth Bear," written in 1959 and published in the *London Magazine* in 1961. The details of the story are drawn from Plath's and Hughes's trip through the American West during the summer of 1959. Norton and Sadie, the husband and wife in the story, are nearing the end of their stay at Yellowstone; both seem tired of sightseeing and each other. Plath's rendering of the park's sulphurous, Hades-like landscape reflects the mood of both protagonists, whose minds seem as ready to rupture as the ground beneath them. Plath subverts the pristine and restorative ideal of the American national park through her descriptions of places such as the "Dragon's Mouth" and "Devil's Cauldron," as well as the "hawks and the shadows of hawks" (*JP* 94) that hover ominously over the couple.

Sadie is fascinated by the park's muddy, steaming landscape and, as Britzolakis notes, is often described with "witchlike imagery" that "hints at occult female powers" (31), as when she bends "over the pit, devout as a priestess in the midst of those vile exhalations" (*JP* 95). Norton, however, experiences a sense of existential unease as he follows Sadie, the ground "a mere shell of sanity and decorum between him and the dark entrails of the earth" (95). Britzolakis sees Sadie as "childish, passive, and fearful" in contrast to her "virile" husband Norton, who treats her with condescension throughout the story. But Plath's presentation of the couple is more nuanced. Norton certainly *sees* himself as Sadie's protector, but Plath does not; Sadie is in fact the more "virile" of the two.

Plath mocks Norton's arrogant self-identification with Adam, as someone who could "will toward him all the animals of the forest" (including, significantly, red foxes): "He saw them, one by one, turn and converge toward the center where he sat, fiercely, indefatigably willing the movement of each hoof and paw" (96). But it is Sadie who actually wills the movements of the bear who kills Norton at the story's end: " 'My bear,' she said, as if she had called it up out of the dark" (103). Plath also mocks Norton's sense of "firm, complacent mastery" by plaguing him with a nagging headache (a condition often associated with women) and sunstroke throughout the story. After Norton "defaulted, overcome by headache," Sadie explores the park on her own; later, she takes control of the wheel after Norton says he is too sick to drive. When he begins to sing an English ballad from his childhood, he soon forgets the words, which Sadie must then supply. Plath also writes that during their walk through the park, Sadie "led him, and he followed" (100). Nevertheless, Norton continues to think of Sadie as a "lamb on a leash," while he is her "protecting god" (99). Plath implies it is Norton's hubris that will lead to his demise. "It never occurred to Norton," Plath writes, "that his wife might outlive him. Her sensuousness, her simple pagan enthusiasms, her inability to argue in terms of anything but her immediate emotions—this was too flimsy, too gossamery a stuff to survive out from under the wings of his guardianship" (98). Plath eventually punishes Norton for his naïve assumptions about Sadie, who proves to possess the more powerful will; as he tries to run off a bear near their tent, we learn that "there was another will working, a will stronger, even, than his" (104). Norton dies at the bear's hands, but not before he hears what is presumably Sadie's "shrill cry—of terror, or triumph, he could not tell" (105). (Hughes, as we will see, presents his own version of this story in *Birthday Letters*.)

"The Fifty-Ninth Bear" shows that long before Plath wrote the *Ariel* poems, she was already experimenting with motifs of female vengeance; Sadie is a forerunner of the murderous female speakers in "Lady Lazarus," "Daddy," and "Purdah." These motifs likewise appear in an early poem, "The Shrike" (1956). There, the female speaker lies beside her husband as he explores vast realms in his "royal dreams"—a phrase that brings to mind Harold's dreams of "royal baroque splendour" (*JP* 50) in "The Wishing Box." The "envious bride" takes on the shape of a malicious, predatory bird not unlike Hughes's hawk in "Hawk Roosting." She

> Cannot follow after, but lies
> With her blank brown eyes starved wide,
> Twisting curses in the tangled sheet
> With taloned fingers,
> Shaking in her skull's cage
> The stuffed shape of her flown mate
> Escaped among the moon-plumaged strangers;
> So hungered, she must wait in rage
> Until bird-racketing dawn

> When her shrike-face
> Leans to peck open those locked lids, to eat
> Crowns, palace, all
> That nightlong stole her male,
> And with red beak
> Spike and suck out
> Last blood-drop of that truant heart. (*CPP* 42)

Like this poem's speaker, Agnes (from "The Wishing Box") too takes on the attributes of a shrike when she sobers up after an afternoon of sherry. In bed, "she would lie stiff, twisting her fingers like nervous talons in the sheets, long after Harold was breathing peacefully, evenly, in the midst of some rare, wonderful adventure" (*JP* 54). Yet the ending of "The Shrike" is antithetical to the end of "The Wishing Box" and more like that of "The Fifty-Ninth Bear." In "The Shrike," the woman takes her revenge upon the male imagination as she takes on the attributes of the Zeusian eagles that pecked Prometheus's liver day after day. If she cannot harness the power to create, then she will embrace the power to destroy. This is a theme Plath will revisit in "Lady Lazarus," "Daddy," and "Purdah" with female speakers who take their revenge upon a male power structure that has denied them admission to their "dreams."

Plath experiments with masculine and feminine identities in her portrayals of marital tension in "The Wishing Box," "Day of Success," and "The Fifty-Ninth Bear." Agnes and Ellen represent passive "feminine" defeat and submission, while Sadie stands for violent, active "masculine" triumph. Agnes and Ellen are subjects of pity and parody, while Sadie inspires fear and terror. These early works may show Plath writing two extreme fantasies in response to the rivalry she was beginning to experience with Hughes. That she continued to return to this subject (and, in the case of "The Wishing Box" and "The Shrike," in such similar language) suggests the extent of her fear of remaking.

PERFORMING ABJECTION

Plath again explored her rivalry with Hughes in "On the Difficulty of Conjuring Up a Dryad," written in 1957. The poem is more subversive than it initially appears. Plath not only engages in a debate about the success of various modes of poetic vision, but she engages specifically with Hughes as she subtly portrays the dilemma of the female writer attempting to find her voice. Significantly, Plath frames her speaker's sense of artistic inadequacy through the metaphor of psychoanalysis:

> "My trouble, doctor, is: I see a tree,
> And that damn scrupulous tree won't practice wiles
> To beguile sight:

> E.g., by cant of light
> Concoct a Daphne;
> My tree stays tree." (*CPP* 66)

The relationship between doctor and patient here parallels that of the male and female writer; like the psychiatrist who will teach his patient to express herself verbally, the male writer will teach his female partner to express herself on paper. Plath explores this dynamic at length in the poem, in which Rose sees "the problem of poetic representation in explicitly sexual, gendered terms" (114). While Plath does not identify her speaker as a woman, she ends the poem with a suggestion of literary sexism that recalls her own position vis-à-vis her husband:

> "No doubt now in dream-propertied fall some moon-eyed,
> Star-lucky sleight-of-hand man watches
> My jilting lady squander coin, gold leaf stock ditches,
> And the opulent air go studded with seed . . .   (66)

Yet Plath's abjection in the face of the male poet is mere performance; despite her protestations to the contrary, she attempts to present herself as the stronger poet in the partnership. Britzolakis writes that Plath ends "On the Difficulty" by "slyly mocking the notion of creative genius"—particularly the Romantic notion that the "poet strives to *incarnate*, through language, a pre-existent fullness of meaning which is supposed to inhere in nature" (86). If Plath is indeed mocking the Coleridgean formula for "creative genius," then the poem is much more complex than it at first appears. Rather than playing the 'abject' partner in what seem to be "confessions of poetic failure, half-humorous laments for an absent sublimity" (Britzolakis 85), Plath instead slyly challenges Hughes's neo-romantic, shamanistic version of artistic creation with her own, less "visionary" (*CPP* 67) style. Indeed, as Uroff suggests, Plath seems to point directly to Hughes in the second stanza of the poem, where she imitates his voice:

> . . . "I shall compose a crisis
> To stun sky black out, drive gibbering mad
> Trout, cock, ram,
> That bulk so calm
> On my jealous stare,
> Self-sufficient as they are." (*CPP* 66)

Although Uroff does not see this allusion to Hughes's style as ironic, an ironic reading suggests Plath's challenge to dominant ideas about poetic creation. As Plath writes in "On the Plethora of Dryads," the companion piece to "On the Difficulty," "No visionary lightnings | Pierced my dense lid" (67). Indeed, in that poem, Plath seems to mock the idea that "quintessential beauty" is visible only to "the paragon heart" (67).

Uroff sees "On the Difficulty" as an explicit admission of Plath's poetic inferiority complex (as many critics read "The Wishing Box"), yet the poem contains indications that Plath was not willing to give in so easily. Plath's description of the supposedly superior visionary imagination as a "hocus-pocus of green angels" that "Damasks with dazzle the threadbare eye" (66) sounds frivolous when compared with the straightforward, no-nonsense approach of the speaker: "My tree stays a tree" (66). Plath, in fact, praises the speaker's own aesthetic when she writes:

> "However I wrench obstinate bark and trunk
> To my sweet will, no luminous shape
> Steps out radiant in limb, eye, lip,
> To hoodwink the honest earth which pointblank
>> Spurns such fiction
>> As nymphs; cold vision
>> Will have no counterfeit
>> Palmed off on it.   (66)

The speaker presents herself as one thing only to subtly reveal herself as another: just as in "Pursuit," where the hunted morphs into the hunter ("One day I'll have my death of him" (*CPP* 22)), here the "weaker" writer cleverly argues for her superiority. The "honest earth" rejects the visionary's attempts at "counterfeit" representation; Plath values Yeatsian "cold vision" above the "hocus-pocus of green angels." At the poem's end, abjection masks the poet's real triumph: "this beggared brain | Hatches no fortune, | But from leaf, from grass, | Thieves what it has" (66). "Beggared" suggests poverty, but also ascetic virtue—hers is a mind that does not overindulge. The notion of stealing, too, suggests an appropriate metaphor for the poem's achievement, for Plath "secretly" manages to put forth a viewpoint completely at odds with the one her speaker supposedly espouses. This is not to say that the speaker is duplicitous, only that Plath feels the need to cloak her real message—in this case, her superior aesthetic sense—behind a veil of abjection and self-contempt, just as she did in "Mr. and Mrs. Ted Hughes's Writing Table." Steven Axelrod's assessment of Plath's "The Colossus" applies equally well to "On the Difficulty": "While seeming to portray the female ephebe as a weak reader, the poem proves her to be a strong misreader" (50).

The poem's form provides further clues as to Plath's intent. Its rigid formal elements—typical of Plath at this time—are perhaps employed ironically. Although Plath may be using formalism to emphasize her speaker's inability to imagine a dryad, as well as her own inability to break from a rigid, formulaic approach, the use of regular form might also be a way of advocating order and precision against the male poet's visionary spontaneity. While the meter varies, the shape of the stanzas—octets with a regular abbaccdd rhyme scheme—remains the same throughout. The first four lines, which are heavy with consonance, vary between pentameter and hexameter, while the last four, which contain more assonance, vary between dimeter and trimeter. Each octet, then, suggests two separate quatrains that have been joined together. While there are numerous compound adjectives in the first four (long) lines of each stanza ("rook-tongued," "hocus-pocus," "dream-propertied," "moon-eyed," "Star-lucky"), Plath abandons this language in the second false quatrains, which have a crystalline, Yeatsian clarity. In each stanza, the second "false" quatrain is more direct, and less ornate, than the first. Plath presents the voice of the Romantic in the first four lines, only to "creatively correct" that voice with her own "cold vision" in the last four. It is as if she is conjuring the Yeats of "A Coat" in these lines, affirming that there is more enterprise in rejecting embellishments and "walking naked." "On the Difficulty" suggests that Plath was very much aware of her position as Hughes's rival even at a time when she told her mother, "There is no question of rivalry" (*LH* 297).

Plath again addressed her rivalry with Hughes through a pair of doubles in "Dialogue over a Ouija Board," which, like "On the Difficulty of Conjuring Up a Dryad," has received little critical attention.[16] Yet this text is important to any discussion of Plath's and Hughes's creative dialogue since it is the only piece of writing in which Plath literally re-creates that dialogue *as* dialogue. Although she attempts something similar in "The Wishing Box," that story is a parodic version of male–female creative rivalry. "Dialogue over a Ouija Board," however, presents a less melodramatic, more autobiographical rendering of the Plath–Hughes conversation.

If "Dialogue" has been overlooked, Hughes may be partially to blame. The verse dialogue does not appear in the main section of *Collected Poems*, but rather in the back of the book, buried amidst Hughes's explanatory notes. In his note on "Dialogue," he tells us that Plath "never showed" (*CPP* 276) the work, but surmises that it was probably written in 1957–8, around the time he and Plath regularly used a ouija board to conjure a spirit named Pan. In fact, Plath had written excitedly to her mother in August 1957 from Cape Cod, telling her she was working on the verse dialogue, "both dramatic and philosophical," which was the first poem she had written in six months (*LH* 324). Did Hughes omit the dialogue from the main manuscript because he assumed Plath was unhappy with it (since she had "never showed" it), or was he uneasy about the poem's content? He offers no explanation in his notes, but instead writes at length about the spirit who controlled the ouija board. (He writes, seriously, that the spirit Pan "could be accurate" (*CPP* 276), and that he had predicted outcomes of football pools.)

Although Plath frequently gives the impression in her letters home that she shared Hughes's interest in the occult, "Dialogue over a Ouija Board" suggests she was ambivalent about participation in such rituals. She mentions Pan and the ouija board only once in her journals, when she wonders "how much is our own

---

[16] Of the major Plath studies, only Rose discusses the poem (briefly); even Uroff, in *Sylvia Plath and Ted Hughes*, overlooks it. Gilbert and Gubar address the dialogue in passing in their chapter on Plath in *No Man's Land*.

intuition working, and how much queer accident, and how much 'my father's spirit'" (400). This passage was written just three days before her first extended burst of rivalrous anger towards Hughes, when she expresses her determination to "make myself & not let myself be made by him" (*J* 401).

In "Dialogue," Plath presents two lovers, Sybil and Leroy, clearly modeled on herself and Hughes. Sybil's first words hint of the tension in the room: "Go get the glass, then" (*CPP* 276), she tells Leroy with an air of exasperation.[17] They have already been arguing, it seems, about whether to use the ouija board, and Leroy has won. This is the first of many instances in which both spouses try to impose their will upon each other. Yet as Sybil frankly admits toward the end of the dialogue, their wills "are strung | To such cross-purposes" (284).

Throughout the work, Sybil's belief in herself becomes contingent upon disbelief in Leroy; her skepticism towards Leroy's authority may even hint at Plath's skepticism in Hughes's modes of authorship. For "Dialogue" is, after all, a work very much concerned with writing itself, as Plath makes clear in her first stanza: "the clock | Has never failed to see our fabling sheared | Down to a circle of letters: twenty-six | In all. Plus Yes. Plus No. And this bare board" (276). Plath positions Sybil and Leroy sitting at a coffee-table "face to face"—a face-off that recalls Plath's (ironically) abject comparison between herself and Hughes in "Mr. and Mrs. Ted Hughes's Writing Table." Here, the "bare board" becomes the symbolic "writing table" where the two poets test their wills. Plath also alludes to her poem "The Other Two" in the first stanza of "Dialogue" when she writes of ghostly doubles watching Sybil and Leroy "With the cold burn dry ice has" (276); in "Dialogue" they are "like marble statues" while in "The Other Two" they are "Heavy as statuary" (68). Plath sets up a complex introduction in which images of the couple's unhappy doubles and metaphorical writing tables engage, and exist, in an uneasy symbiosis. She presents the "bare board" with its "circle of letters" as a kind of blank canvas that both poets will struggle to make their own, for competing interpretations of "letters" are at the very heart of this "dialogue."

Sybil seems reluctant to play with the board from the start, though she has trouble admitting her skepticism to Leroy. When she asks him if he pushes the glass over the letters, Leroy says, "You know I don't," to which Sybil responds, "And still I'm skeptic. I know. I'm being foolish || I suppose. If I didn't trust you at this | I wouldn't trust myself. The fault's my faith | In Pan" (277). Skepticism toward Pan's magic may represent a more general skepticism toward Hughes's beliefs about astrology, the occult, shamanism, and the supernatural. Al Alvarez, who knew Plath and Hughes well during this time, was himself doubtful about Plath's belief in the occult:

---

[17] Gilbert and Gubar note that Plath's choice of name for Sybil's husband, Leroy, is significant: although the name suggests Hughes's "kingly qualities" (Le Roi), this was "also the name that Plath would in a year use for the male playmate whom Sadie bites in 'The Shadow'" (1994: 3.278).

although both of them talked often enough about astrology, dreams and magic . . . I had the impression that at heart their attitudes were utterly different. . . . there was always a sense of his being in touch with some primitive area, some dark side of the self which had nothing to do with the young literary man. . . . he had never been properly civilized—or had, at least, never properly believed in his civilization. . . . So all that astrology, primitive religion and black magic he talked about . . . was a kind of metaphor for the shaking but obscure creative powers he knew himself to possess.   (1971: 24)

But Plath was different:

Her intensity was . . . more intellectual than Ted's. It was part of the fierceness with which she had worked as a student, passing exam after exam brilliantly, effortlessly, hungrily. . . . everything had to be done well and to the fullest. Since her husband was interested in the occult—for whatever clouded personal reasons—she threw herself into that, too, almost out of the desire to excel. And because her natural talents were very great, she discovered she had "psychic gifts". No doubt the results were genuine and even uncanny, but I suspect they were a triumph of mind over ectoplasm.   (1971: 25)

"Dialogue" registers Plath's discomfort with Hughes's occult preoccupations and, at the same time, her anxiety over her own complicity in encouraging them. As Plath had written to her mother in October 1956, "we shall be a team better than Mr. and Mrs. Yeats—he being a competent astrologist reading horoscopes, and me being a tarot-pack reader, and, when we have enough money, a crystal gazer" (*LH* 280). A year later, it seems, she was not so sure.

When Sybil asks Pan about the location and condition of her father, he replies "In plumage." Sybil is astonished by the originality of the image, and begins to wonder whether her skepticism has been misplaced. But when the glass begins to move again, Leroy reads "raw worms," disappointing Sybil, who preferred to envision her father with wings. Leroy mocks her idealism: "You persist in spelling half-hints || Out of a wholeness. Worms, not wings is what | Pan said. A plumage of raw worms" (*CPP* 279). Sybil then immediately moves to discredit Pan's existence: "How | Tedious. That's what we'd say. . . . | I was perfectly right: Pan's a mere puppet | Of our two intuitions" (279). She soon launches more accusations at Leroy:

> . . . you've pampered
> Pan as if he were our first-breached brat
> Fusing two talents, a sort of psychic bastard
> Sprung to being on our wedding night
>
> Nine months too soon for comfort, but a bright
> Boy, prone to compose queer poetry
> In apt iambics, if prodded to recite
> By scoldings, or by subtle praise. Only I,
> Even if you seem pacified, prefer
> To picture some other party speaking through
> Our separate veins and this glass mouth.   (280)

Pan, representative of the two poets' imaginations, is here reduced to a "psychic bastard"—an illegitimate mistake. This portrayal of creative fusion differs starkly from Plath's glowing descriptions of her writing life with Hughes in her letters.

The two soon disagree again about the nature of Pan's message. When asked where he lives, Pan first responds with "In Godpie," an answer that pleases Leroy. But then Pan changes his answer to "In Godhead," which in turn pleases Sybil, who tells Leroy, "You're in a huff | Because Pan bluntly spelt out god's head, not | Your head after all" (282). But Leroy ultimately wins the battle of wills when the two ask Pan, a third time, where he lives and Pan responds, "In core of nerve" (284). "I hope | You're satisfied. My will has evidently | Curtseyed to yours," Sybil says. Exasperated, Leroy attempts to placate her:

> Do we have to battle
> Like rival parents over a precocious
> Child to see which one of us can call
> Pan's prowess our own creation, and not the other's
> Work at all? (284)

But Sybil remains unmoved:

> How can we help but battle
> If our nerves are the sole nourishers
> Of Pan's pronouncements, and our nerves are strung
> To such cross-purposes? (284)

Again, we are far from the model of creative, collaborative marriage that Plath frequently extolled.

Sybil eventually breaks the wine glass, implying that only by doing so will the two be able to reconcile their "two talents" (280). From this point on, the dialogue becomes Yeatsian, incantatory and stylized, and loses its immediacy and prosaic quality. The tone is now Romantic as the two lovers attempt to reconnect their imaginations: as Sybil says, "we grew one | As the glass flew to its fragments.... || Let our backs, now bold, | Oppose what we faced earlier" (285). What they faced, they soon admit to each other, included death and "division": each, it appears, had seen an image of the other dead while Pan still reigned. By killing off Pan, Plath neatly resolves the lovers' conflict: the symbol of their rivalry, their incompatible creative wills, has been swept away. But her solution rings false, for Plath does not truly resolve the tensions between Sybil and Leroy. It is as if she shies away from a deeper exploration of her rivalry with Hughes at the very moment she suggests it exists. We move too quickly from the realm of reality to that of fairy-tale—an ironic progression in light of the skepticism Sybil has shown throughout. Plath has taken the significant step of suggesting, through her autobiographical verse drama, that rivalry exists between herself and Hughes, but she is still unable to offer a way to transform the sorrow that attends the rivalry into innovative art. As Sybil says, "I glimpse no light at all as long | As we two glower from our separate camps, | This board our battlefield" (284).

4

Colonial Contexts

When Sylvia Plath met Ted Hughes, he was the antithesis of the well-mannered, athletic, bourgeois college boys she had dated at Smith. Hughes belonged to a raucous, anti-establishment coterie of young, disaffected Cambridge poets who lived in the St Botolph's Rectory (Lucas Myers bedded down in a former chicken coop, while Hughes often slept in a tent).[1] While Plath longed for acceptance within this rag-tag group of poets, the young men viewed her with both fascination and condescension. On the one hand, with her "exaggerated Ameri-can | Grin" (*CPH* 1045), she embodied the naïve, overeager Yank with no appreciation for nuance or irony. On the other, she represented a physical vitality and health that Hughes found refreshing in the grayish gloom of the postwar years. As he told the *Paris Review* in 1995, "To me, of course, she was not only herself: she was America and American literature in person" (77). In *Birthday Letters*, Hughes often associates Plath's nation with her body: "It seemed your long, perfect, American legs | Simply went on up," he wrote in "St Botolph's" (*CPH* 1052); later, in "18 Rugby Street," he expanded upon this image: "You were a new world. My new world. | So this is America, I marvelled. | Beautiful, beautiful America!" (*CPH* 1058). As these lines suggest, Plath's American identity would prove a barrier to acceptance within a British male literary milieu that did not take women writers, much less American women writers, seriously. (Philip Hobsbaum, for example, invited Ted Hughes to join his creative writing group at Cambridge, but refused Plath admission.[2]) If we are to understand Plath's collaborative relationship with Hughes, we must acknowledge that for him and his friends, Plath was not only a gauche Fulbright scholar seeking admittance to their literary coterie, but a colonial who was, on account of her American origin, sexually alluring.[3] Plath herself seemed to veer between these two identities; although she frequently emphasized her serious intellectual

---

[1] The group included Hughes, Myers, Daniel Huws, Daniel Weissbort, Colin White, and Terence McCaughey. Hughes later remembered that they spent most of their time drinking at the Anchor pub and singing Irish, Welsh, and Scottish folk songs.

[2] Tape-recorded interview with author, Glasgow, October 27, 2000.

[3] Lucas Myers, writing nearly fifty years after leaving Cambridge, somehow remembered that "Sylvia was far more passionate sexually than the average person" (46). Since Myers never had a sexual relationship with Plath, one wonders to what extent his assessment was influenced by Plath's "flashy" (Myers 25) American demeanor.

ambitions in her journals, she also worried that her scholarly pursuits would undermine her femininity. From her earliest days at Cambridge, Plath had to contend with both her sex and her nationality in order to earn the respect of her male peers—especially Hughes.

"HOW AMERICAN"

In 1956, the United States' superior economic and military strength did not guarantee Americans a smooth transition from one side of the Atlantic to the other. In contrast, Plath soon understood that in Britain she appeared a vulgar Roman in the eyes of cultured Greeks. As Bertram Wyatt-Brown wrote in his memoir of the St Botolph years, "In that decade, the English still believed they were meant to rule the world. Americans were thought of as wayward colonists with regrettable accents and pushy manners" (352). Wyatt-Brown, himself an American, noted that the British were often condescending and rude; he and several of his American friends deliberately emphasized their American accents in order "to ward off what we considered the ridiculous, effeminate upper-class English accent that others of us were imitating" (355). It is likely Plath fell under the latter category, for by the time she recorded the "Poets in Partnership" interview with Hughes in 1961, she had acquired an English accent. Yet she too struggled to maintain a national identity in the face of British condescension. Jane Baltzell Kopp, Plath's contemporary at Cambridge, remembered that her friend's Americanisms were ridiculed by their English peers during her first month at Cambridge, while her gold and white Samsonite suitcases inspired "much amazement, incredulity, and humor among the British" (63). Kopp described feeling embarrassed for Plath when she

rode up to a Cambridge bobby and asked him in a Massachusetts accent to suggest "somewhere really picturesque and collegiate" where we might eat. In those days I was self-conscious about the kind of thing the British found ridiculous in Americans. Sylvia absolutely was not, and she managed in the course of her first few weeks in Cambridge to run through most of the classic varieties—sublimely oblivious, I think, all the while. (62)

But Plath, with her acute sensitivity and desire to conform, could not have remained oblivious for long. Her adoption of an English accent was likely a response to her "colonial" insecurities—her growing awareness of her "gauche" American mannerisms, and her sense that Hughes's St Botolph's friends disapproved of her "coffee table propensities" (Kopp 76).

Just as Hughes would feel ill at ease in America, Plath was never completely satisfied with her life in England. Tracy Brain notes that she oscillated "between Anglophilia and Anglophobia" (2001: 54), and that she was critical not only of "American commercialism" but of "English shabbiness" (2001: 57). While Plath's early letters home in the fall of 1955 expressed enthusiasm about Cambridge, they betrayed increasing disappointment as the months wore on and winter set in. During her first semester, she complained about the lack of central heating, the bad weather, and bland British food:

When it is nice here it is 'very very nice, and when it is bad, it is horrid.' I have become used to clouds of frosted air surrounding me as I breathe in the bathtub and to concentrating on the cloud formations outside the dining room windows as I eat my soggy, sludgy mass of daily starch foods.   (*LH* 196)

Although she initially found her attic bedsit and its small gas fireplace quaint (*LH* 183), by February she desperately longed for American conveniences:

I wear about five sweaters and wool pants and knee socks and *still* I can't stop my teeth chattering. The gas fire eats up the shillings and scalds one side and the other freezes like the other half of the moon. I was simply not made for this kind of weather. I have had enough of their sickbay and hospitals to make me think it is better to perish in one's own home of frostbite than to go through their stupid, stupid System. How I miss the Smith infirmary…!   (*LH* 217)

She was also homesick: "Perhaps what I *do* miss most here is the lack of my friends who have known me in my past…. Everyone here is so 'new' and untried" (*LH* 195). Yet perhaps the biggest adjustment Plath had to make was moving from a nurturing women's college with a proud feminist tradition to a decentralized and largely male university. As Plath quipped to her mother, "it seems the Victorian age of emancipation is yet dominant here" (*LH* 219). This environment fueled Plath's anger, but also her insecurities. In the same letter, she wrote, "I am not brilliant enough to invade the professors at the men's colleges" and lamented, "there is no medium for the *kind* of rapport I had at Smith" (*LH* 219).[4] At Cambridge, she must have felt keenly what Steven Axelrod called the "paradox of her education … she had been instructed to value the language of high culture but to doubt her own capacity to employ it" (37). By the spring of 1956, she was confident enough to complain publicly in *Isis* about the shabby treatment women received at Cambridge:

Apparently, the most difficult feat for a Cambridge male is to accept a woman not merely as feeling, not merely as thinking, but as managing a complex, vital interweaving of both. Men here are inclined to treat women in one of two ways: either (1) as pretty beagling frivolous things … worthy of May balls and suggestive looks over bottles of Chablis by candlelight, or, more rarely, (2) as esoteric opponents on an intellectual tennis court where the man, by law of kind, always wins…. A debonair Oxford P.P.E. man demurred, laughing incredulously: "But really, talk about philosophy with a *woman!*" A poetic Cambridge chap maintains categorically: "As soon as a woman starts talking about intellectual things, she loses her feminine charm for me."   (1956: 9)

---

[4] She also told her mother that "In lectures, women are very much the minority" (*LH* 187).

Plath hoped that men and women at the university might someday interact more naturally, "perhaps in supervisions, perhaps in coffee shops . . . playing with ideas where a woman keeps her female status while being accepted simultaneously as an intelligent human being" (9).

"Anglophobia" surfaces in Plath's early poetry, which, notes Paul Giles, is particularly "suffused with American values and attributes" (109). In "Whitsun" (1961), she expresses a profound disappointment with the dreary English seaside that literally paled in comparison with her beloved Nauset. Despite Hughes's attempt to bolster her spirits with a trip to the coast, she finds only "Grownups coffined in stockings and jackets, | Lard-pale, sipping the thin | Air like medicine" (*CPP* 153). In the early "Channel Crossing" (1956) she characterizes the English coastline in similarly bleak terms. Expecting "water drenched | With radiance" she finds "instead, bleak rocks | . . . clouds and chalk cliffs blanched || In sullen light of the inauspicious day" (*CPP* 27). For Plath, only Nauset is radiant; the "sullen" British coast, by contrast, frames an equally sullen land. In "Landowners," written in 1956, the drab British row houses outside the speaker's window emphasize her own "leaden perspective" in Cambridge:

> From my rented attic with no earth
> To call my own except the air-motes,
> I malign the leaden perspective
> Of identical gray brick houses,
> Orange roof-tiles, orange chimney pots,
> And see that first house, as if between
> Mirrors, engendering a spectral
> Corridor of inane replicas,
> Flimsily peopled.   (*CPP* 53)

The claustrophobic architecture is presumably set in contrast to America's endless horizons. The poem suggests an ironic revision of Tennyson's "The Lady of Shalott"—here the speaker is no longer embowered within a turret but sits in a "rented attic," while Camelot has given way to a depressing post-industrial landscape.

Even in Hughes's company, Plath could not always shake off her dissatisfaction with Britain. In "55 Eltisley," Hughes recalled that their first flat "confirmed | Your idea of England: part | Nursing home, part morgue | For something partly dying, partly dead" (*CPH* 1074). By December 1956, Plath wrote to her mother, "Oh, how I secretly hope that Ted finds America the wonderland I feel it is and wants eventually to settle there . . . I would never want to live in England or bring up children here; it is a dead, corrupt country. How I long to get home!"[5] Even as late as 1961, when asked why she liked England by

---

[5] Sylvia Plath to Aurelia Plath, December 1956, Lilly. In a similar letter to Marcia Stern, she wrote, "Ted is staunchly British, but I am hoping that he will see the enormous difference in America & want to settle there eventually. England is no place to bring up children—bad teeth, lousy dentists, careless overworked Mds. It is, really, a dead country" (December 15, 1956, Smith).

a reporter for the *London/American*, she responded, "Because it's about 50 years behind America." Asked what she missed about America, she listed corn on the cob, Nauset Beach, and snow. "There's never any snow, just rain and grey" (Tyler 1961: 7). Although Plath eventually decided to stay in England after her separation from Hughes, this decision may have been motivated by a desire to maintain independence from her mother rather than by a strong preference for life in Britain.

If Plath was impatient with British shabbiness, she was equally annoyed by English pretension. During her second year at Cambridge, in February 1957, she wrote to her mother, "England is so stuffy, cliquey, and plain bad, bad" (*LH* 293). It is likely Plath was voicing her resentment at being snubbed, as she often was at Cambridge. As Lucas Myers claimed, "American universities, in the English Departments at least, were nursery schools compared to Cambridge. Sylvia's effusiveness, which disguised her intelligence, and her seemingly commercial approach to literature . . . exposed her to mockery at Cambridge" (qtd. in Stevenson 315). William Logan's more recent claim that Plath was a poet "formed in the supermarket, with supermarket values" (128) shows that such characterizations have stuck: Plath is still faulted for embodying superficial American materialism. Al Alvarez, as if emphasizing Logan's claim, wrote that when he first met Plath she was "briskly American: bright, clean, competent, like a young woman in a cookery advertisement" (1971: 7).[6] Myers called her "an unusually flashy target" (25) and admitted that he was "embarrassed for her as a fellow American" (32). When Hughes began spending most of his time with Plath, Myers recalled, his "old friends . . . were unable to account for his attraction to her" (45). The St Botolph's crowd even made up a ditty that went "I'd rather have my Ted as he used to be | Than Sylvia Plath and her rich mommy" (45). Kopp remembers a member of the St Botolph circle remarking, "I never, never thought that Ted would marry an *American* girl" (76).

As Brain points out, Plath's British detractors reached new heights of smug reproach in Anne Stevenson's biography:

Some of the oddest contradictions in *Bitter Fame* occur when questions of femininity coincide with those of nationality. English women, Stevenson suggests again and again, just don't behave that way, they don't think that way. Plath's bad example of American femininity is tacitly contrasted with the sophistication, avoidance of *gaucherie*, and indifference to consumer goods incarnated in English women such as Dido Merwin and Olwyn Hughes. (2001: 52)

Such evidence supports Robin Peel's view that, "In England [Plath] is the colonial subject, because that is the way Americans were treated, and that is the way she had come to feel that she was being treated in her marriage" (2002: 107). Myers further confirms this point when he recalls the way Plath was, in fact, treated at Cambridge:

---

[6] Though Plath *did* write to her friend Marcia Stern in late 1956, "God Bless America, land of the Cookiesheet, Central Heating & Frozen Orange Juice!" (qtd. in Peel, 2002: 112).

If, at the time, we had had a tape recorder, it could presently be demonstrated that the view of Sylvia among British graduates was dismissive and not what sometimes is reported. It was pleasant, in a decade when Americans were very rich and the British were poor and, unthinkably, American power was overshadowing that of the British Empire, which itself was unthinkably dissolving—it was pleasant to have on view an American making such a display of herself. (26)

In his memoir of Plath and Hughes, *Crow Steered Bergs Appeared*, Myers takes particular pleasure in lambasting Plath for "making a display of herself" during an afternoon walk to Granchester with Hughes. That day, Plath climbed a stile and recited the "Prologue" of Chaucer's *Canterbury Tales* to a group of cows who, as Hughes later wrote in "Chaucer," gathered round to listen with "astounded attention" (*CPH* 1075). In "Chaucer," Hughes seems as "hypno-tised" by Plath's performance as the cows: "Your sostenuto rendering of Chaucer | Was already perpetual" (1076). But Myers reacted differently when Hughes told him about the incident:

I can't imagine any British university student mounting Sylvia's stile. And I can't imagine any other British student spectator responding the way Ted did. They would either, with a rewarding measure of schadenfreude, have dropped the words, "How American," or have wondered inwardly how one of the pampered scholarship products of wealthy colleges in the richest and most powerful country in the world could have put on a display so obviously calculated....

One can imagine Rimbaud or Verlaine mounting Sylvia's stile, if they had felt like it, in a natural way. But the performance of the poetess *maudite* of our own times and language and friendship was questionably authentic in spontaneity and intention. (48)

Rather than praise her ability to recite the entire "Prologue" from memory, as Hughes does in "Chaucer," Myers deflates Plath's achievement and faults her for a lack of "spontaneity." For Myers, and perhaps many other contempor-aries at Cambridge, Plath was an imposter on two fronts: both as an American laying claim to the words of English poets and a woman aligning herself with a male literary tradition. Hughes, on the other hand, was a rightful heir both of Chaucer and the type of Wordsworthian Romanticism that might lead one to proclaim verse to the fields. It is little wonder that Plath's performance may have come off as "questionably authentic" given the barriers that prevented her integration into both the British nation and its literary canon. Hughes, for his part, was impressed by Plath's performance and sympathized with the shabby treatment she received at Cambridge, which he wrote about in a *Birthday Letters* poem, "God Help the Wolf after Whom the Dogs Do Not Bark":

> The Colleges lifted their heads. It did seem
> You disturbed something just perfected
> That they were holding carefully, all of a piece,
> Till the glue dried. And as if

Reporting some felony to the police
They let you know that you were not John Donne.

            .   .   .   .   .   .

...they let you know, day by day,
Their contempt for everything you attempted,...

            .   .   .   .   .   .

Nobody wanted your dance,
Nobody wanted your strange glitter—your floundering
Drowning life and your effort to save yourself,
Treading water for something to give—
Whatever you found
They bombarded with splinters,
Derision, mud—the mystery of that hatred.   (*CPH* 1060)

Plath's (American) commodification of the poetic voice is a relentless theme in *Crow Steered Bergs Appeared*. One gets the sense throughout that Myers is still slightly embarrassed for Plath, just as he was at Cambridge, and that part of his memoir's aim is to separate "Sylvia's practice of poetic manufacture" (26) from Hughes's more authentic creative process. Myers presents Plath as an embodiment of American capitalism and "shallow American effusion" (51) despite the fact that Plath was a scholarship student raised by a struggling single mother.[7] While he felt Plath was a gifted poet, she was also a typically *American* poet (50) whose "vocation" was "producing and publishing poems as opposed to creating poetry" (42). Plath, in his estimation, was "a familiar type found especially in the American middle class of the period (post-war up to 1968) who was demanding and selfish almost in the manner of a child" (78). Worse, Myers observed, she wrote to please editors, a practice Hughes considered a "terrible thing" (95). (Myers fails to mention that Hughes himself wrote several drama plots with the hope of making money on the BBC, and that he frequently asked Plath for her help in developing these "commercial" plots.) Plath's "view to pleasing a specific editor" is just one more manifestation of her American falseness, which showed, in Myers's opinion, "what fundamentally different sorts of writers" (95) she and Hughes were. While Myers's view represents that of just one person, it has stuck—particularly among Hughes critics, who generally see Plath as the less authentic writer in the partnership. As Keith Sagar wrote, "While Plath searched her thesaurus, Hughes plundered Anglo-Saxon and dialect for the words and rhythms he needed" (2000: 52).

---

[7] As an American, Myers may have been particularly sensitive to the "gauche" foibles of his countrymen and women, and, hence, determined to separate himself from them. Indeed, he is dismissive of the other literary Americans who attempted to join the Anchor pub clique.

"MY NEW WORLD"

Hughes's disaffection with British establishment values may have inspired affection for Plath, who, with her gushing exuberance and long legs, represented a Whitmanesque foil to the careful, methodical spirit of Leavis's literary enquiry and the Movement's subdued verses. While Hughes would eventually chafe against Plath's efforts to "remake" him in an American vein, her national identity was initially a source of liberation. Yet it was also something of an embarrassment, one Hughes attempted to cope with by enfolding Plath, and her work, into a British neo-romantic, mythic tradition. As Paul Giles observes, for Hughes

Plath's American identity is . . . a form of inauthenticity . . . it is always English values which make up the assumed moral focus of the narrative and American attributes which are seen as hyperbolic or otherwise off centre . . . a false façade to be stripped away. . . . The idea here is that Plath's earlier American poems were cerebral exercises, academic in the derogatory sense, and that it took the primitivist landscapes of England to bring her to a realization of her deeper, more authentic self. (106–7)

Letters from Hughes to his English correspondents support Giles's observation. After Hughes met Plath, he assured Olwyn she was "not bla American."[8] Later, in a letter from the *Queen Elizabeth II*, bound for America in June 1957, Hughes pleaded with his sister to give Plath a second chance after a tense meeting at his parents' home in Yorkshire. He wrote that Plath's "vacuous" American mannerisms were simply a protective front:

Her immediate "face" when she meets someone is too open and too nice—"smarmy" as you said—but that's the American stereotype she clutches at when she is in fact panic-stricken. Or perhaps . . . her poise & brain just vanish in a kind of vacuous receptivity— only this american [*sic*] stereotype manner then keeps her going at all. She says stupid things then that mortify her afterwards. Her second thought—her retrospect, is pene-trating, skeptical, and subtle. But she can never bring that second-thinking mind to the surface with a person until she's known them some time. (*L* 99)

Hughes makes clear that Plath's "real" self—the self that is "penetrating, skeptical, and subtle"—is at odds with her "false" American self. After the couple returned to England from America in 1959, Hughes told Myers that Plath's poetry would benefit from the move: "It's much better that she lives in England—her poetry can develop naturally and at leisure here and with a more appreciative audience whereas America would be cramping and stinting and distorting her with that dreadful competitive spotlight."[9] Later Hughes wrote to Aurelia Plath, "Since she left America, she's lost the terrible panic pressure of the American poetry world—which keeps them all keeping up on each other. As a

8 Ted Hughes to Olwyn Hughes, May 1956, MSS 980, Emory.
9 Ted Hughes to Lucas Myers, September 1961, MSS 865, Emory.

result, she's developing her own way & will soon be a considerable genius."[10]
Just two weeks later, he again wrote to Aurelia that "While all those busy
clamorous America whippet poets race round in a circle after their stuffed
fashionable hare (and the publishers all betting drunkenly on them) Sylvia is
beginning to produce some really permanent poetry."[11]

Hughes was initially excited to live in America with Plath: he repeatedly wrote
to Olwyn in 1957 that he was tired of England, which he described as "rotten,"
"complete death."[12] When he landed, he was struck dumb by the wealth he
observed. His letters to his parents during this time are full of wonder, and sound
remarkably like Plath's letters home during her early years in England. From
Wellesley he wrote to his parents in 1957, "What a neighborhood! All the houses
are in their own little grounds." He described in great detail the wedding party
Aurelia threw for him and Plath, and surmised that the size of the party and
status of the guests determined one's class standing in America. Hughes sounds
very much like Plath as he recounts the wedding gifts they received, and the
probable cost. He talks about a "very elite looking" tray, a "huge" pressure
cooker, and a salt and pepper shaker that was "very modern and pleasant to
handle." He also described how well his new silk suit fit him, and noted that it
was made of "Wonderfully expensive material."[13] These observations show that
Hughes was not entirely immune to the prospect of bourgeois contentment.
"Imagine how I enjoy this," he wrote, after tallying the $50 and $100 bills they
received.[14] "This land literally does flow with milk and honey."[15]

Yet the initial excitement faded quickly. The couple's summer on Cape Cod
was restless rather than productive; Hughes claimed he could not work because
he was so disturbed by the cost of the cottage Aurelia had rented for them. He
began to describe America to his English correspondents as artificial, wrapped in
"cellophane" (*L* 106). He complained to his sister that "nobody ever bothers to
get to know anybody except on purely temporary and facetious terms" (*L* 107)
and that "their food is not fresh living stuff but a ten-year preservative, a chemical
concoction."[16] His description of the nation is a narrative of consumption,
waste, and excess—he speaks of the average American living on credit, mocks
the "city man's" naturalist pretensions ("Expensive rods and fat paunches"[17]),
and speaks of "greed, vulgarity, and the horrible superficiality of a race without
any principles."[18] He nevertheless enjoyed teaching his Great Books class at

[10] Ted Hughes to Aurelia Plath, May 1, 1962, Lilly.
[11] Ted Hughes to Aurelia Plath, May 14, 1962, Lilly.
[12] Ted Hughes to Olwyn Hughes, n.d., 1957, MSS 980, Emory.
[13] Ted Hughes to Edith and William Hughes, June 29, 1957, MSS 980, Emory.
[14] Ibid.
[15] Ted Hughes to Edith and William Hughes, summer 1957, MSS 980, Emory.
[16] Ted Hughes to Olwyn Hughes, September 12, 1957, MSS 980, Emory.
[17] Ted Hughes to Edith and William Hughes, summer 1957, MSS 980, Emory.
[18] Ted Hughes to Daniel Weissbort, n.d., 1957, MSS 894, Emory.

the University of Massachusetts, which he later told Myers was "1000 times more valuable than my academic experience at Cambridge."[19] He came to prefer Northampton and Boston to Wellesley, at one point calling Boston his "favorite city."[20]

But he remained suspicious of the nation at large, which he called a "stupid beast," and told Gerald that "Spiritual deadness is a modern American invention."[21] He was appalled by American culture, which seemed to consist of nothing more than newspapers, magazines, and pulp fiction: "women's magazines and men's paper-backs, newspapers . . . make up the shared consciousness of the American people."[22] He reckoned that the "indigenous literary form" was "the advertisement" (*L* 140). One wonders whether Hughes's habit of belittling Plath's fiction stemmed from his feelings toward the culture of the American magazine and its reliance on the advertisement. The fact that, in Hughes's eyes, Plath was pandering to a phony literary culture by pitching her work to this audience may have troubled him more than the actual work itself.

Although Hughes was impressed by Robert Lowell's *Life Studies*, he frequently took swipes at American poetry.[23] To Olwyn he wrote in 1958:

American poetry—there are hundreds of writers producing poems that look at first sight impressive, but this common brilliant style is at second reading a poor cheat—there is a glaze of impermeable plastic cleverness laid over a general nothing. So that, after a year at close quarters with it, I begin to see clearly that the good poets since Robert Lowell are mostly English, still.[24]

One year later, in 1959, he expressed similar thoughts to Daniel Weissbort:

American taste in poetry is basically . . . like their taste in cars. . . . American & English poetry are already as far apart as French & English. I think poetry is either cultivated or perverted or extinguished by national character, & in countries of wrong character the hugest & most excitable geniuses come to nothing. Its [*sic*] my belief that American character is now entering a phase about as favourable to poets as, say, Norway's is. (*L* 140–1)

Three years later, in 1962, he wrote to Bill Merwin, "Are you in the thick of the American new wave? Don't listen to them too closely—the Carlos Williams cult" (*L* 199). Neil Roberts notes that although Hughes wrote most of *Lupercal* in America, the book "reveals no imaginative response whatever" to the nation. On the contrary, Roberts writes, "it is a book that is saturated with English, and specifically Yorkshire, scenes, landscape and wildlife" (2006: 43).

---

[19] Ted Hughes to Lucas Myers, winter/spring 1961, MSS 865, Emory.
[20] Ted Hughes to Gerald Hughes, August 1958, MSS 854, Emory.
[21] Ted Hughes to Gerald Hughes, n.d., 1958, MSS 854, Emory; Ted Hughes to Gerald Hughes, n.d., 1958, MSS 854, Emory.
[22] Ted Hughes to Olwyn Hughes, n.d., 1960, MSS 980, Emory.
[23] I will discuss Hughes's relationship to American confessionalism in more detail in Chapter 8.
[24] Ted Hughes to Olwyn Hughes, summer 1958, MSS 980, Emory.

If Plath's American identity made her, at times, "smarmy" and "vacuous," it also made her sexually intriguing. In *Birthday Letters*, Plath possesses the exotic allure of the Other, and represents an alternative to the somber and stultifying atmosphere Hughes found at Cambridge, where students were still expected to adhere to a nightly curfew, and interactions between the sexes were extremely limited. Plath's national identity was connected to her sexuality from the start: as Hughes recalled in "St Botolph's," her "long, perfect, American legs | Simply went on up" (*CPH* 1052). Several poems in *Birthday Letters* utilize metaphors of colonization as Hughes compares Plath to an African or a Native American, presumably to set her colonial "otherness" into relief. In "St Botolph's" he describes Plath's face as "A rubbery ball of joy | Round the African-lipped, laughing, thickly | Crimson-painted mouth" (*CPH* 1052). In "18 Rugby Street" he describes her eyes as "Two little brown people," and her lips' "aboriginal thickness" (*CPH* 1057). Her nose is "Broad and Apache"; she has a "prototype face | That could have looked up at me through the smoke | Of a Navajo campfire" (1057). In "You Hated Spain," he writes of "The juju land behind your African lips" (*CPH* 1068), while in "The City" (from *Howls and Whispers*), the Plath figure's face is "A desert Indian's, wild, bewildered" (*CPH* 1179). "Black Hair," an uncollected poem that preceded the publication of *Birthday Letters*, imagines Plath as she is brushing her hair. The speaker watches and thinks, "She's Red Indian | And that's why her nose is Red Indian. | And that's why her skin seems so dark" (*CPH* 858). Plath was, as he put it, "My new world" (*CPH* 1058).

Hughes slides, in the first few poems in *Birthday Letters*, from Plath as American to Plath as "native" to Plath as exotic animal. In "Trophies," she becomes the panther of "Pursuit," her earliest poem about him. But this time Hughes is the victim: "The sudden | Look that locked on me | Through your amber jewels | And as I caught you lolling locked | Its jaws into my face" (*CPH* 1054). In "St Botolph's" he calls her fingers "monkey-elegant" (*CPH* 1052), and in "Sam" she is a "Baby monkey | Using your arms and legs for clinging steel" (*CPH* 1049). Hughes writes, in "18 Rugby Street," that "You wanted me to hear you panting," and calls her "A great bird, you | Surged in the plumage of your excitement" (*CPH* 1056–57). He also compares her to a bird in "Fever" when he describes her "baby-bird gape" (*CPH* 1072). In "The Rag Rug" he compares her to a snake (as he also does in "Fulbright Scholars"), hinting at her role in his 'fall': "I was like the snake-charmer—my voice | Swaying you over your heaped coils" (*CPH* 1131). In "The Inscription," Plath, after seeing Assia's inscription, closes Hughes's Shakespeare "Like the running animal that receives | The fatal bullet without a faltering check" (*CPH* 1155). Finally, in "Fingers," Hughes combines animal and exotic metaphors when he compares Plath's fingers to "birds in some tropical sexual | Play of display, leaping and somersaulting" (*CPH* 1168). By casting Plath as "native" and animal, Hughes reinforces Plath's (and woman's) role as mysterious, instinctive, non-rational, and dangerous.

Class is another recurring theme in Hughes's treatment of Plath's American identity in *Birthday Letters*. Hughes often characterizes both Plath and America as wealthy but vulgar, while he identifies himself with English stoicism and understatement. In "A Pink Wool Knitted Dress," for example, Hughes cleverly reverses the usual colonial hierarchy so that it is Plath's mother who is troubled by the transatlantic marriage. Yet his subtle self-defense shows that he does not believe he is wrong for Plath; rather, Plath's mother is swayed by the wrong values. He knows Aurelia Plath sees him as "the Swineherd | Stealing this daughter's pedigree dreams | From under her watchtowered searchlit future" (*CPH* 1064); he is a "U.S. Foreign Affairs gamble" (1065). But, Hughes writes, "No ceremony could conscript me | Out of my uniform" (1064). Hughes suggests that, given the sacrifices the British made for Western democracy, Americans had little right to measure English shabbiness against their own newfound wealth. He also implies that Plath herself is a prisoner of American materialism, while Aurelia, the guardian of the "watchtowered searchlit future" is likened to a totalitarian commandant (in Plath's poetry, it was normally Otto Plath who played this role). Even Plath's pink dress, brought specially from America by her mother, appears frivolous, conspicuous, and inappropriate amidst the post-war gloom. Hughes's old black suit may not be tailored, but it is nonetheless the more fitting attire. It is understated and inconspicuous, right for a man who does not cause scenes—unlike his new wife, who shakes and sobs during the ceremony. We also encounter critiques of Plath's American materialism in "The Blue Flannel Suit":

> . . . Your life
> Was a liner I voyaged in.
> Costly education had fitted you out.
> Financiers and committees and consultants
> Effaced themselves in the gleam of your finish.
> You trembled with the new life of those engines.   (*CPH* 1085)

In "Error," too, he writes of Plath "stripping off | Your American royalty, garment by garment—| Till you stepped out soul-naked" (*CPH* 1121). And in "The Chipmunk," he writes that during their stint on Cape Cod, "You stayed | Alien to me as a window model, | American, airport-hopping superproduct" (*CPH* 1083).

"Your Paris," like "A Pink Wool Knitted Dress," contrasts Plath's gushing vivacity with Hughes's somber, meditative demeanor. Hughes implies that his reaction to the city is the more authentic, and intelligent:

> Your Paris, I thought, was American.
> I wanted to humour you.
> When you stepped, in a shatter of exclamations,
> Out of the Hôtel des Deux Continents
> Through frame after frame,

Street after street, of Impressionist paintings,
Under the chestnut shades of Hemingway,
Fitzgerald, Henry Miller, Gertrude Stein...

.   .   .   .   .   .

I was not much ravished by the view of the roofs.
My Paris was a post-war utility survivor,
The stink of fear still hanging in the wardrobes,
Collaborateurs barely out of their twenties,
Every other face closed by the Camps
Or the Maquis. I was a ghostwatcher.
My perspectives were veiled by what rose
Like methane from the reopened
Mass grave of Verdun. For you all that
Was the anecdotal aesthetic touch
On Picasso's portrait...   (*CPH* 1065–6)

For Hughes, Paris was "only just not German. The capital | Of the Occupation and the old nightmare" (1066). Interestingly, all the writers Hughes lists at the beginning of the poem are American expatriates, and none of them were military combatants during the First World War. Thus, even the American writers Plath admires are suspect. It is only when Plath transcends her American identity that she begins to realize her "true" self, as in "You Hated Spain." Hughes writes how

...Bosch
held out a spidery hand and you took it
Timidly, a bobby-sox American.
You saw right down to the Goya funeral grin
And recognised it, and recoiled
As your poems winced into chill, as your panic
Clutched back towards college America.   (*CPH* 1068)

"The Beach," a companion piece to Plath's "Whitsun," is a variation on the themes in "A Pink Wool Knitted Dress" and "Your Paris." Again, Hughes presents Plath as a materialistic American with no sense of history:

...England
was so poor! Was black paint cheaper? Why
Were English cars all black—to hide the filth?
Or to stay respectable, like bowlers
And umbrellas? Every vehicle a hearse.
The traffic procession a hushing leftover
Of Victoria's perpetual funeral Sunday—
The funeral of colour and light and life!
London a morgue of dinge—English dinge.
Our sole indigenous art-form—depressionist!
And why were everybody's
Garments so deliberately begrimed?

Grubby-looking, like a camouflage? "Alas!
We have never recovered," I said, "from our fox-holes,
Our trenches, our fatigues and our bomb-shelters." (*CPH* 1143)

Hughes reminds us that Britain helped win both world wars, and that any lingering shabbiness is a result of sacrifices endured for democracy—sacrifices most Americans never had to make. His rendition of Plath's "American" voice, here and elsewhere, is shrill and entitled, while her American identity is a source of fantasy and derision.

"PIONEER IN THE WRONG DIRECTION"

Colonial anxieties surface in several poems Plath wrote while visiting the Hugheses in Yorkshire, Hughes's home ground, during the autumn of 1956. There, she wrote that she had experienced a deep connection with the landscape, which she called "Ted's wuthering-heights home" (*LH* 268), and become "a veritable convert to the Brontë clan":

This is the most magnificent landscape . . . incredible hills, vivid green grass, with amazing deep-creviced valleys feathered with trees, at the bottom of which clear, peat-flavored streams run.
  Climbing along the ridges of the hills, one has an airplane view of the towns in the valleys. Up here, it is like sitting on top of the world, and in the distance the purple moors curve away. I have never been so happy in my life; it is wild and lonely and a perfect place to work and read. I am basically, I think, a nature-loving recluse. Ted and I are at last "home." (*LH* 268–9)

Plath's early description of the Yorkshire moors is colored by Emily Brontë's *Wuthering Heights*; she told her mother that she and Hughes "are a happy Heathcliffe [*sic*] and Cathy! Striding about in the woods and over the moors."[25] Plath re-read *Wuthering Heights* in Yorkshire and told her mother that she "really *felt* it this time more than ever" (*LH* 270). Yet she must have understood that comparing herself and Hughes to the doomed protagonists of that novel was an ambiguous gesture. While her identification with Cathy and Heathcliff comprised a rejection of English gentility, she knew that obsession, misery, and death awaited these literary doppelgangers. And while she was awed by the Yorkshire landscape, moor poems such as "Snowman on the Moor," "Two Views of Withens," "Hardcastle Crags," and "Wuthering Heights" hint at what may have existed on the other side of the valleys' silence. These poems suggest that the landscape's beauties and terrors perhaps stood as an objective correlative for her anxieties about her relationship with Hughes, and even the British literary tradition itself.

[25] Sylvia Plath to Aurelia Plath, September 2, 1956, Lilly.

During Plath's first visit to Yorkshire, Hughes and his uncle Walt took her to Top Withens, a ruined farmhouse that, according to local lore, was the site of the original Wuthering Heights. Plath's account of this walk to her mother was exuberant:

> How can I tell you how wonderful it is. Imagine yourself on top of the world, with all the purplish hills curving away, and gray sheep grazing with horns curling and black demonic faces and yellow eyes . . . black walls of stone, clear streams from which we drank; and, at last, a lonely, deserted black-stone house, broken down, clinging to the windy side of a hill. (*LH* 269)

Yet there are hints of unease in this description, such as the "demonic" faces of the sheep and the bleak, "broken down" farmhouse. Plath also bore witness to a disturbing event during this pilgrimage that may have further alienated her from both the landscape and her husband. Hughes later described this incident:

> I was taking her over the moor, to visit the old farmhouse said to be the original of Wuthering Heights.
> Halfway across this moor, a grouse got up out of the heather. It was obviously wounded or sick and just fluttered away and collapsed again. I caught it. My instinct was that if it were sick or wounded, you just killed it. So I killed it. And she went berserk. "How could you do it?" It turned out that grouse were part of her mythology. (qtd. in Peel 2002: 244)

Hughes goes on to describe how when Plath was young she was entranced by a stranger's story about a "heather-bird." Hughes said she "had treasured this vision. . . . From the moment of first meeting her, I used to hear about this wonderful bird. Of course it turned out to be a damned red grouse. And she'd realised this by the time this event happened in Yorkshire. So I'd not only killed this helpless thing in front of her. I'd killed the legendary bird" (244).[26] Although Plath did not record the incident in her journal, Peel notes that she did contemplate writing about it: in a draft of "Wuthering Heights," she mentions a "broken-winged moor bird," though later excised the image (244).

In "Two Views of Withens," "The Snowman on the Moor," "Hardcastle Crags," and "Wuthering Heights," Plath's speakers venture out alone on the moors only to feel themselves shut out rather than let in, taunted rather than welcomed. They go in search of the same things Cathy found there—escape, transcendence, and freedom—but for them, the moorland provides no spiritual solace. Plath's speakers are explicitly *not* Cathy. Because the landscape embodied Hughes, and Hughes, in turn, embodied the landscape, Plath may, in her more insecure moments, have begun to see one as a sinister reflection of the other, and felt that both were intent upon "paring her person down" (*CPP* 63), as she wrote in "Hardcastle Crags." Indeed, the horizons that "ring" the speaker in

---

[26] This article, which originally appeared in *Wild Steelhead and Salmon Magazine*, was reprinted in *The Guardian* (January 9, 1999), Saturday Review, p. 1.

"Wuthering Heights," and then "dissolve and dissolve | Like a series of promises" suggest marital as well as existential anxiety. The speaker's fear that "the wind | Pours by like destiny, bending | Everything in one direction. | . . . trying | To funnel my heat away" (*CPP* 167) recalls Plath's earlier anxieties regarding Hughes's attempt to remake her. Such anxieties would have been particularly acute on Hughes's home ground, where Plath may have feared ending up as isolated and lonely as the characters in *Wuthering Heights*.

Hughes's "Stubbing Wharfe," collected in *Birthday Letters*, suggests that Plath did indeed feel such fears. He remembered the night he and Plath sat in a dim Yorkshire pub amidst the "shut-in | Sodden dreariness of the whole valley, | The hopeless old stone trap of it" and "the moorland | Almost closing above us" (*CPH* 1111). This description is a far cry from Brontë country as Plath described it to her mother. Hughes recalled a more somber mood:

> . . . You having leapt
> Like a thrown dice, flinging off
> The sparkle of America, pioneer
> In the wrong direction, sat weeping,
> Homesick, exhausted, disappointed, pregnant.
> Where could we start living? Italy? Spain?
> The world was all before us. And around us
> The gloomy memorial of a valley,
> The fallen-in grave of its history,
> A gorge of ruined mills and abandoned chapels,
> The fouled nest of the Industrial Revolution
> That had flown. The windows glittered black.   (*CPH* 1111)

Hughes then tells Plath—"pioneer | In the wrong direction"—that they might be able to buy and restore an old manor house in one of the valleys. Plath, however, is distracted by her own thoughts of home:

> You had no idea what I was talking about.
> Your eyes were elsewhere—
> The sun-shot Atlantic lift, the thunderous beaches,
> The ice-cream summits, the whisper of avalanches,
> Valleys brimming gentians . . .
> . . . Where I saw so clearly
> My vision house, you saw only blackness,
> Black nothing, the face of nothingness,
> Like that rainy window.   (*CPH* 1112)

Hughes's poem suggests that the sense of dislocation in Plath's moor poems was due as much to national as to psychic anxieties. Such national anxieties may account for why Plath's speakers experience a deep sense of alienation as they attempt to integrate themselves with the Yorkshire landscape. None succeed in proper Wordsworthian fashion, a fact that suggests Plath was starting to challenge, and set herself apart from, the British literary tradition—a feat she would eventually achieve in *Ariel*.[27]

In Plath's "Two Views of Withens" (1957), the moor is "bare," the weather "colorless," and the farmhouse is "no palace" (*CPP* 72). Her description of Wuthering Heights as "the House of Eros" is ironic, for she was fully aware that Cathy and Heathcliff's love was as destructive, even hateful, as it was passionate. The speaker's companion in "Two Views of Withens," on the other hand, seems unaware of Cathy and Heathcliff's ghostly presence, or the specter of doom that the house barely holds at bay. Instead, he sees a sky full of color where she sees white, pillars where she sees only low, crumbling lintels: "You, luckier, | Report white pillars, a blue sky, | The ghosts, kindly" (*CPP* 72). As in "The Snowman on the Moor," Plath uses the metaphor of pioneering as she presents the speaker traveling "through blurs | Of fog in that hinterland few | Hikers get to" (72). The "blurs of fog" that obscure the "colorless" landscape emphasize the speaker's feeling of both mental and physical disorientation, and suggests that the poem speaks to Plath's sense of unease as a foreigner—both woman and American—in Hughes's native territory. And perhaps the imaginary "House of Eros" she had entered upon her marriage was not living up to expectations either. Was Plath worried, as she watched Edith Hughes "pottering" around her "tiny kitchen" (*LH* 269), that she would eventually inherit this life?[28] Hughes's "Stubbing Wharfe" certainly suggests as much.

Plath revisits similar imagery in "Wuthering Heights," written in September 1961, nearly four years after "Two Views of Withens." Again, the sky is "pale," the sheep stare blankly, and the speaker feels the wind "trying | To funnel my heat away" (*CPP* 167). The imagery of lintel and stone returns here as well: the speaker feels surrounded by ruined farmhouses where "Lintel and sill have unhinged themselves," and where the air communicates only two words, "Black stone, black stone" (168). Plath continues to use the vocabulary of the alienated pioneer: the horizons "dissolve | Like a series of promises, as I step forward," "It is like being mailed into space, | A thin, silly message" (167). The "hollow doorsteps" also suggest "reverse pioneering"—she discovers not virgin land but evidence of death, decay, and abandonment: "Of people the air only | Remembers a few odd syllables" (168). The final image of house lights gleaming

---

[27] Indeed, the pressure for Plath to shed her American identity may account for what Alicia Ostriker calls the "derivative...saving, self-protective primness" of the poems in *The Colossus* (1989: 100; 102), which give a nod to British decorum. For Ostriker, it is only after Plath sheds this academic style for one which is "distinctly American...brusque, businesslike, and bitchy" (1989: 99; 103) that she begins to write good poetry.

[28] Earlier in the visit, Plath had written to her mother (with more than a touch of condescension) that Hughes's parents were "dear, simple Yorkshire folk." She described Edith Hughes's "tiny kitchen," where the Yorkshirewoman spent her time "pottering about, making us starchy little pottages and meat pies," and then added, "(I'll be so happy to have an American kitchen...with orange juice and egg beater and all my lovely supplies for light cookies and cakes!)" (*LH* 269). While Plath never explicitly criticizes the Hugheses, her feeling of American superiority is implicit. (Mrs. Hughes may have felt Plath's snub, for she did not attend her funeral at Heptonstall in 1963.)

"like small change" in the "valleys narrow | And black as purses" (168) suggests that Plath's speaker takes more comfort from the human landscape, with all its material comforts, than the natural one.

While Joyce Carol Oates understands Plath's dilemma as a refusal to integrate her self with different types of consciousness, human or natural—that is, to always stand apart and in trepidation of anything "other"—it may be that the speakers of "Wuthering Heights" and "Two Views of Withens" resist integrating with the landscape for more specific reasons.[29] The landscape in which Plath's speaker feels so alien is that of both Hughes and Brontë—one a husband and literary "father," the other a literary "mother." While both were sources of inspiration, they also fed Plath's colonial insecurity; "the weight | Of stones and hills" (*CPP* 63) may have symbolized the weight of a British literary tradition pressing down on Plath through the eyes of the living (Hughes) and the dead (Brontë). Indeed, the beginning of Hughes's own "Wuthering Heights" boasts a family connection to the Brontës and tells how his uncle's relative "Inherited some Brontë soup dishes" (*CPH* 1080). While this boast may have been ironic, to Plath it would have reaffirmed her husband's connection to Heathcliff, Brontë, and the moors.

While Plath's other moor poems do not engage in an explicit dialogue with *Wuthering Heights*, they still present the speaker as alienated. In "The Snowman on the Moor" (1957), Plath takes on the role of both female victim and colonial subject. As in her other moor poems, she presents a disoriented speaker in a lunar, otherworldly landscape that, according to Tim Kendall, "threatens to extinguish the perceiver's being altogether" (2001: 27). The speaker of "The Snowman on the Moor" recounts a quarrel with her lover, after which she storms out of the house "in fury" (*CPP* 58), taunting him to follow. Although Plath wrote that the poem was about "the vast impersonal white world of Nature against a small violent spark of will" (*J* 583), the content also suggests a quarrel with Hughes; Plath hinted as much when she wrote to her mother that the poem was "about a man & woman fighting in the winter & she running out onto the moors & having a vision."[30] In the poem, the man refuses to follow the speaker out into "a landscape | Of stark wind-harrowed hills and weltering mist" (*CPP* 58), "the world's white edge" (59). Ironically, Plath uses an image frequently associated with Columbus's discovery of America; her speaker, now, makes the reverse journey into an equally perilous and unknown land. Yet leaving the house does the speaker no good—the British landscape belongs to her lover, and she is all but lost in the hostile, shape-shifting country. Plath calls up the imagery of oppositional nationalism in the first line when she writes, "Stalemated their armies stood, with tottering banners" (*CPP* 58). That Plath uses the metaphor of

[29] See Joyce Carol Oates, "The Death Throes of Romanticism: The Poetry of Sylvia Plath," *Southern Review* 9.3 (1973): 501–22.
[30] Sylvia Plath to Aurelia Plath, April 1, 1957, Lilly.

two nations squaring off to describe a lovers' quarrel suggests the poem speaks to national disorientation and anxiety.

Once the speaker is out on the moor, the landscape turns surreal (indeed, the terza rima form recalls Dante's *Inferno*). Soon after she begins her furious night-walk, she meets a giant snowman wearing a belt of "Ladies' sheaved skulls" (reminiscent of Hughes's giant king who "loomed up with your shrunken head" in "The Decay of Vanity" [*CPH* 31]). These are the remains of women who dared to outwit their male superiors, whose "wit made fools | Of kings, unmanned kings' sons." The gruesome ladies warn the speaker, " 'For that brag, we barnacle these iron thighs.' " Although the speaker escapes the snowman's axe, her harrowing experience causes her to return home "humbled," "crying," "brimful of gentle talk | And mild obeying" (59). Presumably the snowman has pursued her for the same reasons he pursued the ladies whose skulls now hang from his belt: she has, like them, tried to outwit a man. Ultimately, the speaker's fiery spark is extinguished.

Hughes's short essay "The Rock," first published in *The Listener* in 1963, suggests that Scout Rock may have been a model for Plath's snowman:

The most impressive early companion of my childhood was a dark cliff, to the South, a wall of rock and steep woods half-way up the sky, just cleared by the winter sun. This was the *memento mundi* over my birth: my spiritual midwife at the time and my godfather ever since. . . . From my first day, it watched. If it couldn't see me direct, a towering gloom over my pram, it watched me through a species of periscope: that is, by infiltrating the very light of my room with its particular shadow. (86)

Hughes's description of Scout Rock brings to mind Plath's snowman, the "Austere, corpse-white || Giant heaved into the distance, stone-hatcheted, | Sky-high" (*CPP* 59). Perhaps her snowman was a surreal manifestation of Scout Rock, a being that embodied Hughes's mental and physical power, or his ability to shadow Plath. In the face of such force, Plath's speaker is daunted into submission. Anxieties of gender and nation merge in the poem, where kings and princes are responsible for the death of their witty female subjects whose "masteries | Amused court halls" (59). The speaker is silenced for her colonial and feminine rebelliousness as she tries to make her way through a landscape haunted by Lear, Heathcliff, and Hughes himself.

After "The Snowman on the Moor" Plath wrote "Mayflower," a patriotic Petrarchan sonnet about the pilgrims' journey to America in 1620. It may be that Plath was pointing out a connection between the pilgrims' brave "forfeiture | Of the homeland hearth to plough their pilgrim way | Across Atlantic furrows, dark, unsure" (*CPP* 60) and her own reverse pioneering. Very soon after "Mayflower" came "Hardcastle Crags." The poem explores the same themes as the other moor poems—it tells the story of a young woman who ventures out alone on the moors, only to be repelled by the violent landscape. This landscape is still identifiably masculine and English: references to granite, black stone, iron, quartz, and grit again bring to mind Hughes's invocation of Scout Rock, while the speaker's comparison of the landscape to "the antique world" suggests colonial anxiety. Here, the cottages are "dark, dwarfed" as in a sinister fairy tale; the "long wind" pares "her person down | To a pinch of flame" (63). The speaker feels she has been cheated by the landscape:

> All the night gave her, in return
> For the paltry gift of her bulk and the beat
> Of her heart, was the humped indifferent iron
> Of its hills . . .

These "antique" elements are "Enough to snuff the quick | Of her small heat out." It comes as little surprise, then, that

> . . . before the weight
> Of stones and hills of stones could break
> Her down to mere quartz grit in that stony light
> She turned back.   (*CPP* 63)

"Hardcastle Crags" might point to the speaker's refusal, or inability, to integrate with a specifically British landscape, which, in Plath's moor poems, is usually hostile and threatening. The fact that this landscape is Hughes's domain undermines self-contained, psychoanalytical readings of poems like "Hardcastle Crags" and "Wuthering Heights," in which these poems are merely reflections of Plath's depressed state of mind. Again, as in "The Snowman on the Moor" and "Two Views of Withens," Plath gives voice to anxieties about her inability to integrate not just with the natural landscape, but, more specifically, with a British husband and a British literary tradition that may have seemed reflections of each other.

A short story version of "Hardcastle Crags" emphasizes the poem's autobiographical nature. Plath's notes for a story titled "Afternoon in Hardcastle Crags" suggest that the characters in the story—and presumably in the poem—were based upon herself and Hughes:

Cold, she resolved, I shall go cold as he. She lay in the grass, not daring to get up for fear Gerald would spot her and spoil her perfect fury of self-pity. Daylong he sat tousled in his mother's parlor in his old RAF sweater, writing poems about water drops and martyred bishops and playing his battered, cracked Beethoven records over and over. Beethoven's deathmask hung waxen and eerie in their bedroom. She had married a genius.

Olwyn saw him famous and suave in a tuxedo, roaring sestinas in a royal godly voice over the BBC, in a dither of actresses, ballet dancers and Italian countesses with a literary flair, while she skulked about choking on cheese rinds like a tear-blind mouse.

Oh, she would make him sorry this last time. She heard the police demanding sternly: "Gerald, what have you done with your wife?" "Why," Gerald said, gnawing absent-minded on a slice of buttered malt bread, "she lost herself on the moor one day about a week ago. Careless girl." Perhaps, Olwyn thought, she would only stay out overnight. She tried to remember the direction back to Gerald's mother's house.

In her mind's eye she turned detective, Sherlock Holmesing a path back up the gravel road.[31]

These notes were typed on the back of a page of Hughes's "The Calm," the same play that appears on the back of the "Daddy" manuscripts. It is not clear whether Plath was using Hughes's manuscript as spare paper, or vice versa. What is clear is that Gerald is a thinly veiled version of Hughes, and the setting is the Beacon ("Gerald's mother's house"). Also, Plath chooses to name her two characters after Hughes's brother and sister. In "Afternoon in Hardcastle Crags," Gerald's writing and burgeoning literary fame, rather than another woman, are the objects of Olwyn's jealousy. While Plath frequently bragged to others about Hughes's "genius," here it is a source of irony.

When Plath attempts to write a "moor poem" about an American landscape, her response to nature is more positive. In "Above the Oxbow," set in western Massachusetts and composed in 1958, Plath extols the orderliness of the landscape, its color, and its connection to human endeavor: "We have not mountains, but mounts," she writes. The land is not pale but "Green, wholly green" (Plath in fact uses the word "green" five times in the poem). On the moors, she finds no trace of human habitation, yet above the Oxbow she gazes down upon "cars," "people," a "Hundred-year-old hotel," and a "state view- | Keeper" who "collects half-dollars for the slopes | Of state scenery, sells soda, shows off viewpoints" (*CPP* 88). Plath's phrases are not ironic; rather she describes a valley abuzz with bourgeois commerce of a distinctly, and unapologetically, American kind. Whereas Hughes frequently uses the image of the horizon in his moor poems to invoke a sense of primeval timelessness—in "The Horses" "the horizons endure" (*CPH* 23) and in "Wind" "the stones cry out under the horizons" (*CPH* 37)—Plath's British horizons offer no real perspective or boundaries; they are "unstable," they "evaporate" and "dissolve" (*CPP* 167). Yet in "Above the Oxbow," Plath celebrates the American horizon:

> ... it's the last cliff
> Ledge will dislodge our cramped concept of space, unwall
> Horizons beyond vision, spill vision
> After the horizons, stretching the narrowed eye
> To full capacity. We climb in hopes
> Of such seeing up the leaf-shuttered escarpments,
> Blindered by green, under a green-grained sky
> Into the blue.   (*CPP* 88)

Plath's "narrowed eye" stretched to "full capacity" brings to mind Emerson's "All-seeing Eye," and suggests she is "rewriting" one of Hughes's moor poems in a distinctly American vein, pitting Emerson against Shelley. "Above the Oxbow" speaks of a transcendental vision that does not overwhelm and frighten. Plath

---

[31] Sylvia Plath, "Afternoon in Hardcastle Crags," Box 139, MSS 644, Emory.

notes from her vantage point that "people stroll | Straightforwardly across the springing green" below, where "All's peace and discipline" (89). While this image brings to mind the sense of security surrounding the houses that "gleam like small change" in "Wuthering Heights," the speaker of "Above the Oxbow" does not feel as if she has been severed from such security. Instead, she is completely integrated into the landscape.

Why was Plath able to write such a poem about the New England hills, but not (with the exception of "The Great Carbuncle") the Yorkshire moors? It is likely Plath's moor poems are concerned with cultural, as well as psychic, alienation. Ultimately, Plath's moor poems may be ironic re-enactments of the pilgrim fathers' journey, which Plath praised in "Mayflower": instead of exploring the new world, she has returned to the old, a "pioneer in the wrong direction." By venturing back to the colonizer's landscape (and by marrying the colonizer) she forfeits some small part of her postcolonial independence. Plath's fantasies of thwarted exploration in the moor poems—of leaving both husband and hearth behind—speak not only to her failed assimilation with the landscape, but with England itself.

5

The Early Dialogue, 1956–1962

During the years of their marriage, Plath's and Hughes's poetic dialogue was both competitive *and* collaborative. At times they strove to show how much their aesthetic styles and thematic concerns differed, as if they feared being "remade" by the other. At other times, in Middlebrook's words, "they were playing an obsessive game of tag with each other's images" (2003: 172). Indeed, the style and themes of some poems from the late fifties and early sixties seem so similar that one is hard pressed to tell whether Plath or Hughes is the author. This is because writing "against" the other was a limiting strategy. Despite their need to keep their aesthetic distance from one another, Plath and Hughes ultimately could not help borrowing images, cadences, and even words. Sometimes they did so to make a point about their differences; at other times, they seemed content to announce their similarities. Their desire to both collaborate and compete helps to explain why the poets seem, paradoxically, so at odds and yet so in tune with each other as they enacted the dynamic Harold Bloom described as "Be me but not me."

AGAINST REMAKING

Although several Plath and Hughes critics have cited examples of mutual "back-talk" in the poets' later work, the poetic dialogue in their earlier poems has received less attention.[1] Hughes himself downplayed the extent of mutual influence during this time, telling Drue Heinz, "I don't know whether our verse exchanged much... not in the early days" (77). Yet careful examination of several early poems, as well as the poets' early correspondence and prose, reveals the extent to which the two poets were engaged, well before *Ariel* or *Birthday Letters*, in a struggle to remain true to a self that was in danger of effacing itself before the other. As we have seen, each felt threatened by the other's attempts at remaking: just as Hughes feared Plath's emasculating influence, Plath felt that Hughes sought to neutralize (and perhaps Anglicize) her

---

[1] Lynda Bundtzen, Susan Van Dyne, Jacqueline Rose, and Diane Middlebrook have emphasized Plath's propensity to "talk back" to Hughes in her *Ariel* poems, while Ekbert Faas, Terry Gifford, Neil Roberts, and Paul Bentley have mainly examined Plath's influence on Hughes since *Lupercal.*

female poetic voice. Rather than defying the other's intentions in person, they defied them in poems that seem to offer up clichés of masculinity and femininity: where Plath puts forth an optimistic, Emersonian view of the natural world, Hughes counters with a colder, more violent aesthetic. Early on, Plath seems to have self-consciously resisted a violent voice in order not to appear to mimic Hughes. Hughes, on the other hand, was determined to counter and even mock Plath's verse when it appeared too neat, too optimistic, and too evocative of Movement decorousness. As he wrote to Olwyn in September 1957, "She doesn't write hard enough, I think."[2] (Since Hughes had earlier boasted to Olwyn that Plath "works herself till she drops," his use of the word "hard" in this instance implies an aesthetic judgment rather than a comment on Plath's work ethic.[3])

Some of Plath's and Hughes's strongest early poems—"The Hawk in the Rain," "Black Rook in Rainy Weather," "Mussel Hunter at Rock Harbor," "Relic," "Wind," "The Great Carbuncle," "View of a Pig"—reveal that the " 'Bluebeard' meets 'abjection' " (128) phenomenon that Jacqueline Rose has observed in their later work began long before *Ariel* or *Crow*. Margaret Uroff was the first to note that Plath's "Black Rook in Rainy Weather," for example, was a response to Hughes's "The Hawk in the Rain."[4] She reads Hughes's poem as a "battle of human endurance against the murderous force of the elements" (77) in which the hawk mocks the speaker's will to live; Plath's rook, on the other hand, represents "poetic vision," not unlike Hughes's thought-fox (78). This reading accords with Uroff's general thesis that in their poetry, Plath and Hughes wage "a continuing debate about the nature of the universe, in which Plath's reservations and Hughes's assertions play against each other" (12). However, a reading informed by ideas of rivalry and remaking offers a different understanding of the Plath–Hughes conversation.

In "The Hawk in the Rain," which was likely influenced by Robert Graves's "Rocky Acres," Hughes's speaker regards the hawk as the still point in an otherwise violent world:[5]

[2] Ted Hughes to Olwyn Hughes, September 12, 1957, MSS 980, Emory.

[3] Ted Hughes to Olwyn Hughes, May 1956, MSS 980, Emory.

[4] "The Hawk in the Storm" (later retitled "The Hawk in the Rain") was published in the *Atlantic* in February 1957, while "Black Rook in Rainy Weather" was published four months later in the *London Magazine* in June 1957. "Black Rook in Rainy Weather" was written after "Ode for Ted," which, according to Neil Roberts, was written two months after "The Hawk in the Rain" (2003: 161).

[5] The second stanza of "Rocky Acres" reads:

> He soars and he hovers, rocking on his wings,
> He scans his wide parish with a sharp eye,
> He catches the trembling of small hidden things,
> He tears them in pieces, dropping them from the sky;
> Tenderness and pity the heart will deny,
> Where life is but nourished by water and rock—
> A hardy adventure, full of fear and shock. (1961: 28)

> I drown in the drumming ploughland, I drag up
> Heel after heel from the swallowing of the earth's mouth,
> From clay that clutches my each step to the ankle
> With the habit of the dogged grave, but the hawk
>
> Effortlessly at height hangs his still eye.
> His wings hold all creation in a weightless quiet,
> Steady as a hallucination in the streaming air.   (*CPH* 19)

The hawk becomes an emblem of humanity in its futile attempt to master the elements, while nature is a malevolent force bent on extinguishing life. Escape is impossible; the hawk, like the speaker, will eventually "mix his heart's blood with the mire of the land" (19). The hawk's mastery of the elements is illusory, as Hughes hints when he calls it "a hallucination in the streaming air" (19). It may seem godlike with its "angelic eye" and "wings that hold all creation," but it controls nothing; its calm repose in the face of the brutal elements is due as much to luck, to catching the weather the "right way," as it is to boldness or skill (19). Admiration for the hawk's will, its strength and repose in the face of violence, ultimately gives way to a terrible realization of mortality.

Although both the storm and the hawk are manifestations of Edmund Burke's "masculine" sublime—or, as Nick Bishop puts it, an " 'outright-masculine' impulse to assert a kind of authority through the strenuous use of language" (1)—the poem's message has more to do with transience and frailty than with power or strength. Hughes's vision in "The Hawk in the Rain" is tragic rather than celebratory; the hawk "suffers" the air, and man barely outruns "the dogged grave." The hawk is less "an ideal to strive for" (Scigaj 28) than a reminder of nature's indifference to ideals; as Paul Bentley writes, "the imagination in Hughes is up against something that resists, limits, oppresses and finally out-flanks its power" (32). Although Keith Sagar claims that in the poem "Art is bringing resolution to what without it would remain uproar" (1992: 99), the hawk's impending fate suggests that nature resists resolution, that "uproar" will always trump artifice.

Plath's "Black Rook in Rainy Weather" must have been inspired by Hughes's poem—the similarities are too striking to ignore. Plath's speaker, walking alone in bad weather, also encounters a bird looming above. Plath makes the bird the centerpiece of a poem that explores, as Hughes's does, the self's place in nature: [6]

> On the stiff twig up there
> Hunches a wet black rook
> Arranging and rearranging its feathers in the rain.
> I do not expect a miracle
> Or an accident

---

[6] Gary Lane notes that the poem was also influenced by Wallace Stevens's "The Man Whose Pharynx Was Bad" (125).

> To set the sight on fire
> In my eye, nor seek
> Any more in the desultory weather some design,
> But let spotted leaves fall as they fall,
> Without ceremony, or portent. (*CPP* 56–7)

While Plath's poem was clearly a response to Hughes's, the differences between the two poems are more interesting than the similarities. Although Uroff says Plath's rook "seems like the fastidious spinster in comparison with Hughes's hawk" (78), Plath's response to "The Hawk in the Rain" does not necessarily qualify as "reservation meets assertion." Plath is playing with the idea of the double, self-consciously inverting Hughes's poem so that her own becomes a kind of distorted mirror-image: where he uses masculine imagery to question man's mastery over nature, Plath uses feminine imagery to assert an essential harmony between humankind and nature. Steven Axelrod has suggested that Plath's use of doubles was a way of subduing her rivalry with Hughes:

As her double, he needed neither to subjugate nor to inspire her. The idea of doubling could eliminate the rivalry between them, just as it lessened the need for intimacy in their marriage. As doubles, they felt no threat to their selfhood, for they were not confronted with an alien presence.... If he was an emanation of her, his accomplishment would count as hers. (194–5)

Yet Plath's use of doubles was also subversive. By "doubling" Hughes's poem with her own, she outwardly paid homage to Hughes; by undermining his poem's premise, she mocked the idea that he was a poetic father-figure. It is as if Plath, in the act of writing (or rewriting), is defining herself both through and against Hughes, borrowing elements of his poem in order to stake a different kind of claim, one that affirms an (American) Emersonian, transcendental vision and subverts Hughes's (British) Burkean sublime; whereas Hughes's understanding of nature resembles that of Shelley's "Mont Blanc," Plath's here is closer to Thoreau's *Walden*. Plath quietly dismantles Hughes's vision, replacing it with her own as she constructs a literary bulwark against what she may have perceived as Hughes's attempts at remaking.

Jacqueline Rose has argued that Plath's desire to enter the domain of the male literary tradition caused her to "[discover] in herself a 'part man'" (117). While we ought not to take this idea literally, we have already seen that Plath was jealous of men's freedom.[7] As several critics have pointed out, Plath underlined a

---

[7] Citing numerous passages from Plath's journals in which she writes enviously of men's autonomy ("my consuming desire to mingle with road crews, sailors and soldiers, barroom regulars...all is spoiled by the fact I am a girl"), Rose writes, "she recognises in herself, not just the desire for man's freedom...but an involuntary slippage, an identification with his sexual pleasure or fantasy, which makes of the woman the surveyed and calculated object of her own desire" (117). Gilbert and Gubar echo Rose when they read Plath's obsessive baby imagery not necessarily as rebirth, but as "escapes from sexual difference" (1994: 3.298).

revealing sentence of John Langdon-Davies's *Short History of Women* when she was a teenager: "Men and women are purely relative terms, and long before the tendencies of our times work to their logical conclusions, men and women, as we know them, will have ceased to exist; and human nature will have forgotten the 'he' and 'she'" (qtd. in Gilbert and Gubar, 1994: 3.275). As we saw in Chapter 1, Plath's journals reveal that such a conclusion appealed to her.

To a certain extent, Hughes encouraged Plath's unconscious identification with the masculine, though he may not have been aware he did so. For example, when he critiqued her poems, he typically celebrated those moments where she exhibited the kind of "hard" imagery Ezra Pound encouraged in his seminal essay "A Retrospect," and criticized the moments that "go soft." Commenting on her poem "Evergreens" in October 1956, he wrote, "It is best where it is hardest," and, in true Poundian fashion, called her phrase "watery radiance" "vague."[8] Hughes's question for Plath, "Do you mean the reflection, or light within water...?" echoes Pound's exacting critical voice.[9] Referring to another unnamed poem in a letter from the same period, he tells Plath, "Everything goes perfectly here until 'Pierced side.' You have been given to think of a side gaping and mangled and bloody, but 'Pierced'—in the context of literal and violent detail, means merely stabbed, with a blade leaving a thin slash, or cut, or small hole. Something like 'Open' would give a much rawer more vulnerable terrible sense."[10] Hughes suggests that Plath's adjective is too cautious, too feminine, that she is afraid to confront her poem's real "rawness." This was the type of aesthetic advice he would dispense throughout the marriage, for he felt (correctly, as it turned out) that Plath had an untapped source of violent energy smoldering under the placid facade, and that she ought to release that violence in her poems. When he wrote to her in October 1956, "Your verse never goes 'soft' like other women's" (*L* 82), she relayed the praise back to her mother, writing "Ted says he never read poems by a woman like mine; they are strong and full and rich ... they are working, sweating, heaving poems" (*LH* 244). Plath was caught in a double-bind: on the one hand she sought to cultivate a masculine "hardness" in her own writing in order to win Hughes's approval, and that of literati still under the spell of Pound and Eliot (note her use of masculine adjectives—"working, sweating, heaving"—in the above letter). On the other hand, she needed to remain sufficiently feminine so that she would not have to compete with Hughes.

In order not to appear as Hughes's rival, Plath may have been hiding her own "wish for masculinity" (Britzolakis 126) by writing poems that seem to feminize Hughes's themes. Paul Giles, speaking of Plath's poetry as a whole, has remarked that she evokes "the lineaments of patriarchal identity only in order to reflect and

---

[8] The phrase brings to mind Pound's contempt, in "A Retrospect," for "dim lands of peace," which represented everything that was wrong with "feminine" Victorian diction.

[9] Ted Hughes to Sylvia Plath, October 23, 1956, Lilly.

[10] Ted Hughes to Sylvia Plath, October 8, 1956, Lilly.

reverse them into virtual figures, ghostly specters, perceived as through a glass darkly" (118). Axelrod too has noted Plath's habit of "*feminization*: a turning of male texts against themselves, an abduction of their language for the antithetical purpose of female inscription" (71). Such a strategy is common among women intellectuals: as Joan Riviere has observed in "Womanliness as Masquerade," "women who wish for masculinity may put on a mask of womanliness to avert anxiety and the retribution feared from men" (35).[11] This idea helps to explain why Plath seems to use feminine imagery in "Black Rook in Rainy Weather" in precise opposition to moments of masculine intensity in Hughes's poem. "Black Rook" is patient where Hughes's poem is urgent; Plath invokes a content, stationary rook rather than a flying, predatory hawk; her language is hesitant and chatty where Hughes's is stylized and bold; her weather is "desultory," the landscape "dull" (*CPP* 57); her light is "minor," her sky "mute" (57); she intersperses her thoughts with domestic images of kitchen chairs and tables; and finally, her natural world is a benevolent conduit to her interior world, whereas nature in Hughes's poem is malevolent and predatory.

Plath also counters Hughes's poem with an American, Emersonian viewpoint. Tim Kendall has discussed Emerson's influence on "Black Rook in Rainy Weather," calling it "a Transcendentalist manifesto" in which the "natural world embodies spiritual truth" (2001: 26). After weighing carefully nature's restorative powers against her own "skeptical" attitude, Plath hesitantly asserts that even nature's "minor light" has the ability to confer "largesse, honor, | One might say love" on the speaker (*CPP* 57). Plath further aligns herself with Emersonian optimism when she declares, "it could happen | Even in this dull, ruinous landscape" (57). The "it" refers to a kind of secular grace that will fortify the speaker against her own self-doubt. Taking her cue from Emerson, Plath allows her speaker to move from a position of self-doubt to fragile self-reliance: by the poem's end, the rook no longer mirrors the speaker's dejected self but has become a manifestation of the self in control. While at the beginning of the poem the speaker utters, "I do not expect a miracle" (56), by the poem's end she declares, "Miracles occur" (57), and decides herself worthy of nature's benediction. Thus the poem moves in the opposite direction of "The Hawk in the Rain"—from self-doubt to self-confidence. Whereas Hughes's speaker is bound to the earth, to the "glutinous physicality of the mud" (Smith 72), Plath's speaker aligns herself with the air. Plath uses an ordered, formal rhyme scheme (ABCDE), in implicit contrast to Hughes, whose natural universe is too brutal for harmony. Hughes's strong, alliterative stresses, as many critics have noted, echo Anglo-Saxon verse; the poem has an almost primitive sensibility. Plath's subtle rhymes, on the other hand, imply that there is a hidden but serendipitous

[11] Britzolakis has likewise commented that "Women with intellectual or professional ambitions, who participate in public discourse, may have a wish for masculinity which they dissimulate in order to avert punishment from their masculine rivals" (126).

order in nature; the poem itself may be the "miracle" for which the poet has waited. Indeed, Plath admired this poem, writing in her journal that it was "Inspiration & Vision expressed through Matter" (350).

Plath's "The Great Carbuncle" engages in a similar type of dialogue with Hughes's "Wind." One of Hughes's strongest poems, "Wind" records a family's awe and terror as they ride out a "stampeding" storm upon the moors inside their home, watching the "Blade-light" of the wind as it cuts through the landscape (*CPH* 36). Here, as in "The Hawk in the Rain," nature is a cold, powerful, amoral force:

> ... The house
> Rang like some fine green goblet in the note
> That any second would shatter it. Now deep
> In chairs, in front of the great fire, we grip
> Our hearts and cannot entertain book, thought,
> Or each other.   (36)

Hughes compares the stormy moors to a treacherous undersea world through which the house perilously drifts. As in "The Hawk in the Rain," the speaker's landscape turns on him with a primeval energy that mocks his faith in shelter and his fragile sense of being. He sees "woods crashing through darkness, the booming hills, | Winds stampeding the fields under the window," yet still ventures out of the house—a transgressive folly for which he is punished by "the brunt wind that dented the balls of my eyes" (36). Again, man is physically punished by nature for daring to strain against it. Hughes offers no Emersonian optimism about the wind's purpose; it does not compel the onlooker to self-awareness or exhilaration, but rather thwarts any human attempt to "experience" its awesome force. If the wind could be said to symbolize anything, it would be negation, annihilation; even "the stones cry out under the horizons" (37). To reinforce this point, Hughes juxtaposes the language of terror and beauty throughout the poem: although the wind is both "luminous and emerald," it nevertheless flexes "like the lens of a mad eye" (36). The house, too, is described as a "fine green goblet," but one which is in danger of shattering. We are far from Wordsworth's bucolic, restorative Lake Country where man and nature achieve mutual harmony.

Plath answers back to "Wind" in "The Great Carbuncle" (1957), again challenging Hughes's dark view of nature with an optimistic, Emersonian vision that stresses nature's benign and restorative effects. Hughes tells us in his notes to Plath's *Collected Poems* that the Great Carbuncle is "an odd phenomenon sometimes observed on high moorland for half an hour or so at evening, when the hands and faces of people seem to become luminous" (*CPP* 276). Such a phenomenon would have offered Plath the perfect opportunity to assert an opposing transcendental view of nature. Her first two lines—"We came over the moor-top | Through air streaming and green-lit, | Stone farms foundering in it"

(*CPP* 72)—reveal that she is engaging in a dialogue with Hughes, whose wind is "luminous and emerald" (36); his house, too, is like a "fine green goblet." Plath's use of "foundering" echoes Hughes's "Winds . . . floundering," while her "streaming" and "sea-bottom" also bring Hughes's water metaphor to mind ("This house has been far out at sea all night"). But where Hughes's family fearfully huddles inside the home, apart from nature, the speaker and her companions in "The Great Carbuncle" delight in walking outside; where Hughes concentrates on the destructive force of the wind, Plath focuses instead on the unmoving, healing quality of the light; and where Hughes's wind appears almost diabolical ("flexing like the lens of a mad eye"), Plath invokes the language of transcendentalism to explain what moves her speaker:

> Some such transfiguring moved
> The eight pilgrims towards its source—
>
> Toward that great jewel: shown often,
> Never given; hidden, yet
> Simultaneously seen
> On moor-top, at sea-bottom . . .   (72)

This "great jewel" has mystical connotations. It is, Plath tells us,

> Knowable only by light
>
> Other than noon, than moon, stars—
> The once known way becoming
> Wholly other, and ourselves
> Estranged, changed, suspended where
> Angels are rumored, clearly
>
> Floating, among the floating
> Tables and chairs. Gravity's
> Lost in the lift and drift of
> An easier element
> Than earth, and there is nothing
>
> So fine we cannot do it.   (72)

Plath again exhibits the optimism at the core of "Black Rook in Rainy Weather," here with even greater confidence in nature's regenerative capacity. She even uses religious language ("pilgrims," "angels") to describe the nature of this "trans-figuring," which invokes images of both Christian rapture and Eastern meditative transcendence (indeed, "The once-known way becoming | Wholly other" echoes lines from Eliot's *Four Quartets*). Plath revels in this liminal state, that place "In a light neither of dawn || Nor nightfall" where the speaker might cross a boundary from one world to another, where "the earth's | Claim and weight" has no hold. Thus Britzolakis's sense that Plath views "the natural object as a recalcitrant and irrecoverable otherness" (85) is undermined here, as is Joyce Carol Oates's famous claim that in Plath's poetry, "There is never any integrating of the self and its experience, the self and its field of perception" (qtd. in Uroff 6). In this poem, the life-affirming gifts of nature *are* recoverable. Plath's seven-syllable lines, which suggest luck, hint at a profound connection between the "uplifting" experience on the moor and the creation of the poem itself.

As in Hughes's poem, Plath's final stanza depicts a domestic interior; yet whereas in "Wind" this interior is protective, in "The Great Carbuncle" contact with the material world destroys the speaker's feelings of transcendence. No longer "floating," the speaker finds, in the house, that "Chairs, tables drop | Down: the body weighs like stone" (73). This line echoes the last line of "Wind," in which "the stones cry out under the horizons." Where Hughes uses the image of stone to emphasize the wind's ferocity and its hostility to man, Plath uses the image to emphasize that the human world is the more hostile environment.[12]

The early poetic dialogue was not one-sided. For example, Hughes's "Relic," which appeared in *Lupercal* in 1960, reads as a response to Plath's "Mussel Hunter at Rock Harbor," probably written during the summer of 1957 while the couple was vacationing on Cape Cod (though the poem's composition history is not clear).[13] Plath's poem—her first *New Yorker* acceptance—was inspired by an early morning walk during low tide at Rock Harbor in Eastham, where she and Hughes had come to collect "Free fish-bait" together (*CPP* 95). In the poem, however, the speaker walks alone, ruminating upon ideas of alienation and vulnerability.[14] The mention of the water-colorists in the first stanza, as well as the speaker's desire to "get the | Good of the Cape light" (95), hints that the speaker herself is an artist, and that her morning walk may be a manifestation of an alienated, artistic sensibility. The fact that the speaker takes the indifferent movements of the crabs and mussels personally—"A sly world's hinges had swung | Shut against me" (95)—further suggests her sense of displacement; she soon forgets about collecting fish-bait and instead focuses on the movements of the "wary otherworld" (96) at her feet, using military imagery ("trench-dug mud," "Camouflaged in mottled mail") to emphasize the hostility she senses in the external world. Toward the end of the poem, she discovers "the husk of a fiddler-crab, | Intact, strangely strayed above || His world of mud" (97). The crab's husk is symbolic of the speaker's feeling of alienation from her environment; she feels kinship with the crab who, like her, was unwilling to take his rightful

---

[12] It would become increasingly difficult for Plath to infuse her moor poems with a sense of Emersonian transcendence, however. Most of Plath's moor poems, as we have seen, express a sense of alienation from her Yorkshire surroundings.

[13] In a journal entry dated August 21, 1957, Plath writes of an afternoon spent watching fiddler crabs; she may have begun composing the poem then. However, "Mussel Hunter at Rock Harbor" was not accepted until June 1958 and was published in *The New Yorker* on August 9, 1958. The other poem accepted by the *New Yorker*, in the same letter, was "Hardcastle Crags," which had been written in 1957. Plath included "Mussel Hunter at Rock Harbor" in a letter to Warren in early June 1958, telling him it was "about the fiddler crabs we found at Rock Harbor when we went to get mussels last summer for fish bait" (*LH* 344). "Relic" was finished by April 1958, when Hughes read it at Harvard's Lamont Poetry Room. It was later published in *Harper's* in November 1958.

[14] The poem was likely influenced by Marianne Moore's "The Fish" and Elizabeth Bishop's "The Fish."

place in the natural order. The speaker wonders if the crab "Died recluse or suicide" (97); either way, she admires the action, which resonates with her own desires, and declares "this relic saved | Face, to face the bald-faced sun" (97).

Hughes's "Relic" focuses not on artistic alienation but on predation and the natural cycle of life and death. As Uroff writes, "It is as if Hughes lifted that word, 'relic,' from Plath's poem and took it as the subject for quite different ruminations" (10). Hughes had in fact written to Olwyn in 1958 that the poems he was writing

for my second book are a little out of favour. They are hard-headed. I have tried so hard to take nothing for granted in matters of cadence & rhythm, that sentiment & warmth has seemed like a proscribed outlaw. In an effort to express myself trenchantly & controlledly, I have kept out softness. . . . I have passed through a necessary stage maybe towards making my writing my own. (*L* 122)

Similarly, in early 1959, he told her

I've a clear idea now of my next kind of poetry, which is my own and not even slightly resembling anyone else's. There is some of it in the progression of the verse in Pike beginning "The jaws hooked clamp and fangs" and it's a sort of verse into which I can put everything. The movement from line to line is irrational but each line is a bald statement. The whole effect is a complete meaning, reduced completely to my sort of music. The careful narrative and subdued development of an idea such as Elizabeth Jennings typifies . . . are as dead to me as Addison.[15]

Here Hughes makes his disdain for the Movement aesthetic quite clear. His statement that his poetry is becoming "my own and not even slightly resembling anyone else's" suggests an anxiety of influence that likely extended to Plath—especially since the two were sharing material at this time. Hughes told Olwyn in summer 1958 that Plath's "Mussel Hunter" was "a beauty . . . very direct & lucid, not so elaborate" (*L* 128). Hughes's admiration for the poem's "direct-ness" accords with his own "hard" aesthetic, but "Relic" takes this directness further. Like Plath's speaker, Hughes's also finds a "jawbone at the sea's edge" where "crabs, dogfish, broken by the breakers or tossed | . . . Continue the beginning" (*CPH* 78). Yet the rotting jawbone does not become an emblem of the alienated self, nor is it endowed with any human nobility, as is Plath's crab husk. It is simply a cog in the wheel of nature, part of an indifferent universe unconcerned with morality. Hughes's poem, like Plath's, is littered with "shells, | Vertebrae, claws, carapaces, skulls" (78), but this refuse offers up no redemptive meaning or message. Whereas Plath goes so far as to name her crab "Columbus," Hughes simply refers to the skeletal shells as "Indigestibles"—detritus that provides no nourishment or sustenance. There is no place, in "Relic," for a meditative encounter between the self and nature: "The deeps are cold: | In that

---

[15] Ted Hughes to Olwyn Hughes, early 1959, MSS 980, Emory.

darkness camaraderie does not hold: | Nothing touches but, clutching, devours" (78). Uroff understands the poem as a dismissal of Plath's "concern for her status in the universe" (10), yet I would argue it reads more like an overt challenge to Plath's attempt to ascribe moral meaning to nature. "Relic" suggests that Plath's vision is sentimental, and offers up a distinctly impersonal, "masculine" version of her experience in which there is no place for "feminine" emotion, pity, or pathos.[16] Hughes, moreover, undermines Plath's formal technique: whereas she writes in careful syllabic meter, he employs irregular rhymes that seem to mock the urge to encase nature within such precise parameters.

Hughes also answered back to Plath's "Sow" in "View of a Pig," which appeared in *Lupercal*.[17] "Sow" is a humorous portrait of a massive, "great grandam" (*CPP* 61) prize hog (who presumably belonged to a neighbor). Plath delights in describing the pig's elephantine physicality—what she calls its "vast | Brobdingnag bulk" (61). The speaker clearly admires this "vision of ancient hoghood" who "lounged belly-bedded on that black compost," refusing to relinquish her primary place in the barnyard pecking order. Plath notes that the inferior sows are surrounded "by a litter of feat-foot ninnies," whereas this sow is free from the burdens of motherhood. The poet spares no tenderness for the other sows and their piglets, who "halt for a swig at the pink teats" of the "Bloat tun of milk | On the move." It is the prize sow, in her haughty irreverence for the brood that surrounds her, who, "monument | Prodigious in gluttonies" (61), wins the speaker's respect. The form of the poem is likewise playful: written in loose terza rima, the tercets alternate syllabic patterns within long and short lines.

Hughes's "View of a Pig" leaves no doubt as to his pig's ultimate fate. Where Plath chose to ignore the threat of the butcher's block, preferring instead to focus on her sow's impressive bulk, Hughes's first line reads, "The pig lay on a barrow dead" (*CPH* 75). Like Plath's, this pig is enormous: "It weighed, they said, as much as three men." Where the intense physicality of Plath's sow impresses, Hughes's pig fascinates on account of its inert lifelessness:

> Such weight and thick pink bulk
> Set in death seemed not just dead.
> It was less than lifeless, further off.
> It was like a sack of wheat.   (*CPH* 76)

Hughes's spondaic monosyllables and unrhyming lines spare no humorous quips for his pig, and seem to remonstrate Plath for her own lighthearted depiction: "It was too dead ... | Its last dignity had entirely gone. | It was not a figure of fun." His pig does not call up human attributes or even human pity. It is "Too dead

---

[16] Nick Bishop writes that "the 'feminine' desire to expand and complete the self, subordinating language to a tool or instrument of the psychological process" exists in "only two of Hughes's first sixty or so poems" (1–2).

[17] Plath's poem was written in early 1957. Hughes included "View of a Pig" in a letter to Olwyn dated summer 1958; Plath sent this poem out to magazines in October 1958.

now to pity," "Too deadly factual." The speaker is disturbed by the sight of the dead pig, but not for the reasons we suspect Plath's speaker might be; rather, he is concerned with practicalities:

> ... Its weight
> Oppressed me—how could it be moved?
> And the trouble of cutting it up!
> The gash in its throat was shocking, but not pathetic.   (*CPH* 76)

Plath's portrait of the barnyard sow must have seemed naïve to Hughes, who understood the reality of farm life. Hughes refuses to romanticize his hog; where Plath's sow eats "seven troughed seas and every earthquaking continent" (61), he observes that a pig's "bite is worse than a horse's— | They chop a half-moon clean out. | They eat cinders, dead cats" (76). As in "Relic," Hughes again seems to chastise Plath for her "feminine" view of nature. To Hughes, Plath's ascription of human attributes and sympathy to the animal world was misguided— violence, not understanding, was at the heart of the relationship between man and nature.[18]

Hughes compared "Sow" and "View of a Pig" during the *Poets in Partnership* interview, in which he and Plath hinted at the extent to which each was writing "against" the other. Their own analysis of the poems' similarities shows how each felt a need to distinguish between their two aesthetics:

> PLATH: I'm sure that anybody comparing these two poems would see an immense difference in the handling, the attitude toward piggery that Ted has and that I have....
>
> HUGHES: Sylvia's pig is a legendary, gargantuan pig, sort of an assembly of all piggishness and excessive piggeryness.
>
> PLATH: [laughs] Oh come now!
>
> HUGHES: Whereas mine is what's left when a pig has disappeared, when, in other words, what's left of the pig when the pig is no longer a pig, when it's a dead pig. And in a way this is the complete reversal of Sylvia's theme. (Hughes and Plath: 1961)

Hughes patronizes Plath's poem: hers is light verse, while his is "dead" serious. Plath registers awareness of Hughes's slight, but all she can do is laugh and offer a meek defense, "O come now!" She must maintain the fiction (in private, but especially in public) that there is no rivalry between herself and Hughes. Yet

---

[18] J. D. McClatchy has read the two poems in similar terms; commenting upon the relationship between them, he praises Hughes's poem for the way he "urges and controls his language and the power it draws from strangeness.... Plath, on the other hand, fusses with piggy banks and parslied sucklings, a constantly shifting metric, long sentences, and a glut of adjectives" (22). McClatchy's critique employs conspicuously gendered language: Hughes, admirably restrained, "controls" and "draws power" while Plath, annoyingly chatty, "fusses" with objects associated with children and the kitchen.

Hughes's admission that his poem is "the complete reversal of Sylvia's theme" hints at his anxiety of influence.

The similarities between these pairs of early poems are too striking to ignore; it is clear that Plath and Hughes are writing back to each other, dismantling each other's versions of the natural world while asserting their own. By challenging Hughes's amoral, predatory universe with a benevolent, optimistic vision, Plath defines herself against Hughes much as she did in "Mr. and Mrs. Ted Hughes's Writing Table." Hughes, in turn, subverts Plath's notions regarding nature's moral order in both "Relic" and "View of a Pig," where there is no "camaraderie" between creatures, much less between creatures and humans. Each in effect revises the other's work in an act of poetic defiance, or what Bloom called "wilful revisionism" (1973: 30)—an effort that would become pronounced in the coming years as Plath's and Hughes's poetic dialogue became more antagonistic.

COMPETITION AND COLLABORATION

In the previous pairs of poems, we have seen that Plath and Hughes attempt to counter the other's voice and view. The couple did not always write "against" each other, however. Many early poems reveal, as Neil Roberts put it, "how difficult it is to . . . attribute particular motifs and even particular textual elements" (2003: 164) to either poet.[19] As we have seen, both shared an intense interest in violence, war, and apocalypse, and sought to strip back the layers of civilization in order to reveal the primal man or woman. Both were also drawn to themes of competition, either among animals, man, and nature, or between man and his inner self. Plath's and Hughes's themes have more in common than is normally presumed—a fact that would eventually intensify the anxiety, and the grief, of influence in their late dialogue.

Although Plath felt compelled to resist Hughes's "strong" aesthetic in much of her early work, some poems, such as "The Shrike" (1956) and "Soliloquy of the Solipsist" (1956), reveal a willingness to experiment with a more violent voice. These early poems, along with "Pursuit," suggest that she did not first learn violent modes of expression from Hughes; he may have even borrowed certain violent imagery from her. As Uroff has noted, Hughes's

---

[19] Even in the early dialogue, Hughes is clearly influenced by Plath's "Black Rook in Rainy Weather" when he writes "Pennines in April," with its final invocation of the Yorkshire landscape "hauling the imagination, | Carrying the larks upward" (*CPH* 68). He may also have been inspired by Plath's Emersonian vision in his "Warm Moors," "Gulls Aloft," and "Snails," poems which put forth an optimistic, non-competitive view of nature: the gulls "Repeat their graces" "in the wind's landward rush" (*CPH* 55) while the "Snails | Climb | The roses" (*CPH* 56). And, as many critics have noted, Plath seems to take on Hughes's doubt in nature's restorative qualities in poems such as "Hardcastle Crags" and "Two Views of Withens."

treatment of man's relationship to the deadly world represented by the animals has changed from the poems in *The Hawk in the Rain*, moving closer to Plath's. In his earlier poems his animals are typically caged, and civilized man appears safe from their fury.... As he later turns to confront this force, he examines more fully its dangerous implications for mankind, and, in so doing, he repeats the view Plath expressed in "Pursuit": violence may thrill, but it also terrifies.   (102)

Uroff has suggested that Hughes's animal poems, and in particular "Hawk Roosting," are "the literary source" of "Daddy," claiming, "The incantatory rhythm, the insistent rhyme schemes, and ritualized figure of the woman speaking [in 'Daddy'] . . . suggest a mind as rigid as the hawk's. Plath's poem shows the limitations of the mind that operates only to rehearse the perfect kill" (159). Yet one of Plath's own poems may be "the literary source" of "Hawk Roosting" (1959). While it is likely that the suggestion of fascism in "Hawk Roosting" did influence "Daddy," it is important to remember that Plath had already laid the groundwork for "Hawk Roosting" in "Soliloquy for the Solipsist," and that Hughes borrowed imagery from Plath.

While Tim Kendall has argued that Keith Douglas's "How to Kill" inspired "Hawk Roosting" (2005: 94), connections between "Soliloquy of the Solipsist" and "Hawk Roosting" suggest that Hughes's defiant, arrogant hawk also owes something to Plath's omnipotent solipsist. Plath wrote "Soliloquy of the Solipsist" in 1956, not long after she met Hughes. The poem, while weaker than her later work, marks a departure from the rigid, stylized verse she had been writing up to this time. In "Soliloquy," Plath lets the speaker's voice guide the poem's form rather than the other way around. And although the poem bears heavy traces of her trademark formalism (four nine-line stanzas with a regular, intricate rhyme scheme throughout), it bears no mark of a thesaurus vocabulary.

The poem begins with a single word in a single line: "I?" From the start, the focus is completely on the self; yet what appears to begin as an exercise in existential pondering soon becomes an assertion of an extreme, Nietzschean romanticism, in which the striving self becomes omnipotent, even Satanic, as it surveys the landscape. The speaker boasts of her power to "Make houses shrink | And trees diminish" as she mocks the mere mortals who cannot guess "that if I choose to blink | They die." She later declares that when she is "in good humor" she colors the landscape in pleasing hues, though in her "wintriest moods, I hold | Absolute power" and "forbid any flower | To be" (*CPP* 37–8). The solipsist's power is never condemned; nor does the poet hint, through irony, that the reader ought to reject the solipsist's outlook as morally problematic. Instead, the speaker's bravado and defiance look forward to the taunting voice of "Daddy" and "Lady Lazarus." The "I" here is all powerful, but also operates alone; it is a perversion of Emerson's all-seeing eye in which the self-glorification of Romanticism disintegrates into the self-obsession of fascism. Here Plath takes on the voice of the predator she had already created in "Pursuit," in which the aggressor's power is both awesome and terrible. In so doing, she anticipates her later poems of female violence, as well as Hughes's

"Hawk Roosting." The poem is a fantasy of power written at a time when Plath and Hughes were at one of the most intense stages of their romantic and literary courtship, spending hours each day writing in close proximity and commenting upon each other's work. Although Hughes says he found the first hints of Plath's Ariel voice in "The Stones," one detects it here as Plath experiments with the dramatic monologue and its liberating aesthetic possibilities.

Jacqueline Rose has rejected Hughes's statement that "Hawk Roosting" is one of "Nature thinking," and insists it is better read as "an emblem of pure identity in its fascist mode" (156). As we have seen, Hughes spoke of the poem in similar terms, telling Ekbert Faas in 1970 that the hawk was like "a fascist" or "some horrible totalitarian genocidal dictator," "Hitler's familiar spirit" (1980: 199). As if corroborating Hughes, Faas notes that there are over twenty personal pronouns in the verse, and writes that the poem "seems to pronounce its deadly verdict like an oracle of destruction" (1980: 67). Yet Hughes denied the suggestion that the poem glorified violence, and justified his characterization by explaining that "what I had in mind was that in this hawk Nature is thinking. . . . When Christianity kicked the devil out of Job what they actually kicked out was nature . . . and Nature became the devil" (1980: 199).

Plath's solipsist provided Hughes with a prototype of ruthless, omnipotent Nature. While Plath's speaker is identifiably human, her power is superhuman. Both poets' speakers are Nietzschean supermen, asserting their will at all costs. It is important to note that Plath had already rehearsed this voice by the time Hughes wrote "Hawk Roosting," and that he incorporated both the sentiment and the language of her poem into his own. Indeed, his first line—"I sit in the top of the wood, my eyes closed"—brings to mind the sense of alienation, remove, and loftiness of Plath's speaker, whose "look's leash | Dangles the puppet-people." From this high vantage point, the hawk, like the solipsist, looks down upon powerless mortals with a sense of disdain: "the earth's face upward for my inspection." Plath's line "I hold | Absolute power" finds a corollary in Hughes's "I hold Creation in my foot" (*CPH* 69), while the solipsist's statement that "if I choose to blink | They die" echoes the hawk's bald assertion of pitiless strength:

> I kill where I please because it is all mine.
> There is no sophistry in my body:
> My manners are tearing off heads—
>
> The allotment of death.
> For the one path of my flight is direct
> Through the bones of the living.
> No arguments assert my right:
>
> The sun is behind me.
> Nothing has changed since I began.
> My eye has permitted no change.
> I am going to keep things like this.   (*CPH* 69)

Hughes takes the voice of Plath's solipsist and hones it to suit the voice of an even more terrifying, "solipsistic" force—his hawk, "Hitler's familiar spirit." Both sought to hone a voice that embodied the will to power.

Plath and Hughes shared a fascination with the subconscious, which was connected to their mutual interest in violence. Although their relationship with this concept was influenced by different experiences—Plath's through psychotherapy, Hughes's through his readings of Blake, Graves, and Jung—both wanted to give voice to what lay in the hidden depths under calm surfaces. They would have agreed with D. H. Lawrence's description of the lake where Diana Crich drowns in *Women in Love*: "so cold . . . and so endless, so different really from what it is on top" (201).

Hughes's "To Paint a Water Lily," written by April 1958 and published in August 1959, is a good example of an attempt to reveal the opposition between what lies above and what lies below. Here, the "green level of lily leaves" hides the primeval scene under the pond's surface, where "Prehistoric bedragonned times | Crawl that darkness with Latin names" (*CPH* 70). Hughes seems to criticize the dominant Movement aesthetic, which rejects "the horror" at the "root" of experience (*CPH* 71) as he points out the dark aspects of the scene his painter has missed. He mocks the artist by juxtaposing military words and phrases such as "bullets," "take aim," "battle-shouts," "death-cries," and "molten metal" (70) with what the artist's "eyes praise": the rainbow colors of the flies and the long, graceful neck of the lily flower. The observer has no sense of the struggle going on beneath the pond's surface, where creatures have "Jaws for heads" and are "Ignorant of age as of hour" (71). Hughes's neat couplets are probably another ironic comment upon Movement "gentility" and use of form as a way of ordering disturbing material. Perhaps for this reason, Hughes found the poem extremely difficult to write, as he told Faas in 1970: "I . . . felt very constricted fiddling around with it. It was somehow like writing through a long, winding tube, like squeezing language out at the end of this long, remote process" (1980: 208). He called the poem "superficial" in a letter to Olwyn in 1960.[20]

Hughes revisits a similar landscape in "Pike," perhaps the most anthologized poem in *Lupercal*. As in "To Paint a Water Lily," placid surfaces hide "submarine delicacy and horror" (*CPH* 85); again, it is the poet's role to expose such discrepancies. Primordial "jaws," "flies," and "darkness" appear here, as they did in "To Paint a Water Lily." But "Pike" is more successful than "To Paint a Water Lily." Because Hughes focuses on only one creature here, rather than an entire pond, he presents a fuller, more powerful totem of what he called "positive violence" (*WP* 255)—the pike is an inheritor of nature's dark but "divine" laws. The addition of a first-person speaker, who is himself "stunned" by the pike's "grandeur," further complicates the poem by emphasizing man's sense of both

---

[20] Ted Hughes to Olwyn Hughes, April 2, 1960, MSS 980, Emory.

connection to and alienation from nature. But the speaker's admiration for the pike is very different from the artist's reverence for nature in "To Paint a Water Lily." This speaker comes to understand his own vulnerability in the face of "life subdued to its instrument" (85). While the speaker says he "dared not cast" for the pike, Hughes implies that the scene's primeval timelessness, rather than the predatory nature of the fish itself, overwhelms and disturbs him. The speaker suddenly perceives the incredible distance between his benevolent view of nature and the reality. In the process, he faces his own mortality:

> A pond I fished, fifty yards across,
> Whose lilies and muscular tench
> Had outlasted every visible stone
> Of the monastery that planted them—
>
> Stilled legendary depth:
> It was as deep as England. It held
> Pike too immense to stir...   (*CPH* 85)

England is imagined not only in geological terms, but historical, political, and even spiritual terms as well. The metaphor is appropriate, for Hughes, in his attempt to wrest control of modern British poetry from the Movement, also seeks to change modern perceptions of "England." As Uroff writes, "The repressed violence which erupts from what is called a lost legendary world is in fact brought into the twentieth century by the poet who creates it" (102). Hughes's England is not that of the post-war welfare state, but Celtic, even pre-Celtic: dark, cold, inhospitable, home to warring factions, "legendary." The pond is a metaphor of England itself; Hughes implies that most of its inhabitants are like the artist in "To Paint a Water Lily," who sees only the civilized surface. Few dare to look below and acknowledge the "horror" that underlies present experience. Hughes, however, demands that man acknowledge his own brutality—"our extraordinary readiness to exploit, oppress, torture and kill our own kind" (*WP* 256)—by acknowledging his distance from nature's "divine" (*WP* 262) laws. As Hughes wrote of his pike and hawk:

I began them as a series in which they would be angels—hanging in the radiant glory around the creator's throne, composed of terrific, holy power.... I wanted to focus my natural world...in a "divine" dimension.... If the Hawk and the Pike kill, they kill within the law and their killing is a sacrament in this sense. It is an act not of violence but of law. (*WP* 262)

Hughes's speaker comes to such a realization at the poem's end, when he tells of "the dream" which "Darkness beneath night's darkness had freed" (*CPH* 86). The encounter with the pike, and history, has brought the speaker closer to self-knowledge. As in "To Paint a Water Lily," Hughes takes it upon himself to write poetry that reflects what is at the bottom of the dark pool, not what glitters upon the surface.

In "Watercolor of Granchester Meadows," probably completed in late February 1959, Plath claimed for herself the violent amphitheater of nature that many critics already saw as Hughes's terrain.[21] The poem consists of four seven-lined stanzas, each with a regular ABABCCA rhyme scheme. Plath's meticulous craftsmanship and pleasing alliteration obscure the essential message of the poem, which is that violence underlies even the most placid mental and physical geographies. Although Granchester is like "a country on a nursery plate," it is also a place where the "blood-berried hawthorn hides its spines with white" (*CPP* 112)—an image that will recur in the later, more violent "Ariel." In the last stanza, Plath juxtaposes a pair of student lovers lolling on the banks of the Cam, "unaware | How in such mild air | The owl shall stoop from his turret, the rat cry out" (112). Like Hughes, Plath is interested in the violence beneath calm surfaces, whether it is natural struggle in a serene landscape, or the struggle of the "ugly and hairy" (*CPP* 160) self to be heard above the platitudes of the "saintly" self, as in "In Plaster." She too is fascinated by the seismic disturbances all but invisible under the polished or "Stilled" (111) veneer of civilization. Yet the disturbance that interests the poet in "Watercolor of Granchester Meadows" goes unnoticed by the lovers. Since Plath and Hughes often took punting trips to Granchester, it is likely that Plath is comparing the young couple to herself and Hughes, perhaps extending her metaphor to suggest that even love can fall prey to unseen threats. For love, too, is "a country on a nursery plate," but just as vulnerable to predators as the defenseless creatures in the poem. The image of the "Black-gowned" students against a landscape of "Arcadian green" further emphasizes their precarious, perhaps even doomed, state. Plath may also be commenting upon art itself, for the poem is a representation of a painting rather than an imagined scene. She might have been making a statement about the "stilled," "small," "bland," "tame," "benign," "droll," and above all "unaware" (111–12) verse of the Movement, in which, as in the watercolor, "Nothing is big or far" (111). Her revealing adjectives suggest that, like Hughes in "To Paint a Water Lily," she is criticizing the artist's limited vision, and, at the same time, announcing that she is aware of the lurking dangers: the final image of owl and rat trumps the first line's spring lamb, which the poet knows will likely be slaughtered.

Plath's "Full Fathom Five" and "Lorelei," which date from 1958, also explore "submarine delicacy and horror" (*CPH* 85) through literal representations of terrors underwater and metaphorical suggestions of the terrors the mind attempts to hold at bay. In "Full Fathom Five," Plath takes inspiration from the famous lines of *The Tempest* to create a metaphor of grief. The father, buried within the

---

[21] Hughes recalled that the poem was composed in early 1957 in one of his notebooks (Notebook 3, MSS 644, Emory). However, Plath suggests in her journal that it was written in February 1959. It is possible she was revising earlier work, or that Hughes simply misremembered the date of composition in his notebook.

turbulent seas of the speaker's mind, surfaces only to tempt her to join him: "Father, this thick air is murderous. | I would breathe water." Like Hughes's pike, the speaker's father is an emblem of "The old myth of origins | Unimaginable"; he resides among "knuckles, shinbones, | Skulls" (*CPP* 93). The speaker is aware that the glassy surfaces hide a "danger" that she must acknowledge but from which she must also protect herself.

In "Lorelei," Plath develops this imagery further. Instead of the dead father beckoning the living daughter to join him, Plath imagines the Rhine sirens calling to her with their "maddening | Song" (*CPP* 94). As Uroff has noted (99), Hughes may have borrowed Plath's image of "Black beneath bland mirror-sheen" (*CPP* 94) for his own "Darkness beneath night's darkness" (*CPH* 86). "Lorelei" bears other similarities to "Pike": both poems are set at night, both invoke the act of literal and metaphorical fishing, both speakers are disturbed by something rising "From the nadir" of the water, "troubling the face | Of quiet" (*CPP* 94), and both implicitly mock the false civilities—the "well-steered country" and "mundane order" (*CPP* 94)—of modern life.

By 1962, when Plath wrote "Elm," she would fuse elements of Hughes's "Pike" with her own surreal landscape as she once again sounded the depths of her psyche:

> I know the bottom, she says. I know it with my great tap root:
> It is what you fear.
> I do not fear it: I have been there.   (*CPP* 192)

Here, Plath gives Hughes's pike a voice. Yet where Hughes's speaker feels a sense of release after contemplating "darkness beneath night's darkness," Plath's speaker simply admits, "I am terrified by this dark thing | That sleeps in me" (193). The elm takes on the pike's "malevolent aged grin," but for Plath, it represents something darker than "the jaws' hooked clamp and fangs" (*CPH* 85). Later, in "The Moon and the Yew Tree," she will again bring Hughes's dark pond to mind when she writes, "the message of the yew tree is blackness—blackness and silence" (*CPP* 173).

Plath again echoes Hughes in "Crossing the Water," a deeply ambiguous love poem that alludes to her husband's "September" and "Pike," as well as back to her own "Lorelei" and the tree poems mentioned above. The poem begins with yet another expression of Hughes's "darkness beneath night's darkness" and her own "Black beneath bland mirror-sheen" in "Lorelei": "Black lake, black boat, two black, cut-paper people." The leaves that surround them are "full of dark advice," while the speaker admits, "Cold worlds shake from the oar. | The spirit of blackness is in us, it is in the fishes" (*CPP* 190). This pastoral is a far cry from the "Arcadian green" Cambridge landscape in "Watercolor of Granchester Meadows." Here, it is as if the prophecy contained in that poem has finally come true: the black-gowned students from the earlier poem now appear bound for Hades, "crossing the water" to a place still and silent as death. The final line,

"This is the silence of astounded souls" (190), may allude to the end of "Pike" and its astounded speaker who emerges from his "dark night" with a sense of renewal and release. In "Crossing the Water," Plath hints that the couple has finally reached "the bottom," "the root," "the horror"—the place she and Hughes had been struggling to bring to words since 1957. (Indeed, Hughes was so impressed with this poem that he titled one of Plath's posthumous collections *Crossing the Water*.)

Even as Plath and Hughes sought to write in voices that were, as Plath told Owen Leeming, "quite, quite different," they were drawn back to the same poetic terrain, continually, as Hughes wrote in "Thistles," "fighting back over the same ground" (*CPH* 147). Whether they were writing competitively or collaboratively, however, both were aware of the threat of remaking, the consequences of which Hughes had already foreseen in his 1956 poem "Bawdry Embraced," dedicated to Plath:

> And so they knit, knotted and wrought
> > Braiding their ends in;
> So fed their radiance to themselves
> > They could not be seen.
>
> And thereupon—a miracle!
> > Each became a lens
> So focusing creation's heat
> > The other burst in flames.   (*CPH* 15)

6

Disarming the Enemy

In the autumn of 1962, Sylvia Plath's worst fears were realized when Ted Hughes began an affair with Assia Wevill. Plath's letters home during this period, like the *Ariel* poems themselves, alternate between the high pitch of rage and the slack, dull tone of resignation. On the same day she wrote to her brother, Warren, that Ted was a bastard, a killer, and a sadist, she told Olive Prouty, "What I have lived through these past three months seems like a dark dream from which I have only the desire to disassociate myself."[1] These varying tones reflect Plath's desire to defeat her "low" abusive anger with a "high" detachment. She was determined to prove to her friends and family that she could prosper without Hughes. As she wrote to Prouty in November 1962, "I simply say I am very happy about the divorce because it frees me for a life of writing in peace. They are disappointed, because they expect me to be full of revenge & frustration."[2] Yet she could not remain so cool in letters to her mother and brother. Her curses flew across the Atlantic in radioactive missives that surely helped Plath hone the voices of "Lady Lazarus," "Daddy," and "Purdah." She complained of Hughes's arrogance and vanity, made outrageous claims about his behavior, and plotted to rid herself of him forever. On October 16, 1962, for example, Plath told her mother that Hughes and Assia wondered why she "didn't commit suicide" since she had tried in the past, and that Hughes told her "how convenient it would be" if she died.[3] Two days later she wrote to Warren about "Ted's fantastic thoughtlessness, almost diabolic—he keeps saying he can't understand why I don't kill myself."[4] Plath's claims in these letters invite skepticism, since Hughes's letters to friends and family immediately after the break-up are filled with both concern and admiration for Plath. As he wrote to his brother, Gerald, in December 1962, "In many of the most important ways, she's the most gifted and capable & admirable woman I've ever met—but, finally, impossible for me to live married to" (*L* 209). Nevertheless, Plath's rage became a source of power, staving off self-doubt and inspiring vengeful vows of self-sufficiency. As she wrote to her mother in October 1962, "He has squelched me, I need no literary help from him. I am going to

[1] Sylvia Plath to Olive Prouty, October 18, 1962, Lilly.
[2] Sylvia Plath to Olive Prouty, November 2, 1962, Lilly.
[3] Sylvia Plath to Aurelia Plath, October 16, 1962, Lilly.
[4] Sylvia Plath to Warren Plath, October 18, 1962, Lilly.

make my own way. . . . I am a genius of a writer."[5] Hughes, in fact, hoped that the separation would produce this effect: as he wrote to Olwyn in late summer, 1962, "as soon as I clear out, she'll start making a life of her own, friends of her own, interests of her own" (*L* 206).

The poems Plath wrote after she separated from Hughes in the autumn of 1962 helped cultivate what has come to be known as 'the Plath myth,' as defined by Sandra Gilbert:

Being enclosed—in plaster, in a bell jar, a cellar or a waxhouse—and then being liberated from an enclosure by a maddened or suicidal or "hairy and ugly" avatar of the self is, I would contend, at the heart of the myth that we piece together from Plath's poetry, fiction, and life, just as it is at the heart of much other important writing by nineteenth- and twentieth-century women. The story told is invariably a story of being trapped, by society or by the self as an agent of society, and then somehow escaping or trying to escape. (1989: 55)

For many critics, what Plath really escaped when she managed to free herself from Daddy's black shoe was less the oppressive ghost of her father than the insidious influence of Ted Hughes.[6] Gilbert, for example, writes that Plath "triumphed" (56) over Hughes in writing *Ariel*, while Margaret Uroff declares that "Not until such late poems as the bee sequence, 'Lady Lazarus,' 'Daddy,' and 'Ariel,' among others, was Plath able to break clear of all influences. . . . Alone, at the end, she was able to hear only her own voice, to write of the topic that interested her most—her self" (217–18).

While other critics have contested this "breakthrough" theory, few observe that Plath did not turn away from Hughes during these months; instead, she plundered his poems for material.[7] Allusions to *The Hawk in the Rain* and *Lupercal*—books Plath could probably recite by heart—abound in *Ariel*. While there are many articles and even one book addressing Plath's role in *Birthday Letters*, Hughes's poetic influence on the *Ariel* poems has remained relatively unexplored. Yet Plath paid close attention to Hughes's poems in the period after the couple separated. *Ariel* presents a caricature of Hughes's poetic femme fatales and animal predators, a fact that complicates many critics' reading of a liberated female voice after the couple's separation. No longer was Plath arguing with Hughes about the role of nature, as she did in *The Colossus*. She looked to his poems now to mock, to impersonate, to emasculate, to argue, and to flaunt a parodic version of her obedient self.

As Hughes himself perceptively observed, Plath employed "a hypnotic technique" in *Ariel*, "imitating somebody, exactly, until at some imperceptible point,

    [5] Sylvia Plath to Aurelia Plath, October 16, 1962, Lilly.
    [6] These critics include Elaine Showalter, Marjorie Perloff, Susan Van Dyne, Steven Axelrod, Sandra Gilbert, and Susan Gubar.
    [7] Those who have contested this theory include Jacqueline Rose, Lynda Bundtzen, Christina Britzolakis, and Robin Peel.

the initiative passes to you, & they begin to imitate you, & can then be controlled—its [*sic*] the fundamental dynamics of the artistic process, but in literature nowhere so naked as in those Ariel poems" (*L* 445). They were, he told Keith Sagar, "about successful 'integration'—violent inheriting of a violent temperament" (*L* 445). Yet many *Ariel* poems speak mockingly to this violent inheritance, for their explosive anger links them back to Hughes and his "instructions" to Plath to release her violent energy. In "The Minotaur," as I pointed out in Chapter 1, Hughes recalled the day he cheered on Plath as she smashed his writing table: " 'Marvellous!' I shouted, 'Go on, | Smash it into kindling. | That's the stuff you're keeping out of your poems!' ||... 'Get that shoulder under your stanzas | And we'll be away' " (*CPH* 1120). In *Ariel*, Plath gives Hughes what he asked for in "The Minotaur," yet now the woman is "More terrible than she ever was" (*CPP* 215).

"Daddy" and "Lady Lazarus," in particular, borrow from Hughes as they attempt, in the psychiatrist R. D. Laing's terms, to "impersonate" the forces that Plath felt had attempted to remake her. In these poems, her speakers become exactly the kind of femme fatale that Hughes had written about in early poems such as "The Woman with Such High Heels She Looked Dangerous," "Bawdry Embraced," "The Drowned Woman," "The Martyrdom of Bishop Farrar," "The Conversion of Reverend Skinner," and "Cleopatra to the Asp." At the same time, "Daddy" and "Lady Lazarus" incorporate elements of Hughes's poems of predation, violence, and torture, such as "Law in the Country of Cats," "Vampire," "Invitation to the Dance," "The Jaguar," "Hawk Roosting," "Thrushes," and "Pike." Plath constructs characters out of Hughes's own words, and gives him back a perversion of his own creation. Like Hughes's Pike, Plath's treacherous females are "stunned by their own grandeur" as they move through a world of "delicacy and horror" (*CPH* 84–5); like the hawk in "Hawk Roosting," their "manners are tearing off heads" (*CPH* 69). These are poems in which, as Bloom writes, "a poet antithetically 'completes' his precursor, by so reading the parent-poem as to retain its terms but to mean them in another sense, as though the precursor had failed to go far enough" (1973: 14). Plath's "completion" of Hughes's poems is ironic: her vengeful heroines speak to the persona that male forces in her life—husband, father, doctor—had "created."

Plath does more than critique a sexist literary construct through her use of the femme fatale. By placing Daddy's daughter and Lady Lazarus in the theater of war and fascism, she also mocks her youthful infatuation with Nietzsche and her glorification of Hughes as *übermensch*—as well as that part of herself that longed for "Something terrible, something bloody" (*JP* 299) the night she met Hughes. By the autumn of 1962, Nietzschean summons to "blood spirit" (*Zarathustra* 1982: 152), which had once excited the young female poet yearning to assert her vision, seemed an embodiment of the patriarchal hegemony she now railed against for personal and political reasons. When, in "Daddy," Plath writes that "Every woman adores a Fascist" (*CPP* 223), she is mocking Nietzsche's Zarathustra, who proclaimed "Brave, unconcerned, mocking, violent—thus wisdom wants us: she is a woman and always loves only a warrior" (153). The self-consciousness of Lady Lazarus's performance, in particular, also mocks Nietzsche's sense, in *The Gay Science*, that women were "first of all and above all else actresses.... they 'put on something' even when they take off everything" (qtd. in Heath 51). Thus, poems like "Daddy" and "Lady Lazarus" may be read less as confessional revenge fantasies and more as a corrective to the "masculine sublime" or "positive violence" that fascinated Hughes, Nietzsche, and Lawrence.[8]

Critics have noted that "Daddy" and "Lady Lazarus" must be read as ironic/parodic performances rather than examples of "an inspirational and sometimes sinister force possessing the poet" (Kendall 2001: 156).[9] Indeed, "Daddy" and "Lady Lazarus" are ironic treatments of Robert Graves's claim that "An English or American woman in nervous breakdown of sexual origin will often instinctively reproduce in faithful and disgusting detail much of the ancient Dionysian ritual" (458). Still, whether critics view Plath's speakers in these poems as triumphant or doomed, most see what Rose calls a clear narrative "from victimisation to revenge" (223).[10] But what seems, in Axelrod's words, like a move

---

[8] Britzolakis notes that "The predominance of blood imagery in the later poetry ... can be seen as an ironic revision of D. H. Lawrence's 'blood-consciousness', which celebrates the cause of a primordial, unconscious, and impersonal life force" (169). Diane Middlebrook further notes that Plath's late poem "Kindness" mocks both Hughes and Lawrence by incorporating elements of Hughes's play *Difficulties of a Bridegroom* and Lawrence's "Rabbit Snared in the Night" ("Poetry" 2006: 168). In *Difficulties of a Bridegroom*, a suitor gives his mistress two roses he has paid for with a rabbit pelt, evoking Lawrence's reference to "the blood-jets of your throat" in "Rabbit Snared in the Night" (1986: 69). In "Kindness," Plath writes of the soullessness of "a rabbit's cry," then ends the poem with the lines, "The blood jet is poetry, | There is no stopping it. | You hand me two children, two roses" (*CPP* 270).

[9] Britzolakis sums up the dominant critical reading of these poems when she writes, "Although Plath's 'confessional' tropes are often seen in terms of ... feminist protest against a monolithic patriarchal oppressor, her self-reflexivity tends to turn confession into a parody gesture or a premise for theatrical production" (151). Kendall writes that Seamus Heaney, offended not so much by Plath's references to Nazis and Jews but to the indecorousness of "Daddy," "fails to credit Plath with the self-awareness to be acting deliberately—to be performing" (2001: 155). Rose reads "Daddy" "as a poem about its own conditions of linguistic and phantasmic production" (230), while Uroff notes that "Plath employs techniques of caricature, hyperbole, and parody that serve to distance the speaker from the poet" (159). Susan Gubar, in *Poetry after Auschwitz*, has emphasized that "Daddy" and "Lady Lazarus" reveal "brilliant insights into a debilitating sexual politics at work in fascist anti-Semitism" (195).

[10] As Judith Kroll put it, "Lady Lazarus, the lioness, and the queen bee are not male-dependent, and they represent triumph over the negative, male-defined aspects of these typical female roles" (11). Although Van Dyne doubts the ultimate efficacy of Lady Lazarus's stand, she still understands the poem as an attempt to "take back" what has been stolen from her: "Rather than be consumed by the fires of sexual jealousy and helpless rage that appear repeatedly in the imagery of the drafts, the speaker wants to separate herself from her fused identity with Hughes, eliminate the threat of his superior position, and finally appropriate his male powers to herself in a consuming gesture of her own fierce territoriality" (1989: 137). Gilbert also reads "Daddy" as a poem of enclosure and liberation (55), while Middlebrook writes that Plath was "saying good riddance to the attitude behind all those poems she had written in which fathers appear larger than life" (2003: 187). For her, "Daddy" and "Lady Lazarus" are poems about the "daughter's enraged recognition, at thirty, of the cost of her emotional collaboration with domination by a strong man" (187).

"from self-subordination to a stance of revolt" (37) comes at too high a cost for the vengeful poet. Plath's effort to draw attention to Hughes's "failure" is as self-defeating as it is self-reflexive: her dangerous, predatory women are not voices of self-assertion, but self-annihilation. By "becoming" dangerous women, Plath's speakers may successfully mock the idea of the femme fatale, the Nietzschean *übermensch*, or the White Goddess, but they are unable to repossess, revitalize, and legitimate the idea of female strength.[11] By parodying Hughes's motifs and language, Plath's speakers cannot help but parody themselves.

PLATH AND *THE DIVIDED SELF*

Before examining Hughes's influence on Plath, we must first turn our attention to the work of R.D. Laing and Sigmund Freud. Plath was interested in psychology, and was likely inspired by ideas regarding impersonation and self-annihilation in Laing's and Freud's work. These psychological models gave Plath the tools with which she would, in Laing's phrase, "disarm the enemy" (48) in her late poems. By performing a Laingian "impersonation" of Hughes through the use of his tropes, Plath enacts the kind of self-annihilating ritual that Freud described in "Mourning and Melancholia," whereby the melancholic mourner who wishes to revenge herself upon the dead (or, in this case, the lost husband) will "succeed, by the circuitous path of self-punishment" (251).

While several critics have discussed the impact of Freud's "Mourning and Melancholia" upon Plath's retaliatory *Ariel* poems, fewer have pointed to the influence of R. D. Laing's groundbreaking *The Divided Self.* It is likely that Plath read *The Divided Self* when it appeared in London in 1960 and that she identified strongly with Laing's romantic depiction of schizophrenia and manic depression, as well as his focus on the conflict between "true" and "false" selves. As Axelrod writes, "Although it is not clear that Plath actually had a copy of Laing's *The Divided Self* in her hands, she would unquestionably have known about the book.... its ideas were in the air. Plath's texts of 1962–63 almost certainly reflect Laing's eloquent evocation of mental illness, employing his metaphors to suggest the dimensions of her own creative crisis" (229).[12] Indeed, there is much to be gained by investigating Laing's influence on "Daddy" and "Lady Lazarus," for the psychiatrist's ideas likely offered Plath a new strategy for competing with her husband.

---

[11] Although Uroff argues that in Plath's late poems, the "goddess is a figure of power and fecundity...in the end an identity to be celebrated and assumed" (223), Britzolakis's view that "Plath's relation to a mythology underpinned by the assertion that 'woman is not a poet: she is either a Muse or she is nothing' is necessarily an ironical one" (57) seems closer to the mark.

[12] Axelrod does not discuss Laing's frequent use of military and torture metaphors or how they might have influenced Plath. Nor does he discuss the ways in which Laing's ideas about engulfment and isolation may have framed Plath's understanding of her relationship with Hughes, and her later attempt to 'impersonate' him in her poems.

In "Mourning and Melancholia," Freud discusses the "impersonation" of the lost object by the mourner, who forms a "narcissistic" relationship with the dead or unfaithful lover, "the result of which is that in spite of the conflict with the loved person the love-relation need not be given up" (249). He continues:

If the love for the object—a love which cannot be given up though the object itself is given up—takes refuge in narcissistic identification, then the hate comes into operation on this substitutive object, abusing it, debasing it, making it suffer and deriving sadistic satisfaction from its suffering. The self-tormenting in melancholia, which is without doubt enjoyable, signifies... a satisfaction of trends of sadism and hate which relate to an object, and which have been turned round upon the subject's own self. (251)

Although Laing and Freud frame their discussions of the relationship between vengeful subject and lost object differently, both agree that the subject's method of revenge involves both impersonation of, or "narcissistic identification" with, the oppressive/lost object, and that such identification results in the subject's self-contempt and even self-annihilation.

While Freud's ideas apply more directly to Plath's psychological condition during her first suicide attempt (she wrote in her journal in December 1958 that Freud's essay was "An almost exact description of my feelings and reasons for suicide" (447)) and the later period when she was "mourning" Hughes, she was likely also influenced by Laing's ideas about exacting revenge through caricature and spiteful impersonation. She would have related to Laing's "schizoid" patients, whose warring "true" and "false" selves waged a constant battle for supremacy. This was a condition Plath felt was her own, and which she described in many poems (notably "In Plaster"). Plath suffered from severe depression rather than schizophrenia; nevertheless, she may have found in Laing's analysis of the divided self a way of understanding or even diagnosing herself. In addition, Laing's statement that life was like a concentration camp for those whose true and false selves were in constant strife may have given Plath the confidence to appropriate the metaphor and experiment with the language of genocide and fascism in "Lady Lazarus" and "Daddy." As Laing wrote:

It is well known that temporary states of dissociation of the self from the body occur in normal people. In general, one can say that it is a response that appears to be available to most people who find themselves enclosed within a threatening experience from which there is no physical escape. Prisoners in concentration camps *tried* to feel that way, for the camp offered no possible way out either spatially or at the end of a period of time. The only way out was by a psychical withdrawal "into" one's self and "out of" the body.... But in the patients here considered, the splitting is not simply a temporary reaction to a specific situation of great danger, which is reversible when the danger is past. It is, on the contrary, a basic orientation to life... the individual whose abiding mode of being-in-the-world is of this split nature is living in what to him, if not to us, is a world that threatens his being from all sides, and from which there is no exit.... For them the world is a prison without bars, a concentration camp without barbed wire. (79)

Plath was likely drawn to Laing's romantic (he called it "existential") understanding of the schizoid condition as one of vision and insight rather than debilitating lunacy, and would have appreciated his references to literature and philosophy. Indeed, to read *The Divided Self* is to experience the uncanny presence of Plath's hand urging one to underline ideas she frequently expressed in her journals and poems. One imagines Plath concurring with Laing's sense that "the inner self splits to have a sado-masochistic relationship with itself" (83) and "If there is anything the schizoid individual is likely to believe in, it is his own destructiveness" (93). Plath herself had expressed a desire to commit violence in her journals, writing, "I have a violence in me that is hot as death-blood. I can kill myself or—I know it now—even kill another" (395).[13] When Laing says that "The schizoid individual exists under the black sun, the evil eye, of his own scrutiny" (112) one imagines Plath assenting. She must have found in *The Divided Self* a validation of her own competing feelings of self-love and self-loathing.

Laing's ideas illuminate Plath's relationship with Hughes and her later treatment of him in "Daddy." For example, Laing speaks of the schizoid's relationship to an intimate "other" in terms that probably resonated with Plath:

> Utter detachment and isolation are regarded as the only alternative to a clam- or vampire-like attachment in which the other person's life-blood is necessary for one's own survival. . . . Therefore, the polarity is between complete isolation or complete merging of identity rather than between separateness and relatedness. The individual oscillates perpetually, between the two extremes, each equally unfeasible. (53)

The schizoid self eventually reaches the point where he needs to "disarm" or "destroy" the other if he is to "prevent himself losing his self" (43)—or to prevent what I have called remaking. Speaking of a particular schizoid patient, Laing wrote, "By destroying, in his own eyes, the other person as a person, he robbed the other of his power to crush him. By depleting him of his personal aliveness, that is, by seeing him as a piece of machinery rather than as a human being, he undercut the risk to himself" (48).[14] Laing uses the metaphor of pertrification (and, frequently, the image of Medusa) to describe the process of "totally disarming the enemy" (note the military metaphor) (48). He writes that "to forgo one's autonomy becomes the means of secretly safeguarding it; to play possum, to feign death, becomes a means of preserving one's aliveness. . . . To turn oneself into a stone becomes a way of not

---

[13] Plath also wrote in her journal, "What unleashed desire there must be in one for general carnage. I walk around the streets, braced and ready and almost wishing to test my eye and fiber on tragedy—a child crushed by a car, a house on fire, someone thrown into a tree by a horse. Nothing happens: I walk the razor's edge of jeopardy" (357).

[14] This patient dreamed that he was "a clam stuck to his wife's body" (48).

being turned into a stone by someone else. 'Be thou hard,' exhorts Nietzsche" (51).

The concentration camp imagery, the Nietzschean will to power, the configuration of the "other" as an enemy in the military sense—all of these ideas find their way into "Lady Lazarus" and "Daddy," as does Laing's idea that at a certain point, the real self "will pour out accusations of persecution at the hands of that person with whom the false self has been complying for years" (100). As Laing sees it, "The individual will declare that this person (mother, father, husband, wife) has been trying to kill him; or that he or she has tried to steal his 'soul' or his mind. That he/she is a tyrant, a torturer, an assassin, a child murderer, etc." (100). This idea lies at the heart of "Daddy," "Lady Lazarus," "The Courage of Shutting-Up," "The Detective," and "The Jailer." Plath, when composing "Daddy," may even have been inspired by Laing's account of a German catatonic who, when asked to speak before a lecture hall, uttered the words, "My father, my real father!" in English, and then began to perform a bitter impersonation of his interrogator. Indeed, the catatonic's repetitive language brings to mind the nursery rhyme cadences of Plath's poem: "You understand nothing at all, nothing at all; nothing at all does he understand. If you follow now, he won't follow, will not follow. Are you getting still more impudent? Are you getting impudent still more? How they attend, they do attend" (29–30).

Laing claims that when the schizoid self can no longer conform to the Other's idea of himself, he produces a caricature of the Other through spiteful impersonation. Discussing a case of a domineering mother and her dutiful daughter, he writes that the daughter covered her face with gaudy rouge, powder, and lipstick until she had achieved a "startlingly unpleasant, clownish, mask-like expression" (103)—a performance that brings Lady Lazarus to mind. Laing writes that "She turned her compliance into an attack, and exhibited for all to see this travesty of her true self, which was both a grotesque caricature of her mother and a mocking 'ugly' version of her own obedience" (104). This is exactly the kind of retaliation I suggest Plath hoped to achieve with "Daddy" and "Lady Lazarus," in which she gives Hughes a "grotesque caricature" of his female poetic figures and "a mocking 'ugly' version" of her obedient (or remade) self. In order to "impersonate" Hughes—just as the young girl painted her face into a distorted version of her mother's—Plath's speakers must exaggerate those qualities she associates with him most strongly.

Plath's adoption of Laing's techniques of "impersonation" may have offered her a way into the Ariel voice while promising a way out of her rivalry with Hughes. If she could successfully disarm the enemy by impersonating him through caricature, she might wrest control of the dialogue and prove herself the strong poet in the partnership. Yet this strategy was ultimately limiting, for it entangled her with the words of her absent husband at exactly the moment she hoped to achieve literary independence.

"LADY LAZARUS"

"Lady Lazarus" traffics in controversial areas: Nazis, concentration camps, and remains of Holocaust victims are the metaphorical props Lady Lazarus uses to draw attention to her performance. While Judith Kroll cites Plath's debt to Kafka's "A Hunger Artist" (154), Gilbert and Gubar note the nod to Coleridge's "Kubla Khan" (1994: 3.290), and Britzolakis discusses the influence of Eliot and Shakespeare, there is reason to look to sources closer to home. "Lady Lazarus" owes much of its theme and imagery to Ted Hughes. Plath reclaims Hughes's poetic material with a vengeance by offering him exactly what he had conjured up in "The Woman with Such High Heels She Looked Dangerous": a woman "painted for the war-path" who will kill men with "the scabbard of her knife," a woman who, "When her blood beats its drum nobody dances" (*CPH* 11). Plath's female speaker must impersonate the male forces that attempt to oppress her *and* parody the femme fatales of Hughes's poems if she is to "disarm the enemy." Indeed, Hughes could be describing Lady Lazarus when he writes, in "The Woman with Such High Heels She Looked Dangerous":

> And when the sun gets at her it is as if
> A windy blue plume of fire from the earth raged upright,
> Smelling of sulphur, the contaminations of the damned,
> The refined fragile cosmetic of the dead.   (11)

Before we turn our attention to Hughes's influence, however, it is important to investigate the earlier genesis of "Lady Lazarus." The poem is essentially a revision of Plath's "Aerialist," which Plath included in her 1957 Cambridge manuscript, "Two Lovers and a Beachcomber," submitted as part of her English examination. "Aerialist" depicts a young girl who each night dreams herself an acrobat balancing "Cat-clever on perilous wire . . . | Footing her delicate dances | To whipcrack and roar | Which speak her maestro's will" (*CPP* 331).[15] As she walks the tightrope she manages to avoid swinging pendulums, only to find that there are more threats to overcome when she lands safely on the ground: "Tiger-tamer and grinning clown | Squat, bowling black balls at her" (331). In a stanza that looks forward to "Lady Lazarus," she writes:

[15] The poem was based on a real dream, which Plath described in her journal: "trying out for a play and being in a huge gymnasium where the clowns and actors were practicing. Everywhere there was the heavy circumstance of menace: I ran, huge weights were dropping on my head; I crossed the slippery floor, and afar off, laughing hobos bowled large black balls at me to knock me down; it was a terrifying time of jeopardy. . . . Black balls, black weights, wheeled vehicles, and the slippery floor: all trying to crush me, moving in heavy blundering attempts, just missing" (*J* 234).

Tall trucks roll in
With a thunder like lions; all aims
And lumbering moves
To trap this outrageous nimble queen
And shatter to atoms
Her nine so slippery lives.   (331–2)

But just at the moment when she is about to escape these instruments, her alarm clock wakes her. Still, she spends her waking hours in fear, trying to shrug off the effects of the dream, nervous that "out of spite, the whole | Elaborate scaffold of sky overhead | Fall racketing finale on her luck" (332).

"Aerialist" is a subversive revision of D. H. Lawrence's "When I Went to the Circus," whose "tight-rope lady, pink and blonde and nude-looking" "turned prettily, spun round | bowed . . . smiled, swung her parasol" (1986: 200). It is likely both Lawrence and Plath are alluding to Nietzsche's metaphor of the tightrope walker in *Thus Spoke Zarathustra*: "Man is a rope, tied between beast and overman— a rope over an abyss. A dangerous across, a dangerous on-the-way, a dangerous looking-back, a dangerous shuddering and stopping" (126). Plath's "maestro" may have been influenced by Nietzsche's jester, whose taunts of weakness cause the tightrope walker to lose concentration and fall to his death. "Forward, lazybones, smuggler, pale-face," the jester cries. "What are you doing here between towers? The tower is where you belong. You ought to be locked up; you block the way for one better than yourself" (131). Plath may have imagined similar leers as she defied convention to find her voice as a writer—to attempt the perilous journey towards "the overman." But Nietzsche approves of the tightrope walker's courage, despite his ultimate failure; thus, the philosopher's exhortations may have inspired Plath to make such a journey herself. Rather than remaining in her tower and observing the world through mirrors, like the Lady of Shalott, Plath's aerialist presses forward.

"Aerialist" offers a metaphor for the challenges faced by the female writer. The young woman's tightrope walk symbolizes her artistry, which she must use to please the male literary audience embodied in both the maestro and the roaring crowd. Plath suggests that the higher the woman artist ascends, the more obstacles are put in her path by the maestros and tiger-tamers of the male literary world. She was not paranoid; after all, her husband's editor at Faber and Faber, T. S. Eliot, had written to his father about his work for the *Egoist*: "I struggle to keep the writing as much as possible in Male hands, as I distrust the Feminine in literature" (qtd. in Gilbert and Gubar 1994: 1.67). Thus the speaker in "Aerialist" may be performing what Joan Riviere has called a "masquerade of womanliness," as I discussed in Chapter 5. Gilbert and Gubar have more recently called this "masquerade" "female female impersonation" (1994: 3.58), in which woman attempts to offer up (often at great cost) a continuity between her "consciousness and costume" (59).[16] The aerialist of

---

[16] As Gilbert and Gubar write, "because this woman of letters, newly conscious of the artifice of her gender, 'played' a public part that was unavailable to most of her ancestresses, she may at times

Plath's poem seems to be performing just this kind of "public" impersonation by amplifying her femininity before the male maestro and his threatening entourage. The speaker is careful to tell us that the aerialist performs "delicate dances" on the wire and that she "curtsies" before she descends to the floor—constructions of a stereotypical demure femininity that seem purposefully exaggerated, like the rouge on a circus performer's cheeks. "Aerialist" further exhibits all the poetic stunts that Plath had mastered by this time. Each six-line stanza conformed to an ABCABC rhyme, displaying her skill with slant rhymes such as "snowflakes" and "acrobatics," "roar" and "wire," "curtsies" and "eyes"; internal rhymes such as "Cat-clever on perilous wire" are also numerous. Plath may be mocking this rigid form as just another extension of her forced walk on the "perilous" wire—performing New Critical, formalist tricks dictated by the male maestro. Just as the aerialist must escape the arena or die, Plath too must escape out of this performance into a poetics that resonate with her more complex and transgressive inner world.

Hughes's "Acrobats," which appeared in *Lupercal*, may have been influenced by "Aerialist," as well as by Lawrence's and Nietzsche's use of this trope. (It is likely Hughes's poem, which he mentioned in a letter to Olwyn in 1958, was written after Plath's "Aerialist.") In "Acrobats," trapeze artists perform high above a circus crowd awed by their performance: "None below in the dumb-struck crowd | Thinks it else but miracle" (*CPH* 73). Hughes's acrobats impress the audience with their "unearthly access of grace, | Of ease." The spectators are particularly moved by the acrobats' mockery of their narrow, sedentary existence, and even, perhaps, of death itself:

> The acrobats flashed
> Above earth's ancient inertia,
> Faltering of the will,
> And the dullness of flesh—
> In the dream's orbit; shone, soared,
> Mocking vigil and ordeal,
> And the prayer of long attempting
> Body had endured
> To break from a hard-held trembling seat
> And soar at that height.   (73)

If Plath's poem was a metaphor for the perils endured by the female writer to aim high, then she may have read Hughes's poem through the lens of her own—as a metaphor of the "ease" with which the male writer was able to ascend to greatness, unhindered by the shadow of the whip-cracking maestro ready to

have found herself far more radically estranged from her aesthetic persona than were her male contemporaries from theirs. On the one hand she was often empowered by her estranged female female impersonation to produce poetry that commented on both the feminine and the masculine from the ironic perspective of the actor who knows that there is a radical gulf between 'me' and 'her.' But on the other, because audiences—both readers and observers—frequently reified the female artist in the feminine role she played, she herself was always in danger of being trapped behind the rigid mask of a self that she secretly despised as inauthentic" (1994: 3.60–1).

pounce below. Hughes's acrobat has become the *übermensch*, successfully jour-
neying over Nietzsche's abyss with no "Faltering of the will." Indeed, as Plath
wrote in her journal, she felt the poem was "a perfect metaphor, really, for
[Hughes] as a poetic acrobat-genius & the desirous & in many cases <u>envious</u>
audience" (368). Plath herself comprised part of that "desirous" and "envious"
audience: when Hughes wrote of his acrobats "Mocking vigil and ordeal," it is
possible Plath misread this line as a mockery of her own aerialist's—that is, the
woman writer's—"vigil and ordeal." Even if Hughes did not intend such a
meaning, Plath could not have helped but read this poem in the context of her
earlier dispirited verse.

"Lady Lazarus" fuses aspects of both "Aerialist" and "Acrobats." Plath takes
her demure but oppressed aerialist and transforms her into a more daring,
arrogant, and grotesque circus performer whose trick is, like Hughes's acro-
bats', evading death. Van Dyne notes that in the drafts of "Lady Lazarus,"
Plath had frequently used the word "love" when speaking of her "enemy"—
for example, an early line from a draft reads, "[My] [Great] Love, [my] [great]
enemy" (1989: 142). Yet by the final draft of the poem the word has vanished:
"the worksheets show a movement from a highly conflicted fusion with an
intimate antagonist toward a defiant separation from stylized, archetypal
representations of male authority" (142). This detail suggests that Hughes,
rather than Plath's father or "the patriarchy," originally personified the great-
est obstacle to her ascent. She looks to "Acrobats" to mock and cajole its
premise: the "miracle" of Lady Lazarus's "comeback" is a grotesque revision of
the "miracle" of Hughes's acrobats' grace. Where the acrobats' performance in
Hughes's poem is stunningly beautiful, Lady Lazarus's is monstrous; where
"Spot-lights sparkle those silver postures" (*CPH* 72) of Hughes's acrobats,
Lady Lazarus possesses "skin | Bright as a Nazi lampshade" (*CPP* 244). Plath
plays with Hughes's images here, deriding his poem's aesthetic of human
triumph, and what she may have read, against "Aerialist," as the grace and
ease of the male writer's ascent.

Lady Lazarus's "comeback" is from her own suicide attempts, provoked by
oppressive male figures who are all "Herr Enemy." In light of "Aerialist," her
"comeback" may also refer to the new woman that she has become, no longer
just a female female impersonator who must please the will of her maestro but
a Laingian female *male* impersonator—a woman who has the proverbial balls
to court the roughest death she can: "I do it so it feels like hell. | I do it so it
feels real" (*CPP* 245). The language here is reminiscent of military men's
blunt aphorisms, particularly General Sherman's "War is hell." If we remem-
ber William Carlos Williams's comment about bad poetry being the stuff of
little girls' fantasies, "sugar and spice and everything nice," and good poetry
being the stuff of little boys' "rats and snails and puppy dog's tales," then
Plath is self-consciously aligning herself with the rats and snails: "They had to
call and call | And pick the worms off me like sticky pearls" (*CPP* 245). This

is a performance in which the "delicate dances" of "Aerialist" (sugar and spice) are cast off for the "big strip tease" which will reveal scars and blood (rats and snails). Lady Lazarus is the resurrection of the diminutive aerialist who barely evaded the wrath of her male captors; in her "theatrical | Comeback" (245–6) she must become more powerful than her former antagonists, whom she now associates not with tiger-tamers but with fascism—an association that rests upon fascism's oppressive masculinity and its concomitant abhorrence of the weak and womanly. Lady Lazarus uses the German "Herr" to address her former antagonists because, in Laing's terms, she must (like Daddy's daughter) impersonate her enemies in order to disarm them; she must become more fascist than the fascists themselves if she is to defeat them. As Jerome Mazzaro has noted, "the new purity that she gains has accomplished exactly what Alfred Rosenberg had imagined for the German race: a superman who can challenge 'Herr God' and 'Herr Lucifer' by having gained self-discipline" (235). In order to renounce the *übermensch*, she must in fact become him—but even this becoming is ironic.[17] The success of Lady Lazarus's female male impersonation depends upon her taking up the maestro's and tiger-tamer's whip, of supplanting the fascist "father." As Van Dyne argues, "The violent fantasy of the poem is informed by the wish to incorporate the forces that threaten to destroy her" (1989: 138). She is not only actress, but director and ringmaster as well (Van Dyne 1993: 57), commanding her tormentors to do as she wills: "Peel off the napkin | O my enemy" (*CPP* 244). Lady Lazarus now embodies the brute male power Hughes had earlier celebrated in "Law in the Country of Cats."

"Lady Lazarus" also alludes to "Quest," which Hughes wrote in 1957 and published in *Grapevine* in 1958. "Quest" depicts a knight's efforts to slay a dragon:

> I know clearly, as at a shout, when the time
> Comes I am to ride out into the darkened air
> Down the deserted streets. Eyes, terrified and hidden,
> Are a weight of watching on me that I must ignore
> And a charge in the air, tingling and crackling bluely
> From the points and edges of my weapons, and in my hair.   (*CPH* 53)

Plath's use of the words "shout," "out," "time," "comeback," "eyes," "terrify," "paperweight," "charge," "air," and "hair" in "Lady Lazarus" gives that poem a verbal texture similar to that of "Quest." Her use of assonance and internal rhyme also resembles Hughes's. Plath's employment of the language and

---

[17] Plath's use of WWII imagery to conflate sex and death makes sense in light of Gilbert and Gubar's observation that during the war, guns were referred to as girls, and big-busted starlets were painted on bomber planes (1994: vol. 3, 227). Plath plays with the idea of the "bombshell" in the figure of Lady Lazarus, who seeks both to arouse and to annihilate: "And there is a charge, a very large charge / For a word or a touch / Or a bit of blood" (246).

rhythms of "Quest" (which in places echoes Browning's "Childe Roland to the Dark Tower Came," Yeats's "Song of Wandering Aengus," and Eliot's "Love Song of J. Alfred Prufrock") suggests that she is partially rewriting the classic (male) quest narrative. In "Lady Lazarus," the dragon becomes the Nazi "Enemy" that threatens to subsume the world in an endless Darwinian struggle-to-the-death. At the end of "Quest," the speaker (who does not possess Lady Lazarus's bravado) imagines himself dying in order to purge his "people" of the menace: his victory "Shall be its trumpeting and clangorous flight | Over the moon's face to its white-hot icy crevasse | With fragments of my body dangling from its hundred mouths" (54). Plath inverts this image: Lady Lazarus will use her mouth to "eat men like air" (*CPP* 247), to conquer the male forces that have, in their incarnation as father/husband and totalitarian dictator, threatened her private and public worlds.

While Plath has been criticized for taking on the persona of a martyr in her later *Ariel* poems, she may have been responding to Hughes's own poems of martyrdom, such as "The Martyrdom of Bishop Farrar," which appeared in *The Hawk in the Rain*. Lady Lazarus takes on many of the attributes of "Bloody Mary," the queen who ordered Farrar's death by burning. Like her, Lady Lazarus is "venomous" (*CPH* 48), a woman in a man's role trying to establish and maintain her control through a show of force. Plath referred to her "aerialist" as a "nimble queen" (*CPP* 332), while in "Stings" she writes, "I | Have a self to recover, a queen" (215). The queen is the ultimate female male impersonator, and, as such, must exaggerate her "maleness" through cruelty, like Queen Mary, or reject female sexuality, like Queen Elizabeth—hence Plath's constant references to vengeful queens in her late poetry. In "The Martyrdom of Bishop Farrar," Bloody Mary ultimately sought to control Farrar's words—his language—which threatened her own authority. By taking on the persona of a Bloody Mary figure in "Lady Lazarus," Plath too attempts to demolish the figures of male authority who would silence *her*—the "comeback" is one from silence to voice, as well as from death to life. Plath reverses the situation of "The Martyrdom of Bishop Farrar" in "Lady Lazarus," where the martyred female challenges the male authority figures who have tortured her. Like Farrar, she too will rise "Out of the ash," but for very different purposes.

Lastly, "Lady Lazarus" owes imagery to Hughes's *The Wound*, a surrealist drama broadcast on the BBC in February 1962, eight months before Plath wrote her poem. As we saw in Chapter 2, this verse drama speaks to anxieties of emasculation: while Ripley, the protagonist, lies wounded on a battlefield, he dreams he is nearly destroyed by a group of women living in a chateau, which he calls a "lousy old brothel" (1995: 106). These women, whom Ripley regards as prostitutes, "all tarted up" (1995: 106), are victims of the sort of torture that Lady Lazarus has endured at the hands of "Herr Doktor" (*CPP* 246). Hughes writes:

FIRST WOMAN: They took me with blood dripping off my chin, my mask was blood and went back over my ears and I'd pulled blood up past my elbows and so I was! And then dragged me from the mob and into the police station, two constables, my toes slapping the steps.

SECOND: The coroner attended, fifteen medical specialists of assorted interests.

THIRD: Experimental psychologists of four countries.

FOURTH: Zoologists of five.

FIRST: Bacteriologists of eight.

SECOND: Anthropologists of seven.

THIRD: With a stuffing of sundries, students and attendants.

FOURTH: While the zinc bench on which they stretched me trembled with the thunder and enthusiasm of the journalists under the windows.

FIRST: They stretched me silently, they accused.

SECOND: Bald domes glistened.

THIRD: Grease oozing among the hair-roots.

FOURTH: Upper lips lifting, quivering.

FIRST: Scalpels descending, quivering.

SECOND: What couldn't they expect?

THIRD: Why, every year dozens disappear, without trace, without a finger-nail or loose hair, and these white jackets already had my canines, roots too, reposing in formalin and I was an extremely interesting case. (1995: 103–4)

Hughes's "stuffing of sundries, students and attendants" bring to mind Plath's "peanut-crunching crowd" (*CPP* 245) who watch as Lady Lazarus performs her "strip tease." Like Hughes, Plath incorporates metaphors of prostitution, madness, and performance as she describes the way Lady Lazarus escapes the death-dealing hands of male tormentors allied with both fascism and science. In *The Wound*, too, policemen and scientists— "these white jackets"—are responsible for "slicing" the women and packing their body parts in formalin. Even Hughes's language resembles Plath's: the "finger-nail" and "loose hair" bring to mind Lady Lazarus's roster of body parts. Her "gold filling," "eye pits," "full set of teeth," and "wedding ring" recall what the "white coats" in Hughes's drama find as they operate on the women:

FOURTH: And what did they find, did they find what they hoped for?

FIRST: Lusted for.

SECOND: Sliced me for.

THIRD: Did they find the gold teeth.

FOURTH: The plastic gums.

FIRST: The glass eyes.

SECOND: The steel skull-plates.

THIRD: The jawbone rivets.

FOURTH: The rubber arteries.

FIRST: The rings.

SECOND: The remains of their darlings.

THIRD: The toe-nails.

FOURTH: The gall-stones.

FIRST: The ear-rings.

SECOND: The hair-pins. (1995: 105)

These women have now become femme fatales who threaten Ripley, and destroy his friend. But by acknowledging the metaphorical torments they have suffered at the hands of their male antagonists, Hughes provides a reason why they have lost their "real" personalities and turned into man-eating monsters. Although the women are a danger to Ripley, we sympathize with their plight; they too are prisoners. They have been damaged, and possibly brainwashed, beyond recognition by a patriarchal society that objectifies them as mere body parts. Rarely does Hughes give such a complex rendering of femme fatales in his work. He may, in fact, have remembered Plath's own accounts of electroshock therapy as he wrote the play. Now Plath exaggerates, parodies, and mocks elements of Hughes's work as she writes her own drama of female rebellion.

Despite Lady Lazarus's vows of revenge, critics worry that her transcendence is ultimately hollow. Rose, for example, is uncomfortable with the reading of Lady Lazarus's ascent as triumphant, and sees instead a reflection "of one of the most classic, and alarming, stereotypes of femininity itself":

To say that Plath creates her own version of this image [female transcendence], that she turns it back against her male oppressors, or raises it up against them, doesn't work when we see that the vision of a terrible and vengeful femininity is so firmly ensconced inside (is in some sense the origins of) the most stereotyped and misogynistic versions of the very image she seeks to transform. (163)[18]

---

[18] Van Dyne likewise writes, "She is hyper-conscious not only of her own feelings, but of her image in others' eyes. . . . perceiving herself as split, as both subject and object, self and other, may be the last vestige of the alienating male perspective she longs to escape from" (1989: 147).

According to this reading, Lady Lazarus is, like Daddy's daughter, manipulated beyond recognition by the very forces she seeks herself to manipulate. Yet Plath seems very much aware of Lady Lazarus as a male fantasy when she likens her "Comeback" to the "big strip tease" (*CPP* 245). Plath is also aware of Lady Lazarus as a clichéd construct when she writes that Lady Lazarus will "eat men like air" (247). Plath knows this is an anticlimactic finale that sounds less like a threat than a resigned admission of powerlessness. Lady Lazarus's identification with fascism and fascist rhetoric must come off as ineffective because this is the language that Plath now closely identifies with Hughes and Nietzsche—the kind of language she must renounce if she is to break free of Hughes's influence. As Alicia Ostriker writes, Lady Lazarus's "incantation is hollow. She is impersonating a female Phoenix-fiend like a woman wearing a Halloween costume... She is powerless, she knows it, she hates it. The reader may fear, but must also pity" (1989: 102). Plath ultimately pities both the aerialist and Lady Lazarus, both the female female impersonator and the female male impersonator, for neither will triumph over the male antagonists who strive to keep the female poet in her place. Plath knows that both personas—abjection and violence—are male creations, male opuses that are perversions of woman. She likely would have agreed with Freud's observations in "Totem and Taboo": "It might be maintained that a case of hysteria is a caricature of a work of art, that an obsessional neurosis is a caricature of a religion and that a paranoic delusion is a caricature of a philosophical system" (12).

"DADDY"

No other poem in the Plath canon has inspired as much critical venom as "Daddy," which many accuse of trespassing upon the memory of Holocaust victims. The poem was published in 1965's *Ariel*, in the midst of George Steiner's and Elie Wiesel's injunctions against literary representation of the Holocaust. Yet when Steiner reviewed the collection in 1965, he was impressed enough with "Daddy" to call it "one of the very few poems I know of in any language to come near the last horror.... It is the 'Guernica' of modern poetry" (1970: 301). Yet even as Steiner celebrated the poem's artistry, he also wondered whether a poet commits "a subtle larceny when he invokes the echoes and trappings of Auschwitz and appropriates an enormity of ready emotion to his own private design" (301). Steiner later expanded upon these concerns in a second essay on Plath, "In Extremis," published four years after "Dying is an Art," in which he famously questioned whether "any human being other than an actual survivor, [has] the right to put on this death-rig" (1970: 305).

Steiner's aggrieved review of Plath in 1969 has framed the literary-critical reception of "Daddy" and "Lady Lazarus" ever since. Critics hostile to confessional poetry, such as Harold Bloom, found in Steiner's review a justification for their own low estimation of Plath's work. For Bloom, the outcry over "Daddy" provided evidence that confessional poetry was not only aesthetically unsound, but morally so; he wrote that Plath's use of Holocaust imagery was "gratuitous and humanly offensive... [just] coercive rhetoric, transforming absolutely nothing" (1989: 3). Irving Howe echoed Bloom in his estimation of "Daddy," claiming that "There is something monstrous, utterly disproportionate, when tangled emotions about one's father are deliberately compared with the historical fate of European Jews. 'Daddy' persuades one again, through the force of negative example, of how accurate T. S. Eliot was in saying, 'The more perfect the artist, the more completely separate in him will be the man who suffers and the mind which creates'" (12). Note how quickly Howe slides from moral to aesthetic outrage here—Plath's offensive use of the Holocaust as a personal metaphor becomes a reason to disparage all confessional poetry. As Rose has shown, many critics hostile to Plath move quickly from "confessional" to "hysterical" to "feminine" to "immoral."[19] The personal, moral, and aesthetic all become intertwined as Plath's alleged lack of form becomes cause for speculation about her hysteria, self-absorption, and self-aggrandizement in "Lady Lazarus" and "Daddy." Even Seamus Heaney—generally an admirer of Plath and an advocate of poetry's moral efficacy—has written that "Daddy" is "so entangled in biographical circumstances and rampages so permissively in the history of other people's sorrows that it simply withdraws its rights to our sympathy" (1988: 165).[20]

I want to counter the idea that in "Daddy" Plath selfishly appropriates the victimhood of those who died in the Holocaust and instead focus on Plath's revision of what she now understood as Hughes's "predatory" aesthetic—that is, the interest in "positive violence" that compelled him to compare his hawk in "Hawk Roosting" to "Hitler's familiar spirit" (Faas 1980: 199).[21] Robin Peel, Al Strangeways, and Al Alvarez have persuasively argued that the Eichmann trial and the Cold War crisis led Plath to fuse the dual discourses of Nazism and nuclear apocalypse in "Daddy" and "Lady Lazarus."[22] Gary Leonard notes that Alvarez, who was close to Plath at this time, visited Auschwitz twice in 1962 and wrote of his experiences there that same year in *The Atlantic Monthly*.[23] Leonard

[19] For Helen Vendler, "Lady Lazarus" and "Daddy" "willfully refuse, for the sake of a cacophony of styles (a tantrum of style), the steady, centripetal effect of thought. Instead, they display a wild dispersal, a centrifugal spin to further and further reaches of outrage" (11).

[20] Of course, "Daddy" has been defended by many critics such as Susan Gubar, Jacqueline Rose, Tim Kendall, Susan Van Dyne, Lynda Bundtzen, Al Strangeways, Christina Britzolakis, Gary Leonard, and Steven Axelrod, who all share a sense that the poem is politically engaged rather than self-absorbed. Most read "Daddy" as a performance of "the female poet's anxiety of authorship" (Axelrod 52). As Gubar put it, "The daughter confronts a symbolic order in which the relationship between the fragile 'ich' and the overpowering national and linguistic authority of Daddy frustrates any autonomous self-definition" (196).

[21] Heather Cam has also pointed to the influence of Anne Sexton's "My Friend, My Friend" on "Daddy."

[22] Alvarez had earlier drawn a parallel between the victims of genocide and the (impending) victimhood of the entire postwar generation, writing, "one of the reasons why the camps continue to keep such a tight hold on our imaginations is that we see in them a small-scale trial run for a nuclear war" (1964: 65–6).

[23] In the article, Alvarez criticized the sentimental commodification of the Holocaust inspired by the Eichmann trial, and pointed out the folly of believing the camps were simply "playgrounds for

believes that Plath discussed the camps at length with Alvarez. Also, as others have noted, representations of the Holocaust were infiltrating popular culture in the late fifties and early sixties: *The Diary of Anne Frank* was released in 1959, followed by *Exodus* in 1960, and *Judgment at Nuremberg* in 1961. Wiesel's *Night* was also published to international acclaim in 1960. And, as Mazzaro has noted, Plath "could not have missed the . . . 'sensational' capture of Eichmann in Argentina in June of 1960. At least three books on the capture and the life of the former Nazi were issued in 1961 from British publishers along with an account by Rudolf Hoess of his activities at Auschwitz" (219). Thus, by 1962, in the wake of these events, Plath had political as well as personal reasons for refuting Hughes's fascination with "positive violence," as well as his general feeling that "the highest human inspiration [is] to be predatory" (Kendall 2005: 97).

While "Daddy" seems to celebrate Nietzschean rhetoric of self-affirmation, Plath in fact rejects such rhetoric by condemning her Nietzschean father, husband, and even former self in the poem. She does so by engaging in a dialogue with T. S. Eliot, whose poetry of abjection, suffering, and humility may have seemed a suitable counter to Hughes's, Nietzsche's, and Lawrence's poetics of assertion. She perhaps arrived at this idea early on at Cambridge, where, Alvarez noted, Leavis had taught that "D. H. Lawrence and T. S. Eliot represent the two warring and unreconcilable poles of modern literature" (1962; 1966: 32). (Eliot had, in fact, attacked Lawrence in *After Strange Gods*.) Despite Plath's increasingly ambivalent attitude towards male modernism, which Christina Britzolakis has charted, Eliot's mournful, elegiac vision of post-Great War Europe in "The Waste Land" must have resonated with Plath at a time when the West was once again on the brink of collapse, just as Eliot's allusions and evasions offered a more appropriate discourse than the rhetoric of strength and violence that Plath, in her anger, now associated with Hughes, Nietzsche, the Nazis, and Cold War politicians.[24] Thus, in "Daddy," the poet retreats from the poetics of violence as the doomed speaker embraces them.[25]

Like the neurotic, paranoid wife in Part II of "The Waste Land," Daddy's stuttering daughter is an allegory for a morally bankrupt, postwar Western society "Scraped flat by the roller | Of wars, wars, wars" (*CPP* 222). "Daddy" laments this new waste land—characterized, like Eliot's, by false prophets ("my Taroc pack"); an outworn religion ("a bag full of God," "I used to pray to

sadists who in another society would have been locked away . . . an aberration best forgotten" (qtd. in Leonard 130).

[24] Britzolakis has called attention to the dialogue between "Lady Lazarus" and "The Love Song of J. Alfred Prufrock," which she sees as a parodic revision of oblique and evasive male modernist discourse: where Prufrock hesitates, Lady Lazarus "tells all" (152).

[25] This reading accords with Britzolakis's view that "Although 'Daddy' seems flagrantly to violate the Eliotic doctrine of 'impersonality' . . . it can equally be seen as pushing it to an unholy extreme: the truly original poet who is in touch with tradition expresses 'the mind of Europe' not merely in its cultural glories but also in its deepest disgrace" (190).

recover you"); images of war and industrialization ("barb wire snare," "Luft-waffe," "Panzer-man," "An engine, an engine | Chuffing me off like a Jew"); nostalgic memories of pre-war Europe ("The snows of the Tyrol, the clear beer of Vienna"); an inability to communicate ("I could hardly speak," "I could never talk to you"); different polyphonic registers ("I began to talk like a Jew"); the use of German ("Ach, du"); the juxtaposition of different discourses ("Barely daring to breathe or Achoo"); shifting identities ("I think I may well be a Jew"); allusions to the restorative powers of water ("In the waters off beautiful Nauset"); references to suicide ("At twenty I tried to die"); images of bones and corpses ("I thought even the bones would do"); the Gothic ("The vampire who said he was you"); repetition and verbal tics ("You do not do, you do not do"); the ironic use of apostrophe ("O You") and nursery rhymes (*CPP* 222–4). Most import-antly, however, both poems bemoan, in their allusions to dysfunctional marriages and sexual relationships, the degenerative states of their respective societies. Yet Plath pushes this trope to its extreme: there is absolutely no chance for regeneration in "Daddy." Neither the murdered Jews nor the speaker, who has killed her husband, will bear children. And, as several critics have suggested, it appears as if the speaker herself wills her own death at the end of the poem in the line, "I'm through." Whereas the end of "The Waste Land" suggests the hopeful possibility that the land will be set in order, no such hope exists in "Daddy," which ends not with an invocation of peace, but a murder that alludes, in its images of hateful villagers and torture, to a pogrom. Such imagery suggests that the age of mass-murder will continue unabated: Plath's speaker is trapped in a new hell, one that recalls Eliot's "rats' alley | Where the dead men lost their bones" (57).

   Yet Plath was not only engaging in a counter-revision of Hughes through Eliot. She also borrowed from her husband's work as she assembled her case against his aesthetic. Van Dyne, Bundtzen, and Middlebrook have all pointed out that "Daddy" was written on the back of Hughes's play "The Calm", an "absurd existential" (Bundtzen 78) revision of Shakespeare's *The Tempest*. Yet Hughes's war poem "Out" has remained an overlooked source for Plath's most controversial work.[26] Hughes recorded "Out" on the BBC in July 1962, a month before he left Court Green.[27] (Hughes had begun his affair with Assia Wevill in June.) Middlebrook says the poem was part of the cache of Hughes's work that Plath angrily swiped from Court Green that September while he was traveling with Assia (2003: 219); however, the words "BBC" and "Observer" appear in Plath's handwriting on the left-hand corner of a draft at Emory.[28] This suggests Plath had sent the poem out to these venues before Hughes left Court

[26] "A Secret," "The Applicant," "Eavesdropper," "Medusa," "The Jailer," "Lesbos," "Lyo-nesse," and "Amnesiac" were also written on the back of *The Calm*. See Bundtzen's *The Other Ariel*, 78–82, for a detailed discussion of the ways in which Plath may have incorporated elements of *The Calm* into "The Jailer," "Amnesiac," "A Secret," and "Lyonesse."
[27] "Out" was collected in *Wodwo*.   [28] Ted Hughes, "Out," Box 60, MSS 644, Emory.

Green. Regardless, Plath borrowed extensively from "Out"; in her anger towards Hughes that autumn (both "Daddy" and "Lady Lazarus" were written in October 1962), she mockingly revised his work.[29]

In "Out," Hughes presents a father in a state of continual but ineffectual recovery from "the four-year mastication by gunfire and mud" that was the Great War. The son is the father's "luckless double, | His memory's buried, immovable anchor, | Among jawbones and blown-off boots, tree-stumps, shellcases | and craters" (*CPH* 165). In the second part of the poem, as Tim Kendall notes, Hughes is "rewriting Christian resurrection" (2005: 101) in his evocation of a dead soldier emerging, Lazarus-like, from a cave as "a baby." But while Kendall finds in this section "release . . . for the war-dead" (101), there are several disturbing images and stylistic devices which belie such release—images and rhythms Plath would incorporate into "Daddy": "The lulling of blood in | Their ears, their ears, their ears, their eyes | Are only drops of water and even the dead man suddenly | Sits up and sneezes—Atishoo!" (*CPH* 165–6). The "reborn" infantryman finally emerges from his cave "with the eyes | Of an exhausted clerk" (166)—hardly a triumphant resurrection. In the poem's final section, "Remembrance Day," Hughes uses the image of paper poppies, which Plath will later borrow, to again undermine the idea of resurrection. For Hughes, the artificial poppies do not stand for national mourning and healing but the senselessness of state-sanctioned slaughter. Hughes sees the poppies as a kind of "opium of the people," "Today whoring everywhere," that mitigate the rage and sadness of those left behind—feelings, in his mind, that should never be tamed or nullified. "It is years since I wore one," the speaker declares. "So goodbye to that bloody-minded flower. || You dead bury your dead" (166).

Stylistically, there are several obvious connections between this poem and "Daddy." Hughes's soldier sneezes "Atishoo!" while the speaker of "Daddy" can hardly "breathe or Achoo" (*CPP* 222); and Hughes's "their ears, their ears, their ears, their eyes" makes use of the repetitive tic that critics will come to associate with Plath.[30] Hughes writes that the war held his speaker's "juvenile neck bowed to the dunkings of the Atlantic," while Plath describes Daddy as having a "head in the freakish Atlantic" (*CPP* 222). Plath will also use imagery of rebirth and resurrection in "Lady Lazarus," though she will do so ironically.

The poems are connected in thematic ways as well. Both "Out" and "Daddy" deal with a child's relationship to a distant soldier-father who has somehow alienated or disappointed that child. The speakers of both poems are their fathers' "luckless doubles" (*CPH* 165)—inheritors of their psychic wounds,

---

[29] While Middlebrook comments briefly upon the influence of Hughes's "The Road to Easington" on Plath's "The Bee Meeting" (219), she does not mention the allusions to "Out" in both "Daddy" and "Lady Lazarus."

[30] In "Daddy" alone she gives us "You do not do, you do not do," "wars, wars, wars," "Ich, ich, ich, ich," "And my Taroc pack and my Taroc pack," "Panzer-man, panzer-man," "the brute | Brute heart of a brute like you," "get back, back, back to you," and "I do, I do" (*CPP* 222–4).

victims of their fathers' wars. Both poems declare a renunciation. Hughes's speaker says "goodbye" to the empty, hypocritical rituals of remembrance, and in the process attempts to clear his own mind of the war's debris. In effect, he seeks relief from his father's (and his father's war's) hold upon him. Plath exaggerates themes and language she finds in "Out" in order to say goodbye, or rather good riddance, to fatherly oppression in "Daddy." The two poems arise from similar, angry impulses to assert their speakers' independence from a silenced or silencing father and bankrupt state elders who demand filial loyalty and sacrifice. Neither will collude in false pieties; instead, both will speak out, in their different ways, against the forces anchoring them to the sins of the father. Both have found themselves inhabiting nightmare worlds where, as Hughes put it, "the sun has abandoned, and where nobody | Can ever again move from shelter" (*CPH* 165). For Plath, the swastika is "So black no sky could squeak through" (*CPP* 223). Just as Hughes's speaker refuses to wear the poppy, Daddy's daughter will no longer *be* the metaphorical poppy, "a canvas-beauty puppet on a wire" who has been symbolically "whoring" (*CPH* 166) herself to father, husband, and state—all of whom have reduced her to propaganda.[31] As so often happens in Plath's poetic responses to Hughes, her words are stronger, louder, more self-consciously vulgar (and perhaps American) than Hughes's restrained voice: where Hughes writes with Gravesian eloquence, "Goodbye to all the remaindered charms of my father's survival" (166), Plath ends simply with the famous "Daddy, daddy, you bastard, I'm through" (224). "Daddy" mocks the genteel pieties of "Out," replacing them with an angrier and less reverent criticism of the father. Where Hughes rejects the hypocrisy of a government that creates a national day of mourning to honor the millions it carelessly sent to death, Plath blasts the bloodthirsty appetites of the entire patriarchy—father, husband, and commanders-in-chief. As usual, Plath one-ups Hughes by taking elements of his own work and grossly distorting (or "impersonating") them, giving Hughes an exaggerated reflection of the world, and world-order, he has presented.

Although the tone of "Daddy" bears some resemblance to that of Plath's earlier "Soliloquy of the Solipsist" and "The Shrike," "Daddy" differs in its refusal to sanction the supremacy of the "monstrous 'I'" that characterized several of Hughes's poems—particularly "Hawk Roosting," which Uroff sees as a major influence on "Daddy" (158–9). Daddy's daughter is ultimately defeated by her own hatred, rage, and lust for vengeance, none of which will bring her any closer to wholeness. Plath wants to show us that Nazism is *not* natural; Daddy's daughter clearly makes the wrong decision when she takes on the guise of a predator and ultimately chooses to endorse the cycle of violence—both personal and historic—that she initially sought to escape. "Daddy" offers a revision of what happens when man takes on the cold predatory gaze of Hughes's

---

[31] As Middlebrook has noted, Plath's negative treatment of poppies in "Poppies in July" and "Poppies in October" both allude to Hughes's poppies in "Out" (2003: 219).

hawk: not triumph, but defeat. In order to "disarm the enemy," as in "Lady Lazarus," she must impersonate him; ultimately the speaker and Daddy switch places at the end of the poem, when Daddy himself becomes the metaphorical Jew tortured for fun by "the villagers" as she, now in the place of the Nazi, passively watches the gruesome spectacle. Plath suggests that the speaker's Laingian transformation was not redemptive, for there is no hint here of legitimate rebirth in the exhausted "I'm through" but rather a deep resignation—or even death. The ridiculousness of Daddy's daughter's predatory inspiration reveals the futility, rather than the beauty, of the fascist or "sadist" imagination that Plath, in her rage, now associated with Hughes.[32] And yet, the poem is much too tied to Hughes to allow Plath to "break" from his influence. Plath achieves nothing here that will allow her to escape Daddy's black shoe. Instead of retreating from "the enemy," she attacks, tangling her words and life further with the very force from which she seeks to disengage.

Despite Plath's renunciation of Hughes's aesthetic of violence in "Daddy" and "Lady Lazarus," her own interest in violence, coupled with her feelings of betrayal at the hands of her husband and father, make it hard to believe that she condemned her speakers absolutely. In "Stone Boy with Dolphin" (1957/8), a story based on Plath's first meeting with Hughes, Dody Ventura burns to "walk into *Phèdre* and put on that red cloak of doom. Let me leave my mark" (*JP* 299). She later fantasizes about the rewards of martyrdom:

I will bear pain, she testified to the air . . . Through suffering, wisdom. In her third-floor attic room she listened, catching the pitch of last shrieks; listened: to witches on the rack, to Joan of Arc crackling at the stake, to anonymous ladies flaring like torches in the rending metal of Riviera roadsters, to Zelda enlightened, burning behind the bars of her madness. What visions were to be had came under thumbscrews, not in the mortal comfort of a hot-water-bottle-cosy cot. Unwincing, in her mind's eye, she bared her flesh. Here, strike home. (*JP* 299)

While Plath treats her youthful fascination with dangerous women (and men) ironically in "Daddy" and "Lady Lazarus," Dody's earlier musings suggest that Plath's "act" in her later poems may not be *all* performance. But Plath cannot have it both ways. It is only when she shifts from an examination of the aesthetic of violence and interrogates instead the act of writing in "Ariel" that she is able to distance herself from Hughes's imagined gaze.

---

[32] Sylvia Plath to Aurelia Plath, October 18, 1962, Lilly. Plath had underlined many passages regarding sadism in Erich Fromm's *The Art of Loving*, which was apparently found on her bedside table the morning after her suicide. Consider one of the many passages on this topic that Plath underlined: "The active form of symbiotic fusion is domination or, to use the psychological term corresponding to masochism, sadism. . . . He inflates and enhances himself by incorporating another person, who worships him. . . . The sadistic person is as dependent on the submissive person as the latter is on the former; neither can live without the other. The difference is only that the sadistic person commands, exploits, hurts, humiliates, and that the masochistic person is commanded, exploited, hurt, humiliated" (20). (Plath's copy of this book is at Emory.)

7

Tracking the Thought-Fox

In "Daddy" and "Lady Lazarus," Plath had attempted to wrest control of her dialogue with Hughes by mocking his adulation of "positive violence" and "impersonating" his femme fatales. Although she was attempting to criticize Hughes's use of the masculine sublime, Plath's fantasies of fascism elicited critical outrage for the very same reason Hughes's "Hawk Roosting" had: in the eyes of many, the two poets had adopted ambiguous moral stances toward their murderous speakers. Yet there were other, more personal reasons why these poems did not allow Plath to "break" from Hughes. Plath rooted her versions of transcendence in a debilitating anger by parodying what she perceived as her husband's aesthetic; when her speakers take on the personas of the vengeful White Goddess, they do so to showcase the absurdity, rather than the triumph, of that feminine guise. It was only when Plath abandoned her metaphors of murder and focused instead on the act of writing in "Ariel" that she was able to forge a truly triumphant poetic voice—one that did not drive her deeper into Daddy's black shoe, as "Daddy" and "Lady Lazarus" had, but allowed her to emerge from "stasis in darkness." Although she continued to borrow words and imagery from Hughes in order to "answer back" to him, she now did so in order to put forth an active version of feminine creation, and to declare that her poems were "indefatigable hoof-taps" (*CPP* 270) as opposed to Hughes's "neat prints" (*CPH* 21). Yet the momentum of "Ariel" could not sustain itself. Some of Plath's late poems, particularly "Sheep in Fog," "Words," and "Edge," look back to Hughes's poems with longing, resignation, and sadness. As Plath's depression worsened, her resentment towards her husband and poetic rival, which had earlier fueled her rage, became a measure of defeat. Plath writes of her perceived failure to achieve the poetic end she desired as her literary landscape turns "Starless and fatherless, a dark water" (*CPP* 262).

"ARIEL" IN DIALOGUE

Susan Van Dyne, Lynda Bundtzen, and Neil Roberts have all commented upon the relationship between Plath's "Burning the Letters" (1962) and Hughes's early poem "The Thought-Fox," generally agreeing that Plath is "throwing down the gauntlet" in a contest over whether Hughes's "impersonal" lines or

her "cri de coeur" (Bundtzen 2001: 54–5) will stand the test of time.[1] This
interpretation rests on the fact that Plath wrote "Burning the Letters"—a poem
based upon her burning of Hughes's papers after she learned of his affair with
Assia Wevill—on the other side of Hughes's "The Thought-Fox." Van Dyne
speculates that this was no accident (1993: 38), that Plath's image of dogs
"tearing a fox" to death (*CPP* 205) was a rebuttal of Hughes's feelings about
"The Thought-Fox," which he made public during a 1961 BBC broadcast:

Long after I am gone, as long as a copy of the poem exists, every time anyone reads it the
fox will get up somewhere out in the darkness and come walking towards them.... It will
live forever.... And I made it. And all through imagining it clearly enough and finding
the living words.   ("Capturing Animals," 20–1)

Hughes here draws upon Robert Graves, who wrote in *The White Goddess* that
"True poetic practice implies a mind so miraculously attuned and illuminated
that it can form words ... into a living entity—a poem that goes about on its own
(for centuries after the author's death, perhaps) affecting readers with its stored
magic" (490). Plath may have been mocking Hughes's arrogance when she called
her dying fox's cry "immortal" (*CPP* 205).

By the time Plath wrote "Burning the Letters" in August 1962, "The
Thought-Fox" had become Hughes's most famous poem. It was first published
in the *New Yorker* in August 1957 (ten months before Plath's first *New Yorker*
acceptance), and received the 1958 Guinness Award, a substantial cash prize
awarded annually to the best poem published in Britain. "The Thought-Fox"
established Hughes's reputation as an animal poet who tracked his creatures
through his poems with the surefooted instinct of a hunter. It makes sense, then,
that in a poem about the destruction of her husband's "letters," ("here is an end
to the writing" (*CPP* 204)), Plath would choose to respond or "talk back" to the
poem that Hughes held most dear, and that was most emblematic of his poetic
persona.

Plath's tussle with Hughes's "The Thought-Fox" in "Burning the Letters"
suggests that she was particularly preoccupied with her husband's poem and its
self-assured version of (male) creation. It comes as little surprise, then, that Plath
decided to re-engage in her debate with "The Thought-Fox" two months later in
"Ariel," the poem that has come to represent her struggle to achieve independ-
ence from her "fathers"—Otto Plath, Ted Hughes, and the male modernist
tradition—out of whose shadow she struggled to emerge.

Plath wrote "Ariel" on her thirtieth birthday, October 27, 1962, about two
months after Hughes left Court Green. This date must have represented the
end of an old life and the beginning of something quite new. Plath knew that

---

[1] Van Dyne writes that Plath's poem "defies Hughes's visionary equation of his own poetic
genius with the mysterious powers of nature" (1993: 41) while Roberts claims that Plath finds
"something troubling about ... [Hughes's] confidence that the poem is immortal" (2003: 167).

her first real poetic "breakthrough" had occurred three years earlier, on her twenty-seventh birthday, while she and Hughes were guests at Yaddo. There, she had written the seven-part "Poem for a Birthday," which recounted a troubled woman's recovery from mental illness. Plath had been suffering from writer's block in the weeks preceding that birthday, and had turned to Hughes, as she often did, for help; after he set her breathing and concentration exercises, she wrote two poems that pleased her (*J* 518). It is likely Hughes prompted Plath to come up with the ideas for "Poem for a Birthday" several days later; a paper in his archive lists ideas for the sequence in both poets' handwriting, suggesting that they brainstormed together.[2] When Plath finished the sequence, she knew she had hit a new note, and confided to her journal that the poems had freed her (521). After Plath's death, Hughes would claim that the emergence of her "real" or "reborn" self dated from "Poem for a Birthday" (*WP* 467).

Thus on her thirtieth birthday, Plath may have remembered her earlier "breakthrough" and Hughes's role in prompting it. One can easily imagine Plath, in her angry and prideful state of mind that autumn, determined to write another successful birthday poem—this time, without Hughes's help. It is possible, then, that Plath had a motive in writing "Ariel"—that before she set pen to paper, Hughes was in the back of her mind, together with her "Poem for a Birthday" and its theme of rebirth. Plath, who always strove to outdo her past achievements, may have willed herself that day to write a poem that would record and sanctify the emergence of her truest self yet—the self that needed nobody, not even her husband or her children. Such a poem, if good enough, would confirm that Hughes's abandonment had freed her to become an even more powerful poet.

Plath's "arrow" in "Ariel," as Van Dyne has noted (1993: 123), is an inversion of the same image mentioned in both *The Bell Jar* and the *Journals*, in which man is the arrow, woman the bow.[3] In "Ariel," the female speaker becomes the arrow, ignoring her "child's cry" in her single-minded pursuit of transcendence. Yet "Ariel" is less concerned with "the fiery transubstantiation of the female subject," as Van Dyne has suggested (1993: 119), than it is with the act of writing itself. During this time, Plath woke around 4 a.m., after her sleeping pills wore off, and wrote until her two children awoke, usually around dawn. "Ariel" is a record of those inspired hours when she was suddenly able to write the poems that, as she told her mother, would make her name (*LH* 468). Plath's positioning of her speaker in a quiet room, presumably a study, sitting before a window as the sun rises and her child wakes suggests that the poem is a comment upon the

[2] Box 138, MSS 644, Emory.

[3] Plath may also be alluding to one of Hughes's early reviews, quoted earlier, in which the reviewer referred to Hughes's poems "as direct as an arrow from a bow" (Seymour: 1958).

imaginative ascent engendered by poetic inspiration: the speaker's journey upon
Ariel parallels Plath's creation of the poem itself.

Much of the critical commentary on "Ariel" emphasizes its "hurtling velocity"
(Van Dyne 1993: 120), and seems to insist that the poem somehow wrote itself:
that Plath is, in the words of Tim Kendall, "an oracular poet writing as if taking
dictation" (2001: 206). Yet there is reason to believe that Plath's composition
was as considered as it was inspired. Plath's friends reported that Ariel, the horse
Plath rode at her local riding stable, was a far cry from the svelte mare in
the poem (Middlebrook 2003: 192); Anne Stevenson went so far as to call the
horse "elderly" (272). Nor was Plath herself an experienced rider—according to
Kate Moses, who interviewed Plath's riding teacher, she was not skilled enough
to gallop in October of 1962 (Middlebrook 2003: 327). Most likely, then, Plath
invented, rather than recalled, her wild ride upon Ariel.

What she may have in fact recalled as she sat down to compose was Hughes's
"Phaetons," published five years before "Ariel" in 1957:

> Angrier, angrier, suddenly the near-madman
> In mid-vehemence rolls back his eye
> And lurches to his feet—
>
> Under each sense the other four hurtle and thunder
> Under the skull's front the horses of the sun
>
> The gentle reader in his silent room
> Loses the words in mid-sentence—
>
> The world has burned away beneath his book
> A tossing upside-down team drags him on fire
> Among the monsters of the zodiac.   (*CPH* 33)

Plath had observed this poem's gestation over the course of at least one draft: an
early typescript of "Phaetons," entitled "The Horses of the Sun," shows editorial
suggestions in Plath's handwriting.[4] (Plath most likely typed the poem, as
Hughes never typed his own work.) Hughes's poem, like Plath's, draws upon
the myth of Phaethon, mentioned (among other places) in Plato's *Timaeus*. In
the story, Phaethon asks his mother about the identity of his father and discovers,
to his amazement, that he is the son of the sun-god, Helios. Doubtful about his
legitimacy, he immediately sets out to find Helios and question him face to face.
When Helios reassures him that they are, in fact, father and son, Phaethon
demands further proof, and asks if he may ride Helios's sun-chariot through the
heavens. Helios, in a moment of indulgence, agrees, but quickly realizes that
Phaethon is not strong enough to control the powerful sun-horses who draw the
chariot. He asks Phaethon not to go, but when Phaethon refuses, Helios implores
him to take the middle path through the heavens so as not to plunge the earth
into fire or ice. Phaethon takes off and discovers too late that his father was right;

---

⁴ Ted Hughes, Notebook 2, MSS 644, Emory.

he is not strong enough to control the chariot. The horses veer from the middle path, scorching the earth with fire when they ride too low, freezing the land and ocean when they ride too high. A distressed Zeus looks on and decides he must put an end to the catastrophic ride, and so he destroys the chariot, and Phaethon, with a thunderbolt.

Stylistically, "Ariel" and "Phaetons" are quite different, although both build momentum, and halt that momentum when necessary, through the use of dashes. But Plath is most interested in responding to the Phaethon story itself, or at least to Hughes's version of it. Hughes's poem is about a reader who is so engrossed in the story of Phaethon's wild ride that he imagines himself being dragged into another realm by the powerful sun-horses. In "Ariel," however, Plath's speaker *is* Phaethon. This speaker could not be more different than Hughes's "gentle" reader. She is in control of her own words, while Hughes's reader is swept away by someone else's. Plath's speaker focuses so intently on her journey that she ignores her child's cry; Hughes's reader, on the other hand, distractedly loses his words "in mid-sentence." Although both are transformed by the poem's end, the transformations are very different: Hughes's speaker becomes disoriented and loses his grip on reality, while Plath's harnesses the energy of her imaginary sun-horse and uses that energy to propel her to the poem's conclusive end. Whereas Hughes's speaker resembles a victim, Plath's is more like a predator; where he is passive, she is active.

Plath may have chosen to echo Hughes's poem, and the Phaethon myth, in "Ariel" because Phaethon's story touches upon ideas of authority, legitimacy, rebellion, and hubris that interested her at this time. Phaethon takes the sun-chariot because he needs to prove to himself that he is indeed his father's son, and thus capable of steering the wild horses; however, he rebels from his father's authority when he refuses to acknowledge that he is too weak to control the chariot. Plath plays with this idea in "Ariel," fashioning herself as the rebellious and unruly daughter determined to show off her poetic skill to her literary fathers, including Ted Hughes. Yet, unlike Phaethon, Plath's speaker remains in control of her metaphorical sun-horse even up to the moment of annihilation; importantly for Plath, that moment is "suicidal"— willed rather than ordained. She has, in fact, outwitted Zeus's thunderbolt. It seems as if Plath's speaker delights in veering from the middle path here, that she means to provoke her poetic fathers by writing poetry that embraces extremity rather than moderation.

Plath also looked back, in "Ariel," to Hughes's "Constancy," written in 1957 or 1958 but never collected.[5] "Constancy" itself bears some similarity to "Phae-tons," which suggests that Hughes was still preoccupied with the ideas of

---

[5] A draft of "Constancy," along with "Crow Hill," can be found in a 1958 letter from Ted Hughes to Olwyn Hughes, MSS 980, Box 1, ff 7, Emory.

freedom, transcendence, speed, and weightlessness that marked Phaethon's jour-
ney. These ideas propel "Constancy," like "Ariel," forward:

> The rivers are flowing, the air moving,
> The landmark mountains are lasting: this persisting
> Pig-headedness of the earth is not resisting
> Time, but a rider astride it arriving.
>
> The cloud of the mind climbs, declines,
> The flowing of rivers a stay to its going,
> The caress and press of the air sole knowing
> Of its own being, and the mountain stones
>
> Buttress awhile the cloud of the mind
> As it leans to them. Braced against object
> Body claims permanence like a muscle locked,
> Never doubts that grip on ground;
>
> But the mind's cloud is a coming and going
> Of airs and dews that shape it and colour
> And dusts floating, and for all its mountain pillow
> Cannot affirm hardier being.
>
> On every instant the earth arrives...
> Wide the feet brace, strong, as the hands
> Haul against that massive careerer, but the mind's
> Clouds are under its hooves.   (*CPH* 54)

Plath may have borrowed images of moving air, the rider and horse, hilly
landscape, and even similar vocabulary ("dew," "haul") from Hughes when
she wrote "Ariel," but her point is very different. In "Constancy," Hughes
compares the physical (mountains, rivers, the earth) to the metaphysical ("the
cloud of the mind") and finds that the mind, while sure of its superiority,
"Cannot affirm hardier being" (54) than nature. Hughes allows little doubt
that the "mountain stones" will endure long after the mind's cloud has evapor-
ated: the earth is the one constant that the mind must lean upon for strength.

Plath's poem is more ontologically and stylistically confident than "Con-
stancy," eschewing Hughes's long lines for shorter ones, replacing his slow,
ponderous rhythms ("The rivers are flowing, the air moving, | The landmark
mountains are lasting") with two- and three-word lines that mock the steady beat
of "Constancy" and the theme of constancy itself. In "Ariel," the mind at full
gallop rushes past the solid elements as it pursues its goal—the creation of the
poem. Ariel's rider feels no need to look to the earth for support or reassurance, as
the mind does in "Constancy." The one "constancy" for Plath is the supremacy
of the imagination in the moment of creation; no elements or physical obstruc-
tions will hinder her rider. Plath rejects Hughes's masculinized landscape of
mountain and stone, which serves as "a stay" to the mind's "going," and replaces
it with the more feminine landscape of "tor" and "furrow," the latter a "sister" to
the speaker's equine vehicle of escape. Nothing in this landscape holds the

speaker back from her transformative journey deeper into the self, from "stasis" (or "constancy") into motion. Where Hughes stresses the need for the mind to remain "grounded" in the physical, Plath instead celebrates the mind's deliverance from its earthly encumbrances. Again, Plath strives to present a more confident, less passive version of Hughes's work: while Hughes's "body" may lean on rock, river, and stone in order to establish its "grip on ground" (54), Plath's speaker has no need of such support—she has the ability to change shape at will, to "unpeel" and "melt" into sea and dew. In "Constancy," the air and "dew" are what "shape" and "colour" the mind, but in "Ariel," the mind *becomes* the dew, simply through a force of will. Plath seems to embrace the glorious recklessness of the Phaethon figure in the moment before his fall, where Hughes finds, instead, a warning about man's arrogance and hubris. Again, Plath mocks Hughes's equivocation and asserts her own strength and daring.

The most significant Hughes poem with which "Ariel" engages in dialogue, however, is "The Thought-Fox." "Ariel" borrows heavily from this poem, which suggests that Plath is answering back to her husband, as she did in "Burning the Letters." Although Plath wrote "Ariel" quickly, there is no doubt she thought carefully about its construction. As Van Dyne points out, there are three handwritten drafts in the Smith archive; in the first draft most of the poem is written out in full sentences, but by the third, Plath has cut the lines in half (1993: 126). As in "Burning the Letters," Plath skillfully manipulates poetic technique, methodically constructing her lines to achieve the desired effect of speed. It is through this effect, says Van Dyne, that Plath "progressively obliterates the distance and difference between the speaker and the animal energy of her horse" (1993: 119). Such "animal energy," as Plath well knew, was what characterized Hughes's greatest poems: in "The Thought-Fox," "The Jaguar," "Hawk Roosting," and "Thrushes," Hughes strove to use language that would reveal how animals are "Triggered to stirrings beyond sense" (*CPH* 82). In his poems, animal instincts are heightened by the sense that the poet, too, is acting upon instinct as he writes. This is how Hughes described the writing process in "Capturing Animals": "The special kind of excitement, the slightly mesmerized and quite involuntary concentration with which you make out the stirrings of a new poem in your mind.... This is hunting and the poem is a new species of creature, a new specimen of the life outside your own" (*WP* 12). This idea is the basis of "The Thought-Fox," in which the poet is led through the poem by the animal he tracks. Plath employed this same strategy in "Ariel" when she cut her lines to produce the illusion of speed and to emphasize the fusion of animal and poet; as in "The Thought-Fox," the poet-speaker relies on the animal to guide her through the poem and ultimately lead her to its conclusion.

Reading "Ariel" alongside "The Thought-Fox" strengthens the idea that Plath's signature poem is more concerned with poetic inspiration and the act of writing than the destruction and creation of an unfettered (or ungendered) self. From the outset of both "Ariel" and "The Thought-Fox," Plath and Hughes invoke symbolic animals to guide them on their journey across the blank page. Both Plath's horse and Hughes's thought-fox become linked, throughout the course of their respective poems, to creativity. Each poem begins in darkness: Hughes's opens at "midnight moment's" (*CPH* 21) while Plath's first line is "Stasis in darkness" (*CPP* 239). Although this darkness defines a natural landscape—for Hughes a forest, for Plath "tor and distances" (239)—the poet is not actually situated in these landscapes but inside a room, where the poet-speaker is writing. Hughes makes this explicit in "The Thought-Fox," in which the speaker describes himself "Beside the clock's loneliness | And this blank page where my fingers move" (21). In "Ariel" we do not discover this detail until Plath writes of the child's cry sounding through the wall, suggesting that the speaker has been, like Hughes's, alone in the act of writing—possibly also sitting before a "blank page" watching her fingers move.

The darkness in the first line of each poem is literal: Hughes's speaker writes at midnight, Plath's just before dawn. Yet this darkness is also figurative in that it represents, for both poets, the stasis of the imagination in the moment before creation. Hughes emphasizes this idea in his second stanza, in which the star, emblematic of celestial guidance, fails to appear and provide the poet with a clear sense of direction:

> Through the window I see no star:
> Something more near
> Though deeper within darkness
> Is entering the loneliness: (*CPH* 21)

The poet must look inward rather than outward in order to find direction for his words: this vague, enigmatic force that will guide the poet on his internalized journey is described in the first stanza as "something else" and in the second stanza as "something more near." Plath uses the same words in "Ariel" to describe the mysterious force that sets her mind (as well as her body and horse) racing: "Something else || Hauls me through air—" (*CPP* 239). In both poems, the use of the word "something" refers both to poetic inspiration and to the imagined animal that leads the poet to the source of the poem deep inside the self. Both the fox and the horse, then, serve similar purposes—they represent "Something else" that allows the poets to move beyond the "midnight moment" or "Stasis in darkness" in which there is "no star" to guide them. The phrase "Something else" is noteworthy for its appropriate vagueness: it speaks to the impossibility of literally naming the force that drives the poem, and suggests that the protean nature of poetic inspiration can only be captured through metaphor. The force is a wild animal in motion, shape-shifting throughout the course of each poem (here a horse, there an arrow), eluding both reader and writer who seek to capture its essence. That Plath, like Hughes, would also choose the words "something else" to describe the force that drives her speaker's writing seems conscious rather than coincidental.

There are other ways in which Plath responds to "The Thought Fox." Like Hughes's fox, Plath's horse is "a body that is bold to come || Across clearings" (*CPH* 21). (She also resembles the wild, threatening horse that pursues the protagonist of Hughes's "The Rain Horse," yet another influence on "Ariel.") Both poems follow similar trajectories: like "The Thought Fox," which begins in a midnight forest, expands into a "widening, deepening greenness," then contracts again to a "hole of the head" (21), "Ariel" too moves from stasis to the more expansive "tor and distances" (*CPP* 239) to finally contract into the "red || Eye" (240) of the rising sun. Each poem, then, expands and contracts from beginning to end. There is the sense, in both poems, that this trajectory has given the poets the momentum to break through a barrier: for Hughes the moment occurs when the fox "enters the dark hole of the head" (*CPH* 21) while Plath's speaker aims straight into the sun. In each case, the deepest corners of the imagination are penetrated.

Both poets also play with the word "eye." In each poem, the eye stands outside the poet's domain, looking in. Hughes's speaker first imagines the "Two eyes" of the thought-fox outside his window, then later spies "an eye" again as the fox comes into his room (21). Plath's red eye, the "cauldron of morning" (240)—that is, the sun—also rises outside the writer's window. There is something almost oracular about these "eyes"—not only do they allow each speaker to "see" into the creative process, but both lead the poet toward his or her ultimate "vision." Hughes's speaker will follow the thought-fox to its end on the printed page, while Plath's finds fulfillment by aiming straight into the rising sun. In each case, the writer achieves his or her vision with the aid of an all-seeing "eye" that works in conjunction with the writer's self, that is, his or her "I." As symbols of the racing mind in the process of creation, these roving eyes stand in contrast to the "stasis in darkness" out of which each speaker struggles to emerge. It is perhaps no coincidence that both speakers position themselves before a window—another device that allows them to "see" beyond the confines of the room, and, by extension, the bounded self.

Plath's invocation of Lady Godiva may also have been a way of answering back to Hughes, since Lady Godiva's decision to ride naked on her horse through the streets of Coventry was prompted by her husband's dare. Plath may have imagined herself re-enacting this dare in "Ariel," stepping up to Hughes's poetic challenge and proving to him that in her metaphoric nakedness she is empowered rather than humiliated. This move relates to Plath's decision to "bare all" in poems such as "Lady Lazarus" and "Daddy," where she subverts the power of her interrogators and torturers by "confessing" what she has suffered under their custody. Thus, like Lady Godiva, Plath dignifies what might otherwise be understood as humiliating— discussing a botched suicide attempt, for example, in "Lady Lazarus."

Plath's galloping horse also subtly mocks Hughes's slinking fox. Horses are larger, stronger, and faster than foxes; by analogy, Plath's poem will merit the same kind of comparison to Hughes's. Hers is the "stronger" of the two, the one

with the more intensely rhythmic momentum, the more resounding final cres-
cendo. Unlike Hughes's speaker, she will not wait passively for the poem to sneak
into the mind; she will ride after it (or ride with it) as an active participant in the
creative process. Hers is the more daring of the two speakers, the one willing to
take more risks with her poetry: riding a galloping horse surely requires more
courage than tracking a fox. Whereas Hughes's fox displays what could crudely
be called female characteristics—it is timid, quiet, moves "delicately" while
setting "neat prints" on the snow (*CPH* 21)—Plath's horse, although referred
to as "God's lioness" (*CPP* 239), displays stereotypically male characteristics of
strength, agility, speed, and recklessness. When we consider that Plath's self-
identification with the shooting arrow was meant, at some level, to undermine
the docile, sexist platitudes of women like Mrs. Willard in *The Bell Jar*, and that
the speaker of "Ariel" is a working mother who ignores her child's cry in order to
finish her poem, it seems likely that the galloping, jumping mare also works to
mock the culturally imposed confines of gender. Plath's poems, as Marianne
Moore lamented, were not decorous; at any moment they could rise up, throw
the reader off, and pursue their own course. Hers were poems which could not
be tamed.

   Finally, it is likely that "Ariel" was also influenced by another Hughes poem,
"The Horses," from *The Hawk in the Rain*. Both poems begin at "the hour-
before-dawn dark" (*CPH* 22) in a formless landscape where the color of the air
and sky are indistinguishable. The mood changes when the sun rises and
Hughes's speaker sees the horses in the valley below, "steaming and glistening
under the flow of light" (23). The speaker becomes exuberant and runs toward
them, "Stumbling in the fever of a dream" (22). He has emerged out of darkness,
into the light; out of stillness into motion. This progression may have influenced
"Ariel," in which the speaker begins at a similar point of "Stasis in darkness,"
then gathers momentum as the sun rises. In both poems, the rising sun is a
catalyst for transcendence; both speakers are transformed in the moments be-
tween night and day. In "The Horses," the speaker "erupts" as the sun emerges
out of the dark—"Orange, red, red erupted" (22)—while the sunrise in "Ariel"
causes the speaker to shape-shift into weightless, ethereal substances that allow
her to ascend into "the red ‖ Eye." And needless to say, horses play a central role
in each speaker's moment of transcendence, "carrying" them from one realm to
another. Plath's horse, however, is a far cry from Hughes's horses, who "made no
sound. | Not one snorted or stamped, | Their hung heads patient as the horizons"
(22–3).[6] Where Hughes's speaker hopes he will be able to recapture the moment
("In din of the crowded streets... | May I still meet my memory in so lonely a
place" (23)), Plath's speaker *becomes* the moment. Again, where Hughes is
passive, Plath is active.

   ------

   [6] In Plath's and Hughes's copy of Ernest Jones's *On the Nightmare*, Plath had underlined "Some-
times Witches turned men into horses for the purpose of riding on them to the Sabbath" (205).

"SHEEP IN FOG," "EDGE," AND "WORDS"

Harold Bloom's understanding of the toll of rivalry between living and dead poets helps illuminate Plath's bleak psychological state during her final weeks, when she wrote "Sheep in Fog," "Edge," and "Words":

To attain a self yet more inward than the precursor's, the ephebe becomes necessarily more solipsistic. To evade the precursor's imagined glance, the ephebe seeks to confine it in scope, which perversely enlarges the glance, so that it rarely can be evaded. As the small child believes his parents can see him around corners, so the ephebe feels a magical glance attending his every movement. The desired glance is friendly or loving, but the feared glance disapproves, or renders the ephebe unworthy of the highest love, alienates him from the realms of poetry. Moving through landscapes that are mute, or of things that speak to him less often or urgently than they did to the precursor, the ephebe knows also the cost of an increasing inwardness, a greater separation from everything extensive. The loss is of reciprocity with the world, as compared to the precursor's sense of being a man to whom all things spoke.   (1973: 105–6)

The profound feeling of resignation that marks the poems reveals Plath's anxiety that Hughes would forever remain ahead of her poetically. Indeed, one of her frequent complaints to her mother in late 1962 and early 1963 was that Hughes's fame had skyrocketed while she had been left to languish in obscurity, on her own, with two babies. If "Ariel" was an attempt to forge a poetic self and a poetic method distinct from Hughes's, then "Sheep in Fog," "Edge," and "Words" suggest that the loss of the poetic "father" was not worth the wild ride upon his borrowed chariot.

   Like "Ariel," "Sheep in Fog" also describes a horse ride, but here the speaker's mood is defeatist rather than triumphant; as Kendall has written, "the hope of rebirth has disappeared, to be replaced by resignation" (2001: 190). The poem was written in December 1962, then revised in January 1963 when Plath was living in a London flat with her two young children during one of the coldest winters in Britain's history. In her letters home during this period, she speaks mainly of her mental and physical exhaustion and her constant battles against colds and flu. The letters bear no trace of the terrible rage that had marked her autumn poems; now she was calm, controlled, and very much aware of the long and lonely road ahead. In one of her last letters to Olive Prouty, she wrote:

I must just resolutely write mornings for the next years through cyclones, water freeze-ups, children's illnesses & the <u>aloneness</u>. . . . I desperately want to make an inner strength in myself, an independence that can face bringing up the children alone & in the face of great uncertainties.[7]

---

[7] Sylvia Plath to Olive Prouty, January 22, 1963, Lilly.

In these letters, Plath no longer flings insults at her estranged husband; instead, she speaks about her old love for him, calling him "beautiful," "kind," and "dear" at turns.[8] She even blames Assia Wevill for Hughes's betrayal, claiming Assia had "brutalized Ted beyond belief."[9]

These letters give a sense of Plath's state of mind when she wrote the final version of "Sheep in Fog" on January 28, 1963 (an earlier version was written the previous month). Like "Ariel," this poem presumably was inspired by an early morning ride on a horse over the North Tawton landscape. This time, however, the mood is deathly somber:

> The hills step off into whiteness.
> People or stars
> Regard me sadly, I disappoint them.   (*CPP* 262)

Plath's introduction to the poem for a BBC radio program reads, "In this poem, the speaker's horse is proceeding at a slow, cold walk down a hill of macadam to the stable at the bottom. It is December. It is foggy. In the fog there are sheep" (*CPP* 295). Her emotionless description mirrors the benumbed state of the speaker, who has lost the will to live. Plath no longer uses enjambment to create the illusion of motion; here the horse's slow walk is emphasized by at least two end-pauses in every stanza. As Kendall has noted, the exuberant repetition that characterized the earlier *Ariel* poems is gone, as are the question marks and exclamation points (2001: 192). The tone now is dull and flat. The only striking use of internal assonance and consonance comes in the last line of the poem, in which the siren song of the soft vowels in "Starless," "fatherless," "dark," and "water" (*CPP* 262) tempts the speaker ever closer to the abyss.

The tone of "Sheep in Fog" echoes the first few stanzas of Hughes's "The Horses." Plath's poem embraces a static world in which the speaker resists the imaginative leap of "Ariel"—vision, both literal and figurative, is shrouded in fog. Thus Hughes's depiction of a still, remote landscape where the air is "evil," the light is "iron," and the morning is "cast in frost" may have appealed to Plath that December—suddenly his "grey silent world" (*CPH* 22) seemed much more hospitable than it had in October, when she had escaped "Stasis in darkness" on Ariel. In "Sheep in Fog," however, Plath's dawn world is, like Hughes's, cold and desolate: the "flower left out" (*CPP* 262) and the mention of rust suggests decay, while the train reminds one of other trains in *Ariel*, bound for a dark destination.[10] Likewise, "dolorous bells" and the double reference to "morning" (mourning) further prepare the reader for the final stanza, in which the speaker ponders the lure of her own death (262). Plath's line "My bones hold a stillness" (262), suggests Hughes's "frost-making

⁸ Sylvia Plath to Olive Prouty, January 22, 1963, Lilly.
⁹ Sylvia Plath to Olive Prouty, December 15, 1963, Lilly.
¹⁰ Tim Kendall notes that "Daddy," "Metaphors," "Getting There," "Totem," and "Sheep in Fog" all employ "sinister" train metaphors (2001: 176).

stillness" (22), while her second stanza—"The train leaves a line of breath. | O slow | Horse the color of rust" (262)—also owes something to Hughes's line, "Where my breath left tortuous statues in the iron light" (22). Plath's "All morning the | Morning has been blackening" (262) echoes Hughes's "blackening dregs of the brightening grey" (22), while her "far | Fields" appear to be a version of Hughes's moors. Whereas in "Ariel" and "The Horses" the scene gradually brightens, the morning only blackens in "Sheep in Fog"; the "heaven" at the poem's end suggests none of the brightness or redemptive beauty of the sunrise in "The Horses" or "Ariel." Plath's speaker now resembles Hughes's in "Phaetons," dragged into an equally dark "heaven" by forces beyond her control.[11]

In a lecture originally delivered to the Wordsworth Trust in 1988, Hughes revealed that in earlier drafts of "Sheep in Fog" Plath had again made use of the Phaethon myth. In her first draft she had written, "The world rusts around us | Ribs, spokes, a scrapped chariot," and then, four lines later, "I am a scrapped chariot" (*WP* 195); Plath also referred, in the same draft, to the body of the fallen Phaethon as "a dead man left out" (195). These discarded lines highlight the flight and fall trajectory from "Ariel" to "Sheep in Fog"; as Kendall has written, the movement from one poem to another "is the movement from the red heat of Phaethon's life-affirming, self-destructive adventure to its wrecked and sombre aftermath" (2001: 192). They also reveal the extent to which Plath may have intended to comment upon her poetic rivalry with Hughes. The rebellious daughter who attempted to prove her legitimacy in "Ariel" now seems less confident about her ability to master the poetic forces she had harnessed so skillfully only a few months earlier. Hughes himself admitted as much when he described how "quite suddenly, the *Ariel* inspiration has changed. The astonishing, sustained, soaring defiance of the previous eight weeks has suddenly failed. Or rather has reversed" (*WP* 198).

In his analysis of the poem, Hughes says Plath's invocation of the Phaethon myth in "Ariel" was partly "an attempt to soar (plunge) into the inspirational form of her inaccessible father" (*WP* 200–1), and suggests that Plath's reference to Phaethon's dead body in "Sheep in Fog" is "the spirit that was also her resurrected father" (202). He touches upon this idea several times in his essay, writing that "In the poem 'Ariel' she had fused her heart—her whole being— into the sun's red eyes, as a triumphant Phaeton reaching her Father" (206) and, later, that "Sheep in Fog" was an attempt "to deal with terrible news about her father and her fateful bond with him" (210). He even goes so far as to suggest that "the body of her father" was "the Chrysalis" of the *Ariel* voice (202).

---

[11] Hughes's "Pibroch," which was published in 1960, was another influence on "Sheep in Fog": Hughes's final lines, "This is where the staring angels go through. | This is where all the stars bow down" (*CPH* 180) are precursors of Plath's final lines, "They threaten | To let me through to a heaven | Starless and fatherless, a dark water" (*CPP* 262).

Hughes here makes clear (as he would in *Birthday Letters*) that his interpretation of *Ariel* rested upon Plath's obsession with Otto Plath rather than her feelings of marital betrayal. "Sheep in Fog," with its dark vision of a "fatherless" heaven, supported Hughes's thesis; this is one reason, as Bundtzen suggests, he chose to include it in his version of *Ariel* (2001: 103–4).[12]

"Sheep in Fog" is a kind of anti-"Ariel," but not for the reasons that Hughes suggests. Needless to say, Hughes did not interpret the reference to the father at the end of "Sheep in Fog" as a reference to himself, nor does he ever mention that Plath's images of Phaethon might allude to his own poem concerning the myth. Yet the image of Phaethon's wrecked chariot (uncovered by none other than Hughes himself) suggests that "Sheep in Fog" may have been Plath's way of saying that her attempt to prove her own legitimacy in the face of her poetic "father" came at too high a cost.

Just as "Sheep in Fog" is the "sombre aftermath" (Kendall 2001: 192) of "Ariel," so too is "Edge" the somber aftermath of the murderous impulse in "Lady Lazarus" and "Purdah." That impulse has now turned inwards, yet the stunt which the woman of "Edge" performs is much more horrific than that of her man-killing *Ariel* sisters. "Edge," which was written on February 5, 1963, is often read as Plath's artful substitute for a suicide note, or, as Judith Kroll writes, "transcendence through completion" (145). But her point may be more ironic. The poem may have been a message for Hughes: Plath's speaker now performs the part of the White Goddess, only this time she has no strength left to demolish the myth. Plath implies (however unfairly) that for Hughes, she served as a manifestation of the White Goddess because, as Graves had written, "woman is not a poet: she is either a Muse or she is nothing" (446).

Hughes's "Dark Women" (later entitled "The Green Wolf") likely influenced "Edge."[13] "Dark Women" was written in August 1962, and published in the *Observer* on January 6, 1963, a little over a month before Plath committed suicide on February 11.[14] (Hughes told Keith Sagar that Plath found "Dark Women" amidst his papers while he was in Spain with Assia Wevill in September of 1962 (*L* 720).[15]) Hughes's poem incorporates typical Plathian images, such as

---

[12] Plath did not include "Sheep in Fog" in her final *Ariel* manuscript, a gesture that suggests she may have been aware that the poem undermined the collection's intended narrative of rebirth. In fact, she may have agreed with Hughes's assessment that the poem was "the epitaph and funeral cortège of the whole extraordinary adventure dramatized in the poems of *Ariel*" (*WP* 207). For a detailed analysis of Plath's original *Ariel* manuscript see Marjorie Perloff's "The Two *Ariels*: The (Re)Making of the Sylvia Plath Canon."

[13] Hughes's later title, "The Green Wolf," refers to a passage in Frazer's *The Golden Bough* in which villagers in Normandy burn a man dressed in green in order to ensure the harvest (Scigaj 103). The imagery of paralysis and menacing flowers in "The Green Wolf" may also have influenced Plath's "Paralytic," written on January 29, 1963.

[14] Its original title was "Event in a Cave Drama" (Box 59, MSS 644, Emory).

[15] Hughes told Sagar that his "Out" and "The Road to Easington" were among Plath's papers after she died, and that he thought the latter had influenced "The Bee Meeting" (*L* 720).

night flowers, stars, dew, hair, and mouths, and mimics her stylistic tic.[16] The last
four stanzas read:

> I watch it approaching but I cannot fear it.
> The punctual evening star,
> Worse, the warm hawthorn blossoms, their foam,
>
> Their palls of deathly perfume,
> Worst of all the beanflower
> Badged with jet like the ear of the tiger
>
> Unmake and remake me. That star
> And that flower and that flower
> And living mouth and living mouth all
>
> One smouldering annihilation
> Of old brains, old bowels, old bodies
> In the scarves of dew, the wet hair of nightfall.   (*CPH* 159–60)

Hughes's original title, "Dark Women," refers to Ama, a figure of the Cabbala who,
as Scigaj puts it, "is the destructive aspect of Binah or Understanding.... Ama
attests to the arduous labor needed to achieve any goal and the necessity of
disrupting and destroying the old self-image to create fertile ground for personality
growth" (103). Scigaj also points out that in traditional representations, the "Dark
Mother," as Ama is known, "is depicted as a gigantic Mother Superior completely
shrouded in black" (103). Plath may have had Ama in mind while composing
"Edge," her own poem about self-destruction that seemingly takes place under the
auspices of that "dark mother," the moon. The moon may be a manifestation of
Ama, who is "used to this sort of thing"—that is, the surrender of the old self in
order to achieve "perfection." She is characterized, like Ama, as being dressed in a
long black, witch-like cape ("Her blacks crackle and drag"). Plath also echoes
Hughes's image of the "deathly perfume" of night flowers: "She has folded |
Them back into her body as petals | Of a rose close when the garden || Stiffens
and odors bleed | From the sweet, deep throats of the night flower" (*CPP* 273).

"Edge" was probably also influenced by Hughes's "New Moon in January,"
published on January 6, 1963—the same day as "Dark Women"—in the
Observer. This poem, too, was in the batch of Hughes poems that Plath took
while Hughes and Assia were in Spain; Hughes told Sagar it was in her flat when
she died (*L* 720). Plath's depiction of the moon in "Edge" as impassive ("noth-
ing to be sad about") recalls Hughes's moon, a "head, severed while staring, | Felt
nothing, only | Tilted slightly" (*CPH* 167); she echoes Hughes's "faint-shriek"
in "Her blacks crackle." Hughes ends "New Moon in January" with a nihilistic
image—"zero | Itself loses consciousness"—which finds its correlative in Plath's
dead woman. Plath may also be responding, in "Edge," to what appears to be an
early unpublished draft of Hughes's "Full Moon and Little Frieda," originally

---

[16] Plath's "The Bee Meeting" also alludes heavily to "Dark Women."

entitled "Frieda's Early Morning," possibly among the manuscripts Plath saw while Hughes and Assia were in Spain. In his poem, Hughes uses the words "razor's edge" and "roses," and refers to "massively-golden Jupiter, hanging there in the orchard."[17] Jupiter looks on benevolently as the father watches his child sleep. Plath's all-seeing moon, on the other hand, stares indifferently at the dead body of the mother and her children.

By the time Plath realized Hughes was engaged in an affair with Assia Wevill, she may have felt that by rejecting Graves's reductive understanding of the woman poet, she was freeing herself from Hughes's influence—this notion was part of Plath's irony in "Lady Lazarus" and "Daddy." But by "Edge," Plath has decided that her speaker will in fact "surrender" to Graves's (and, hence, what she perceived then as Hughes's) understanding of the female poet:

A woman who concerns herself with poetry should, I believe, either be a silent Muse and inspire the poets by her womanly presence ... or she should be the Muse in a complete sense: she should be in turn Arianrhod, Blodeuwedd and the Old Sow of Maenawr Penardd who eats her farrow, and should write in each of these capacities with antique authority. She should be the visible moon: impartial, loving, severe, wise.   (1948: 447)

Plath again "impersonates" one of Hughes's female stereotypes—the deathly Goddess.[18] Plath aligns her speaker with the Goddess at the poem's end, when the Goddess makes an appearance as the moon. This Goddess is the presiding spirit of "Edge," and has "folded" the speaker back into her own system just as the speaker has folded her dead children back into her body. The images of barrenness and sterility further suggest that Plath imagines her speaker joining the ranks of the Goddess, who is childless. Hughes's abandonment of Plath for a childless woman may have embittered her even more toward the White Goddess myth, and inspired a new determination to "give" Hughes what he "wanted"—a cold, cruel, childless muse to whom he must sacrifice himself. Thus, one way to read the poem, as with "Daddy" and "Lady Lazarus," is as ironic performance aimed at Hughes.[19]

Plath probably realized Hughes would recognize her allusions to his "Dark Women," "New Moon in January," and as Middlebrook has argued, "Full Moon and Little Frieda" in "Edge"—that she had "folded" his own poems into hers.[20] Plath may also have looked to "Full Moon and Little Frieda," which

[17] Ted Hughes to Olwyn Hughes, December 1962, MSS 980, Emory.
[18] The poem's Cleopatra imagery ("My resolution's plac'd, and I have nothing | Of woman in me; now from head to foot | I am marble-constant; now the fleeting moon | No planet is of mine" (V.ii.238–41)) looks back not only to Shakespeare's play, as Kroll has noted, but also to Hughes's "Cleopatra to the Asp"; Graves had also listed Cleopatra as "an incarnation" of the White Goddess (Kroll 146).
[19] Hughes's poem "Moonwalk," in *Birthday Letters*, shows, however, that he may not have felt the full rage behind Plath's irony.
[20] Middlebrook writes, "it appears that some of the poem's imagery, specifically that of the milk—a full bucket in Hughes's poem, an empty pitcher in Plath's—and the moon, may have been a response to the call she heard in 'Full Moon and Little Frieda'" ("Poetry" 1994: 170).

was published on January 27, 1963 in the *Observer*, when she wrote "Words" on February 1. The pail of milk that Frieda lifts in "Full Moon and Little Frieda" is a "mirror | To tempt a first star to a tremor" (*CPH* 182), an image Plath uses, in "Words," to very different effect when she writes, "From the bottom of the pool, fixed stars | Govern a life" (*CPP* 270). The "echoes" of Hughes's poem provide her with an image of fatalism and drowning. Plath's pool image also plays with the reflection between Frieda and the moon at the end of Hughes's poem, when "The moon has stepped back like an artist gazing amazed at a work | That points at him amazed" (*CPH* 183). The image of two artists engaged in an act of mutual admiration might once have existed as an ideal between Plath and Hughes, but now the image served as a bitter reminder that the marriage of true minds had disintegrated. "Words" speaks directly to Plath's poetic dialogue with Hughes, and suggests that despite her attempts to "disfigure" his words, their echoes still rang in her ears. Like "Sheep in Fog" and "Edge," the poem is static, somber, and resigned. The revisionary energy of "Ariel" has all but disappeared—now the words are "riderless." Plath comes close, here, to saying that the poetic venture has failed her; the sap left in the axe's wake "Wells like tears" (*CPP* 270).

According to "A Dream," which Hughes later published in *Birthday Letters*, the last lines in "Words" came from him: "Not dreams, I had said, but fixed stars | Govern a life" (*CPH* 1119).[21] If Plath was disturbed by Hughes's "echo" of her work, Hughes's attempt to reclaim "his" lines from Plath in "A Dream" show that the reverberation of her echoes now troubled him. Plath's words had come full circle. Like the moon and child in "Full Moon and Little Frieda," Hughes stares back at Plath, staring back at him.

---

[21] Steven Axelrod maintains that the image came from a passage in *King Lear* that Plath had underlined in her edition of the play: "It is the stars | The stars above us, govern our conditions" (4.4.34–37). He mentions that the phrase "fixed stars" also occurs in Milton, Roethke, and Lowell (76), while images of axes, echoes, and wood can be found in the work of Roethke, Dante, Whitman, Lowell, and Pound (75).

8

Hughes's Plath

In a letter to Andrew Motion regarding a biography of Sylvia Plath, Ted Hughes wrote, "The main problem with S.P.'s biographers is that they fail, at the outset, when they embark on the book they hope will sell a lot of copies, to realize that the most interesting and dramatic part of S.P.'s life is only ½ S.P.—the other ½ is *me*" (qtd. in Malcolm 201). As Janet Malcolm showed in *The Silent Woman*, any serious exploration of Plath's poetic legacy must consider the role of Hughes as, in Sarah Churchwell's words, "author, editor, reader, protagonist, occasional publisher and chief financial officer of Sylvia Plath, Inc."[1] Hughes's role as Plath's editor, however, has caused much suspicion among Plath scholars. Marjorie Perloff, Jacqueline Rose, and Churchwell, for example, have been dismayed by what they see as Hughes's censorship of Plath, while even his more sympathetic critics, such as Diane Middlebrook, Tim Kendall, and Malcolm, have questioned his decision to destroy Plath's last journal. As Kendall neatly put it:

Jacqueline Rose's claim that [Hughes] "deprived feminism of a positive identity and selfhood" merely by changing the running order of *Ariel* illustrates the level of scrutiny and accusation which Hughes was obliged to endure. Nevertheless, his frank admission that he had destroyed one of Plath's journals and lost another did little to prove that he was a responsible keeper of the flame.[2]

Because there have been so many explorations of Plath's archive, and, in particular, Hughes's rearrangement of Plath's *Ariel* poems, I have chosen to focus in this chapter on Hughes's "reading" of Plath in his prose.[3] While this topic, too, has been the subject of recent scholarship, questions regarding Hughes's management of Plath's posthumous legacy remain. Was he attempting to "creatively correct" Plath by aligning her with a British romantic tradition rather than an American confessional one? Did he continue to regard his dead wife as a rival? Was he promoting Plath as a member of his own particular poetic "school,"

---

[1] Sarah Churchwell, "Love at the Barre," *Times Literary Supplement* (December 17, 2004).

[2] Tim Kendall, "Famous nearly Last Words," *Times Literary Supplement* (November 26, 2004).

[3] See Jacqueline Rose's *The Haunting of Sylvia Plath*, Janet Malcolm's *The Silent Woman*, Lynda Bundtzen's *The Other Ariel*, Diane Middlebrook's *Her Husband*, and Marjorie Perloff's "The Two Ariels" for detailed discussions of Hughes's editorial stewardship of Plath's *Ariel*, *Collected Poems*, *The Bell Jar*, and unabridged *Journals*.

using her considerable achievement to bolster his own ideas about poetry, or did he feel Plath needed *his* support to achieve a place in the canon? And lastly, how did her literary portrayals of him affect his critical portrayals of her?

Feminist critics have long complained that Hughes's comments about Plath betray a condescending male sensibility that refuses to give the woman poet her due.[4] In the writings of Robert Lowell, Al Alvarez, Peter Davison, and Ted Hughes, Plath is often presented as a passive medium of her poetry rather than an active creator who had endured years of intellectual discipline in order to refine her craft. Hughes in particular often characterizes Plath as possessed, oracular, a vessel through which some "other" poetic spirit speaks. But, as we will see, this is the way Hughes thought of poetic inspiration generally. Although Hughes seems to be "authoring" Plath's life in his various introductions to her work, he is also re-authoring his own, reasserting his own aesthetic prerogatives, and co-opting Plath back into his own poetic "system." Once we examine Hughes's prose writings about Plath in the context of dialogue and rivalry rather than through the lens of masculine chauvinism, we begin to see that these writings were extensions of the poets' intertextual relationship.

Hughes, in his writings on Plath, imagines himself speaking to her, for her, and with her. He is conscious of his role as her reader, for he knows her work intimately, but he is equally conscious of being her "writer" as he sets down his own account of her aesthetic. During the sixties, seventies, and eighties, Hughes's Plath is (like him) a poet of the highest mythic order, not a purveyor of tawdry secrets: she is the heir of Lawrence, not Lowell. Since Hughes had come to see Plath's poetry as part of a project that belonged to "we" rather than "I," his insistence on his "version" of Plath grew out of his sense that she was his poetic partner and collaborator. What critics often read as arrogant male bullying on Hughes's part ("tyrannical interpretation" in Churchwell's words (1998: 117)) is understandable when we recognize that he was defending his own reading of *himself* and his personal aesthetic when he defended his reading of Plath. For Hughes felt that their work was a joint effort; as he told Drue Heinz in 1995, "I see now that when we met, my writing, like hers, left its old path and started to circle and search" (77). Yet Plath still posed a threat to his poetic selfhood, even after her death; by making her his "double,"

---

[4] Sarah Churchwell has commented upon these writings at length. Churchwell claims, as Rose has, that Hughes refuses "to be textual subject, rather than author, of writings about Sylvia Plath. Ted Hughes writes about Plath as if his readings are definitionally textual rather than biographical and others' readings are biographical rather than textual" (1998: 100). Taking her cue from Malcolm, who drew upon a detective story motif in *The Silent Woman*, Churchwell sees Hughes as the archetypal male detective who must solve both the mystery of Plath's works and the "crime" of her death (1998: 103) and suggests that "what Malcolm terms a context over 'ownership' is, in fact, a struggle for authorship" (1998: 105). She views the struggle through the lens of feminism, and concentrates on Hughes's tendency—as other male critics had done before and since—to present Plath in gendered terms, as both a nurturing mother and enigmatic priestess. (Rose also discusses this tendency in *The Haunting of Sylvia Plath*.)

Hughes not only promoted his preferred aesthetic, he contained and controlled the rivalry. Reading Hughes's prose pieces about Plath reveals how closely he aligned her poetry with his own; how, in effect, he came to see her poems as an extension of his own work—even when those poems were hurtful. As Hughes wrote to Donald Hall in 1963 of Plath's *Ariel*, "What a feat! For a change, and at last, somebody's written in blood" (*L* 226).

INTRODUCING SYLVIA PLATH, 1965–82

When *Ariel* was published in the UK in March 1965, Hughes promoted it relentlessly to correspondents. To János Csokits he wrote in 1967, " 'Ariel' by Sylvia, is in a class apart. She truly became the most phenomenal genius just before she died. In English there is nothing quite so direct & naked & radiant— yet complicated & mysterious at the same time" (*L* 272). Likewise, he told Richard Murphy in March 1965, "she was incapable of writing a line that wasn't unique & inspired" (*L* 240). In May 1966 he wrote to Plath's mother about an article he was writing on *Ariel*: "I do not wish to set afloat the impression that she was just another ordinary person and the poems were some sort of fluke which in time we shall see through. I wanted to give a suggestion of the extreme temperatures of her genius. I don't think there's any avoiding the fact that she will become a literary legend—already is" (*L* 257). Later, in 1981 he dissuaded Keith Sagar from taking Hugh Kenner's hostility toward Plath seriously, writing, "I read those Ariel poems as a climb—not a fall.... I tell you all this to qualify your attitude to the notion of her as a young woman hurtling to disintegration shedding rags of poetry—leaping into Aetna & bursting into flames as she fell.... Mustn't underestimate her humour either" (*L* 445–46). Such letters suggest that Hughes had taken on the role of Plath's "agent," promoting her work just as she had his.

In his longer, published works on Plath, Hughes's attempts to explain "the extreme temperatures of her genius" became forced and, at times, melodramatic. Hughes frequently suggested that Plath was a passive observer of her own creativity with no real agency of her own; that she was, as he put it, "only the flimsy, brittle husk of what was going heavily and fierily on, somewhere out of reach inside her" (1982: 90). Despite his confidence that Plath was, as he told Heinz, "a genius" (77), he rarely acknowledged Plath's discipline and intellectual labor, except to say that in her earlier poems she consulted "her Thesaurus and Dictionary for almost every word" (1965; *WP* 161). In a 1965 article for the *Poetry Book Society Bulletin* titled "Sylvia Plath," Hughes reduced her "process" to something romantic, strange, and unknowable—"just like her" (1965; *WP* 162). In the 1966 *Tri-Quarterly* article "Notes on the Chronological Order of Sylvia Plath's Poems," he wrote that "Her poetry escapes ordinary analysis in the way clairvoyance and mediumship do... she had free and controlled access to depths formerly reserved to the primitive ecstatic priests, shamans and Holy men, and more recently flung open to tourists with the passport of such hallucinogens as LSD" (82). She was an "initiate into the poetic order of events" (1966: 82).

Not only is Hughes's Plath passive, she is frightened by what was happening inside her "internal furnace" (1982: 91); as Hughes wrote in a 1971 *Observer* article, "Publishing Sylvia Plath," "she herself was a little afraid of her poems" (*WP* 165). Hughes often portrays her as a vessel: when Plath found her "true" voice, he wrote in "Sylvia Plath and Her Journals," "It was as if a dumb person finally spoke" (*WP* 185). Consider the following excerpts from this article, which first appeared in *Grand Street* in 1982:

The importance of these diaries lies in the rich account they give of her attempts to understand this obscure process, to follow it, and (in vain) to hasten it. As time went on, she interpreted what was happening to her inwardly, more and more consciously, as a "drama" of some sort. (1982: 88)

. . . in her poems and stories . . . she felt her creative dependence on that same process as subjection to a tyrant. (90)

It would not be so impressive if she were not so manifestly terrified of doing what she nevertheless did. At times, she seems almost invalid in her lack of inner protections. (91)

The seriousness, finally, of her will to face what was wrong in herself, and to drag it out into examination, and to remake it—that is what is so impressive. (91)

Her new Ariel self had evolved for the very purpose of winning this battle, and much as she would have preferred, most likely, to back off and live in some sort of truce, her next step was just as surely inescapable. (96)

She forced the poem ("Elm") back into order, and even got a stranglehold on it, and seemed to have won, when suddenly it burst all her restraints and she let it go. (97)

All her poems are in a sense by-products. Her real creation was that inner gestation and eventual birth of a new self-conquering self. (98)

Reading these various accounts of Plath's "inner process," it is not difficult to understand how she would become, in Rose's words, "the Marilyn Monroe of the literati" (26)—a vulnerable, troubled, beautiful woman who produced some memorable art but who, inevitably, was unable to defeat her inner demons.

This was a pattern of characterization which began with Lowell's notorious 1965 introduction to *Ariel*, in which he cast Plath as a Lady Lazarus figure hurtling towards her own destruction. Lowell's clichés are by now familiar, particularly his comparisons between Plath and "Dido, Phaedra, or Medea" (vii), and his insistence upon her teleological drive toward suicide, described as "appalling and triumphant fulfillment" (ix). But perhaps the most damaging misunderstanding of Plath occurs when Lowell writes that "Sylvia Plath becomes herself, becomes something imaginary, newly, wildly and subtly created—hardly a person at all" (vii) when she wrote the *Ariel* poems. (Lowell later wondered, in a letter to Hughes, whether he should have been more "impersonal" in his introduction, but figured that most readers would already know "at least as much as I let out.")[5]) Hughes echoes Lowell's language in his own assessment of Plath's achievement: in 1966, just a year after Lowell's introduction, he wrote in the *Tri-Quarterly* article that she "became herself" after she found her Ariel voice (86). Hughes's use of the same phrase may not have been accidental. He had surely read Lowell's introduction and, while he disagreed with Lowell's estimation of her poetry as "personal, confessional" (vii), he nevertheless presented Plath in a similar way, even using the metaphor of hallucination (1966: 82) as Lowell had (vii). While Hughes resented the implication that Plath was a confessional poet, his understanding of her poetry as intimately linked to whatever "was wrong in herself" (1982: 91) ironically supported Lowell's view.

Hughes never wavered in his teleological assessment of Plath's work. In a 1971 *Observer* article responding to Al Alvarez's review of *Crossing the Water*, he maintained that only Plath's *Ariel* poems constituted her "good" work (*WP* 165) and that everything else was "weaker" or "poor" (164–5). In his ambivalent 1977 introduction to *Johnny Panic and the Bible of Dreams*, he famously characterized Plath's prose work as vastly inferior to her later poems, while in his 1981 introduction to Plath's *Collected Poems*, he emphasized the weakness of the earlier poems that nonetheless helped her "chart the full acceleration towards her final take-off" (*WP* 174).[6] He had previously hinted at his own role in this "take-off" when he wrote, in the 1971 *Observer* article, that the Ariel voice was something "we had been trying to get flying for a number of years" (*WP* 165). While some scholars, such as Churchwell, have criticized Hughes for taking too much credit for Plath's development, this comment is actually one of the rare occasions in which Hughes acknowledges his presence in Plath's writing life—a topic he tends to avoid. Hughes was wary of positioning himself as an actual influence on Plath, preferring instead to play the part of the midwife who helped her to deliver "the growing brood" (1981: 14; *WP* 172), as he called her poems.

In most of his prose writings on Plath, Hughes continuously cites his critical authority as Plath's husband but fails to explore how the dynamic of their creative marriage might have shaped her poems. Instead, he focuses on Plath's "inner" dilemmas, her fascination with the ritual of rebirth, and the trauma of her father's death. In effect, he wrote himself out of Plath's story by failing to explain exactly how "they" ("we") got Plath's Ariel poems "flying." Hughes was caught in a double bind: if he discussed his poetic dialogue with Plath, or even hinted at his

---

[5] Robert Lowell to Ted Hughes, October 8, 1966, MSS 644, Emory.

[6] Hughes also mentioned, in this introduction, that he had labeled all of her poems up to the end of 1955 "juvenalia," and included a small selection at the back of the book. Given the fact that Plath was 23 in 1955, this decision struck many, particularly Rose, as a disservice to Plath, despite Hughes's insistence that she "had set these pieces... firmly behind her and would certainly never have republished them herself" (*WP* 173). While this may be true, Hughes's demarcation appeared to many to be motivated by self-interest, for he began dating Plath in 1956. Yet given the couple's sense of shared aesthetic purpose, it is not surprising that Hughes relegated Plath's earlier, more formal poems to "juvenalia."

own influence, he would contradict his own characterization of her as a "solitary genius," to use Jack Stillinger's phrase—someone who arrived at her "true" voice by fighting her own battles within the self. Hughes was also aware that any claims he made about Plath's work, positive or negative, would likely be greeted with skepticism. As he wrote to Lowell in 1966, "I realised well enough that whatever I said in praise would sound, as you say, like uxorial fatuity, and that anything I might say in detraction would be something much worse" (*L* 264). But ultimately, as Hughes told Lowell, "her poems are public property as well as my private life, and I felt I must say one or two things" (*L* 264).

While Hughes's statements about Plath do at times sound reductive, one must remember that such characterizations mirror his understanding of the internal creative process. Hughes's attitude toward the role of the poet is Romantic, Coleridgean; his reluctance to grant Plath agency as a writer stems not so much from chauvinism, but from his own beliefs about poetic inspiration. Hughes thought that all poets, male and female, were vessels of the muse, and that all Western poets should reclaim their true inner self from the tyranny of the rational mind. As he wrote to a graduate student in 1992, "I have never really felt much interest in objective descriptive writing for its own sake—or in writing about anything that I couldn't regard as the 'dramatisation' of a purely internal psychodrama" (*L* 622). In "Myth and Education" (1976), he wrote that the imagination "can be called religious or visionary" (*WP* 151). As he explained to Lucas Myers, "In the middle ages vision was a common way of thinking, a kind of controlled dreaming awake. Now we are so stupidly self-conscious that this perfectly commonplace gift has hidden itself completely" (qtd. in Myers 9). Myers, for his part, wrote that for Hughes, "Poetry was the expression and the inner life was the substance. He attended to and developed his inner life more consistently than anyone I have encountered apart from advanced Buddhist practitioners" (2).[7]

Hughes hesitates to place Plath in her historical or social context (including the context of their marriage) because he gives primacy to the poet's inner voice rather than to history or literary relationships. This is one of the many reasons Hughes would find himself so at odds with a later generation of literary critics who were trained to regard the notion of the "poet as prophet" as naïve. Not only did Hughes's pronouncements on Plath seem colored by male arrogance, they seemed an outdated and simplistic understanding of the writing process. Hughes surmised as much in 1998 when he wrote to János Csokits, "I've got to the point

---

[7] Hughes explained this belief in detail when he wrote to Aurelia and Warren Plath about his play, *The House of Aries*, about a man "searching for the SELF . . . for reunion with the whole being from which it has become, by its character, cut off." He also wrote that "a division has been created in the Self, between a briskly busy discursive thought-process, logical, with an air of infallibility and precision, arrogant because it thinks it works according to eternal rational laws, and the whole emotional animal life of consciousness which is on the whole impressionable, passive, and only positive in its intuitions." (December 1960, Lilly).

where the blood-flow is all that interests me—the finger-tip on the aorta. . . . Everything the critically-armed modern litterateur is equipped to demolish."[8] When critics complain that Hughes too often emphasizes Plath's fascination with death and rebirth, they are equally uncomfortable with his location of Plath's creativity as something completely self-contained—or, as Hughes put it in 1981, "an enclosed cosmic circus" (*WP* 174).

Read alongside his prose about other poets, Hughes's writings on Plath seem less sexist. In an article titled "Context," published in the *London Magazine* in 1962, he applied a similar understanding of the poetic process to Coleridge, Blake, Wordsworth, Yeats, and Mayakovsky:

The poet's only hope is to be infinitely sensitive to what his gift is, and this in itself seems to be another gift that few poets possess. According to this sensitivity, and to his faith in it, he will go on developing as a poet, as Yeats did, pursuing those adventures, mental, spiritual and physical, whatever they may be, that his gift wants. Or he will lose its guidance, lose the feel of its touch in the workings of his mind, and soon be absorbed by the impersonal lumber of matters in which his gift has no interest, which is a form of suicide, metaphorical in the case of Coleridge, actual in the case of Mayakovsky. . . . At the moment of writing, the poetry is a combination, or a resultant, of all that he is . . . and for the time of writing he can do nothing but accept it. If he doesn't approve of what is appearing, there are always plenty of ways to falsify and "improve" it . . . his other faculties are only too ready to load it with their business, whereon he ceases to be a poet producing what poetry he can and becomes a cheat of a kind, producing confusion.   (*WP* 1; 3)

When we read that for Hughes, "to live removed from this inner universe of experience is also to live removed from ourself, banished from ourself and our real life" and that "The struggle truly to possess his own experience . . . to regain his genuine self, has been man's principal occupation" ("Capturing Animals," 1967; *WP* 23–4), his inability to separate Plath's poems from her struggle for self-individuation appears consistent with his more general understanding of creativity. As he told Ben Sonnenberg in 1982, "Her whole opus is a record of the process that most poets (the ones that count) have gone through secretly (and unconsciously) before they can really begin" (*L* 451).

Hughes's interest in shamanism, which he likened to a "flight to the goddess," probably also influenced his reading of Plath. In an unidentified group of notes about the universal goddess in the Emory archive, Hughes wrote,

It [shamanism] reappears, in quite pure form, in civilized and not particularly religious individuals, as the healing process of a psychic illness, and then it brings the gifts of healing or poetry. The essential experience of the Shaman is purely psychic, a magical flight to the goddess, and a return to worldliness with something divine, a cure, an inspired answer, some kind of blessing which everybody recognizes.[9]

---

   [8] Ted Hughes to János Csokits, January 29, 1998, MSS 895, Emory.
   [9] Ted Hughes, unidentified notes on the universal goddess, Box 115, MSS 644, Emory.

He continued, "The scheme behind my poetry, as I see it, and insofar as there is one, could be described as the negotiations with the goddess, outside any particular religion. The goddess is the ancient one—Isis, Hecate etc.—but Universally Nature simply, creatress and destroyer."[10] Thus we should not be surprised to read in an unpublished essay on Plath's poetry that "The White Goddess pervades all Sylvia Plath's poetry."[11] Hughes's *Shakespeare and the Goddess of Complete Being* confirms that his obsession with the Goddess and application of a mythic "code" extended beyond his writings on Plath. (Indeed, Hughes even went so far as to call T. S. Eliot a "shamanic healer" (*L* 617)). As Terry Eagleton wrote in his review of Hughes's Shakespeare book:

Secretly governing the whole of Shakespeare's work, so Ted Hughes informs us, is an algebraically exact equation, the first part of which concerns the Great Goddess and the second the Goddess-destroying God.... The Shakespeare who emerges from this book is uncannily familiar. He is a poet of primitive violence, animal energies, dark irrational forces and incessant sexual strife. In fact he is, by a remarkable coincidence, a mirror image of the Laureate himself.[12]

Frank Kermode wrote that a librarian would be "tempted to catalogue this book under 'Hughes' rather than under 'Shakespeare.'"[13] John Carey's more charitable point might just as well apply to Hughes's writings on Plath: "Whatever his deficiencies as a Shakespeare critic... he is undoubtedly himself a leading poet, and if we take the simple step of reading his book as a commentary on his own poetry rather than Shakespeare's it at once becomes quite sane and informative."[14]

Yet it is questionable whether Hughes's constructions of Plath, like Plath's constructions of Hughes, are accurate. Alvarez's short memoir about Plath in *The Savage God* (1971) contradicts many of Hughes's assertions about his wife.[15] The memoir exhibits both sexism and armchair psychology, as well as the same kind of typecasting in which Hughes and Lowell indulged (for example, Alvarez describes Plath, during the last night he saw her alive, as "a priestess emptied out by the rites of her cult" (26)). Yet Alvarez restores Plath's agency, writing of her exemplary craftsmanship and technique as few had at that time. He praised her "rhymes and half-rhymes, the flexible, echoing rhythms and off-hand collo-quialisms" (17), her "hard-earned skills and discipline" (18), and her tireless ability to rewrite her poems until she was satisfied with them (18). He also gave

[10] Ibid.

[11] Ted Hughes, Notes on Sylvia Plath's "Totem" and "The Munich Mannequins," Box 115, MSS 644, Emory.

[12] Terry Eagleton, "Will and Ted's Bogus Journey," *Guardian* (April 2, 1992).

[13] Frank Kermode, "Ted Hughes Charges at Shakespeare," *Sunday Telegraph* (April 5, 1992).

[14] John Carey, "Shaman Scandal," *Sunday Times* (April 5, 1992).

[15] After Plath's death, when Alvarez talked openly about his friendship with Plath, Hughes accused him of breach of trust, and the two had a falling out. Nevertheless, Alvarez does not fall squarely into a pro-Plath or anti-Hughes camp.

Plath credit for her stylistic innovation, for "breaking down the old, inert moulds, quickening the rhythms" (19). He suggested that Plath worked hard to achieve these stylistic effects and, importantly, that she was no stranger to rewriting—a habit that calls Hughes's oracular assessment into question.[16] Alvarez also said Plath "scarcely mentioned her father" in conversation with him, and insisted that her poems were "purely poems, autonomous" (23). This comment echoes a remark Plath made to Peter Orr in October 1962 during a recording for the BBC program "The Poet Speaks": "Young women come up to me and say 'How do you dare to write, how do you dare to publish a poem, because of the criticism, the terrible criticism, that falls upon one if one does publish?' And the criticism is not of the poem *as poem*" (168).

It is likely Plath would have been frustrated with many critics' refusal to consider her poems as "purely poems, autonomous" works of art which were not synonymous with the self. She may also have been disappointed by Hughes's refusal to acknowledge the happiness she found in the writing process, which he continually characterized as a struggle or battle. Alvarez, in contrast, acknowledged Plath's contentment after writing a well-wrought poem: "just as the suicide adds nothing at all to the poetry, so the myth of Sylvia as a passive victim is a total perversion of the woman she was. It misses altogether her liveliness, her intellectual appetite and harsh wit, her great imaginative resourcefulness and vehemence of feeling, her control" (1971: 33). Again, Plath confirmed Alvarez's words in her interview with Orr. When he asks, "basically this thing, the writing of poetry, is something which has been a great satisfaction to you in your life, is it?" Plath responded, "Oh, satisfaction! I don't think I could live without it. It's like water or bread, or something absolutely essential to me. I find myself absolutely fulfilled when I have written a poem, when I'm writing one. . . . I think the actual experience of writing a poem is a magnificent one" (172). That sense of fulfillment—however fleeting it was in reality—is something Hughes rarely captured in his writings on Plath.

PLATH, HUGHES, AND CONFESSIONALISM

When Plath complained that she was trapped inside a "glass caul," she might have been speaking of her entire generation of poets, on both sides of the Atlantic. As Peter Davison remembered, "Young poets in the mid-1950s, still overshadowed by the sequoias of Frost, Pound, Eliot, Stevens, Cummings, Marianne Moore, and William Carlos Williams, had taken refuge in a formal elegance that they were beginning to outgrow" (11). Adrienne Rich agreed:

---

[16] For example, Hughes wrote that the *Ariel* poems were written "as one might take dictation, where she ignores metre and music." ("Sylvia Plath," draft of article on *Ariel* for the *Poetry Book Society Bulletin* 44, February 1965, Box 114, MSS 644, Emory.)

"In those years, formalism was part of the strategy—like asbestos gloves, it allowed me to handle materials I couldn't pick up bare-handed" (qtd. in Davison 40). Rich, Lowell, and Plath had all practiced formalism early on, but knew instinctively that something needed to change. As Lowell wrote, "Poets of my generation and particularly younger ones have gotten terribly proficient at these forms. They write a very musical, difficult poem with tremendous skill.... It's become a craft, purely a craft, and there must be some breakthrough back into life" (qtd. in Davison 2). This breakthrough came in the form of Lowell's *Life Studies* in 1959, which many critics have hailed as the most influential postwar American poetry collection.[17] Plath was a student of Lowell's during the fifteen months she and Hughes spent in Boston during 1958–9; in his class she also met Anne Sexton. Lowell's and Sexton's verse had a profound impact upon Plath, as she told Orr in 1962:

I've been very excited by what I feel is the new breakthrough that came with, say, Robert Lowell's *Life Studies*, this intense breakthrough into very serious, very personal, emotional experience which I feel has been partly taboo. Robert Lowell's poems about his experience in a mental hospital, for example, interested me very much. These peculiar, private and taboo subjects, I feel, have been explored in recent American poetry. I think particularly the poetess Ann Saxton [*sic*], who writes about her experiences as a mother, as a mother who has had a nervous breakdown, is an extremely emotional and feeling young woman and her poems are wonderfully craftsman-like poems and yet they have a kind of emotional and psychological depth which I think is something perhaps quite new, quite exciting. (168)

Hughes did not want to include Plath in the confessional camp, however. Confessional poetry was an American phenomenon that had its roots in Puritan spiritual autobiography. Hughes situated himself within a British Romantic tradition that, though cousin to confessionalism, preferred to explore states of mind rather than private, personal histories. Lowell's and Sexton's airing of dirty laundry struck Hughes as slightly vulgar, and typically American. As he wrote to Weissbort in 1959, "AutoBiography is the only subject matter really left to Americans. The only thing an American <u>really</u> has to himself, & <u>really</u> belongs to, is his family. Never a locality, or a community, or an organization or ideas, or a private imagination" (*L* 140). Confessionalism fit into an American literary tradition that had been shaped by Whitman's intense individualism, but it received a colder reception in postwar Britain; there, all traces of extremism were treated with suspicion by the Movement poets, who saw a link between Romanticism and fascism. Hughes, of course, rejected the Movement. Yet his inclusion in Alvarez's anthology and his fascination with violence did not necessarily mean that he approved of confessionalism, with its emphasis on personal tragedy and taboo. Hughes did not want Plath to write directly about

---

[17] Davison called *Life Studies* "the most influential book of American poetry for a generation" (3).

her time at McLeans's or her suicide attempts. He wanted her to approach these events through myth and metaphor, which he felt were absent in Lowell's and Sexton's work. He may have thought that the emerging confessional genre pushed Plath in the wrong direction—back toward her breakdowns, back toward hysteria, back toward America, and perhaps toward a burgeoning feminism. Hughes was still firmly ensconced within a British tradition that found such a poetics slightly embarrassing, slightly uncouth—as Plath herself had been perceived during her first few months in Cambridge.

But Plath was inspired by the daring work of Lowell and Sexton, as her comments to Orr make clear. In her journal, she wrote that reading Lowell after Richard Wilbur and Adrienne Rich was "like good strong shocking brandy after a too lucidly sweet dinner wine" (465). Lowell's famous lines from "Skunk Hour"—"My mind's not right. | [...] I myself am hell; | nobody's here—" (2003: 191–2)—must have resonated deeply with Plath and given her the confidence to shed her decorous formalism. Lowell often paired Sexton and Plath in his poetry class, a setup which pleased Plath, who wrote that Sexton "has very good things, and they get better" (*J* 475): "She has none of my clenches and an ease of phrase, and an honesty" (*J* 477). Heather Cam has shown that Plath's "Daddy" is heavily indebted to Sexton's "My Friend, My Friend," while Davison speculates that Plath may have gotten her "bell jar" metaphor from Sexton, who had penned the lines "I tapped my own head; | it was glass, an inverted bowl" in her poem "For John, Who Begs Me Not to Enquire Further" (144).[18] In 1959, Plath wrote to Lynne Lawner that she admired Robert Lowell "immensely" and that Sexton "has the marvelous enviable casualness of the person who is suddenly writing and never thought or dreamed of herself as a born writer: no inhibitions" (qtd. in Davison 175). Sexton, for her part, later thought that Plath "may have influenced Lowell" (Davison 177). Interestingly, it was when Plath enrolled in Lowell's course that she began admonishing herself, in her journal, not to show her poems to Hughes (*J* 467, 484).

Plath may have carried confessionalism across the Atlantic when she and Hughes left Boston for London in December 1959; certainly Alvarez had been keeping tabs on the Americans and watching for similar developments in Britain. In 1962, as we have seen, he published an anthology of "extremist" poets with Penguin, entitled *The New Poetry*, in which he famously "attacked the British poets' nervous preference for gentility above all else, and their avoidance of the uncomfortable, destructive truths both of the inner life and of the present time" (1971: 21). Alvarez felt that his essay vindicated Plath's aesthetic perspective, for she spoke of it to him "often and with approval, and was disappointed not to

[18] The poem itself was a response to John Holmes's advice to Sexton to stop writing about personal, traumatic experiences. Holmes had said, "I distrust the very source and subject of a great many of your poems, namely, all those that describe and dwell on your time in the hospital. . . . It bothers me that you use poetry this way. It's all a release for you, but what is it for anyone else except a spectacle of someone experiencing release? . . . Don't publish it in a book" (qtd. in Davison 144).

have been included among the poets in the book" (22). (Alvarez only included British poets, apart from Lowell and Berryman, in the first edition, but included Plath and Sexton in the second.) Plath mentioned the book to Orr in 1962 when he asked her about the state of English poetry:

I think it is in a bit of a strait-jacket, if I may say so. There was an essay by Alvarez, the British critic: his arguments about the dangers of gentility in England are very pertinent, very true. I must say that I am not very genteel and I feel that gentility has a stranglehold: the neatness, the wonderful tidiness, which is so evident everywhere in England is perhaps more dangerous than it would appear on the surface.   (168)

In the late 1950s, however, Plath did not have much choice but to embrace gentility, to play the part, as Davison described her, of "a 'regular' girl, full of smiles" with "a gee-whiz semblance of naivete" (158–9). The 1960s would yield viable alternatives for women, but in the late fifties, Plath's person, as well as her poetry, was still trapped inside a "glass caul"—one that her poems, along with those of Rich and Sexton, would help to shatter. As Alicia Ostriker has suggested, shedding formalism was a particularly powerful way for the woman poet to shed patriarchal language altogether. "For Rich," Ostriker writes, "and for the many writers who have been influenced by her, the inherited language is what history was for Stephen Dedalus: a nightmare from which they are trying to escape" (1986: 68). Hughes, Lowell, Alvarez, and Davison fail to make this connection when discussing Plath's stylistic "breakthrough," which they attribute instead to an "inner" psychological victory.

   Although Hughes would later express hostility toward the confessional genre, he shared Lowell's belief about the direction in which modern poetry needed to travel. While Hughes and Lowell came from very different literary, national, and economic backgrounds, both felt a profound desire to break away from the rigid, formal verse that had reigned in the academy for so long. For both, this meant discovering a new aesthetic that substituted a wilder, more instinctive energy for restraint and decorum; they shared a belief that modern poetry needed to be revitalized, and that this revitalization needed to come from an "inner" source, whether it be traumatic personal experience or nature's primal life-force. The impulse, in both cases, was Romantic, Lawrentian. Lowell would reject the idea that personal crises and dirty laundry were not suitable subjects for poetry, as the poet and Tufts professor John Holmes had told Anne Sexton in 1959. Hughes, for his part, would rebel from the current aesthetic by forging a style that had more in common with the kinds of ancient poetic practices described in *The White Goddess*. As we have seen, he felt that modern English poetry had lost touch with its "magical" Celtic roots, and sought to revive the bardic note. Though on opposite sides of the Atlantic, both Lowell and Hughes were reared in cultures in which personal propriety, fastidiousness, and decorum governed social behavior; Lowell found Brahmin Boston just as suffocating as Hughes found Cambridge. Hughes hinted as much when, after meeting Lowell in Boston in 1958, he told

Lucas Myers "his whole tempo is perfect Botolph." He also told Myers that Lowell's new poems, which would eventually be published in *Life Studies*, "are a complete change in style and to my mind much more exciting that his earlier stuff,"[19] and boasted to his parents that Lowell considered his poem "Pike" "a masterpiece" (*L* 139). Both sought to strip away the layers of "civilization" to reveal something deeper, truer—as did Alvarez, who admired Lowell and included him in the Penguin *New Poetry* anthology of 1962 that so influenced Plath. Alvarez, poetry critic at the *Observer* from 1959 to 1977, was one of the few to mention Lowell's influence in his review of *The Hawk in the Rain* ("Lowell prowls about").[20] Alvarez knew that Hughes "never properly believed in his civilization" (1971: 24), and that the same might be said of Lowell.

In the late fifties, Hughes frequently expressed admiration for Lowell in letters from America, calling him, at one point, "easily the best of all the Americans under fifty—easily & far away" and "the most charming and likable American I've ever met" (*L* 139). But his initial enthusiasm for Lowell's work waned over the years—perhaps as a result of his own increasing sense of alienation from America and the American poetry scene. Hughes criticized Lowell's work to W. S. Merwin in 1962, writing that his translations were "10x more interesting than his own poems."[21] Myers remembers Hughes saying of Lowell in the 1970s, " 'I don't really like him' with an expression of distaste" (91). In 1976, Hughes wrote to Daniel Weissbort that Lowell's work was "totally ersatz, it is all stage performance, even the careless, slovenly, loose shuffling off of imperfect approximations, on his way to closer sincerities" (*L* 372).

Hughes was rather dismissive of Lowell's and Sexton's influences on Plath, or the possibility that Plath may have influenced *them*. In 1966, Hughes sent Aurelia Plath a draft of an article he had written for a symposium on *Ariel* which was to appear in the *Tri-Quaterly* magazine, as well as a long letter explaining how he had come to write it. The letter leaves little doubt that he did not see her as a member of the confessional school, and that he saw himself as Plath's advocate, attempting to explain "the extreme temperatures of her genius" to the world:

I wanted to set in the forefront, at as early a stage in the great inevitable exegesis as possible, the claim that Sylvia was not a poet of the Lowell/Sexton self-therapy, or even national therapy, school, but a mystical poet of an altogether higher—in fact of the very highest—tradition.... There is simply nobody like her. I've just finished re-reading all Emily Dickinson for a small selection, and my final feeling is that she comes quite a way behind Sylvia. As for Lowell, etc, if he is a fine doctor, she is a miracle healer. There is no comparison. But I want to avoid seeming to set myself up as the high priest of her mysteries—and so I've limited myself in these notes to the lowest order of editor's facts.[22]

      [19] Ted Hughes to Lucas Myers, spring 1958, MSS 865, Emory.
      [20] Al Alvarez, "Tough Young Poet," *Observer* (October 6, 1957), 12.
      [21] Ted Hughes to W. S. Merwin, February 26–27, 1962, MSS 866, Emory.
      [22] Ted Hughes to Aurelia Plath, May 19, 1966, Lilly.

Hughes is not entirely wrong here, for Plath was not, strictly speaking, a confessional poet in the style of Lowell and Sexton; her work also incorporates mythic elements.[23] In the published article, Hughes admitted that Plath "shares with them the central experience of a shattering of the self, and the labour of fitting it together again or finding a new one," but felt her poetry was ultimately "quite different" from anything by them. Their "final world is a torture cell walled with family portraits," while Plath's "autobiographical details" are set "out like masks, which are then lifted up by dramatis personae of nearly supernatural qualities" (1966: 81). Hughes received aggrieved letters from Lowell and Sexton after this article appeared in 1966, and apologized to both. In his reply to Lowell, he wrote:

I dragged you and Anne Sexton in because the linking of your three names in every blessed review has become an automatic reflex that seems to me to obscure differences that are much more important than the links, and a main obstacle to anybody approaching her poems.... I was trying to define Sylvia's poetry as something that moves in spirit or in the dimension of spirit rather, and to distinguish it in this way from yours and Anne Sexton's which seem to me to share at least this, that they move in the dimension of nature and society. (*L* 264)

Although Hughes went on to say that "I brought you both in because without the combined operation of you and Anne Sexton Sylvia would never have written what she finally did" (*L* 265), he would not link Plath to Lowell's and Sexton's work in a published piece until 1995.

It comes as little surprise that Plath's most confessional period came after she separated from Hughes—this was yet another way for Plath to convince herself she was moving away from his influence and closer to her own voice. For Hughes, however, poems like "Daddy" and "Lady Lazarus" were egregious. He may have felt that by excluding some of the more extreme confessional poems from the *Ariel* manuscript, he was not only protecting his personal reputation, but also Plath's poetic reputation. He felt the confessional label trivialized her work, and made her poems seem ordinary. He perceived a threat to Plath's literary legacy—and perhaps through hers, his own—particularly in the wake of John Bayley's negative review of her *Collected Poems* in 1981. Hughes called Bayley's review "a tortuous effort to domesticate her to her most conventional work, misread her artistic motives, with the ultimate conjurer's

[23] Jacqueline Kroll advanced these ideas in her book on Plath, *Chapters in a Mythology*, arguing that Plath was not a confessional poet but was rather influenced by archetypal myths, particularly those in Graves's *The White Goddess*. This claim alarmed Rose, who wondered whether "there might be a problem in such an inheritance, that it might function as male projection and fantasy..., that the archetype might be hellish, might be taken on—for Plath certainly takes it on—at considerable cost" (153). This is exactly the kind of criticism Hughes anticipates when he says he does not want to set himself up as "the high priest of her mysteries," and perhaps accounts for his reluctance to mention his own role in Plath's writing life or influence on her work.

flourish of demonstrating what an ordinary little sparrow she was—a hectic ordinary sparrow even a very talented ordinary sparrow but still a sparrow."[24] As Hughes's anger over Bayley's review makes clear, he thought of himself as her strongest advocate—the one person who understood the true nature of her genius. His greatest fear was that Plath would be regarded as "ordinary," and that critics would—as Bayley had—attempt "to domesticate her to her most conventional work." Ironically, critics would accuse Hughes of the same charge—"domesticating" Plath's work in order to save his own reputation.

When Hughes rejects Plath's association with confessionalism, he situates her as a member of his own "school," a poet who, like him, rejected the refined cadences of the Movement and embraced a wilder, more Lawrentian aesthetic. But Plath was the heir and beneficiary of both Hughes's and Lowell's approaches, which she fused in her later poetry. In both "Lady Lazarus" and "Daddy," for example, Plath fuses confessional elements, such as her suicide, failed marriage, and anger at her husband and father, with Hughesian motifs of folktales, witchcraft, magic, and prophecy. Indeed, it is likely that her change in style had as much to do with this British–American cross-fertilization as it did a psychological "breakthrough." As Paul Giles has remarked, "Plath's most incisive work emerges from neither an adherence to American idealist poetics, nor a straightforward conversion to indigenous British romanticism, but rather from the points of transition between these different positions. . . . she not only constructed an artful rhetorical voice but also embodied within her verse conflicts between different intellectual and poetic traditions" (110). Hughes's discomfort with labeling Plath a confessional poet prevented him from seeing the transatlantic hybridity of her work.

By 1995, Hughes had gained a different perspective on confessional poetry. In his *Paris Review* interview, he implied that confessionalism was something in which all poets, including Shakespeare and Milton, indulged. He even went so far as to include Plath within an American confessional school that included Lowell and Sexton:

The novelty of some of Robert Lowell's most affecting pieces in *Life Studies*, some of Anne Sexton's poems and some of Sylvia's, was the way they tried to throw off that luggage, the deliberate way they stripped off the veiling analogies. Sylvia went furthest in the sense that her secret was most dangerous to her. She desperately needed to reveal it. You can't overestimate her compulsion to write like that. She had to write those things— even against her most vital interests. She died before she knew what *The Bell Jar* and the *Ariel* poems were going to do to her life, but she had to get them out. She had to tell everybody . . . like those Native American groups who periodically told everything that was wrong and painful in their lives in the presence of the whole tribe.[25] It was no good doing it in secret; it had to be done in front of everybody else. Maybe that's why poets go

---

[24] Ted Hughes to Frances McCullough, September 29, 1981, MSS 644, Emory.
[25] Heinz's ellipses.

to such lengths to get their poems published. It's no good whispering them to a priest or a confessional. And it's not for fame, because they go on doing it after they've learned what fame amounts to. No, until the revelation's actually published, the poet feels no release. In all that, Sylvia was an extreme case, I think.   (75–6)

Hughes's willingness to link Plath to Lowell and Sexton reflects his own aesthetic shift during the 1990s. For this was around the time he was preparing *Birthday Letters*—his most confessional work—for publication. His comments about Plath might apply equally well to his own "compulsion" to reveal his "dangerous secret." As he told Keith Sagar in July 1998 (and other corres-pondents such as Seamus Heaney and Ben Sonnenberg), he felt he had made a grave error by staying silent about Plath's death. Writing of his feelings about Plath was

A thing that I too had always thought unthinkable—so raw, so vulnerable. . . . And so dead against my near-inborn conviction that you never talk about yourself in this way—in poetry. . . . But there is no way I could have gone on letting all that business gag me, knowing, with Sylvia's reputation as my environment, I could never escape with her onto the other levels. . . . So I don't care what people say. It has worked for me—better than I'd thought possible. Though I now see that any traumatic event—if writing is your method—has to be dealt with deliberately. . . . My high-minded principal was simply wrong—for my own psychological & physical health. It was stupid.   (*L* 720)

After years of dismissing confessional poetry, Hughes finally embraced the aspect of Plath's aesthetic that he had long dismissed; *Birthday Letters* was in fact more overtly autobiographical—confessional—than anything Plath had ever written. His decision to abandon his "high-minded" aesthetic principles in favor of a raw style shows that Plath still exerted a powerful influence years after her death.

Hughes believed Plath was a genius, and took his custodianship of her work and legacy seriously. Although he had been wounded and angered by many of Plath's *Ariel* poems, he was perhaps more upset by others' refusal to give Plath her due as a major poet, and stunned that there was any disagreement about her genius. It is ironic that he found himself so at odds with feminist critics, since both worked toward the same goal—to promote Plath's work and secure her a prominent place in the canon. Like aggrieved parents, each party fought for custody of Plath's legacy. Hughes, of course, knew that his writings about Plath gave him a rare opportunity to reach the masses. As custodian of Plath's work—"keeper of the flame," as Kendall put it—he was able to reach a much wider reading public, since Plath's popularity far outstripped his own. He admitted as much to Daniel Weissbort, writing that he was "only a moderate draw by comparison with Sylvia."[26] Yet he felt that the readers who constituted this audience misunderstood Plath's poetry, and needed to hear "the truth" about her (for example, that she was "Laurentian," not "women's lib"). While

---

[26] Ted Hughes to Daniel Weissbort, December 3, 1960s, MSS 864, Emory.

Hughes felt he was looking out for Plath's best interests, all of his writings about her constitute a kind of self-promotion, since he still thought of her as his partner in poetry, if not in love. Such a strategy meant that Plath became a double rather than a rival. Yet, when it came time to answer back to Plath's late verse with his own, he was less willing to play the role of supportive critic and collaborator. There, Hughes abandoned the detached persona of "her husband," which he had cultivated in his prose writings. In his later poetry, he was finally able to voice his anger, and his grief, as he became drawn deeper into a dialogue with his lost wife.

9

Crow and Counter-revision

In 1998, Ted Hughes admitted to Keith Sagar what many critics had probably assumed but never claimed in print: that *Crow* had been a way to work through the devastation of Sylvia Plath's suicide. Hughes's first impulse after her death had been to approach the tragedy through the guise of Orpheus, but, as he told Sagar, he quickly rejected this impulse: "I thought it would be too obvious an attempt to exploit my situation—I was too conscious of that obviousness." He had "despised" the confessional school of Lowell and Sexton, and felt a "moral reluctance" to use Plath as poetic material. Only by approaching her life and death "obliquely, through a symbol" would he be able to honor her "creatively." Hughes admitted that "in retrospect, I can see that it began to emerge in exactly this fashion in *Crow*," though he was still "too close to the experience" of Plath's suicide to "turn deadly negatives into triumphant positives" (*L* 719; 718). Only during the last year of his life was Hughes ready to recognize the extent to which his earlier poems had been influenced by, and entwined with, those of Sylvia Plath.

Hughes critics, in their efforts to divorce the work from the life (antithetical to the efforts of many Plath scholars, in this regard), have been hesitant to make such a connection: none of the major Hughes scholars gives more than a passing nod to Plath's influence on *Crow*.[1] Most focus instead on Hughes's critique of modernity through his use of the epic, the trickster myth, folk tales, shamanism, and violence. Scigaj's reading is representative in this respect: "*Crow* contains a critique of Protestant Christianity as denying personality growth by repressing instinctual life, and of modern science as alienating humans both from nature and from inner life by valuing only objective fact and quantifiable analysis" (123). While this reading is insightful, Hughes critics consistently, almost willfully, refuse to connect Crow's encounters with vengeful females to the ghostly presence of Plath. While it would be reductive to claim that the only way to read *Crow* is in dialogue with Plath, the focus thus far on the trickster tale and shamanism has occluded analysis that considers the roles of Plath's influence

---

[1] These include Terry Gifford, Keith Sagar, Neil Roberts, Paul Bentley, Leonard Scigaj, and Ekbert Faas. Faas, in a short chapter on Plath and Hughes in *The Achievement of Ted Hughes*, wrote that *Crow* "has its roots in the Plath mythology" (1983: 117) but does not credit Plath's poetry as an actual influence on Hughes. Instead, he focuses on "Hughes's ongoing concern with the rescue of a desecrated female at the hands of an equally disintegrated male" (117).

and rivalry. Hughes is largely responsible for this critical bias, since he asked
scholars to avoid any mention of his personal life in their work and pleaded for a
hermetic, New Critical approach. In 1974 he asked Sagar to exclude all bio-
graphical details from his forthcoming book, writing, "It would be ideal if your
book concerned the verse alone as if nothing at all were known about me
personally—as if my name were a pseudonym." He also asked Sagar to include
only one photograph, since he felt that photographic exposure "intensifies my
sense of being 'watched'.... It sharpens, in any reader, the visual image of
me, making the telepathic interference correspondingly more difficult to coun-
ter" (*L* 348). Later, in 1988, increasingly embittered by "the Babel of the Plath
industry," he reiterated to Sagar that "the world of biography is a world of lies."[2]

Hughes critics have dutifully obeyed his instructions. When asked about his
sources, Hughes often pointed scholars toward Eastern literature or literary-
anthropological texts such as *The White Goddess* and *The Golden Bough*. When
Faas wrote to Hughes expressing "surprise at the confessional nature of the
Gaudete lyrics" (1980: 137), for example, Hughes told him the work was not
confessional at all, but based upon his dreams and "a collection of South Indian
vacanas... translated by A. K. Ramanujan" (137). During a 1977 interview, Faas
again suggested to Hughes that the "the underlying story" in *Crow* was "some
kind of autobiographical myth," to which Hughes defensively replied "Why
autobiographical? It's just a way of getting the poems" (213). Faas took Hughes
at his word and declined to push his insight about the "confessional nature" of
Crow or *Gaudete* any further. What Plath is, Hughes is not, the critical thinking
goes. Hughes later told his daughter, Frieda, to avoid writing about autobio-
graphy directly in her poems, that such writing always came off as "false."
Instead, he advised her to seek alternate metaphors that would help her find an
"escape route": "The emotions of a real situation are shy, but if they can find a
mask they are shameless exhibitionists. So—look for the right masks" (*L* 678).
Crow may have been Hughes's own "mask."

While there is little doubt that books about "primitive" literature and sham-
anism, which Hughes was reviewing throughout the sixties, enabled him to
clarify his subject and direction, one must also take into account his ongoing
dialogue with Plath as a major influence on the first collection begun after her
death.[3] In fact, the idea of *Crow* was entangled with Plath's suicide from the start.
Scigaj reports that a mere three weeks after Plath's death, Leonard Baskin asked
Hughes to write a poem entitled "The Anatomy of Crow," which Baskin
planned to print alongside some of his Crow drawings. Baskin, a Smith professor

[2] Ted Hughes to Keith Sagar, June 10, 1988, British Library.
[3] Hughes wrote excitedly to Lucas Myers in August 1964 about a "magnificent" book called
Shamanism, by Mircea Eliade, which he was reviewing for the *Listener*. This seems to have been his
first sustained encounter with the subject. He told Myers, "You'll be glad to know that your (& my)
obsession with physical disintegration, being torn into fragments & fitted together again, is the great
Shaman initiation dream" (*L* 235).

who had befriended Plath and Hughes during Plath's stint at the college, hoped the commission would propel Hughes "from despair to activity" (Scigaj: 144). Although it would take time for Hughes to give full voice to Crow, by 1968 he wrote to Baskin that the project he had initially abandoned had "assumed epic proportions" (Scigaj: 144).[4]

In *Crow*, Plath's and Hughes's positions have essentially reversed, as Margaret Uroff has noted: "Plath is now triumphant, and Hughes, if not defeated, is at least fully aware of that possibility" (224).[5] Just as Plath had felt a female "anxiety of authorship" in relation to Hughes and male writing generally, Hughes now felt oppressed by Plath's literary ghost, which had temporarily silenced him.[6] (As he told Sagar, he had been "floundering in creative lassitude" (Middlebrook 2003: 230) from 1963 to 1965.) And just as Plath had found herself incapable of successfully mourning Hughes's absence in *Ariel*, Hughes was in turn unable to mourn her in *Crow*. Indeed, many of the Bloomian and Freudian concepts that applied to Plath now also apply to Hughes, who exhibits traits of both melancholic mourning and the anxiety of influence as he engages in a dialogue with his lost wife.[7]

Freud wrote that when a person dies, "opposition [to mourning] can be so intense that a turning away from reality takes place and a clinging to the object through the medium of a hallucinatory wishful psychosis" occurs ("Mourning" 244–5). *Crow* exhibits a kind of "hallucinatory... psychosis" similar to Plath's *Ariel*, as Uroff first observed, both collections are heavily marked by surrealism, as well as "sardonic humor, caricature, hyperbole, parody" (223). Like the vengeful heroines in "Daddy," "Lady Lazarus," and "Purdah," Crow is a repository of violence and hatred, a nihilist speaking in what Hughes called "super-ugly" language, who travels through a nightmarish landscape in his quest for renewal. Indeed, Hughes's blunt, stripped-down language in *Crow* brings to mind Plath's similarly bare aesthetic in her late poems. As Hughes wrote to Sagar in 1973, "I simply tried to shed everything.... My idea was to reduce my style to the simplest clear cell—then regrow a wholeness and richness organically from that point" (*L* 340). Similarly, he told Faas, "The idea was originally just to write

---

[4] Hughes began working on the *Crow* poems in 1964 with "Eat Crow"; however, the first *Crow* poem, "A Disaster," was not published until July 22, 1967. The last *Crow* poem, he told Sagar, was written the week before Assia Wevill's suicide in March 1969, an event that "knocked Crow off his perch" (*L* 719). To Ben Sonnenberg he wrote that "the animal has altered out of all recognition. Crow no longer says anything for me" (November 13, 1969, MSS 924, Emory).

[5] While Uroff was the first to point out Plath's influence on *Crow*, she does not examine specific poems in which Hughes engages in an intertextual dialogue with Plath. Nor does she consider Hughes's anxiety of influence in her analysis, or how this anxiety compelled him to revise Plath's work.

[6] See pp. 45–92 in Gilbert and Gubar's *The Madwoman in the Attic* for an account of female "anxiety of authorship."

[7] Hughes was no stranger to the kind of self-accusation that, according to Freud, haunts the melancholic mourner. As he wrote to Leo and Ann Goodman after Plath's suicide, "That's the end of my life. The rest is posthumous" (May 8, 1963, Smith).

his songs, the songs that a Crow would sing. In other words, songs with no music whatsoever, in a super-simple and super-ugly language which would in a way shed everything except just what he wanted to say without any other consideration" (1980: 208).

Plath, too, had indulged in "super-ugly" language in "Daddy" and "Lady Lazarus," and for similarly nihilistic purposes; those poems had also drawn extensively upon military imagery and the motif of war. As Uroff writes, "Crow's style is not so much a matter of stripped-down language as of a bold and defiant posture. In this he resembles no one more than the speakers of Plath's late poems who never flinch in their attacks" (202). There are even parallels between Plath's and Hughes's composition processes. The *Crow* poems, like those in *Ariel*, were written very quickly, as Hughes told Faas: "There was no planning in the poems themselves. Most of them were revealing to me as I wrote them and they usually wrote themselves quite rapidly" (1980: 98). Hughes also admitted that after he wrote the poems, "I had the sensation of having done something taboo and very horrible" (1980: 98); Plath likewise told Peter Orr, in *The Poet Speaks* interview, that she was interested in poetry that broke taboo. Hughes critics rarely draw such parallels; instead, they tend to reproduce Hughes's own mystical and esoteric explanations of his work. Yet Hughes's notebooks at Emory show that he was thinking about Plath while composing *Crow*. In one there is a description of a dream in which Plath came back to life:

Dreamed as if all night Sylvia had been brought back to life. The great hope was that she could see the children. There was some drug which would do it—but if she died again, that was final. And so she was brought back, & was absolutely herself—except some photos shown me later showed the death had had some effect on her. . . . But then there was another version of the dream in which I met her and we were at Smith—busy meeting all her Smith friends. She greatly surprised . . . by the success of Ariel. . . . She dug a hole in the main path at Smith (one that doesn't exist) and there we buried her manuscript—the black book. It was her mother's decision to bring her back briefly in this way. I composed something on the insanity of it and its effect on one. But the whole dream . . . immensely detailed and vivid. The strangeness of her presence after so much death—the thousand little details how long death showed its effect in her behaviour. The dramatic mood—that she was back only for that day.[8]

This passage, which was written between drafts of two Crow poems, suggests that it was not just the memory of Plath herself that troubled Hughes, but her writing, her "black book," which they bury together in the dream.

Both collections were, and continue to be, controversial. "Daddy" and "Lady Lazarus," as well as other poems in *Ariel*, have been repeatedly attacked for their allegedly excessive narcissism, lack of style, and moral bankruptcy. *Crow* was denounced for similar reasons. Roy Fuller was upset by "the pathological

---

[8] Ted Hughes, Notebook 10, Box 57, MSS 644, Emory.

violence of its language, its anti-human ideas, its sadistic imagery" (qtd. in Bentley 1997: 27), while Geoffrey Thurley called *Crow* an "inhuman, even brutal book," and wondered "whether Hughes's abandonment of a human perspective is ultimately justifiable" (27). Paul Bentley's understanding of *Crow* echoes frequent critical assessments of Plath's "Daddy": "regression or disintegration is pushed back the farthest, to a stage where all attempted identifications fail and where language itself becomes reified to the point of apathy as Crow remains unable to solidify himself into any signifier" (1997: 31).

Thus, there is much to be gained by considering *Crow* as part of Hughes's revisionary dialogue with Plath. In *Crow*, Hughes speaks to Plath in poems that simultaneously address language, writing, and moments of originary "naming" in the context of violent sexual relationships between men and women. Many poems in *Crow* reveal a deep anxiety about women's ability to "silence" men's language, as well as emancipated women's role in shaping "the mother tongue." In his treatment of these themes, Hughes is engaged in a counter-revision of Plath, who had written of "the father's" attempt to silence women's language in poems such as "The Detective," where the speaker's mouth is "hung out like brown fruit | To wrinkle and dry" (*CPP* 209), "The Courage of Shutting-Up," in which the speaker's tongue is cut out and "Hung up in the library with . . . | . . . the fox heads, the otter heads, the heads of dead rabbits" (*CPP* 210)—a clear reference to Hughes—and "Daddy," where the daughter can "hardly speak." Ultimately, *Crow* presents a distorted mirror image of *Ariel*: where Plath feared the silencing authority of "the father," Hughes fears the theft or suppression of language by "the mother."

REVISING THE "MOTHER TONGUE"

When Hughes writes of giant vulvas and vaginas that silence and suffocate men in *Crow*, he is voicing the same concerns felt by an earlier generation of male modernists, who worried that the intrusion of female discourse into public, intellectual, and literary life would sully the language and lower literary standards.[9] Hughes expressed this anxiety in his letters to Sagar, where he

---

[9] Gilbert and Gubar read the overtly masculinist and phallocentric modernist aesthetic (what T. E. Hulme called "the knife-order") as a way to exclude women: "a reaction-formation against the rise of literary women became not just a theme in modernist writing but a motive for modernism" (1994: 1.156). They methodically trawl through the literary history of the sexes to find that twentieth-century male writers revisit themes of male impotence (Hemingway, Faulkner, Lawrence), cuckoldry (Joyce), female hysteria (Eliot), or, alternatively, "female potency" (Yeats) in their work, and suggest that such patterns were not only due to the cataclysm of the Great War or the increasing fragmentation and mechanization of Western society, but anxiety about the success and even dominance of women's writing in the literary marketplace (36). Gilbert and Gubar also remind us that in 1975 Harold Bloom wrote, "the first true breach with literary continuity will be brought about in generations to come if the burgeoning religion of Liberated Woman spreads from its clusters of enthusiasts to dominate the West.

railed against the state of literary studies as feminism gained ground in the academy. English literature, he said, now had "nothing to do with the original concern, enjoyment of books."[10] Echoing the male modernists, he expressed frustration toward what he felt to be the increasing ignorance of the English people, writing, "you need to nurse your under-exposed reader along like some mollycoddled, spoiled child who will squall and abuse you if you say anything he doesn't know.... It's the ultimate triumph of the old law: if he can read, hang him."[11] While Hughes does not mention feminism as a cause for the disintegration of "cultural life," many of his letters to Sagar from this period complain bitterly about the feminist-driven Plath industry, which Hughes regarded as an amorphous enemy. His increasing frustration with the politicization of literary studies and what he saw as the concomitant "deterioration" of culture were likely tied to his feelings of contempt toward "the Sylvia Plath Society," or, as he put it more bluntly, the "crazies."[12]

In *The Hawk in the Rain* and *Lupercal*, Hughes's anxiety about Plath's literary ambition was subtle and muted; there, strong male speaker-warriors tend to dominate powerful female antagonists. In *Wodwo*, *Gaudete*, and especially *Crow*, however, Hughes is no longer sure of the male's power. His speakers are now hunted and victimized by women, and martyred for enduring women's torments. At the center of this battle between the sexes is, to paraphrase Susan Gilbert and Sandra Gubar, a war of and over words themselves.

Though Nathalie Anderson has called *Crow* "a feminist's nightmare" (101), she has defended Hughes's treatment of women as a way to register his opposition to a "rational" modernity that denies the sanctity of both women and mother nature. "If rationalism perceives the female principle as 'a horror', 'a whore and a witch'," writes Anderson, "then Hughes must portray such a horror in order to present rationalism accurately" (98).[13] Yet *Crow* nonetheless offers striking support to Gilbert and Gubar's thesis that "a major campaign in the battle of the sexes is the conflict over language, and, specifically, over competing male and female claims to linguistic potency" (1994: 1.228). Male modernists, they write,

---

Homer will cease to be the inevitable precursor and the rhetoric and forms of our literature then may break at last from tradition" (1994: 1.131).

[10] Ted Hughes to Keith Sagar, July 9, 1994, British Library.

[11] Ted Hughes to Keith Sagar, April 27, 1993, British Library.

[12] Ted Hughes to Keith Sagar, July 9, 1992; December 2, 1993, British Library. In a letter to his brother, Gerald, in 1972, Hughes called Plath "the laureate of Women's Lib." (Ted Hughes to Gerald Hughes, n.d. 1972, MSS 854, Emory.)

[13] Anderson later admits, however, that "If part of Hughes's point is that the Western (male) intellect must recognize and embrace its intuitions, its emotions, its connectedness, its sexuality, that laudable precept nevertheless rests on an identification of the female as intuitive, emotional, connected, and sexual—an object available to be embraced, rather than a fully realized partner, a complex subjectivity" (107).

met their own awareness that they now shared (indeed were confined to) the language of... women with intensified fantasies about what they *as men* could do with that common language. In general, these masculine linguistic fantasies fall into four categories: 1) a mystification (and corollary appropriation) of the powers of the *materna lingua* itself; 2) a revision of the *materna lingua* which would assert (male) power over it; 3) a recuperation (or wish for recuperation) of what are seen as the lost powers of the *patrius sermo*; 4) a transformation of the *materna lingua* into a powerful new kind of *patrius sermo*. (253)

Crow is often engaged in a battle to break free from the "great mother," or what D. H. Lawrence termed the "Mater Magna" in *Women in Love*. In "Song for a Phallus," "Revenge Fable," "Oedipus Crow," and "Crow and Mama," Crow attempts to kill or escape oppressive mother figures who seek to silence him, just as Plath seeks to destroy or defeat equally silencing, oppressive father figures in *Ariel*. In "Crow and Mama," this anxiety of female (literary) influence is particularly acute: Crow's mother "closed on him like a book | On a bookmark" (*CPH* 219). These lines accrue greater significance when we consider how often Crow or other male speakers in the collection become stalled in their attempts to write, just as in "Daddy," the daughter finds herself unable to speak in the presence of the father. In Hughes's "A Bedtime Story," for example, the male speaker attempts to "write his autobiography" (*CPH* 246) but gives up after realizing that his mind and body are unable to sustain the effort. In "In the Land of the Lion," the male speaker's life "stood frontispiece to a book | . . . The work of a lifetime." Yet that work will remain unread, "kicked aside," or even "burned": it "flies in space | Unopened, | A parenthesis | Like a bullet-hole into which a person's whole life vanished—" (*CPH* 261). So many poems interrogate the utility of words—and do so in dialogue with Sylvia Plath—that Crow's quest seems to be motivated not only by a yearning for spiritual fulfillment but a desire to be "Himself the only page," as Hughes writes in "Crowego" (*CPH* 240).

Throughout his career, Hughes repeatedly criticized Christianity in general and Protestantism in particular for abolishing the mother-goddess figure, a "murder" he dramatizes in "Revenge Fable," where a male kills his mother "With numbers and equations and laws" (*CPH* 245). While Hughes considered himself a feminist of a particular sort, his Gravesian understanding of woman as deity/muse was repeatedly attacked by feminist critics, who equated his nostalgia for the Goddess and interest in "primitive" literature with nostalgia for a lost patriarchal culture—a time before women had broken from their traditional roles as male servants or muses, and before men had been emasculated by Christian theology and capitalism.[14] Graves had helped set the tone for such

---

[14] As Gilbert and Gubar write, "Where the male precursor had had an acquiescent mother-muse, his heir now confronted rebellious ancestresses and ambitious female peers, literary women whose very existence called the concept of the willing muse into question" (1994: 1.130).

nostalgia, writing in *The White Goddess* that "the prime causes of our unrest" were "that of a patriarchal God, who refuses to have any truck with Goddesses and claims to be self-sufficient and all wise" (475).

Hughes's desire to expose the bankruptcy of patriarchal theology and modern rationalism is in some ways akin to Graves's, as is his depiction of woman as femme fatale. Thus Hughes returns, again and again in *Crow*, to the biblical creation story, portraying it as the beginning of the end. In "Apple Tragedy," for example, he reinterprets the creation myth and recasts Eve, rather than the serpent, as the instigator of the Fall. Eve, drunk on cider that God has maliciously provided, seduces the serpent "And gave him a wild time" (*CPH* 250). Victimized by his wife's adultery, Adam tries to hang himself, whereupon Eve cries " 'Rape! Rape!' " By casting Eve as an early feminist, Hughes implies that patriarchal society is on the brink of yet another Fall. Hughes returns to biblical motifs in "Fragment of an Ancient Tablet," in which the poet "unearths" an artifact that reasserts a biblical/patriarchal authority over women. Women's deceitful natures are exposed in the poem's juxtaposition of what lies "Above" and "Below"—a stylistic device that recalls the classic Western allegorical binaries of heaven and hell, soul and body, reason and passion. Hughes invokes these binaries by comparing the inviting details of woman's face (above) to her womb and vagina (below), the source, the poet intimates, of her true nature. Above lie "the well-known lips, delicately downed," "her brow, the notable casket of gems," "her perfect teeth," "a word and a sigh," and "the face, shaped like a perfect heart." Below, however, is the "beard between thighs," "the ticking bomb of the future," "the belly with its blood-knot," and "gouts of blood and babies" (*CPH* 254).[15] The conceit of biblical excavation allows Hughes to voice an anti-feminist polemic and to endow his own words with the sanctity of a "lost" patriarchal authority. At the same time, he distances himself from the anonymous author of this fragment and positions himself as the passive receiver of the law, like Moses.

Hughes's frequent references to the creation story in *Crow* had personal resonance, for Plath often characterized him as "Adamic" in her letters and poems. It is as if Hughes is trying to regain that original balance of power and wrest control of the dialogue back from Plath's mocking, taunting late poems. The *Crow* poems' emphasis on women's duplicity may also have stemmed from

---

[15] Jacqueline Rose notes that this poem draws heavily upon Jung's *Symbols of Transformation*, in which he writes, "The double being corresponds to the mother-imago: above, the lovely and attractive human half, below, the horrible animal half" (161), as well as from *King Lear*:

> Down from the waist they are Centaurs,
> Though women all above:
> But to the girdle do the Gods inherit,
> Beneath is all the fiends: there's hell, there's darkness,
> There is the sulphurous pit—burning, scalding,
> Stench, consumption; fie, fie, fie! Pah, pah!   (IV.vi.126–31)

Hughes's hostile encounters with feminist scholars during this period. As Hughes told Sagar, between 1970 and 1972, around the time *Crow* was published, "Sylvia's poems & novel hit the first militant wave of Feminism as a divine revelation from their Patron Saint." Soon, he said, "Sylvia's reputation" became "my environment" (*L* 719–20)—his own suffocating version of Daddy's black shoe. He spoke of the intense "opposition" to him in literary and academic circles in the US (he even felt stares in bookshops) and wondered why more men did not support him. He had come to the conclusion that he simply had to "delete the U. S. from all my reckonings.... I can't go lecturing/reading to raise my stakes—because I meet crazies."[16] Hughes had literally been "silenced" by his dead wife's female supporters.

The desire to repossess the "mother tongue," then, helps account for why so many poems in *Crow* return to the biblical moment of creation and focus upon the acquisition of language. In "Crow's First Lesson," for example, God attempts to teach Crow to speak his first word, "love." Crow cannot bring himself to utter the word, and instead "convulsed, gaped, retched" as if reenacting Daddy's daughter's rhetorical stutter ("Ich, ich, ich, ich") and voicelessness ("I could hardly speak") (*CPP* 223). Suddenly, "woman's vulva dropped over man's neck and tightened. | The two struggled together on the grass. | God struggled to part them, cursed, wept—" (*CPH* 211). Crow flies "guiltily" away from the scene while man and woman continue to fight. The specter of the giant vulva silencing man at the originary moment of naming reflects anxiety about the potentially emasculating effect of women's language upon the male voice; for Hughes, it may also reflect a more personal anxiety that Plath had come to dominate the literary dialogue, and that she had effectively and literally silenced *him*.

In "The Battle of Osfrontalis," Hughes connects words to the pernicious aspects of modernity that prevent man from experiencing spiritual enrichment. No longer do words give voice to song and prayer; instead they have become the servants of capitalism, lending their power to "Life Insurance policies," "warrants," and "blank cheques" (*CPH* 213). Equally troubling, words have been co-opted by women: "Words came in the likeness of vaginas in a row," "Words came in the likeness of a wreathed vagina," "Words infiltrated guerilla labials" (214). ("Labials" is a linguistic term that describes a type of consonantal sound produced with both lips ("b" and "p"), though it also echoes "labia.") That Hughes uses the word "guerilla" to describe these "labials" suggests not only women's allegedly secretive maneuvers to possess or repossess the language, but the violent insurrection of the words themselves, which have "infiltrated" the labials. The use of military metaphors to describe language parallels Plath's use of the same trope in "Daddy," where the daughter struggles to take possession of

---

[16] Ted Hughes to Keith Sagar, December 2, 1993, British Library.

the language from the totalitarian father. Hughes adopts a stance antithetical to
Plath's: where Daddy's daughter attempts to defeat the male forces that have
silenced her, Crow must "take back" language from the destructive, vengeful
mother.

In "Crow Tries the Media," Crow's inability "to sing" (*CPH* 231) about a
lost, nameless woman is again linked to the illegitimacy of words, which Hughes
depicts as feminine:

> Oversold like detergents
> He did not even want words
> Waving their long tails in public
> With their prostitute's exclamations.   (*CPH* 231)

Here Hughes links words to female themes of domestic consumption and
household chores. But Hughes pushes the identification between words and
women even further, likening language itself to a whore or loose woman.
Words, like women, are not to be trusted; they sell themselves to the highest
bidder. In Crow's fallen universe, words have lost their purity. Crow cannot use
them "to sing" because they cannot convey the depth and profundity of his song;
nor can the poet fulfill his role as prophet if he regards words themselves as
broken, used, and sullied.

In "A Disaster" the word is again depicted as feminine through vaginal and
mammary imagery: "Ravenous, the word tried its great lips | On the earth's
bulge, like a giant lamprey— | There it started to suck" (*CPH* 226). It is soft, it
"oozes," and it is "all mouth." The phrase "all mouth" explicitly equates the
word with feminine anatomy and, at the same time, recalls Plath's use of the
phrase "I am all mouth" (*CPP* 131) in "Poem for a Birthday." Hughes continues
to draw upon Plath's imagery from "Poem for a Birthday" in "A Disaster,"
writing that Crow saw the word "sucking the cities | Like the nipples of a sow"
(*CPH* 226), lines which echo Plath's "I suck at the paps of darkness" (*CPP* 136).
The feminized word devours the living "Till there were none left, | All digested
inside the word" (*CPH* 226). Here Hughes again alludes to Plath's recurring
mouth imagery in "Poem for a Birthday" ("all mouth," "All-mouth," "mother
of mouths," "this mouth," "frog-mouth," "fish-mouth," "the mouth of a door,"
"candle's mouth," "mouth-hole"), and her supplication to the *materna lingua*
when she writes, "Mother, you are the one mouth | I would be a tongue to.
Mother of otherness | Eat me" (*CPP* 132). He also recalls her depiction of a
ravenous woman intent upon swallowing time itself: "Time | Unwinds from the
great umbilicus of the sun | Its endless glitter. || I must swallow it all" (*CPP* 133).

"The word," in "A Disaster," is personified as a murderous woman who, like
Lady Lazarus, possesses no eyes and attempts to destroy men. Hughes wrests
control of the dialogue with Plath here, assaulting her words with his own until,
as in "The Battle of Osfrontalis," they "retreat," leaving Crow victorious. For the
word

> ...could digest nothing but people.
> So there it shrank, wrinkling weaker,
> Puddling
> Like a collapsing mushroom.
> Finally, a drying salty lake.
> Its era was over.
> All that remained of it a brittle desert
> Dazzling with the bones of earth's people
>
> Where Crow walked and mused.   (*CPH* 226–7)

Hughes ascribes feminine attributes to the word when he characterizes it as weak and shrinking; its inability to "digest" anything other than "people" suggests that it is confined to the (female) vernacular and incapable of articulating high (masculine) ideas. The "collapsing mushroom" calls up the image of a deflated penis, while the "salty lake" combines traditionally feminine imagery of water and tears. When Hughes declares "Its era was over," he wills the revision of *materna lingua* to *patrius sermo*, a necessary part of Crow's quest for a place that has dodged the wrecking-ball of modernity and a time before words lost their (phallic) strength. It is the very weakness of words that accounts for the ravaged state of the world; in the Christian era, they are no longer the medium of divine communication or inspiration, but power and mammon. Hughes implies causality here: when women lost their "divinity," so too did words. As Robert Graves wrote in *The White Goddess*:

It is true that in English-speaking countries the social position of women has improved enormously in the last fifty years and is likely to improve still more now that so large a part of the national wealth is in the control of women—in the United States more than a half; but the age of religious revelation seems to be over, and social security is so intricately bound up with marriage and the family...that the White Goddess in her orgiastic character seems to have no chance of staging a come-back, until women themselves grow weary of decadent patriarchalism. (458)

A revitalized, remasculinized language will aid Crow in his epic effort to achieve harmony and divinity because that language will take him back to a time and place that has not cut itself off from the godhead.

As we have seen, Plath revised Hughes's totemic poem, "The Thought-Fox," in "Ariel," asserting that her "indefatigable hoof-taps" were more powerful than his "neat prints." Hughes seems to have recognized the allusion, for he engages in a dialogue with "Ariel" in two Crow poems, "Crowcolour" and "Bones." In "Crowcolour," Hughes borrows Plath's images in his depiction of Crow's blackness: the lines "He was as much blacker | Than any negro | As a negro's eye-pupil" (*CPH* 243) recall Plath's "Nigger-eye | Berries cast dark | Hooks—" (*CPP* 239). Hughes's dialogue with Plath is more complex in "Bones," whose title, like "Ariel," refers to the actual name of the horse at the center of the poem. But in Hughes's revision, Plath's powerful mare has been stripped of her finesse:

> Bones is a crazy pony.
> Moon-white—star-mad.
> All skull and skeleton.   (*CPH* 259)

From the outset of "Bones," several clues hint that Hughes is responding to
Plath. His opening stanza is a tercet, like Plath's opening stanza in "Ariel," and
utilizes similarly short lines. (The rest of Hughes's poem alternates between
tercets and single lines.) Hughes begins each line with a stressed syllable, just as
Plath does in "Ariel"; both poems' first lines also start with a dactyl. Hughes
echoes Plath's internal assonance in her third line ("Pour of tor") with internal
consonance in his own: "All skull and skeleton." Like Plath, Hughes announces
the horse's gender in the fourth line. "Her hooves pound," Hughes writes,
echoing Plath's "indefatigable hoof-taps" in "Words" and her repeated image
of hooves in "Years." Yet "Bones" revises the momentum and vitality of Plath's
powerful female persona in "Ariel." Ariel is now just a "crazy pony" who appears
not as Pegasus but Thanatos, perhaps an allusion to Plath's rider's "Suicidal"
drive (*CPP* 240). "Who has broken her in? | Who has mounted her and come
back | Or kept her?" (*CPH* 259), Hughes writes, using sexual imagery that speaks
to the difficulty and danger of harnessing the possessed rider in "Ariel," whom he
associates with Plath. Hughes invokes images of the femme fatale, reminiscent of
Plath's dangerous women, when Bones torments those male "heroes" who want
"a ride": "She lifts under them, the snaking crest of a bullwhip" (259). Ulti-
mately, he links Bones's, and perhaps Plath's, "craziness" to her willful refusal to
be controlled: "Every effort to hold her or turn her falls off her | Like rotten
harness" (260). Plath's Ariel has been transformed from "God's lioness" to "the
stunted foal of the earth" (260) in an act of revision which, like "A Disaster,"
seeks to "write back" to Plath and counter her own revisionary impulse.

Although neither "Bones" nor "Ariel" addresses the concept of the word,
Hughes's counter-revision nonetheless speaks to male anxiety about women—in
this case, his wife—taking control of language and riding off (or off course) with
it. Britzolakis notes that the image of horse and rider has been a recurring motif
in art since Plato first aligned the soul with a charioteer in the *Phaedrus*; from the
Renaissance onward, the image of the rider was used to denote the "hierarchical
relation between reason and passion, soul and body" (183). Passion was aligned
with the horse, and reason with the rider, whose duty was to hold passion at bay.
Freud again used the metaphor in *The Ego and the Id*, in which he aligned the
rider with the ego "who has to hold in check the superior strength of the horse
[the id]" (qtd. in Britzolakis 183). Plath subverted this trope in "Ariel" by
allowing her rider to sublimate her will to that of the horse, inverting the
hierarchy of reason over passion. Hughes's revision of Plath's horse as a willful,
deathly, sexual predator allows him to emphasize and punish this subversion.
Plath's speaker's assertion, "I | Am the arrow" (*CPP* 239), claims a phallic voice
that must be silenced in Hughes's revision if he is to take control of the dialogue.

As Hughes writes in "Crowego," "His wings are the stiff back of his only book, | Himself the only page—of solid ink" (*CPH* 240).

WORDS AS WEAPONS

Hughes continues to decry the inefficacy of words in "Crow Goes Hunting," which, like "A Disaster" and "Crow Tries the Media," relies heavily upon weapon imagery while engaging in a dialogue with Plath. This time, Hughes alludes to Plath's "Burning the Letters," in which, as we have seen, she used the metaphor of hunter, hound, and fox to invoke her own "hunt" and destruction of Hughes's "letters."[17] Hughes reverses Plath's symbols and compares his "words" to "a lovely pack" of hounds that Crow sets after a hare. The hare continually eludes the words. It first shape-shifts into "a concrete bunker," whereupon Crow changes the words to "bombs." When the bombs blow up the bunker, its shattered pieces morph into "a flock of starlings"; the words then change to "shotguns" that try to shoot the birds down. After more shape-shifting, the hare finally eats Crow's words, leaving Crow (ironically, Scigaj notes) "Speechless with admiration" (*CPH* 236). Nature has outwitted the human urge to document, classify, and deconstruct, and has transcended the "trappings" of human rationalism. The triumph of the hare represents a Gravesian triumph of nature over human artifice, and the passive, nurturing feminine over the aggressive, destructive masculine.[18] Hughes may also be enacting a reversal of Plath's allusion, in "Burning the Letters," to the story of Artemis and Actaeon, in which Artemis turns Actaeon into a stag after he sees her naked and leaves him to be devoured by his own hounds.[19]

Perhaps no other poem in *Crow* speaks to Hughes's tragic, revisionary dialogue with Plath as much as "Lovesong," which uses motifs of war, weaponry, hunting, and writing to depict the speaker's battle with his lover. Although the first line asserts "He loved her and she loved him," we soon realize that these two lovers want more of each other than they can have. Hughes uses metaphors of cannibalism to suggest the extent to which both sought to "devour" the other: "His kisses sucked out her whole past and future or tried to | He had no other

[17] See Chapter 7 for a more detailed discussion of "Burning the Letters."

[18] As Graves wrote, "there seems no escape from our difficulties until the industrial system breaks down for some reason or other, as it nearly did in Europe during the Second World War, and nature reasserts herself with grass and trees among the ruins" (482).

[19] Ovid's version in *The Metamorphoses* tells that Artemis punished Actaeon for boasting that he was a better hunter than she. It is also possible that Hughes is alluding to an image from Shakespeare's *Twelfth Night*: "That instant was I turn'd into a hart; | And my desires, like fell and cruel hounds, | E'er since pursue me" (I.i.21–3). Hughes will use similar imagery in "Epiphany" when he encounters a man selling a fox cub in London: "My thoughts felt like big, ignorant hounds | Circling and sniffing around him" (*CPH* 1117).

appetite | She bit him she gnawed him she sucked | She wanted him complete inside her" (*CPH* 255). Hughes's reference to biting recalls the night Plath bit his cheek at the St Botolph's party and places the poem squarely within an autobiographical, confessional tradition more typically associated with Plath. Hughes further hints that the poem is as much about writing and rivalry as it is about a tragic love affair when he writes that "Her embrace was an immense press | To print him into her bones" (255) and later,

> His words were occupying armies
> Her laughs were an assassin's attempts
> His looks were bullets daggers of revenge
> Her glances were ghosts in the corner with horrible secrets
> His whispers were whips and jackboots
> Her kisses were lawyers steadily writing   (255)

Images of torture soon replace images of weapons as the couple struggles to efface each other:

> His promises were the surgeon's gag
> Her promises took off the top of his skull
> She would get a brooch made of it
> His vows pulled out all her sinews . . .
> Her vows put his eyes in formalin
> At the back of her secret drawer
> Their screams stuck in the wall   (255)

Hughes's hospital imagery and metaphors of surgery allude to Plath's "The Surgeon at 2 a.m.," in which a surgeon dismembers a body in a metaphor of "revision":

> It is a statue the orderlies are wheeling off.
> I have perfected it.
> I am left with an arm or a leg,
> A set of teeth, or stones
> To rattle in a bottle and take home,
> And tissue in slices—a pathological salami.
> Tonight the parts are entombed in an icebox.
> Tomorrow they will swim
> In vinegar like saints' relics.   (*CPP* 171)

While Rose (134) and Britzolakis (72, 209) have read Plath's surgeon as male, her references to blood, the color red, and flowers, which she usually associates with female speakers, indicate that the surgeon may be a woman. Rather than tending "the colossus" of the male literary tradition, the female surgeon will now wield control with her scalpel/pen, reassembling the body or "corpus" of male writing to her own specifications. In "Lovesong," Hughes portrays himself as the female surgeon's male victim.

In addition to his allusions to "The Surgeon at 2 a.m.," Hughes may be responding to Plath's use of weapon imagery in "Daddy" and "The Courage of Shutting-Up," where "artillery" and "the muzzles of cannon" (*CPP* 209–10) threaten the female speaker, as well as her metaphors of torture in "Lady Lazarus" and "The Jailer." In "The Jailer," Plath takes the trope of bodily dismemberment to its extreme in a fantasy of torture: "I die with variety— | Hung, starved, burned, hooked" (*CPP* 227). Like "The Jailer," "Lovesong" too uses torture as a metaphor for the symbolic silencing Plath and Hughes sought, perhaps unconsciously, to perpetrate upon each other. The last lines of "Lovesong"—"In their entwined sleep they exchanged arms and legs | In their dreams their brains took each other hostage || In the morning they wore each other's faces" (*CPH* 256)—echo those of "The Jailer" in their admission of both rivalry and melancholic mourning:

> I imagine him
> Impotent as distant thunder,
> In whose shadow I have eaten my ghost ration.
> I wish him dead or away.
> That, it seems, is the impossibility.
>
> That being free....
>   ... what would he
> Do, do, do without me?   (*CPP* 227)

"Lovesong," however, is more than an anxiety-ridden revision of "The Surgeon at 2 a.m.," "The Courage of Shutting-Up," "Lady Lazarus," and "The Jailer": it is a mournful confession of the realities of poetic rivalry. In this respect, "Lovesong" differs from other poems in *Crow* that speak to the "war of words" between the sexes—and between Plath and Hughes in particular—in that male and female are equally to blame for the loss of self enacted at the poem's end. While "Lovesong" still exhibits the same male anxiety of female influence that appears in "A Disaster" and other *Crow* poems, it also acknowledges "the surgeon's gag" that the male literary tradition had placed upon women's expression. When Hughes writes that "His words were occupying armies," he acknowledges his complicity as an "imperial" force colonizing the woman writer. Yet he also holds Plath responsible: if his words are an army, hers are assassins hiding in wait for a clear shot. Both sides have blood on their hands. Ultimately, "Lovesong" registers the secret fear that Plath had harbored since the earliest days of the marriage—that she would "become" Hughes, that he would "remake" her. Hughes, too, shared this fear of remaking: "In the morning they wore each other's faces" (*CPH* 256).

Such anxieties would continue to surface in later years. Consider Hughes's "Mother-Tongue," which dates from the 1990s:

> Now she sways over a cello.
> The hairs of the bow
> Are the hairs of my body miraculously lengthened.
> She regards them as hers.

> She uses them with abandon, flings her arm
> And the hand holding the bow.
>
> The strings of the cello are the fibres
> Of the umbilicus
> We shared long ago. So long ago
> My memory of our sharing it, in the cave mouth,
> Is lost, far beyond the event horizon,
> In the black hole
> Out of which her music still pours.   (*CPH* 860–1)

It is perhaps no coincidence that some of the imagery in "Mother-Tongue" recalls Hughes's earlier elegy for Plath, "Cadenza," published in *Wodwo*:

> The violinist's shadow vanishes.
>
> The husk of a grasshopper
> Sucks a remote cyclone and rises.
>
> The full, bared throat of a woman walking water,
> The loaded estuary of the dead.
>
> And I am the cargo
> Of a coffin attended by swallows.
>
> And I am the water
> Bearing the coffin that will not be silent.   (*CPH* 148–9)

In "Cadenza," the music of the violin is drowned out by the voice of the dead woman, just as in "Mother-Tongue" the woman usurps the speaker's "music." In each case, the speaker reluctantly relinquishes his voice to the female—an act which initiates an apocalypse, as if the woman's voice has the power to alter the landscape itself. In "Mother-Tongue" all is reduced to a "black hole"; in "Cadenza" "the whole sky dives shut like a burned land back to its spark" (149), while images of cyclones and grasshopper husks recall the Book of Revelation. Later, in "The Hidden Orestes," a *Howls & Whispers* poem, the speaker recounts the story of Electra, an obvious double of Plath. Hughes imagines Electra's husband

> alarmed
> By the uncanny masculine voice
> That now and again, before she's aware of it,
> Bursts from between her lips
> With a demonic snarl.   (*CPH* 1175)

These poems suggest that Hughes never completely overcame the anxiety of female influence that went hand in hand with Plath's posthumous presence in his writing life. For Hughes, even in death, Plath "will not be silent" (*CPH* 149).

10

The Old Factory Demolished:
Wodwo to *River*

Ted Hughes's editorial re-engagement with Sylvia Plath's work after her death meant that he again assumed the role of collaborator, as he had throughout the early years of their marriage. Although he felt duty-bound to promote Plath's work, he was all too aware of the toll this task took upon his own writing life. He often complained, after Plath's and Wevill's deaths, of a debilitating writer's block, and constantly claimed he had allowed himself to become distracted by the Plath "fanstasia." But it was mainly grief that stood in the way of his ambition. He told Lucas Myers in 1984,

I keep writing this and that, but it seems pitifully little for the time I spend pursuing it. I wonder sometimes if things might have gone differently without the events of 63 & 69. I have an idea of those two episodes as giant steel doors shutting down over great parts of myself, leaving me that much less, just what was left, to live on.   (*L* 489)

In 1976, he wrote about Plath's death to his old friend Daniel Huws:

Sometimes I think I ought really to try and write it all out, as I've occasionally started doing, and then other times I ought to forget it, vanish, and start again somehow. I met a healer/spiritualist last week who told me to lie flat on the earth, splay out my arms and legs, and let it all go—release it into the astral. I feel she might be right. But then I feel you have to deal with it, too—if only to put an end to "evasion". What's certainly wrong is staggering along year after year, neither dealing with it nor letting it go.   (*L* 381)

While Hughes did not publish confessional elegies about Plath during this time, as he later would in *Birthday Letters*, he nevertheless assimilated Plath's poetic strategies into his work throughout the sixties, seventies, and eighties. *Wodwo*, *Gaudete*, and *Remains of Elmet* engage with her work on a variety of levels: at times, Hughes continues to revise Plath; at others he comes close to elegizing her; still elsewhere he incorporates her loose rhymes and short lines without any revisionary intent. The *Moortown* poems eschew her influence altogether, though this "break" from Plath would be short-lived. Thus, while several collections in the decades following Plath's suicide may appear to ignore her death, closer analysis reveals that Plath's shadow hovers over many of these poems—poems in which he was "neither dealing with it nor letting it go."

THE SURREALIST IMPULSE: *RECKLINGS, WODWO,*
AND *GAUDETE*

Hughes has said his experimentation with surrealism came as a result of his engagement with the *Bardo Thödol,* the Tibetan Book of the Dead, which he first read in 1959–60 (Scigaj 7). Yet Plath's poems may have also increased his interest, for she had always been drawn to surrealist art, particularly that of Giorgio de Chirico and Paul Klee. Between 1963 and 1966 Hughes was in the process of organizing Plath's poems and publishing *Ariel* at the same time he was composing many of the *Recklings* and *Wodwo* poems; thus it is not surprising that he would have been influenced by the surrealism and apocalyptic grandeur of Plath's late work. The psychic turmoil Hughes experienced after her tragic death may also have pointed him toward surrealism; as Leonard Scigaj has written, "Plath's suicide may have thrown the surrealistic mode into overdrive" (87). Indeed, in his notes on *Wodwo,* Hughes wrote that after Plath's death, he realized that his "old factory had been demolished, and that I would have to start again elsewhere with a different product."[1]

Hughes first began to experiment with surrealism in the early sixties. "Memory," for example, shows the influence of Plath's Roethkean "Poem for a Birthday." "Memory," eventually collected in *Recklings* (1966), was first published in the *Times Literary Supplement* in 1961, which means it was most likely written after "Poem for a Birthday," whose composition Hughes dates to November 1959. "Memory" uses surrealism to describe the state that precedes the physical self. The last line of Hughes's first stanza, "Mother, mother, mother, what am I?" (*CPH* 129) echoes Plath's "Mother, you are the one mouth | I would be a tongue to. Mother of otherness | Eat me" (*CPP* 132) from the "Who" section of "Poem for a Birthday." Throughout "Who," the speaker uses metaphors of the shed and greenhouse to describe her mental state; she variously describes herself as "a root, a stone, an owl pellet," and says, "I must remember this, being small" (*CPP* 132). In "Memory," the speaker uses similar metaphors of the cellar to describe the process of "remembering." The speaker says, "A mouse buds at the washboarding. A nose | of ginger spider weaves its hairs toward me" (*CPH* 129). Plath writes, "Let me sit in a flowerpot, | The spiders won't notice. | My heart is a stopped geranium" (*CPP* 131). Hughes echoes this last line when he writes, "If I stop my heart and hold my breath || The needle will thread itself" (*CPH* 129). Hughes's "Nose wavering to investigate me" brings to mind Plath's "Dogbody noses the petals," while his "I fly up flustered | Into the winter of a near elm" echoes her "These halls are full of women who think they are birds." Hughes also alludes to the "Witch Burning" section of "Poem for a Birthday": his "Hands of light, hands of light" (*CPH* 129) bring us back to

---

[1] Ted Hughes, "Notes on Published Works," Box 115, MSS 644, Emory.

Plath's "I am lost, I am lost, in the robes of all this light" (*CPP* 136). Hughes's poem, like Plath's, shows the influence of Roethke, but his use of repetition ("Mother, mother, mother," "Hands of light, hands of light"), questions, exclamation points, and surrealism, all speak to Plath's influence. Plath's poem was more successful, however: where "Poem for a Birthday" depicts the process of mental breakdown and recovery, "Memory" is vague about its subject, sounding imitative rather than innovative. Other poems from *Recklings* also show Plath's influence: "Last Lines" incorporates elements of Plath's "Tulips" and "In Plaster," "Stealing Trout on a May Morning" looks to "Ariel," while "A Match" alludes to "The Snowman on the Moor" and "Hardcastle Crags." Hughes's "Love, love" (*CPH* 114) in "Plum-Blossom" echoes the same phrase in Plath's "Fever 103°," "Burning the Letters," "Nick and the Candlestick," and "The Couriers."

Wodwo (1967) lacks the stylistic and thematic unity of *The Hawk in the Rain* and *Lupercal*. The collection comprises poems written both before and after Plath's death—an event, Hughes admitted, that is reflected in the poems' order. He told János Csokits in 1967 that the book was "a record—for me—of a rather baffled time" and that all of the poems in the first part of *Wodwo* "were before the event, and yet seemed related to it"; he also wrote that the stories were "episodes of the event." Those poems written before Plath's suicide he deemed "prophetic." Hughes went so far as to say that "The Suitor," a short story in Part II of *Wodwo*, "is a story of death & the maiden & is a prophecy—I wrote it in 1962, January, almost under dictation. The Suitor is me, the man in the car is me, the girl is Sylvia, the stranger is death, & the situation turns me into an animal" (*L* 274). The letter to Csokits provides an unusually candid account of Plath's "influence," however indirect, upon Hughes's writing; very rarely does he admit to any kind of a connection—aesthetic or personal—between Plath and his own work during the sixties and seventies. He expressed a similar conclusion to Nick Gammage in 1993, writing that all the prose works in *Wodwo* were "prophecies about my own life. One or two others I wrote a bit later made this so clear, I stopped writing stories.... I became convinced that everything I wrote would somehow come true" (*L* 644).

We have seen that Plath was probably influenced by *Wodwo* poems such as "New Moon in January," "Out," "Full Moon and Little Frieda," "Dark Women," and "Pibroch." But the influence also ran in the other direction. "A Wind Flashes the Grass," published in 1966, was likely influenced by Plath's "Elm," while Hughes's "Ghost Crabs" owes something to Plath's "Mussel Hunter at Rock Harbor." Plath's "Mary's Song," written on November 19, 1962, probably influenced one of the more apocalyptic poems in *Wodwo*, "Karma." The food and religious imagery of "Mary's Song"—"The Sunday lamb cracks in its fat" (*CPP* 257)—suggests humankind's ravenous appetite for destruction and murder, one that often stems from religious differences. The same religion that dutifully observes the Sabbath will be responsible for the Holocaust; the Scientific Revolution, which helped put a man on the moon, also gave mankind the efficient killing machine that was Auschwitz. Mary understands that hatred will eventually sabotage even the noblest human ideals; the lamb cracking in its fat symbolizes the hypocrisy, gluttony, and greed that underlies the "holocaust" of human existence.

Hughes echoes Plath's apocalyptic overtones in "Karma," composed, according to his notebook, sometime in 1965–6 and published in the winter of 1966.[2] "Karma" is the first Hughes poem to use Holocaust imagery and invoke the names Dresden and Buchenwald; it tells a story of human destruction and genocide similar to "Mary's Song." Hughes writes of how "The seven lamented millions of Zion | Rose musically through the frozen mouths | Of Russia's snowed-under millions" (*CPH* 168), reflecting Plath's imagery of the Holocaust dead: "Their thick palls float || Over the cicatrix of Poland, burnt-out | Germany. | They do not die" (*CPP* 257). In both cases, the cries of the dead refuse to be silenced. Hughes again echoes these lines, and the word "cicatrix" in particular, when he writes of the blood of African-American slaves "Skywriting across the cortex" (*CPH* 168). He also echoes Plath's heart metaphor ("It is a heart, | This holocaust I walk in") with his own images of heart and blood ("the heart, a gulping mask, demands, demands | Appeasement | For its bloody possessor"). Hughes uses the word "fatten" while Plath uses "fat" twice. His point is similar to Plath's as he evokes food and female imagery:

> And a hundred and fifty million years of hunger
> Killing gratefully as breathing
> Moulded the heart and the mouth
>
> That cry for milk
> From the breast
> Of the mother
>
> Of the God
> Of the world
> Made of Blood.   (*CPH* 168)

While "mother" most likely refers to the White Goddess rather than the Virgin Mary, Hughes felt that the latter was a manifestation of the former. In Plath's poem, too, the world is "made of blood": Mary laments how "the world will kill and eat" her "golden child" (*CPP* 257).[3]

---

2 Ted Hughes, Notebook 8, MSS 644, Emory.

3 Hughes's "Boom," published in the *New Statesman* in October 1966, was also influenced by "Mary's Song." Hughes also draws on imagery from Plath's 1957 poem about the Holocaust, "The Thin People," in "Public Bar T.V.," with its depictions of weakened refugees unable to find sustenance in a parched land.

Hughes's use of surrealism in "Scapegoats and Rabies," which was composed in 1965–6, published in the *New Statesman* in 1967, and included in the American version of *Wodwo*, echoes that of "Lady Lazarus" and "Daddy."[4] His depiction of a First World War general suffering hellish visions evokes Lady Lazarus's memories of torture: his "Nothing remains of the *tête d'armée* but the skin— | A dangling parchment lantern || Slowly revolving to right, revolving to left" (*CPH* 188) echoes Plath's "my skin | Bright as a Nazi lampshade" (*CPP* 244) and "I turn and burn" (*CPP* 246). Hughes's soldiers' "laced-up eyes" (189) recall the dismembered bodies of Keith Douglas's speakers, but they also bring Lady Lazarus's mutilated face to mind. His "terrible engine of the boots" (187) recall Plath's "An engine, an engine | Chuffing me off like a Jew" (*CPP* 223) as well as the boot imagery in "Daddy."

Hughes continued in the surrealist mode in *Crow* (1970), which I discussed in Chapter 9, and *Gaudete* (1977), which was originally written as a screenplay as early as 1964.[5] *Gaudete* tells the story of the Revd Nicholas Lumb, who is abducted by spirits while his double is sent back into the human world. The book is divided into two parts—Prologue and Epilogue. The Prologue tells the story of Lumb's double as he wreaks havoc upon Lumb's friends and family, while the Epilogue, a long sequence of lyric poems, tells of the real Lumb's experiences in the spirit world. Scigaj writes that these poems are "written to the goddess of nature . . . after having achieved spiritual rebirth" (167), yet Plath's memory also haunts the Epilogue. The "you" of the poem does at times resemble a nature goddess, but she also resembles Plath. Frequently, the two identities merge together, which is not surprising given the fact that Plath was, for Hughes, a manifestation of the White Goddess (a part she played willingly until *Ariel*).

The woman in the Epilogue is lost and wounded, and only the speaker can save her. She is a vestige of the lost bride in *Crow*. Hughes had already written of the myth of Orpheus and Eurydice in *Orpheus* (1973), but, as he later told Sagar, this approach to Plath's suicide had been too obvious. *Gaudete* shows Hughes attempting to rewrite the story of Orpheus and Eurydice through the figures of Lumb and "the goddess":

> My legs, though, were already galloping to help
> The woman who wore a split lopsided mask—
>
> That was how the comedy began.
> Before I got to her—it was ended
>
> And the curtain came down.
>   .   .   .   .   .
> She fell into the earth
> And I was devoured.   (*CPH* 361)

---

[4] Ted Hughes, Notebook 8, MSS 644, Emory.
[5] Ted Hughes to Assia Wevill, January 31, 1964, MSS 1058, Emory.

As in *Crow*, Hughes attempts to integrate his real relationship with Plath with his personal myth. The Hughes figure/speaker becomes a martyr, while the Plath figure is both the cause of his undoing and the key to his restitution. While his description of her uses the imagery of Greek and Minoan myth, the imagery of the lion and the act of riding also recalls "Ariel":

> She rides the earth
> On an ass, on a lion.
> She rides the heavens
> On a great white bull.
>
> She is an apple.
> Whoever plucks her
> Nails his heart
> To the leafless tree.   (*CPH* 363)

Here Hughes melds the imagery of Eve, the Fall, and the Goddess, while perhaps alluding to Plath.

Hughes had admitted to Aurelia Plath that he felt a tremendous amount of guilt over Plath's suicide, writing in March 1963, "if there is an eternity, I am damned in it" (*L* 215). But by turning the real story into myth—by recasting himself Orpheus, or Lumb, or Crow, and Plath as the lost bride, Great Mother, or White Goddess—he found a distancing mechanism. If both he and Plath were directed by forces beyond their control, then neither was to blame for destroying the other's life: their story was preordained. This idea reaches its apotheosis in the teleological trajectory of *Birthday Letters*, in which the love story is doomed by fate. But we also see glimpses of the strategy in *Gaudete*. There, Plath and Hughes are thinly disguised:

> I turned
> I bowed
> In the morgue I kissed
> Your temple's refrigerated glazed
> As rained-on graveyard marble, my
> Lips queasy, heart non-existent
>
> And straightened
> Into sun-darkness
> Like a pillar over Athens
>
> Defunct
>
> In the blinding metropolis of cameras.   (*CPH* 364–5)

Hughes's reference to Plath and the media glare he endured after her death is so obvious here that it is difficult to understand how critics have been able to persist in ignoring her role in this work.

Although T. S. Eliot's *Four Quartets* is the most obvious poetic influence on the Epilogue (particularly in the third and penultimate poems), Plath's voice is also present. As Hughes told Terry Gifford and Neil Roberts in 1979, "I wanted the language [in *Gaudete*] open and clear—conductive of narrative current— above everything I wanted a flowing and accelerating current of narrative momentum . . . something between a primitive painting, a mosaic, and a slightly speeded up early silent film—a sense of that—where things are simultaneously comic, horrible and beautiful" (*L* 429). Two years later he described Plath's *Ariel* voice to Sagar in similar terms: it was naked, "all little dramas. More like some painting, or music, than any other poetry" (*L* 445). Indeed, the style of *Gaudete* does at times resemble Plath's. For example, the following section makes use of Plathian cadences, syntax, imagery, dashes, question marks, and short lines:

> A bang—a burning—
> I opened my eyes
> In a vale crumbling with echoes.
>
> A solitary dove
> Cries in the tree—I cannot bear it.
>
> From this centre
> It wearies the compass.
>
> Am I killed?
> Or am I searching?
>
> Is this the rainbow silking my body?
> Which wings are these? (*CPH* 373)

The passage's stylistic features bring *Ariel* to mind, while the rebirth and wing imagery recall Plath's "Poem for a Birthday," particularly the "Flute Notes from a Reedy Pond" section. It is Hughes, now, who borrows Plath's language to aid his epic of rebirth. He will do so again in *Cave Birds* (1978), in poems such as "The Interrogator," "The Plaintiff," "The Executioner," and "The Accused," which answer back to Plath's "The Detective" and "The Jailer." Hughes's "The Plaintiff," especially, seems to be deliberately written in Plath's voice to suggest that she is the plaintiff and he is the defendant in the ongoing public trial of their marriage. Note the moon imagery, exclamation points, short lines, and the quickly changing metaphors—all features of Plath's late work:

> These are the wings and beak of light!
>
> This is your moon of pain—and the wise night-bird
> Your smile's shadow.
>
> .   .   .   .
>
> How you have nursed her!
>
> Her feathers are leaves, the leaves tongues,
> The mouths wounds, the tongues flames
>
> The feet
> Roots (*CPH* 423)

"Bride and Groom Lie Hidden for Three Days," a surrealist *Cave Birds* poem in which a couple "assembles" each other, hopefully imagines the moment when the lost bride and groom "bring each other to perfection." The assembly occurs after a disaster of some kind—the bride finds the groom's eyes "Among some rubble"—suggesting that the bride and groom are a post-apocalyptic Adam and Eve. Here, however, there is no serpent waiting in the wings; both man and woman attend to the other's creation "gasping with joy, with cries of wonderment" (*CPH* 438). The poem offers a counter-image to the trope of bodily dismemberment in Plath's poems ("The Stones," "The Applicant," "Lady Lazarus"): here the couple does not tear each other apart, but rather reassembles each other with "infinite care." Hughes re-imagines the insidious "city of spare parts" (*CPP* 137) Plath had written of in "The Stones," and offers an alternative vision, a return to the early promise of marriage. *Gaudete* and *Cave Birds* may have been reflections of a "complex Jungian dreamworld" (166), as Hughes told Sagar, but they were also reflections—no matter how well disguised in surrealism—of Hughes's grief for Plath.

REMAINS OF ELMET

Remains of Elmet (1979) marked Hughes's departure from the surrealism of *Wodwo*, *Crow*, and *Gaudete*, and a return to the realism of earlier moor poems such as "Wind," "The Horses," and "Crow Hill." Yet, despite its naturalistic overtones, *Remains of Elmet* is dominated by the same sense of terror, foreboding, and doom that marked many of the poems in *Crow*.

Hughes wrote the collection in response to a series of black and white photographs of the Calder Valley taken by Fay Godwin.[6] The "remains" of the book's title refers to the remains of the valley and its people, as well as the remains of the dead—specifically, the dead of the First World War and the dehumanized victims of the Industrial Revolution. As in Seamus Heaney's *North*, archaeology metaphors are interspersed throughout the volume in order to give a sense of the region's brutal history. In fact, the volume is influenced throughout by Heaney's *North*, which had been published four years earlier. As Hughes told a BBC reporter in 1980:

I use Elmet then to signify not just a rather vaguely-featured Celtic and criminal and nonconformist inheritance, but a naturally-evolved local organism, like a giant protozoa, which is made up of all the earlier deposits and histories, animated in a single glance, an attitude, an inflection of speech. If you imagine all those things distilled into a lens, with filters and distortions peculiar to the ingredients, then the characteristics of this lens would be, in a sense, *Remains of Elmet*. (qtd. in Scigaj 255)[7]

---

[6] Hughes had in fact suggested that he and Godwin collaborate as early as 1971 (*L* 376).
[7] "Elmet," BBC Radio 3, Prod. Fraser Steel, recorded 3 May 1980.

In "Long Screams," for example, Hughes could be writing about the victims of the Somme or a tribal battle: "Unending bleeding. | Deaths left over. | The dead piled in cairns | Over the dead. | Everywhere dead things for monuments of the dead" (*CPH* 460). But unlike Heaney, Hughes chronicles capitalist as well as political violence. In several poems, the horrors of the Industrial Revolution are linked explicitly with those of the First World War. As Hughes writes in "First, Mills," one prepared the path for the other: "First, Mills | and steep wet cobbles | Then cenotaphs" (*CPH* 462). *Remains of Elmet* is an elegy for a time and a place before "the railway station | That bled this valley to death" (462).

The First World War and the Industrial Revolution are not the only events upon which Hughes ruminates: Plath's spirit and words also haunt these poems. Personal and historical tragedy intersect, particularly in the many moor poems which dominate the volume. When Hughes revisits this landscape, its significance is forever changed by his wife's grave in Heptonstall cemetery in the Calder Valley. Hughes mourns Plath alongside the legions of dead Lancaster Fusiliers whose graves cover the hillsides; these poems are elegies for a time and a place, but also for a lost youth, a lost wife, and the lost promise of Hughes's first marriage. Just as Hughes was the unspoken object of many of Plath's moor poems, so Plath is now Hughes's object as he assimilates her bleak metaphors into his own moor poems.

Hughes's critics have been reluctant to ascribe to the poems any connection with Plath.[8] Nevertheless, several poems engage in a grief-propelled dialogue with Plath through allusions to the Wuthering Heights story, which, as we have seen, Plath used as a personal metaphor for her relationship with Hughes. Now Plath had become Cathy's ghost, who roamed the moors and tormented Hughes for his transgressions. Four poems in *Remains of Elmet* extend the Wuthering Heights conversation Plath had begun years earlier: "Two Trees at Top Withens," "Top Withens," "Emily Brontë," and "Haworth Parsonage" all refer back to the novel and the actual journey Hughes took with Plath to Top Withens, the alleged site of Wuthering Heights, during her 1956 visit to Yorkshire. As we have seen, Plath wrote about that trip in her journal, her letters to her mother, and in her poems "Two Views of Withens" and "Wuthering Heights," both of which evince sadness and resignation. Hughes's Top Withens poems express similar sentiments.

"Top Withens" alludes to the promise of Hughes's and Plath's early years together, and, simultaneously, mourns the loss of that promise. The ruins of the original Wuthering Heights provide Hughes with a metaphor for the early hope of his marriage: "Pioneer hope squared stones | And laid these roof slabs, and wore a way to them" (*CPH* 486). The act of building a house corresponds

---

[8] Leonard Scigaj focuses on the influence of Taoist philosophy (236–9), while Terry Gifford and Neil Roberts discuss the volume as one in which Hughes "can continue with unique directness his interest in the relationship between human and elemental processes" (233).

to the attempt to build a solid foundation in a "pioneering" marriage, where both husband and wife would treat each other as equal artists. "How young that world was!" he writes, "The hills full of savage promise" (486). Hughes imagines that the owners of Wuthering Heights resisted the temptation to move to America, despite ubiquitous stories of its abundance. Yet he implies it was the wrong decision: "The dream's fort held out— | Stones blackening with dogged purpose. | But at the dead end of a wrong direction" (486). The Yeatsian "dream's fort"—the marriage of true minds—was not so inhabitable after all. Hughes may have felt guilty for convincing Plath to move back to England from America, where, he now imagines, she may have been happier. But, Hughes writes, "Now it is all over" (487). The ruin of Wuthering Heights reflects, as it did for Cathy and Heathcliff, the ruin of their love and the impossibility of their partnership.

Several lines in "Top Withens" allude to Plath's "Wuthering Heights" (1961): Hughes's "And the skylines, howling, closed in" echoes Plath's "The horizons ring me like faggots," while Plath's image of the horizons dissolving "Like a series of promises" brings to mind the sense of "Pioneer hope" that was squandered in Hughes's poem. Like Hughes, Plath also described the house's ruins—"Hollow doorsteps go from grass to grass; | Lintel and sill have unhinged themselves" (*CPP* 168). Hughes's mention of "Stones blackening" may allude to Plath's "Black stone, black stone," as well as her use of the same phrase in other moor poems such as "The Snowman on the Moor" and "Hardcastle Crags." Her depiction of the wind as deathly ("I can feel it trying | To funnel my heat away" (*CPP* 167)) matches Hughes's: "The wind swings withered scalps of souls" (*CPH* 487). In Hughes's "Two Trees at Top Withens" the language is similarly pessimistic: the two trees "Play the reeds of desolation" (457).[9] The poem responds to Plath's "Two Views of Withens," which recounts the speaker's sense of foreboding upon viewing the ruins of Wuthering Heights. While Hughes had used such imagery before in his landscape poems—and indeed Plath's "Wuthering Heights" owes something to Hughes's earlier moor poems, particularly "Wind"—his engagement with the Wuthering Heights story reflects a desire to add his own voice to the burgeoning myth of his marriage to Plath.

Hughes gives an account of the Withens hike in two later poems, "Two Photographs of Top Withens," and "Wuthering Heights." The former was published in Hughes's 1994 revised version of *Remains of Elmet*, titled *Elmet*. It is written in the style of the *Birthday Letters* poems—confessional, autobiographical, fatalistic, and nostalgic—and recalls a famous photograph Hughes took of Plath sitting in one of the sycamore trees atop the hill. Although Plath

---

[9] Presumably, one of these is the tree upon which Plath perched while Hughes took her photograph on their first hike to Top Withens, and which he later wrote about in "Wuthering Heights."

smiles in the photograph, and gushes about the possibility of buying and renovating Top Withens, Hughes implies that both knew neither could withstand "the empty horror of the moor" (*CPH* 841). In a line that recalls Plath's dismal vision in her earlier "Two Views of Withens," he calls Wuthering Heights "a fouled nest" from which "Emily's dream has flown" (*CPH* 841). Hughes implies that Plath's desire for the two of them to "become" Cathy and Heathcliff was a self-fulfilling prophecy of death and doom. He echoes the repetitive wind and stone imagery in Plath's "Wuthering Heights" when he writes of the

> Mad heather and grass tugged by the mad
> And empty wind
> That has petrified or got rid of
>
> Everything but the stones.
> The stones are safe, being stone.
> Even the spirit of the place, like Emily's,
>
> Hidden beneath stone.   (*CPH* 841)

Hughes draws an implicit comparison between the Wuthering Heights story and Plath's life when he writes, "Nothing's left for sightseers—only a book" (841). He ends the poem with contrapuntal images of permanence and transience that allude to his marriage. The two trees still stand together, "unchanged," but the woman whose photograph he snapped years ago was, even then, "a ghost."

By recalling the visit, and by comparing Plath to both Brontë and Cathy, Hughes suggests that Plath had inherited Brontë's death-wish as well as her literary ambition. Hughes saw numerous parallels between Plath and Brontë— both were writers alternately repressed and romantic, both were fascinated by wild landscapes, and both died young. Both were also, for Hughes, manifestations of the White Goddess who became entwined with the myth of their literary creations. Just as Hughes read Plath's heroines as manifestations of her real self rather than performances, so he read Cathy as Brontë. In "Emily Brontë," Hughes imagines the writer in love with the bleak moor-wind whose "kiss was fatal" and draws an implicit comparison with Cleopatra when he writes of "The stream she loved too well | That bit her breast" (*CPH* 485). Hughes's depiction of Brontë is, as Lucasta Miller has noted, both clichéd and reductive: "Creative women, he seems to be saying, are terrifying and vindictive creatures" (280). Later, others would accuse him of the same reductive typecasting of Plath in *Birthday Letters*. In "Wuthering Heights," a *Birthday Letters* poem, he begins to conflate the two women and their alleged death-wish early on: "The moor | Lifted and opened its dark flower | For you too" (*CPH* 1080). Hughes compares Plath to Brontë throughout the poem; by the end, they begin to merge into one:

> And the stone,
> Reaching to touch your hand, found you real
> And warm, and lucent, like that earlier one.

> And maybe a ghost, trying to hear your words,
> Peered from the broken mullions
> And was stilled. Or was suddenly aflame
> With the scorch of doubled envy. Only
> Gradually quenched in understanding.   (1082)

Hughes's final poem in *Remains of Elmet*, "The Angel," again makes clear that the ghost of Plath is one of the presiding "spirits" of the collection. The poem recounts a dream Hughes had before Plath's death, in which he saw an apocalyptic angel flying over the moors, "made of smoking snow" and "cast in burning metal" (492–3). The dream, he later told Scigaj, was a premonition of Plath's suicide; the angel's "strange head-dress" made of a satin square "foreshadowed the white square of satin covering Sylvia's face when Hughes first viewed the body" (Scigaj 253). In the poem, Hughes writes, "When I next saw that strange square of satin | I reached out and touched it" (*CPH* 493). As Scigaj notes, "The Angel" is a revision of "Ballad of a Fairy Tale" in *Wodwo*, which is slightly darker. In that poem, Hughes writes that he does not touch the square of satin covering Plath's face, yet by *Remains of Elmet*, he imagines himself doing so. "The Angel" recalls the Wuthering Heights story in its evocation of a woman-spirit haunting the moors by night, and vanishing before the moment of contact, and, like others in *Remains of Elmet*, emphasizes the connection between Plath and Hughes and Cathy and Heathcliff. Scigaj writes that the angel, which also takes the form of a swan, is a manifestation of an international folklore motif in which the mortal man possesses the "swan maiden... or divine princess only until she recovers her feather garment from his possession or until he breaks a taboo" (253). Although the dream foretells Plath's death, "The Angel" is also a narrative of self-recrimination in which Hughes castigates himself for breaking a taboo (through adultery) and losing the "divine princess."

"Cock-Crows" (1978), one of the final poems in *Remains of Elmet*, shows the influence of Plath's "Ariel" quite clearly. Hughes is not so much rewriting Plath here as he is inheriting her innovations, and applying them to his own work. However "Cock-Crows" is not as successful as "Ariel," partly because Plath's influence is so obvious; in this instance, imitation does not yield innovation, as it did in *Crow*.

"Cock-Crows" begins at the same point as "Ariel": with the self in darkness.

> I stood on a dark summit, among dark summits —
> Tidal dawn splitting heaven from earth,
> The oyster
> Opening to taste gold.   (*CPH* 491)

"Ariel" opens with the line "Stasis in darkness" (*CPP* 239); both speakers are poised before sunrise on the brink of experience. Hughes's next line, "Tidal dawn splitting heaven from earth," draws upon Plath's sea imagery in her second and third lines: "Then the substanceless blue | Pour of tor and distances" (*CPP* 239). Hughes's use of the word "splitting" also echoes Plath's "The furrow | Splits and passes" (239). His "oyster | Opening to taste gold" mimes the widening of perspective that takes place in "Ariel," while his tasting metaphor brings Plath's "Black sweet blood mouthfuls" to mind. Yet the "I" of "Cock-Crows" simply observes the emerging dawn, and listens to the sounds of the cocks crowing across the valley; unlike the speaker of "Ariel," the self is passive.

Hughes situates his speaker on a hill amidst the moors, as Plath did. His speaker hears the cocks "Bubbling deep in the valley cauldron," a line which borrows Plath's "cauldron of morning" from "Ariel." Hughes goes on to depict the gathering sounds of the cock-crows in sexual language that echoes the propulsion of Plath's metaphorical horse:

> Then one or two tossed clear, like soft rockets
> And sank back again dimming.
>
> Then soaring harder, brighter, higher
> Tearing the mist,
> Bubble-glistenings flung up and bursting to light
> Brightening the undercloud,
> The fire-crests of the cocks—the sickle shouts,
> Challenge against challenge, answer to answer,
> Hooking higher,
> Clambering up the sky as they melted,
> Hanging smouldering from the night's fringes.   (*CPH* 491)

The "bursting to light" is a more prosaic version of Plath's "Foam to wheat," while "Hooking higher" echoes Plath's "Berries cast dark | Hooks—" (*CPP* 239), as well as other hook imagery in Plath's work.[10] Hughes's "melted" repeats Plath's "The child's cry || Melts in the wall" (*CPP* 239) while his "magical soft mixture boiling over, | Spilling and sparkling into other valleys" again brings Plath foaming ("glitter of seas") and cauldron metaphors to mind. There is also an echo of "foam" and "glitter" in Hughes's "glow-swollen" in the next stanza. Yet Hughes's poem picks up where Plath leaves off—at the moment of sunrise when "the last spark died, and the embers paled" (*CPH* 491). Plath's "red eye" of the sun has become just a dying spark—perhaps a reference to the actual end of the journey she romanticized in "Ariel." Hughes implies there is no magic moment that will carry his speakers heavenward; rather, the moment is ephemeral, and leads not to transcendence but to the workaday world, "the smoke of towns." He suggests something similar in "Roe-Deer," in which a dawn encounter with a pair of deer ends prosaically—the deer scatter (Hughes invokes

---

[10] Variations of the word "hook" appear in "Words for a Nursery," "Zoo Keeper's Wife," "Tulips," "Blackberrying," "Three Women," "Elm," Berck-Plage," "Burning the Letters," "The Detective," "The Munich Mannequins," "Gigolo," and "Mystic."

Plath's cauldron metaphor again when he writes that they leave "Into the boil of big flakes") and the snow erases their hoof prints, "Revising its dawn inspiration | Back to the ordinary" (513). Where Plath leaves us forever in the moment of transport and exhilaration, Hughes suggests that such journeys into the self ought to lead outward, eventually.

Although Plath is rarely mentioned as an inspiration for *Remains of Elmet*, the collection is indebted to her words and images. Hughes not only writes of the historical changes that have scarred the Calder Valley, but the personal cataclysms that have changed the terrain of his own life: the impact of the Industrial Revolution and the First World War on the region mirrors the world-altering impact of Plath's death. *Remains of Elmet* chronicles how all have made their mark upon Hughes's real and psychic geographies.

MOORTOWN AND BEYOND

The poems of *Moortown Elegies* (1978), later published in *Moortown* (1979), mark a departure from the bleak moor poems of *Remains of Elmet* and the surrealism of *Crow, Cave Birds*, and *Wodwo*.[11] *Moortown*, in fact, marks perhaps the biggest stylistic shift of Hughes's career. Part of the reason the poems sound so different from Hughes's earlier work is that Hughes has, for the time being, disengaged himself from his dialogue with Plath. The poems are "unsentimental, antipastoral" (Scigaj 264) portraits of farm life written from the farmer's perspective. Hughes told János Csokits that the poems were "bits and pieces" written between 1971 and 1977, when his "main concern and focus" was farming.[12] (Hughes was, at this time, helping his wife, Carol, and father-in-law, Jack Orchard, run a farm he had bought near Court Green.) The births and deaths of lambs and calves, the dehorning of bulls, the mating of cattle, and the travails of spawning salmon are all relayed in long-lined, prosaic verse. Scigaj reports that Hughes intended the poems to be immediate and accurate, true to the experience of the moment, rather than events later recrafted into literary artifacts: "in the great majority of the poems he deliberately sought to copy down the details fresh, as near as possible to the day of the actual occurrence, in a rough, pocket journal sort of verse" (262).

Like *Birthday Letters*, *Moortown* is characterized by long, unrhyming lines, few stanza breaks, and little distance between poet and speaker. While one

---

[11] Paul Keegan notes that the Faber and Faber edition of *Moortown* (1979) included "three works previously published in limited editions by the Rainbow Press—*Prometheus on His Crag, Moortown Elegies*, and *Adam and the Sacred Nine. . . .* Hughes later regretted the bundling of these works together with the 'Moortown' sequence proper, which he later republished as *Moortown Diary* (1989)." What I refer to here as *Moortown* is "the 'Moortown' sequence proper," which was published as a separate sequence in Hughes's *Collected Poems* under the title *Moortown Diary*.

[12] Ted Hughes to János Csokits, September 1980, MSS 895, Emory.

might venture that *Moortown* lays the poetic foundation for the style of *Birthday Letters*, there is much less artifice in the earlier volume, and no esoteric imagery. As Hughes wrote to Michael Hamburger about life on the farm, "The whole thing is too interesting to resist. It's reconnected me to the only world I belong to in any way—which I felt I was beginning to lose" (*L* 365). The poems' unsentimental vignettes of rural life suggest the influence of Seamus Heaney and Patrick Kavanagh. Plath's influence is relatively absent; apart from a few phrases ("Blue | Dusk presses into their skulls | Electrodes of stars" (*CPH* 505); "the wind | Presses outer space into the grass" (*CPH* 511)), Hughes seems to have jettisoned her language, imagery, and motifs altogether.

The poems of *Moortown* may be "antipastoral" in their unflinching descriptions of the farmer's life, but they belong, nonetheless, to the pastoral tradition. It is as if Hughes is prescribing an antidote to the disease he described in *Remains of Elmet*; the trauma of the Industrial Revolution and the First World War can only be "cured" through a re-engagement with nature on its own terms. While Hughes was already best known as an animal poet before *Moortown*, these "animal poems" are very different from his previous ones. Here the animals are not wild, and, thus, not romanticized; unlike Hughes's pike, jaguar, and hawk, they inhabit the domestic realm. They inspire loyalty, affection, and pity rather than awe. Nature had obviously been a source of wonder before *Moortown*, but that wonder was usually tinged with fear; here there is more pathos than violence. Death is no longer a Satanic avatar, as it was in *Crow*; it has become a manifestation of the benevolent chaos of nature rather than a bullet fired from the underworld.

Stylistically, there are fewer question marks and explanation points in the *Moortown* poems, most of which are at least a page long without stanza breaks. The long lines in loose blank verse give these poems a very different tone than those in previous collections. The overall impression is one of relaxed observation—which is why they sound so different from Plath, whose *Ariel* poems tend to be either deliberately flat or high-pitched. As Hughes himself admitted to a graduate student in 1992, the *Moortown* poems, along with some pieces in *River*, were the only instances in his *oeuvre* of "objective descriptive writing" as opposed to the "'dramatisation' of a purely internal psychodrama" (*L* 622). There is no place for Nietzsche in these poems; Lawrence is only half-audible.

The strict realism suits Hughes well. The poems' lack of self-censure or self-pity is refreshing; it is as if Hughes has finally found a way to free himself from the currents of guilt, anger, and despair that run through his poetry from *Wodwo* on. By focusing intently on the daily life of farm animals and the demands of farm labor, he avoids the kind of imaginative encounters with esoteric motifs so often tied to pain. Despite the poems' overt autobiographical genesis (their "pocket journal" tone), *Moortown* is less personally revealing than those collections that use surrealism to approach the traumas of Hughes's life, such as *Crow* and *Gaudete*.

Hughes's move away from esoteric motifs and surrealism may have been inspired by his reading of Seamus Heaney. Though *Moortown* was published in 1979, many of the poems in the collection date from the early- to mid-seventies. Hughes would have read Heaney's *Death of a Naturalist* and *Door into the Dark*, with their startling metaphors of farm labor, by the time he began composing his *Moortown* poems. Hughes's poems, though less lyrical and metaphorical than Heaney's, nevertheless use a similar plainspoken, Frostian diction, as in "Struggle," a poem which recounts the birth of a calf: "We had been expecting her to calve | And there she was, just after dawn, down. | Private, behind bushed hedge-cutting, in a low rough corner" (*CPH* 508). Similarly, in "New Year Exhilaration," Hughes draws upon the Yorkshire vernacular, just as Frost and Heaney had drawn upon their local vernacular. Hughes writes:

> People
> Walk precariously, the whole landscape
> Is imperiled, like a tarpaulin
> With the wind under it. "It nearly
> Blew me up the chymbley!" And a laugh
> Blows away like a hat.   (508)

As in the case of Plath and Hughes, it is sometimes difficult to distinguish Hughes's influence on Heaney—who credited Hughes's "View of a Pig" as one of the poems that inspired him to begin writing—from Heaney's influence on Hughes. However, it is clear that with *Moortown*, Hughes has moved away from those topics he and Plath had pursued together, such as war, violence, and competition. The life-and-death struggles in nature are now recast as a birth-weakened calf attempting to walk rather than a wild hawk fighting the wind. Nature is no longer red in tooth and claw. While *Moortown* appears to be an unimportant chapter in the Plath–Hughes dialogue, it is Hughes's distance from Plath that allows us to see, in retrospect, the extent to which his previous poems drew upon hers. By turning to farm life—a topic with which Plath had little familiarity—Hughes finally finds a subject that is "his" alone.

The quiet, plodding cadences of these poems, however, could only be sustained for so long. Hughes soon re-engages in his dialogue with Plath in "Earth-numb," part of the 1979 Faber edition of *Moortown*. Here, Hughes once again revises Plath's "Ariel"—indeed, the poem might be described as "Pike" meets "Ariel." Hughes sets his poem during a dawn fishing outing, and employs Plathian metaphors of electrocution and surgery to describe the effect of the river's "awakening" on the speaker. As in "Ariel," dawn marks the moment of individual transformation:

> And bang! The river grabs at me
>
> A mouth-flash, an electrocuting malice
> Like a trap, trying to rip life off me—
> And the river stiffens alive,

The black hole thumps, the whole river hauls
And I have one.
A piling voltage hums, jamming me stiff—
Something terrified and terrifying
Gleam-surges to and fro through me
From the river to the sky, from the sky into the river

Uprooting dark bedrock, shatters it in air,
Cartwheels across me, slices thudding through me
As if I were the current—
Till the fright flows all one way down the line   (*CPH* 541)

Hughes's "As if I were the current" echoes Plath's "I | Am the arrow," while his imagery of a natural force "grabbing" at the speaker, as well as the phrases, "the whole river hauls" and "shatters it in air," remind one of Plath's "Something else || Hauls me through air—"(*CPP* 239). Like Plath, Hughes imagines himself possessed by a life force normally beyond grasp; for both poets, the liminal dawn setting is a metaphor for the awakening of the self. At the end of Hughes's poem, however, the speaker turns his attention to the fish he has caught. Thus what initially appeared to be a poem of self-transformation along the lines of "Ariel" subverts the reader's expectations: the exhilaration of the first few stanzas ends bluntly in an image of "the steel spectre of purples | From the forge of water | Gagging on emptiness || As the eyes of incredulity | Fix their death-exposure of the celandine and the cloud" (*CPH* 542). Hughes refuses to yield to the romantic impulse that propelled most of the poem. In the end, the speaker is left only with a dead fish rather than a deeper level of self-awareness. Unlike most of Hughes's "Ariel" "revisions," "Earth-numb" is a successful assimilation of Plath's motifs; here Hughes borrows Plath's images yet transforms them into a very Hughesian poem.

    In *River* (1983), Hughes's subject is no longer the farm, but the life of the river, and the life-and-death struggles of the creatures within it. The poems share the same observant focus on nature that marked *Moortown*. The style of *River*, however, differs from that of *Moortown* in that Hughes uses more artifice; the poems are closer to lyric poetry than the prosaic "pocket-journal" style he had used previously. *River* is less naturalistic as well. Poems such as "The River" and "Last Night" strike a grandiose, mythic tone more reminiscent of *Crow*. And man is no longer nature's caretaker, as in *Moortown*; the poems revert back to Hughes's earlier, more violent representations of nature. "Last Night," for example, is reminiscent of "Pike" in its invocation of the river's "evil": "An evil mood | Darkened in it. Evil came up | Out of its stillest holes, and uncoiled | In the sick river . . . | . . . I stood in a grave | And felt the evil of fish" (*CPH* 665). Likewise in "After Moonless Midnight," the fish wait for the speaker with "torpedo | Concentration" and "savagery" (659). "The River," on the other hand, recalls Eliot's "The Dry Salvages" as Hughes mythologizes the "brown god": "It is a god, and inviolable. | Immortal. And will wash itself of all deaths"

(*CPH* 664). The river itself, the speaker implies, will also wash him of all deaths. Thus the river becomes the focal point and presiding spirit of the collection, while the metaphor of fishing is used again and again as a conduit to one's own personal depths, as in "Go Fishing":

> Join water, wade in underbeing
> Let brain mist into moist earth
> Ghost loosen away downstream
> Gulp river and gravity
>
> Lose words
> Cease (652)

River is relatively free of Plath's influence, and at first glance it appears Hughes has been able to liberate himself from the dialogue with his dead wife. However, his frequent uses of marriage and death metaphors (or "Copulation and death" as he puts it in "Low Water" (*CPH* 670)), which he applies mainly to spawning salmon, suggest the memories of Plath and Assia Wevill are not far from his mind. Images of ravenous "female" flowers in *Flowers and Insects* also reveal the specter of Plath, even if her influence on that short collection is relatively insignificant.

Hughes's period of respite from his dialogue with Plath would be short lived, as *Capriccio*, *Birthday Letters*, and *Howls and Whispers* revealed. In "Systole Diastole," a *Capriccio* poem, the male speaker tries to escape an oppressive ghost by immersing himself in nature. He soon finds, however, that he cannot hide or outrun her:

>   ... he hid his heart
> He implanted it in the belly
> Of a flower, where pollen might repair it
>
> It was desperate magic he tried it
> Soaked his deranged heart the torn god
> In the nectar of an orchid a lily
>
> A tiger lily almost a lotus
> But the crying lioness found it
> Though she had died of thirst her ghost found it
>
> And tore up the flower, with ghost fangs
> And carried his heart back to her lair, in his chest
> Where her ghost could gnaw at it, lick at it, guard it (*CPH* 786–7)

It would take a less guarded, more confessional approach to Plath's death, in *Birthday Letters*, to make Hughes believe that he had, on some level, exorcised this "ghost." Yet, as we will see, his attempt to free himself from Plath would only entangle him further with her memory.

11

Fixed Stars: *Birthday Letters*

There is an undated, untitled poem in one of Ted Hughes's notebooks in the Emory archive, written in the same style as many of the *Birthday Letters* poems. What sets this poem apart from those in the published collection is the speaker's relentless assault on himself for making a decision that, as he writes, cost three lives:

> The train pushes along the same track—
> What is coming is all future
> Before me stands yesterday
> But like the wall of a prison.
> Yesterday should be tools—weapons—
> Not a prison.
>
> Heart anchors in yesterday, maybe has sunk.
> Why am I compelled to this same
> Crime over and over like a ghost
> Trying to expiate?
> I have no eternity to wear out—
> Just a few years.
>
> Why can I not say: it was a mistake.
> Before God, it was a mistake.
> Yes, it cost a life. It was a mistake.
> It cost two lives—three. It was a mistake.
> Why go on slavishly leaving her
>
> Leaving my happiness, which she is, she is.
> Leaving her over and over. Going back
> And leaving her weeping again, over and over.
> It feels like bewilderment and it is.
> It moves me like a puppet, and I am.
> In this I have lost freedom.
> I have lost power to dream, I am my dream.
>
> So I see it simply.
> Where is the strength to break from this prison

> To turn the tables on this trickery,
> To make it my play. To sit and see it performed
> By masks other than my own.
> To sit freed of it, to leave the theatre refreshed.[1]

Hughes's break with Sylvia Plath and subsequent affair with Assia Wevill are the "crime," the "mistake." This poem and others like it in his notebooks were never published, perhaps because they gave too much away.[2] Hughes may also have felt they would give ammunition to radical feminists who blamed him for Plath's death. Yet this poem, even more than those in *Birthday Letters*, gives a profound sense of the crippling guilt Hughes experienced after Plath's and Wevill's suicides. It also speaks to the psychological and creative paralysis that afflicted him during this time; as he wrote to Lucas Myers in 1987, "I've let my life be hijacked" (*L* 537). The poem helps to explain why, in 1998, Hughes told Keith Sagar that if he had written about Plath less guardedly twenty-five years earlier, he would have been able to mourn in a healthier manner and put the episode behind him: "I have wondered ... if an all-out attempt much much earlier to complete a full account, in the manner of those BL, of that part of my life, would not have liberated me to deal with it on deeper, more creative levels—i.e. where the very worst things can be made positive" (*L* 718).[3] He later wrote to Kathleen Raine:

those letters do release the story that everything I have written since the early nineteen sixties has been evading. It was in a kind of desperation that I finally did publish them—I had always thought them unpublishably raw and unguarded, simply too vulnerable. But then I just could not endure being blocked any longer. How strange that we have to make these public declarations of our secrets. But we do. If only I had done the equivalent 30 years ago, I might have had a more fruitful career—certainly a freer psychological life. Even now, the sensation of inner liberation—a huge, sudden possibility of new inner experience. Quite strange.[4]

---

[1] Ted Hughes, Notebook 11, Box 57, MSS 644, Emory.

[2] Part of another poem from the same notebook reads:

> ... He is a spider of love,
> Not loving but catching up in webs of love,
> The women who touch him, where they die. Yes
> Where they die; And, dying
> Grow his face; And, dead, hang
> In the web with his long face.
> On their dead souls. He is what he has swallowed.
> And if this were a parable, a metaphor only,
> It would be painful enough. It is real.
> (Notebook 11, Box 57, MSS 644, Emory.)

[3] Hughes told Herbert Lomas he began writing the *Birthday Letters* poems in 1972 (*L* 731).

[4] Ted Hughes to Kathleen Raine; part of a letter Frieda Hughes quoted when accepting the Whitbread Prize on her father's behalf in 1999. Box 2, MSS 1014, Emory.

These letters, and others like them, suggest that the publication of *Birthday Letters* gave Hughes the "inner liberation" he had desperately sought since Plath's death; finally, it seemed, he had regained his "lost freedom" and "power to dream." As he wrote to his son, Nicholas, in 1998, since Plath's suicide he had been "living on the wrong side of the glass door . . .

> That thickening thickening glass window between me and that real self of mine which was trapped in the unmanageable experience of what had happened with her and me. And so—because I could never break up the log-jam . . . never open the giant plate glass door of it, that real self of mine could never get on with its life, could never join me and help me get on with my life. (*L* 712)

Publishing the poems helped him, he wrote, experience "a freedom of imagination I've not felt since 1962" (*L* 713). (Interestingly, Hughes uses a metaphor similar to Plath's bell jar here, and characterizes himself in the same way he often wrote about Plath: as someone struggling to allow his "real self" to triumph over his "false self.")

Yet, like *Ariel*, *Birthday Letters* is driven by equally rivalrous and elegiac impulses—competing claims for what John Burt Foster has called "independence and subordination" (37). Hughes continued his revisionary dialogue with Plath in *Birthday Letters*, "creatively correcting" her work as he challenged her constructions of him as an aggressive, violent "man in black." Through his revision of Plath's poems and person, Hughes rewrites (and attempts to re-right) not just her story, but his part in that story. Indeed, a remark by Hughes's publisher, Matthew Evans, suggests the extent to which the poems were motivated by Hughes's desire to defend himself against Plath's charges. As Evans told the *New York Times* after Hughes's death, "The publication was a very important moment for him. He was putting another side, and there was a great deal of understanding after that book was published."[5]

Like many classic elegies, *Birthday Letters* says as much about the elegist as the elegized.[6] As Peter Sacks has demonstrated:

[5] Sarah Lyall, "Ted Hughes, 68, a Symbolic Poet and Sylvia Plath's Husband, Dies," *New York Times* (October 30, 1998).

[6] The divided critical response to *Birthday Letters* calls attention to the text's ambivalence about its own status: reviewers either claimed that Hughes had attempted to have the last word in his drama with Plath, or that he had offered himself up guilty as charged. In the *New Republic*, for example, James Wood called the poems "little epidemics of blame" (31) while Katha Pollit, in the *New York Times*, wrote that *Birthday Letters* "presents itself as an unambiguous rebuke to those who saw Sylvia Plath as Ted Hughes's victim . . . Here, we are to believe, is The Truth About Sylvia . . . she was beautiful, brilliant, violent, crazy, doomed; I loved her, I did my best to make her happy, but she was obsessed with her dead father, and it killed her" (March 1, 1998). Michiko Kakutani, on the other hand, read the poems as "remarkably free of self-pity, score-settling and spin; rather, they draw a deeply affecting portrait of the couple's marriage while attesting to Mr. Hughes's own impassioned love for Plath. . . . They are clearly the work of a poet writing out of the deepest core

Few elegies can be fully read without an appreciation of their frequently combative struggles for inheritance... the heir apparent must demonstrate a greater strength or proximity to the dead than any rival may claim; but he must also wrest his inheritance *from* the dead. More than a mere ingestion, some act of alteration or surpassal must be made, some device whereby the legacy may be seen to have entered a new successor.   (37)

Sacks believes that such "combative struggles" are part of the process of healthy mourning, and allow the living poet to overcome feelings of guilt and grief which might otherwise paralyze both his life and art. Most poems in *Birthday Letters* seek to declare independence from Plath even as they appear to submit to her influence; indeed, what Sacks called the "combative struggle for inheritance" is so prevalent and pervasive that it is difficult to understand how Erica Wagner could claim that the collection is "is no attempt to have 'the last word' in an 'argument'; it is not an answer to any accusations" (18). In contrast, the poems frequently subvert the traditional consolatory and conciliatory functions of elegy; indeed, there are nearly as many instances of self-elegy as elegy in the collection. If Hughes can show that part of him "died" with Plath, he establishes his right to mourn over those who suffered no comparable loss, and proves himself Plath's most rightful heir and elegist.

The mixture of humility, rivalry, and self-aggrandizement in *Birthday Letters*, as in *Ariel*, recalls Freud's depiction of the melancholic mourner in "Mourning and Melancholia":

If one listens patiently to a melancholic's many and various self-accusations, one cannot in the end avoid the impression that often the most violent of them are hardly at all applicable to the patient himself, but that with insignificant modifications they do fit someone else, someone whom the patient loves or has loved or should love.... we perceive that the self-reproaches are reproaches against a loved object which have been shifted away from it on to the patient's own ego.... They are not ashamed and do not hide themselves, since everything derogatory that they say about themselves is at bottom said about someone else. Moreover, they are far from evincing towards those around them the attitude of humility and submissiveness.... On the contrary, they... always seem as though they felt slighted and had been treated with great injustice. All this is possible only because the reactions expressed in their behaviour still proceed from a mental constellation of revolt, which has then, by a certain process, passed over into the crushed state of melancholia.   (248)

In both *Ariel* and *Birthday Letters* the mourned object, which the mourner has struggled to put to rest, has "the last word" as Freud predicted: "in regression from narcissistic object-choice the object has, it is true, been got rid of, but it has nevertheless proved more powerful than the ego itself" ("Mourning" 252).

of his being" (*New York Times*, February 13, 1998). Seamus Heaney similarly declared the poems "miraculous.... The immediate impression is one of wounded power healing and gathering and showing its back above the depths where it has been biding. To read it is to experience the psychic equivalent of 'the bends'" (*Irish Times*, January 27, 1998).

In *Birthday Letters*, Hughes was caught in a double-bind: as much as he tried to salvage what he called "my own psychological and physical health" (*L* 720) by grieving for Plath and revising her poems and person, he nevertheless conjures her back in an effort to regain his "closest" reader. Although Hughes felt that writing *Birthday Letters* would put Plath's ghost to rest—he suggested to Keith Sagar that the collection was "the funeral, & the mourning" (*L* 541)—his frequent expressions of anger towards Plath and his constant references to her poems undermine this attempt, just as Plath's allusions to Hughes's poems in *Ariel* undermine her declarations of independence from her husband.[7]

DISINHERITING THE DEAD

Birthday Letters owes much to Thomas Hardy's *Poems of 1912–13*, which elegize his wife, Emma Gifford. Like Hardy, Hughes ceaselessly questions himself and his ghostly wife about the circumstances of their marriage, and her death. What Sacks has said of Hardy—that he sought "not only to review but to *revise* his marriage" (239)—is also true of Hughes. But perhaps the most important traits both collections share are their accusatory attitude toward the dead and their subversion of traditional elegiac forms. Writes Jahan Ramazani, "Though critics have tended to shrink from the disquieting guilt, aggression, and narcissism in Hardy's love elegies, these poems instance the work of melancholia, fraught as they are with recriminations and self-recriminations, their affection intertwined with hostility" (48). Hardy is "angry at his dead wife and angry with himself for having this anger. . . . Never in the canonical tradition of elegy had a poet vented such anger at the dead person for betraying him. . . . she leads him on, abandons him, and even in this way sickens him" (48; 51). As we will see, Hughes expresses a similar hostility toward Plath for "abandoning" him; however, this hostility is complicated by literary rivalry. Ultimately, Plath's words themselves become the target of Hughes's aggression.

Even those poems in *Birthday Letters* that initially read as highly traditional "subordinate" elegies contain subversions that hint at the desire for independence. On the surface, "Daffodils" seems to invoke all the characteristics of traditional elegy: it pays tribute to the dead using a pastoral, floral motif common to the Western elegy since the Greeks; it looks toward springtime as a symbol of

---

[7] Tracy Brain has pointed to the way Hughes uses "Hesitant words and questioning syntax" to argue that he refuses "any one meaning or privileged viewpoint" in *Birthday Letters*. She claims that he is "self-conscious about his own narrative fallibility" because he understands "how slippery any biographical truth can be" (2001: 181–2): "the 'Plath' so incessantly addressed by Hughes's speaker, is a poetic character who is no more stable or real as 'Plath' than the object of any intensely felt love poem" (181). But it is still hard to ignore the fact that these poems are about an actual marriage, and that Hughes *was* remembering a "real" Plath rather than inventing a "poetic character." Obviously Hughes's memories of his dead wife are not to be unquestionably regarded as "fact," but neither should we pretend that there is no actual, historical addressee.

renewal and rebirth; and it mourns the dead by means of a substitutive, consolatory symbol in the daffodils themselves, which Hughes associates with Plath when he describes their "wet shocks shaken" (recalling Plath's ECT) that "Opened too early" (*CPH* 1126).[8] Yet there are other ways in which "Daffodils" departs sharply from the benign, "subordinate" elegy. Like Eliot's "The Waste Land," "Daffodils" quietly subverts traditionally restorative images of April and springtime, which are not symbols of rebirth but reminders of the lost object's death in a universe gone awry, just as Ophelia's flowers "become the signs of madness" (Sacks 85). The imagery of Plath gathering daffodils recalls Eliot's "mad" hyacinth girl (based on his own wife, Vivienne) who becomes a symbol of neurosis later in the poem. Like Eliot's speaker in the garden, the speaker in "Daffodils" mourns the lost woman and his own lost youth. Throughout the poem, Hughes laments the fact that he and Plath felt obliged to sell their daffodils, and suggests that their urge to "convert everything to profit"—including, presumably, poetry—was an error that doomed their marriage: "The crop thickened faster than we could thin it. | Finally, we were overwhelmed | And we lost our wedding-present scissors" (*CPH* 1126). If the flowers are meant to stand, in part, for poems, then Hughes suggests that it may have been poetry itself, and the poetic rivalry between the couple, that "overwhelmed" the marriage. But ultimately, the responsibility for converting "everything to profit"—that is, the "overwhelming" need to attain success in the literary marketplace—lies with Plath, who is portrayed as the one cutting the daffodils, busily "snipping their stems" as Hughes imagines their "soft shrieks."

Interestingly, it is the male speaker who cuts the daffodils in an earlier version of the poem published in *Flowers and Insects* (1986). There, Hughes drew upon metaphors of torture and rape as the speaker remembers how much he enjoyed the "deflowering":

> To each scared, bright glance
> I brought a defter cruelty. So many times
> Slid my fingers down her slenderness,
> Felt for the source, her chilly fount,
> The watery flicker she peered from,
> And nipped her off close to the bulb.   (*CPH* 711–12)

In *Birthday Letters*, however, Plath becomes responsible for severing the daffodils from Mother Earth; thus images of rape in the first version are transformed into castration in the second. Sacks stresses that successful mourners are able to renounce their grief by transposing it onto a substitutive symbol for the dead (flower, flute, etc.). While it seems that Hughes "turns" Plath into flowers in

---

[8] Sacks writes that flowers traditionally "serve not only as offerings or as gestures for respite but also as demarcations separating the living from the dead" (19). In "Daffodils," Hughes may be alluding to Ben Jonson's "Slow, Slow, Fresh Fount" ("Nature's pride is now a withered daffodil"), or Whitman's "When Lilacs Last in the Dooryard Bloom'd."

"Daffodils," what she actually "becomes" is the scissors used to cut and sell them: "your scissors," which are lost and buried in the soil with "blades wide open" (1126), invokes both phallic and feminine imagery typically associated with a femme fatale. In the end, Plath is not transformed into the reconstitutive daffodils but "an anchor, a cross of rust," suggesting she is the cross Hughes must bear. As elsewhere in *Birthday Letters*, Plath is both victim and perpetrator. Indeed, there is more than a hint of the "combative struggle for inheritance" at the end of the poem when Hughes writes that the daffodils—typically symbols of remembrance and renewal—"return to forget you" each spring.

"Robbing Myself" also uses several traditional elegiac conventions, including pastoral motifs (lingering remnants, like flowers, of the ancient vegetation gods) and light imagery. The poem describes Hughes's journey back to Court Green in the days before Plath's suicide to check on the house and retrieve food for himself and her. The first stanza, in which the road to Devon seemed "unnatural and familiar, | A road back into myself" (*CPH* 1150), recalls the opening lines of Dante's *Inferno*. Reunion with the lost woman propels the journey, as it did for Dante and Orpheus. Hughes describes his happiness at uncovering his cache of vegetables and fruit, contrasting the "warm" "sweetness" of the potatoes with the frigid cold and snow outside. Images of pastoral abundance in the form of potatoes, apples, and flowers position the poem squarely within the tradition of elegy, as do Hughes's allusions to spring and rebirth as he handles the stock: "It was a nest | Secret, living, the eggs of my coming year, | Like my own plump litter, my secret family, | Little earthen embryos... || My spring prayers still solid" (1150). Unaware of the looming "disaster," the young, hopeful Hughes walks through the house and regards its rooms and furniture tenderly, intimating that the house "Waited only for us," and that it lay sleeping peacefully like "an unborn baby." The space even seems blessed by the "stained church-windows" next door, which cast their glowing light onto the house—a conventional elegiac motif, like flowers and spring, which suggests the promise of immortality. Yet none of Hughes's hopes for his future reconciliation with Plath will come to pass. The fruit would eventually rot, the flowers die; Plath would never eat the potatoes and apples he packed for her; the house would never again know their presence. Hughes's hopes are about to die along with Plath, as is a part of Hughes himself; he calls himself a "ghostly trespasser" and compares the house to "my darkened, hushed, safe casket" (1151). At the poem's end, he suggests that he "lost the treasure," or "robbed himself," when he left Plath; yet his identification with the dead Plath symbolically "robs" her of her rightful place in the elegy. It is as if he is attempting to displace her, to become himself the object of his own elegy, and again cast himself as a casualty of Plath's death. Freud called this strategy "narcissistic identification" ("Mourning" 251) with the dead, and argued that it showed an unwillingness to properly distance oneself from the lost love object. Here Hughes takes revenge on Plath "by the circuitous path of self-punishment" (Freud, "Mourning" 251), just as Plath did in *Ariel*.

Other poems in *Birthday Letters* enact what Sacks has described as part of the process of healthy mourning, that is, "moving from nature to artifice": " 'turning' from the object of his love to a sign of her . . . is [the] substitutive turn or act of troping that any mourner must perform" (5). Hughes performs such "turning" several times throughout the collection when he represents Plath not as a living being but as a figure in a painting or photograph. Still, these poems of "healthy" mourning nevertheless engage in a struggle for power between the dead and the living, and highlight "the elegist's need to draw attention, consolingly, to his own surviving powers" (Sacks 2). In poems that enact the turn from nature to artifice, such as "Fulbright Scholars," "Portraits," "Perfect Light," and "Drawing," Plath becomes a static, silent image. These poems efface and displace her by forcefully asserting the living poet's voice over the dead. Sacks's understanding of healthy elegiac mourning may elucidate elegies in which the poet memorializes a non-writer, but his argument becomes harder to sustain when the elegist elegizes not only a fellow poet, but a former wife whose abandonment caused him personal pain and professional setback. Here, the combative struggle between living and dead is particularly intense, and cannot be neatly resolved by turning the elegized into a substitutive "symbol."

In "Black Coat," Hughes presents Plath as a "paparazzo sniper" and likens her eye to a camera lens that "tightens" around him; he protests when she reduces him to image, and admonishes her "eye's inbuilt double exposure" (*CPH* 1109). Yet if Plath is guilty of this kind of "diplopic error" (1109), so too is Hughes. *Birthday Letters*, in fact, opens with a static image of Plath that also offers the reader a "double exposure" of sorts. In "Fulbright Scholars," Hughes remembers the moment he first laid eyes on his future wife in a publicity photograph of the incoming American prize-winners. He writes of Plath's hair, face, and smile, and then links this memory with his first taste of a peach in an allusion to both the Fall and Eliot's "The Love Song of J. Alfred Prufrock." Hughes engages in a struggle for power from the very beginning of the collection when he presses Plath into a two-dimensional image—one he's not even sure he remembers ("Maybe I noticed you")—and then goes on to suggest that she was the cause of his own "fall." She becomes a silent temptress whose "exaggerated American | Grin" (*CPH* 1045) should have served as sufficient warning not to buy what she was selling.

Likewise, in "Portraits," Hughes presents Plath as an image in a portrait painted by a friend at Yaddo. Hughes admires the painter's rendition of Plath, which seems more lifelike than Plath herself. He seems to prefer the flattened, passive image to the live and unruly person: "You deepened, | Molten, luminous, looking at us | From that window of Howard's vision of you. | Yourself lifted out of yourself" (*CPH* 1110). The painter's act of aesthetic reproduction—replacing nature with artifice—is itself "doubled" at the poem's end, when Hughes refers to Plath's poem "Medallion," which presents a painterly image of a dead snake. Whereas the portrait of Plath enlivens her in "a flaming of oils," Plath's poem merely portrays the "thing's dead immortal doppelgänger" (1111). Moreover,

Hughes suggests that Plath is drawn to the snake, as the painter says, " 'Because it's evil. It's evil, so it thrills you.' " Plath's attempt to transform nature to artifice is linked to her fascination with death and "evil," whereas the artist's attempt to paint Plath is aided by benevolent female muses or "Spirits" (1109). Again we are reminded of Hughes's suggestion in "Fulbright Scholars" of the connection between Plath and the Fall. By "turning" Plath into an image, Hughes achieves a consolatory substitutive metaphor; yet in doing so he suggests she is better off as passive muse (inspiring the male painter and poet) than as active artist. The metaphorical act of "taming" Plath by way of freezing her in portraiture recalls Robert Browning's "My Last Duchess," which may itself allude to Browning's rivalry with his wife, Elizabeth.

In "Perfect Light," Hughes again freezes Plath into a static image as he describes a photograph of her sitting among the Court Green daffodils with her children. Hughes "revises" Plath in this poem so that she appears as a paragon of gentle femininity. He compares her to the Virgin Mary ("Mother and infant, as in the Holy portrait"), and repeats the word "innocence" three times within the space of the short poem (*CPH* 1136). While Hughes uses the traditional motifs of elegy—it is springtime, the sunlight is "perfect," and Plath is surrounded by flowers—he is nevertheless engaged in a combative struggle with Plath, for by turning Plath into a consolatory substitutive metaphor (the photograph itself), he also turns her into an idealized, benignly feminine earth mother and, in the process, turns the reader away from the volatile images she projected in *Ariel.* She becomes more virginal here, and less like the angry, dangerous women in "Daddy," "Purdah," and "Lady Lazarus." Hughes attempts to reinscribe Plath's image as that of a nurturing mother in order to counter what he sees as the false image of Plath as feminist martyr. "Perfect Light" is nostalgic and sentimental, and exhibits the same need that Aurelia Plath felt, when she published *Letters Home,* to offer a happier version of "her" Plath to the public. Nowhere else in *Birthday Letters* is Plath more idealized—"There you are, in all your innocence, | Sitting among your daffodils, as in a picture | Posed as for the title: 'Innocence' " (1136)—and yet no portrait of Plath could be further from the one she offered in *Ariel,* which subverted traditional patriarchal assumptions about fifties femininity. Significantly, Plath is not idealized as a writer, but as a mother, as she is in "Remission," where she is one among the "sorority of petals." "Your words were lost in the camera" (1136), Hughes writes, effectively silencing Plath the poet.

RESURRECTING THE WHITE GODDESS

While some poems in *Birthday Letters* turn Plath passive, others portray her as the perpetrator of violence and a femme fatale. In these poems, Hughes often identifies Plath with the masculine, as soldier or assassin, and himself with the feminine, as nurse or midwife, in an effort to reverse her portrayals of him as the "man in black." By doing so, Hughes recasts Plath as an embodiment of the White Goddess, just as Robert Graves had done to Laura Riding—an identification that, as we have seen, Plath parodied in several *Ariel* poems. For if Plath is a manifestation of the vengeful Goddess, Hughes's suffering and punishment at her hands will have been for the sake of poetry, since the White Goddess normally tormented those who sought her inspiration.[9] As Graves wrote, "The reason why the hairs stand on end, the eyes water, the throat is constricted, the skin crawls and a shiver runs down the spine when one writes or reads a true poem is that a true poem is necessarily an invocation of the White Goddess, or Muse, the Mother of All Living, the ancient power of fright and lust—the female spider or the queen-bee whose embrace is death" (490). In her bee poems, Plath parodied this idea, just as she parodied the "positive violence" of Hughes's femme fatales and animal predators in "Daddy" and "Lady Lazarus." Throughout *Birthday Letters*, however, Hughes undoes Plath's earlier parodic revisions. She thus becomes for Hughes, as in "Moonwalk," "The Ancient Mariner's Death-in-Life woman | Straight off the sea's fevered incandescence | Throwing black-and-white dice. | A sea saracen and cruel-looking" (*CPH* 1069).

In "St Botolph's," which memorializes his first encounter with Plath, Hughes writes, "You meant to knock me out | With your vivacity" (*CPH* 1052). Like Plath, he uses the language of war and violence to characterize the fateful meeting, and adds that she left a "swelling ring-moat of tooth-marks" that would brand his face "for good" (1052). The poem is a revision of Plath's famous journal passage about their meeting, and is the first of many works in *Birthday Letters* in which Hughes attempts to characterize Plath as the more violent partner in the relationship. In "Trophies," which alludes heavily to Plath's "Pursuit," Hughes again revises that first meeting at the St Botolph's party by portraying himself as Plath's quarry. Referring to the hair-raising effect of the White Goddess, Hughes describes his emotions while reading "Pursuit" "After forty years": "The whiff of that beast, off the dry pages, | Lifts the hair on the back of my hands. | The thrill of it" (*CPH* 1054). When he refers to Plath's "Pursuit" (which itself alluded to Hughes's early "The Jaguar"), he engages in a self-conscious, intertextual dialogue and act of revision. *She* now becomes the panther that tracked *him* down:

---

[9] For a more extensive treatment of Robert Graves, Laura Riding, and the White Goddess, see Amber Vogel, "Not Elizabeth to His Ralegh," in *Literary Couplings*. Vogel notes that "even a reader as astute as Randall Jarrell was led to say of Riding, 'I believe that it is simplest to think of her as, so to speak, the White Goddess incarnate, the Mother-Muse in contemporary flesh' " (231). Riding herself noted "the offensiveness of the characterization of *me* as 'a living incarnation' of Robert Graves's 'The White Goddess' " (qtd. in Vogel 235).

> ... The sudden
> Look that locked on me
> Through your amber jewels
> And as I caught you lolling locked
> Its jaws into my face. The tenacity
> Of the big cat's claim
> On the one marked down and once disabled
> Is a chemical process—a combustion
> Of the stuff of judgement.
>
> .   .   .   .   .   .
>
> ... With a laugh I
> Took its full weight. Little did I know
> The shock attack of a big predator
> According to survivors numbs the target
> Into drunken euphoria. Still smiling
> As it carried me off I detached
> The hairband carefully from between its teeth
> And a ring from its ear, for my trophies.   (*CPH* 1054)

Hughes notes that he only takes Plath's headband as she carries him off. In "18 Rugby Street" he similarly emphasizes Plath's role as the hunter/panther (and again uses military imagery), writing, "I can hear you | Climbing the bare stairs, alive and close, ... | That was your artillery, to confuse me: | Before coming over the top in your panoply | You wanted me to hear you panting" (*CPH* 1056).

In "The Shot," Hughes again engages in a "combative struggle" with Plath, whom he likens to a "high-velocity bullet" as she "ricocheted" through her "Alpha career" (*CPH* 1053):

> You were undeflected.
> You were gold-jacketed, solid silver,
> Nickel-tipped. Trajectory perfect
> As through ether. Even the cheek-scar,
> Where you seemed to have side-swiped concrete,
> Served as a rifling groove
> To keep you true.   (1053)

Hughes goes on to claim that Plath's bullet, aimed at her father, actually hit him. Thus elegy begins to resemble self-elegy as Hughes reverses the terms of "Lady Lazarus." Here Plath is the deadly assassin who aims her rifle directly at him. He in fact alludes to "Lady Lazarus" in the last line of the poem when he refers to what he has managed to salvage: "A wisp of your hair, your ring, your watch, your nightgown" (1053). In Plath's poem, Lady Lazarus, who has been reduced to "A wedding ring," insists that there is "a charge, a very large charge | For a word or a touch | Or a bit of blood | Or a piece of my hair or my clothes" (*CPP* 246). Hughes alludes to this "charge," which he feels he has paid, in "The Shot." Woman becomes weapon, as in "The Inscription":

> The wound she had given herself, striking at him
> Had given herself, that had emptied
> From her hands the strength to hold him against
> The shock of her words from nowhere, that had
> Fatally gone through her and hit him.   (*CPH* 1155)

Hughes's "The Rabbit Catcher" is perhaps the most explicit example of score settling in *Birthday Letters*. Plath's "The Rabbit Catcher," as I have mentioned, draws on D. H. Lawrence's "Cruelty and Love" and "Rabbit Snared in the Night" in its portrayal of Hughes as a sadistic hunter "excited" (*CPP* 194) by the prospect of killing defenseless creatures. Hughes's "The Rabbit Catcher" is a revisionary act of self-defense. "What had I done?" he asks at the outset, establishing his innocence. It was Plath, he suggests, in her "dybbuk fury" (*CPH* 1136), who overreacted to the situation that day. He emphasizes that he is the rational partner when he writes that he followed her into the car because he feared she would "do something crazy." Hughes takes on the feminine role as Plath takes on the masculine: "I simply | Trod accompaniment," he writes, "carried babies, | Waited for you to come back to nature" (1137). Hughes presumably means for Plath to come back to her female nature, which is hidden beneath her (masculine) "iron" look. Plath, however, refuses to carry babies and provide lunch; instead, Hughes does these things ("I'd brought food"). She is "inaccessible": "Your Germanic scowl, edged like a helmet, | Would not translate itself" (1137). Hughes again uses military imagery to describe Plath; her "Germanic scowl" recalls the Nazi imagery she used to describe him in "Daddy" and "Lady Lazarus." She is the one in command, whereas he simply "sat baffled. | I was a fly outside on the window-pane | Of my own domestic drama.... | And I | Trailed after like a dog" (1137).

When Plath tears up a rabbit trap, Hughes offers his own side of the story: he suggests she did not understand "Country poverty" or "Ancient custom." He presents himself, as he did in "The Owl," as more attuned to nature than Plath, who, he writes, "cared nothing for rabbits" (1138). Hughes, however, fails to mention that Plath's rage was directed squarely at him, for she already suspected that he was attracted to Assia Wevill, as her poem "Event," written on the same day she composed "The Rabbit Catcher," makes clear. (Both poems were written just three days after David and Assia Wevill's first visit to Court Green in late May 1962; Hughes would begin his affair with Assia in June.) Hughes evades culpability in this "domestic drama," beginning and ending his poem with a series of questions meant to fill the reader's mind with doubt as to Plath's mental state, and thus his own guilt. At the poem's end, Hughes intimates that it was not his actions that motivated Plath's rage, but her own hysteria:

> In those snares
> You'd caught something.
> Had you caught something in me,
> Nocturnal and unknown to me? Or was it
> Your doomed self, your tortured, crying,
> Suffocating self? Whichever,
> Those terrible, hypersensitive
> Fingers of your verse closed round it and
> Felt it alive. The poems, like smoking entrails,
> Came soft into your hands.   (1138)

Hughes portrays Plath as she portrayed him at the end of her "Rabbit Catcher"—as a cruel and merciless hunter. In Hughes's version, however, Plath's "weapon" is not the trap itself, but her "terrible, hypersensitive... verse." Hughes undermines his earlier portrayal of Plath as victim ("tortured, crying, | Suffocating" (1138)) with an image of Plath as perpetrator.

Plath is similarly masculinized in other poems that invoke the very imagery of war and violence she had earlier turned on Hughes. In "Child's Park," Hughes draws upon Plath's use of nuclear holocaust motifs in "Fever 103°" when he writes of her "homicidal | Hooded stare," her "fury," her "plutonium secret" at "the core" of her "Inferno," and her "radioactive" Eden (*CPH* 1086–7). In "Black Coat" he portrays himself as the unwitting victim of Plath's murderous rage when he compares her mind to a rifle: "I had no idea I had stepped | Into the telescopic sights | Of the paparazzo sniper | Nested in your brown iris" (1109). In "Setebos" he alludes to Shelley's "Adonais" as he paints himself Plath's victim ("I crawled | Under a gabardine, hugging tight | All I could of me, hearing the cry | Now of hounds" (1129)).[10] He is her victim again in "9 Willow Street," in which he attempts to refute Plath's identification of him with the vampire figure. After finding a sick bat on Boston Common, Hughes attempts to cradle it and "lift it again to tree-bark safety" despite its snarls (1089). He eventually lets the bat bite his finger in order to free it, only later to realize that he could have caught rabies. Given his dual understanding of himself as Plath's protector and victim throughout *Birthday Letters*, it seems clear that the bat is aligned with Plath. Hughes inverts Plath's vampire motif here when he intimates that it was she, not he, who drew blood.

---

[10] Stanza 31 of "Adonais" reads:

> Midst others of less note, came one frail Form,
> A phantom among men; companionless
> As the last cloud of an expiring storm
> Whose thunder is its knell; he, as I guess,
> Had gazed on Nature's naked loveliness,
> Actaeon-like, and now he fled astray
> With feeble steps o'er the world's wilderness,
> And his own thoughts, along that rugged way,
> Pursued, like raging hounds, their father and their prey.

"YOU COULDN'T HAVE DONE IT"

Instead of declaring the permanence and immortality of Plath's poems in the face of her death, as Shelley had done of Keats in *Adonais* (and as Hughes himself had done in his earlier prose writings on Plath), Hughes implies that Plath's writing was the weapon with which she wounded herself, her family, and him. Thus, her poetic achievement, which a traditional elegy would have celebrated, is strangely muted, negated, and even regretted. Hughes repeatedly implies that Plath would not have died—and a part of him would not have died with her—had she not become a writer. He insists her writing opened up the channels of communication between herself and her dead father, who eventually "possessed" her. Yet Hughes never effaces Plath's work completely because he continually reinscribes that work onto the page in his revisions of her poems.

Hughes first links Plath's writing with mental illness in "The Tender Place," which confirms Plath's psychosis through a description of the shock therapy she received before she met Hughes. While the poem evinces tenderness toward the disturbed and mistreated subject, and even views the psychiatrists in language that echoes Plath's own description of ECT ("Somebody wired you up. | Somebody pushed the lever. They crashed | The thunderbolt into your skull" (*CPH* 1050)), "The Tender Place" nonetheless leaves little doubt that Hughes perceives Plath as flawed. He intimates that Plath's words, like her, are wounded or sick. He implies that her electroshock therapy had lasting effects on her language, and that her voice

> Came up, years later,
> Over-exposed, like an X-ray—
> Brain-map still dark-patched
> With the scorched-earth scars
> Of your retreat. And your words,
> Faces reversed from the light,
> Holding in their entrails.   (1051)

Here, words are both victim and perpetrator, much like Hughes's depictions of Plath herself; at the poem's end, they take the form of an actual wound. (Hughes used the same image to describe Plath's words in "The Rabbit Catcher," where "The poems, like smoking entrails, | Came soft into your hands" (1138)).

In "Moonwalk," Plath's "words" are "Like bits of beetles and spiders | Retched out by owls" (*CPH* 1069); in "Drawing" she uses a "poker infernal pen" (1071); in "A Dream" her father's coffin is her "Strange letter box" (1119). Hughes suggests, as he had in his prose writings, that Plath feared her own words: in "Dream Life" her poems follow her with their "blood-sticky feet" (1135); in "9 Willow Street" he writes "your new sentence | Tortured you . . . / Every letter a needle" (1089); and in "Suttee," he is aghast at what he has helped to deliver—"And the tongues of those flames were your tongues. | I had delivered an explosion | Of screams that were flames" (1140). Likewise, in "Apprehensions," "Your writing was also your fear, | At times it was your terror" (1134):

> It hid in your Schaeffer pen—
>
> That was its favourite place. Whenever you wrote
> You would stop, mid-word,
> To look at it more closely, black, fat,
> Between your fingers—
> The swelling terror that would any moment
> Suddenly burst out and take from you
> Your husband, your children, your body, your life.
> You could see it, there, in your pen.
>
> Somebody took that too.   (1134)

Here writing is a malignant act. As elsewhere in *Birthday Letters*, Hughes insists that Plath is not responsible for her words, that she has been possessed by her inner demons and is merely a vessel for their rage. "Apprehensions" alludes to Plath's own "Apprehensions," written in May 1962, which portrays a speaker trapped in a claustrophobic psychic landscape ("Is there no way out of the mind?" (*CPP* 195)). Yet nowhere in her poem did Plath refer to writing as the source of this malaise. In fact, Plath suggested that writer's block, rather than writing itself, was the true source of her speaker's depression when she wrote that she experienced "Cold blanks" in which "There is no talk of immortality" (*CPP* 196). Whereas Plath's poem implied it was the blank page that caused her anxiety—her fear of *not* being able to write—Hughes revises Plath's text to suggest that the cause of her "apprehension" was the process of writing itself.

Although Hughes wants to forgive Plath and explain her hurtful words, he relegates her to doll-status in "The Ventriloquist," in which she relies on him like a child. Hughes, in contrast, is Plath's protector: "With your arms around my neck | I ran through a thorny wood.... || You sobbed against my chest. | I waded the river's freeze" (*CPH* 1159). He is a knight-errant rescuing the damsel in distress from the beast within herself. Similarly, in "9 Willow Street," he presents Plath in need of rescuing as she attempts to write "in a paralysis of terror-flutters | I hardly understood. I folded | Black wings round you, wings of the blackness | That enclosed me, rocking me, infantile, | And enclosed you with me" (1088). In "The Blue Flannel Suit," too, Plath is construed as weak and vulnerable, this time as she prepares for a day of teaching at Smith. The professionally preened working woman does not appear confident but "helpless," her head "pathetically tiny," her posture "dummy stiffness." Hughes does not see a brilliant and successful woman before him but rather "the lonely | Girl who was going to die" (1086).

Hughes negates the anger of Plath's late poems by ascribing it to a force she can neither handle nor understand. "Fever," for example, presents a very different portrait of Plath than her own "Fever 103°," in which the heroine achieves transcendence and liberation from an oppressive patriarchy. Hughes undermines Plath's speaker's assertions of (sexual) independence and existential freedom from the objectifying gaze of her male lover; as Plath wrote, "Not him, nor him | (My selves dissolving, old whore petticoats)— | To paradise" (*CPP* 232). In his revision of the poem, which emphasizes Plath's dependence on him as "nursemaid" (*CPH* 1072) when she fell ill during their honeymoon, Hughes erases the triumph of "Fever 103°" by focusing on Plath's infirmity; at the start of "Fever," he tells us Plath "lay helpless and a little bit crazy" (1072). Whereas Plath's speaker had declared in "Fever 103°," "I am too pure for you or anyone. | Your body | Hurts me as the world hurts God" (*CPP* 232), Hughes gives us another version of the poem in which he spoons food into Plath's "baby-bird" gape (an image that likens her to both animal and child) and wipes her "tear-ruined face" as she sobs " 'Help me' " and " 'I'm going to die' " (*CPH* 1072). Although Hughes does not borrow imagery directly from "Fever 103°," he nevertheless calls Plath's powerful narrative of female transcendence into question with his own "revision." While his intent may have been to restore Plath's "true" personhood, thereby rescuing her from the distortions of feminists, his emphasis on her sickness in "Fever" nevertheless emphasizes her instability and "hysteria." He also makes clear his own sacrifices as her caretaker so that he, not Plath, becomes the martyr.

Hughes enacts a similar effacement of anger in Plath's late work in "Sam," yet another revision of "Ariel." Here, Plath does not masterfully command her mare but instead loses control as the spooked horse gallops away with her: "You lost your reins, you lost your seat" (*CPH* 1049).[11] Alluding to her poems, Hughes again refuses to ascribe agency to Plath. "You couldn't have done it. | Something in you not you did it for itself," he writes (1049). Hughes explicitly links "Sam" to "Ariel" when he writes "That gallop | Was practice, but not enough, and quite useless" (1050); he further alludes to her suicide when he says that she flung herself under his feet and "lay dead" after she struggled off the horse. He replaces the image of Plath as Lady Godiva riding high on "God's lioness" with the reality of a scared young woman barely hanging on to life.

"Sam," like the other poems in which Plath is a passive medium of her own words, reinforces Hughes's own version of "the Plath myth": that, essentially, she had not meant what she said in her last poems, and that another force had been speaking through her. Hughes feels it is his responsibility, now, to reinterpret or "translate" those last words in order to exonerate Plath (and, in doing so, also to exonerate himself). He does this again in "The Bee God," where he writes that "You did not want me to go but your bees | Had their own ideas. . . . || Your face wanted to save me | From what had been decided" (*CPH* 1141). The bees— clearly meant to stand for feminist scholars—do not listen, however; they are

---

[11] The poem is based on a real incident in which Plath lost control of a horse during a riding outing.

"Deaf to your pleas as the fixed stars | At the bottom of the well" (1142). (Hughes, of course, invokes Plath's "Words" here.) Similarly, in "The Inscription," Hughes rewrites what was presumably a late attempt at reconciliation during which Plath "begged | For assurance" that they would be together by the summer. Here Plath is a far cry from the vengeful heroines of "Daddy" and "Lady Lazarus," even when she sees Assia's inscription in his Oxford Shakespeare: "She read the inscription. She closed it | Like the running animal that receives | The fatal bullet without a faltering check | In its stride, she started again | Begging for that reassurance and he gave it | Over and over and over and over" (*CPH* 1155).

In "Astringency," Hughes implies that a sinister force, which Plath did not understand, invented her metaphors. When she compares a rock in the Charles River to a lariat, Hughes observes it was

> The sole metaphor that ever escaped you
> In easy speech, in my company—
> Past the censor? Past the night hands?
> Past the snare
> Set in your throat by whom? Who caught all
> That teeming population, every one,
> To hang their tortured eyes and tongues up
> In your poems? To what end? The constrictor
> Not to be tugged out, or snapped.   (*CPH* 1094)

In "The God," Hughes again relieves Plath of agency and depicts her as an uncomprehending vessel of her own words as she writes "Elm":

> The little god flew up into the Elm Tree.
> In your sleep, glassy-eyed,
> You heard its instructions. When you woke
> Your hands moved. You watched them in dismay
> As they made a new sacrifice.
> Two handfuls of blood, your own blood,
> And in that blood gobbets of me,
> Wrapped in a tissue of story that had somehow
> Slipped from you.   (*CPH* 1164)

Here Plath is "uncomprehending," dismayed by her poem that "had somehow | Slipped" from her pen. Hughes implies they are both victims of the "little god" that all but forced Plath to "sacrifice" her well being for her writing. Hughes relies on the same formula in "The Hands," in which he ascribes all of Plath's hurtful or self-destructive actions to an invisible, Satanic manipulator. In the hospital, recovering from her suicide attempt, Plath "got help to recognise | The fingerprints inside what you had done. | You could not believe it" (*CPH* 1161). These hands wore her poems "like gloves" and left "big fingerprints" "Inside those words you struck me with" (1162). Yet unlike other poems in *Birthday*

Letters, "The Hands" hints that the speaker is now trapped in his own "black shoe" of melancholic mourning:

> Sometimes I even think that I too
> Was picked up, a numbness of gloves
> Worn by those same hands,
> Doing what they needed done, because
> The fingerprints inside what I did
> And inside your poems and letters
> And inside what you did
> Are the same.   (1162)

This is one of the most poignant moments in *Birthday Letters*. Here, Hughes does not try to blame, forgive, or revise Plath. Instead, he admits to resenting Plath's revisions of his poems, which he now responds to with his own, perhaps equally hurtful, counter-revisions. Yet he also aligns himself with Plath's achievement and reputation in a gesture that has struck some critics as appropriation: as he wrote in "The Blackbird"—ostensibly referring to a jail sentence—"Your sentence was mine too" (1148).[12]

In "Remission," Hughes recasts Plath as an Earth-Mother, and insists that she

> ...flourished only
> In becoming fruitful—in getting pregnant,
> In the oceanic submissions
> Of giving birth. That was the you
> You loved and wanted to live with.
>
> .   .   .   .   .   .
>
> That was the you you shared with the wild earth.
> It was your membership
> Of a sorority of petals and creatures
> Whose Masonic signs are beauty and nectar
> In the love-land, the Paradise
> Your suicide had tried to drag you from.   (*CPH* 1113)

This portrayal of Plath as most "herself" when pregnant is one we have seen in Hughes's earlier prose writings on Plath, where he continually draws upon metaphors of motherhood to elucidate the process by which she labored her poems into existence (as he does in "Suttee"). Here, however, motherhood is no longer simply a metaphor for the delivery of Plath's writing (and her "true self"), but has become the only state in which Plath was truly happy. By characterizing her as happiest when mothering, Hughes implies that Plath would have been more content had she not become a writer and opened the channels of communication between herself and her dead father. By folding her back into "a sorority of

---

[12] Sarah Churchwell has commented that Hughes maintains his "position is finally that of 'co-author': he may share her punishment, but he also writes her 'sentences'" (2001: 134).

petals" he emphasizes her femininity—she is the "joy-being Venus of Will-endorf"—and her distance from the "hands" who urged her to write and to hurt those she wrote about. He echoes "Remission" in "Red" when, in his effort to negate Plath's fascination with "Blood-red" motifs, he invokes Marian imagery (Bundtzen 2001: 181) and remembers how "blue silks from San Francisco | Folded your pregnancy" (*CPH* 1170). In "Ouija," too, he suggests that she would have suffered less had she pursued a non-literary course. There, the spirit Pan tells Plath:

> "Fame will come. Fame especially for you.
> Fame cannot be avoided. And when it comes
> You will have paid for it with your happiness,
> Your husband and your life." (1078–9)

In "The Rag Rug," Hughes experiences a sense of contentment as Plath works on her rug. While the act of braiding or weaving (which features prominently in elegies) has long been a metaphor for writing (Sacks 18), Hughes initially ignores its symbolic implications and focuses instead on the sense of relief it allotted him and Plath: "It freed me. It freed you." He remembers a scene of patriarchal domestic harmony when he was the speaker, she the audience:

> Whenever you worked at your carpet I felt happy.
> Then I could read Conrad's novels to you.
> I could cradle your freed mind in my voice,
> Chapter by chapter, sentence by sentence,
> Word by word: *The Heart of Darkness,*
> *The Secret Sharer.* The same, I could feel
> Your fingers caressing my reading, hour after hour,
> Fitting together the serpent's jumbled rainbow.
> I was like the snake-charmer—my voice
> Swaying you over your heaped coils. (*CPH* 1131)

Plath's submission takes on an erotic element as Hughes imagines her "fingers caressing my reading." He hypnotizes and controls his subject. Engaged in an act of homemaking rather than writing, Plath poses no threat either to him or herself. (Hughes feels similarly calm when Plath draws instead of writes in "Drawing": "As you drew | I felt released, calm" (*CPH* 1071).) Hughes here identifies Plath with a serpent, an association that again suggests that Plath is an agent of doom. The reference to Conrad's *Heart of Darkness* likewise portends a journey that will end with a face-to-face encounter with "the horror."

Years later, after reading Plath's journal, Hughes realizes "What furies you bled into that rug." Plath was not as calm as she had appeared:

> Was I the child or the mother? Did you braid it,
> That umbilicus between us,
> To free yourself from my contraction or was it

> Pushing me out and away? Did you coil it,
> Your emergency magic operation,
> To draw off the tangle of numb distance
> Secreting itself between us?   (1131)

Hughes leaves aside his anxiety of influence here in a startling moment of candor. Braiding becomes a metaphor for intertextuality and literary dialogue, while the metaphor of labor prompts the question of who had "created" whom. Indeed, this metaphor in particular hints at the sense of claustrophobia and competition within the creative marriage. Hughes acknowledges Plath's resentment toward him and effectively dismantles his earlier memory of her as his silent, passive audience. The braiding did not signal a "remission" at all, but simply a sublimation of his wife's anger. Hughes now recognizes that the "braiding" of their words altered Plath's "blood," and his "nerves and brain." It may not have been for the best. As he wrote in "9 Willow Street,"

> . . . Alone,
> Either of us might have met with a life.
> Siamese-twinned, each of us festering
> A unique soul-sepsis for the other,
> Each of us was the stake
> Impaling the other. We struggled
> Quietly through the streets, affirming each other,
> Dream-maimed and dream-blind.   (*CPH* 1088)

Hughes goes on to describe himself as Plath's parasite, writing how he "Hung on you, fed on you," and later wondered whether their "collaboration" had produced anything of value: "What a waste! | What did our spectre-blinded searching reach | Or wake to, that was worth it?" (1089). The sick bat that locks onto Hughes's finger at the end of the poem further recalls, as I have noted, the motif of vampiric attachment both poets had explored in their work. These brief admissions of parasitism (rather than symbiosis) contradict Hughes's deterministic suggestion that the ghost of Otto Plath drove them apart. Hughes's admissions of his rivalry with Plath are among the most moving moments in *Birthday Letters*, for they are clear-eyed assessments of one of the main sources of tension within the marriage—not Plath's devotion to her dead father, or her depression, but the rivalry itself.

Birthday Letters, like *Ariel*, is a failed work of mourning. Yet, as in *Ariel*, the failure to mourn the lost lover and rival—a failure enacted through frequent expressions of self-abasement, self-pity, and anger—resulted in an innovative book of poems. While it is still too early to predict the place *Birthday Letters* will occupy in the twentieth-century poetry canon, it will likely assume, along with Donald Hall's *Without* and Paul Muldoon's "Incantata," a position of prominence among the late century's elegiac sequences. This suggests that even within the most intense literary rivalries, imitation can lead to innovation, for in both

Ariel and *Birthday Letters* engagement with the lost rival opened up new modes of expressive and aesthetic possibility. Indeed, it is not only Hughes's expressions of tenderness toward his lost wife that makes *Birthday Letters* so poignant, but his bursts of anger. It is this anger—towards Plath, her illness, her ambition, and her writing—that ultimately suggests the depth and profundity of Hughes's loss. *Birthday Letters* is a fitting final homage to Plath, for no other book by Hughes reveals the grief of influence—and the influence of grief—so intimately. Both *Birthday Letters* and *Ariel* show that, much as the poets sought to purge their lives and their work of each other, they were never able to do so. The compulsion to engage with the other's words in their final collections was driven not only by rivalry, anger, and grief, but the need to continue a poetic dialogue that began the night Plath first quoted Hughes's poem to him. Neither would ever find a closer reader. Indeed, what Plath prophesized to her mother two months after she met Hughes would eventually come to pass, though in markedly different terms than those she had once envisioned: "the world will come to see him in the light of my look, even as I shall be the most beautiful woman in the blazing sun of his belief in me. So there it is, the two of us."[13]

---

[13] Sylvia Plath to Aurelia Plath, May 10, 1956, Lilly.

Bibliography

Note: All unpublished material from Emory, Lilly, Smith, and the British Library is cited in the footnotes. The following is a list of published sources only.

Alexander, Peter F. *Leonard and Virginia Woolf: A Literary Partnership* (New York: St. Martin's Press, 1992).

Allen, Walter. "London Letter," *New York Times Book Review* (January 29, 1961).

Alvarez, Al. "Tough Young Poet," *Observer* (October 6, 1957), 12.

—— (ed.). *The New Poetry*, rev edn (London: Penguin, 1962; 1966).

—— "The Literature of the Holocaust," *Commentary* 34 (November 1964), 65–9.

—— *The Savage God: A Study of Suicide* (London: Weidenfeld and Nicolson, 1971).

—— *Where Did It All Go Right?* (London: Richard Cohen, 1999).

—— "Ted, Sylvia and Me," *Observer* (January 4, 2004).

Anderson, Nathalie. "Ted Hughes and the Challenge of Gender," in Keith Sagar (ed.), *The Challenge of Ted Hughes* (New York: St. Martin's Press, 1994), 91–115.

Anonymous. "Verse in Brief," *New Yorker* (April 19, 1958), 144.

Axelrod, Steven Gould. *Sylvia Plath: The Wound and the Cure of Words* (Baltimore: Johns Hopkins University Press, 1990).

Badia, Janet. "The 'Priestess' and Her 'Cult': Plath's Confessional Poetics and the Mythology of Women Readers," in Anita Helle (ed.), *The Unraveling Archive: Essays on Sylvia Plath* (Ann Arbor: University of Michigan Press, 2007), 159–81.

Becker, Jillian. *Giving Up: The Last Days of Sylvia Plath* (New York: St. Martin's Press, 2002).

Beer, John. *Post-Romantic Consciousness* (Basingstoke: Palgrave Macmillan, 2003).

Benstock, Bernard. "Non-Negotiable Bonds: Lillian Hellman and Dashiell Hammett," in Whitey Chadwick and Isabelle de Courtivron (eds), *Significant Others: Creativity and Intimate Partnership* (London: Thames and Hudson, 1993), 173–87.

Bentley, Paul. "Depression and Ted Hughes's *Crow*, or through the Looking Glass and What Crow Found There," *Twentieth Century Literature* 43.1 (1997), 27–40.

—— " 'Hitler's Familiar Spirits': Negative Dialectics in Sylvia Plath's 'Daddy' and Ted Hughes's 'Hawk Roosting,' " *Critical Survey* 12.3 (2000), 27–38.

Bishop, Nick. "Ted Hughes and the Death of Poetry," in Keith Sagar (ed.), *The Challenge of Ted Hughes* (New York: St. Martin's Press, 1994), 1–10.

Bloom, Harold. *The Anxiety of Influence: A Theory of Poetry*, 2nd edn (Oxford: Oxford University Press, 1973; 1997).

—— "The Sorrows of American-Jewish Poetry," in *Figures of Capable Imagination* (New York: Seabury Press, 1976), 247–62.

—— (ed.). *Sylvia Plath* (New York: Chelsea House, 1989).

Brain, Tracy. " 'Your Puddle-jumping daughter': Sylvia Plath's Midatlanticism," *English* 47 (1998), 17–39.

—— *The Other Sylvia Plath* (London: Longman, 2001).

Britzolakis, Christina. *Sylvia Plath and the Theatre of Mourning* (Oxford: Oxford University Press, 1999).

Bundtzen, Lynda K. "Poetic Arson and Sylvia Plath's 'Burning the Letters.'" *Contemporary Literature* 39.3 (1998), 434–51.

—— *The Other Ariel* (Amherst: University of Massachusetts Press, 2001).

Burke, Edmund. *A Philosophical Enquiry into the Origins of Our Ideas of the Sublime and Beautiful* (1757; Oxford: Oxford University Press, 1998).

Cam, Heather. " 'Daddy': Sylvia Plath's Debt to Anne Sexton," *American Literature* 59.3 (1987), 429–32.

Carey, John. "Shaman Scandal," *Sunday Times* (April 5, 1992).

Castronovo, David. *Beyond the Gray Flannel Suit: Books from the 1950s that Made American Culture* (New York: Continuum, 2005).

Churchwell, Sarah. "Ted Hughes and the Corpus of Sylvia Plath," *Criticism* 15.1 (1998), 99–132.

—— "Secrets and Lies: Plath, Privacy, Publication and Ted Hughes's *Birthday Letters*," *Contemporary Literature* 42.1 (2001), 102–48.

—— *The Many Lives of Marilyn Monroe* (New York: Henry Holt, 2004).

—— "Love at the barre," *Times Literary Supplement* (December 17, 2004).

Conquest, Robert (ed.). *New Lines* (London: Macmillan, 1956).

—— (ed.). *New Lines II* (London: Macmillan, 1963).

Cooper, Brian. "Sylvia Plath and the Depression Continuum," *Journal of the Royal Society of Medicine* 96 (2003), 296–301.

Davison, Peter. *The Fading Smile: Poets in Boston from Robert Lowell to Sylvia Plath* (New York: Knopf, 1994).

Day, Philip. "A Pride of Poets," *Sunday Times* (June 26, 1960).

De Beauvoir, Simone. *The Second Sex* (1949), trans. and ed. H. M. Parshley (New York: Vintage, 1989.

Douglas, Keith. *Keith Doulgas: Poems Selected by Ted Hughes* (London: Faber and Faber, 1964; 2006).

Dyson, A. E. "Ted Hughes," *Critical Quarterly* 1.3 (1959), 219–26.

Eagleton, Terry. "Will and Ted's Bogus Journey," *Guardian* (April 2, 1992).

Eddins, Dwight. "Ted Hughes and Schopenhauer: The Poetry of the Will," *Twentieth Century Literature* 45.1 (1999), 94–109.

Eksteins, Modris. *Rites of Spring: The Great War and the Birth of the Modern Age* (Boston/New York: Mariner Books, 2000).

Eliot, T. S. *Collected Poems 1909–1962* (New York: Harcourt Brace, 1968).

Ennis, Stephen. "Sylvia Plath, Ted Hughes, and the Myth of Textual Betrayal," *Papers of the Bibliographical Society of America* 101.1 (2007), 63–71.

Faas, Ekbert. *Ted Hughes: The Unaccommodated Universe* (Santa Barbara: Black Sparrow Press, 1980).

—— "Chapters in a Mythology: Sylvia Plath and Ted Hughes," in Keith Sagar (ed.), *The Achievement of Ted Hughes* (Athens: University of Georgia Press, 1983), 107–24.

Fainlight, Ruth. "Sylvia and Jane: Women on the Verge of Fame and Family," *Times Literary Supplement* (December 12, 2003).

Feinstein, Elaine. *Ted Hughes: The Life of a Poet* (London: Weidenfeld and Nicolson, 2001).

Foster, John Burt. *Heirs to Dionysus: A Nietzschean Current in Literary Modernism* (Princeton: Princeton University Press, 1981).

Freud, Sigmund. "Mourning and Melancholia," in *Standard Edition of the Complete Psychological Works of Sigmund Freud*, vol. 14, trans. James Strachey (London: Hogarth Press and the Institute of Psycho-Analysis, 1953; 1973), 243–58.

Friedan, Betty. *The Feminine Mystique* (1963; New York: Norton, 2001).

Fromm, Erich. *The Art of Loving* (London: Allen and Unwin, 1957; 1960).

Fuller, Roy. "Views," review of *Crow*, by Ted Hughes, *The Listener* (March 11, 1971), 296–7.

Gay, Peter. "Introduction," in *Basic Writings of Nietzsche*, trans. and ed. Walter Kaufmann (New York: Modern Library/Random House, 2000).

Ghose, Zulfikar. "The Hawk Above London Zoo," *Western Daily Press* (February 22, 1961).

Gifford, Terry, and Neil Roberts. *Ted Hughes: A Critical Study* (London: Faber and Faber, 1981).

Gilbert, Sandra. " 'A Fine White Flying Myth': Confessions of a Plath Addict," in Harold Bloom (ed.), *Sylvia Plath* (New York: Chelsea House, 1989), 49–65.

—— and Susan Gubar. *The Madwoman in the Attic: The Woman Writer and the Nineteenth-Century Literary Imagination*, 3rd edn (New Haven: Yale University Press, 1979; 1984; 2000).

—— and —— *No Man's Land: The Place of the Woman Writer in the Twentieth Century*, vol. 1: *The War of Words* (New Haven: Yale University Press, 1994).

—— and —— *No Man's Land: The Place of the Woman Writer in the Twentieth Century*, vol. 3: *Letters from the Front* (New Haven: Yale University Press, 1994).

Giles, Paul. "Double Exposure: Sylvia Plath and the Aesthetics of Transnationalism," *Symbiosis* 5.2 (2001), 103–20.

Gill, Joanna. " 'My Sweeney, Mr. Eliot': Anne Sexton and the 'Impersonal Theory of Poetry,' " *Journal of Modern Literature* 27.1/2 (2003), 36–56.

—— (ed.), *The Cambridge Companion to Sylvia Plath* (Cambridge: Cambridge University Press, 2006).

Gordon, John. "Being Sylvia Being Ted Being Dylan: Plath's 'The Snowman on the Moor,' " *Journal of Modern Literature* 27.1/2 (2003), 188–92.

Gordon, Lyndall. *T. S. Eliot: An Imperfect Life* (New York: Norton, 2000).

Graves, Robert. *The White Goddess: A Historical Grammar of Poetic Myth*, 2nd edn (New York: Farrar, Straus and Giroux, 1948; 1975).

—— *Collected Poems*, 2nd edn (Garden City, NY: Doubleday, 1958; 1961).

Gubar, Susan. *Poetry after Auschwitz: Remembering What One Never Knew* (Bloomington/Indianapolis: Indiana University Press, 2003).

Hainsworth, J. D. "Ted Hughes and Violence", *Essays in Criticism* 16.1 (1965), 356–9.

Hall, Donald. *Without* (New York: Houghton Mifflin, 1998).

—— *The Best Day the Worst Day: Life with Jane Kenyon* (Boston/New York: Mariner Books, 2006).

Harris, Mason. Review of *The Bell Jar*, by Sylvia Plath. *West Coast Review* 8 (1973), 54. Reprinted in Linda Wagner-Martin (ed.), *Sylvia Plath: The Critical Heritage* (Abingdon: Routledge, 1989), 108.

Heaney, Seamus. "Hughes and England," in Keith Sagar (ed.), *The Achievement of Ted Hughes* (Manchester: Manchester University Press, 1983), 14–21.

—— "The Indefatigable Hoof-taps: Sylvia Plath," in *The Government of the Tongue* (London: Faber and Faber, 1988), 148–70.

—— "A Wounded Power Rises from the Depths," *Irish Times* (January 27, 1998).

Heath, Stephen. "Joan Riviere and the Masquerade," in Victor Burgin, James Donald and Cora Kaplan (eds), *Formations of Fantasy* (London/New York: Methuen, 1986), 45–61.

Horder, John. "Desk Poet," *Guardian* (March 23, 1965).

Howe, Irving. "A Partial Dissent," in Harold Bloom (ed.), *Sylvia Plath* (New York: Chelsea House, 1989), 5–15.

Hughes, Ted. "Ted Hughes Writes," *Poetry Book Society Bulletin* (September 15, 1957).

—— *The Hawk in the Rain* (London: Faber and Faber, 1957).

—— *Lupercal* (London: Faber and Faber, 1960).

—— "Context," *London Magazine* 1.2 (February 1962).

—— "The Poetry of Keith Douglas," *Listener* (June 21, 1962), 1069–72.

—— "The Poetry of Keith Douglas," *Critical Inquiry* (Spring 1963).

—— "The Rock," *Listener* (September 19, 1963), 421–3.

—— "The Rat Under the Bowler," *Saturday Night* (November 1963), 21–7.

—— *How the Whale Became* (London: Faber and Faber, 1963).

—— "Introduction," in *Keith Douglas: Poems Selected by Ted Hughes* (London: Faber and Faber, 1964; 2006), ix-xii.

—— "The Rock," in *Writers on Themselves* (London: BBC, 1964), 86–92.

—— "Sylvia Plath," *Poetry Book Society Bulletin* 44 (February 1965).

—— "Notes on the Chronological Order of Sylvia Plath's Poems," *Tri-Quarterly* 7 (1966), 81–8.

—— *Wodwo* (London: Faber and Faber, 1967).

—— "Capturing Animals," in *Poetry in the Making: An Anthology of Poems and Programmes from Listening and Writing*, 2nd edn (London: Faber and Faber, 1967; 1982), 15–21.

—— *Crow: From the Life and Songs of the Crow* (London: Faber and Faber, 1970).

—— "Publishing Sylvia Plath," *Observer* (November 21, 1971).

—— "Myth and Education," in Geoff Fox et al. (eds), *Writers, Critics and Children* (London: Heinemann, 1976).

—— *Gaudete* (London: Faber and Faber, 1977).

—— "Introduction," in Sylvia Plath, *Johnny Panic and the Bible of Dreams* (London: Faber and Faber, 1977), 11–13.

—— "Introduction," in *Sylvia Plath: Collected Poems*, ed. Ted Hughes (London: Faber and Faber, 1981).

—— "Sylvia Plath and Her Journals," *Grand Street* 1.3 (1982), 86–99. Reprinted in *Winter Pollen*, ed. William Scammell (New York: Picador, 1995), 177–90.

—— *Winter Pollen: Occasional Prose*, ed. William Scammell (New York: Picador, 1995).

—— "Ted Hughes: The Art of Poetry, LXXI" (interview with Drue Heinz), *The Paris Review* 134 (1995), 54–94.

—— *Difficulties of a Bridegroom* (New York: Picador, 1995).

—— *Collected Poems* (New York: Farrar, Straus and Giroux, 2003).

—— and Sylvia Plath "Two of a Kind: Poets in Partnership," Interview with Owen Leeming, *Third Programme*, BBC, London, January 18, 1961 (National Sound Archives, British Library).

Ingelbien, Raphael. "Mapping the Misreadings: Ted Hughes, Seamus Heaney, and Nationhood," *Contemporary Literature* 40.4 (1999), 627–58.

John-Steiner, Vera. *Creative Collaboration* (New York: Oxford University Press, 2000).

Kakutani, Michiko. "A Portrait of Plath in Poetry for Its Own Sake," review *of Birthday Letters*, by Ted Hughes, *New York Times* (February 13, 1998).

Kaufmann, Walter. *Nietzsche: Philosopher, Psychologist, Antichrist* (1950), 4th edn (Princeton: Princeton University Press, 1974).

Kendall, Tim. *Sylvia Plath: A Critical Study* (London: Faber and Faber, 2001).

—— "Famous nearly last words," *Times Literary Supplement* (November 26, 2004).

—— "Fighting Back Over the Same Ground: Ted Hughes and War," *Yale Review* 93.1 (2005), 87–102.

—— *Modern English War Poetry* (Oxford: Oxford University Press, 2006).

Kenner, Hugh. "Sincerity Kills," in Gary Lane (ed.), *Sylvia Plath: New Views on the Poetry* (Baltimore/London: Johns Hopkins University Press, 1979), 33–44.

Kermode, Frank. "Ted Hughes Charges at Shakespeare," *Sunday Telegraph* (April 5, 1992).

Kopp, Jane Baltzell. " 'Gone, Very Gone Youth': Sylvia Plath at Cambridge, 1955–1957," in Linda Wagner-Martin (ed.), *Sylvia Plath: The Critical Heritage* (Abingdon: Routledge, 1989), 61–80.

Kroll, Judith. *Chapters in a Mythology: The Poetry of Sylvia Plath* (New York: Harper and Row, 1976).

Krook, Dorothea. "Recollections of Sylvia Plath," in Edward Butscher (ed.), *Sylvia Plath: The Woman and the Work* (New York: Dodd, 1977).

Laing, R. D. *The Divided Self: An Existential Study in Sanity and Madness*, 3rd edn (London: Tavistock, 1960; London: Penguin, 1990).

Lane, Gary. "Influence and Originality in Plath's Poems," in Gary Lane (ed.), *Sylvia Plath: New Views on the Poetry* (Baltimore/London: Johns Hopkins University Press, 1979), 116–37.

Lawrence, D. H. *Phoenix: The Posthumous Papers of D. H. Lawrence*, ed. Edward D. McDonald (New York: Viking, 1936).

—— *Selected Poetry*, ed. Keith Sagar, 2nd edn (London: Penguin, 1972; 1986).

—— *Women in Love* (1920; New York: Bantam, 1996).

—— *The Man Who Died* (1931; London: Heinemann, 1950). (Sylvia Plath's copy).

—— *Lady Chatterley's Lover* (1928; New York: Barnes and Noble, 2005).

Leavis, F. R., and Denys Thompson. *Culture and Environment* (London: Chatto and Windus, 1933).

Leonard, Gary M. "Sylvia Plath and the Reporting of the Holocaust in the Popular Press," in Sanford Pinsker and Jack Fischel (eds), *Holocaust Studies Annual 1991* (New York: Garland, 1992).

Logan, William. "You must not take it so hard, Madame." *Salmagundi* 135/136 (2002), 127–48.

Lowell, Robert. "Foreword," in Sylvia Plath, *Ariel* (New York: Harper and Row, 1965).

—— *Collected Poems*, ed. Frank Bidart and David Gewanter (New York: Farrar, Strauss and Giroux, 2003).

Lyall, Sarah. "Ted Hughes, 68, a Symbolic Poet and Sylvia Plath's Husband, Dies," *New York Times* (October 30, 1998).

McClatchy, J. D. "Short Circuits and Folding Mirrors," in Gary Lane (ed.), *Sylvia Plath: New Views on the Poetry* (Baltimore/London: Johns Hopkins University Press, 1979), 19–32.

McGann, Jerome. *The Textual Condition* (Princeton: Princeton University Press, 1991).

Magee, Bryan. *The Philosophy of Schopenhauer* (New York: Oxford University Press, 1983).

Malcolm, Janet. *The Silent Woman: Ted Hughes and Sylvia Plath* (London/Basingstoke: Papermac Macmillan, 1994).

Matovich, Richard M. *A Concordance to the Collected Poems of Sylvia Plath* (New York: Garland, 1986).

Mazzaro, Jerome. "Sylvia Plath and the Cycles of History," in Gary Lane (ed.), *Sylvia Plath: New Views on the Poetry* (Baltimore/London: Johns Hopkins University Press, 1979), 218–39.

Merwin, W. S. Review of *The Hawk in the Rain*, by Ted Hughes, *New York Times Book Review* (October 6, 1957).

Meyers, Jeffrey. "Terminator: The Legacy of Ted Hughes," *Virginia Quarterly Review* 80.2 (2004), 219–32.

Middlebrook, Diane. *Anne Sexton: A Biography* (Boston: Houghton Mifflin, 1991).

—— *Her Husband: Hughes and Plath—A Marriage* (New York: Viking Press, 2003).

—— "Stevens in the Marriage of Sylvia Plath and Ted Hughes," *Wallace Stevens Journal* 30.1 (2006), 45–51.

—— "The Poetry of Sylvia Plath and Ted Hughes: Call and Response," in Jo Gill (ed.), *The Cambridge Companion to Sylvia Plath* (Cambridge: Cambridge University Press, 2006), 156–71.

Miller, Jean Baker. *Toward a New Psychology of Women*, 2nd edn (Boston: Beacon Press, 1976; 1986).

Miller, Lucasta. *The Brontë Myth* (New York: Anchor Books, 2001).

Milton, Colin. *Lawrence and Nietzsche: A Study in Influence* (Aberdeen: Aberdeen University Press, 1987).

Moses, Kate. *Wintering: A Novel of Sylvia Plath* (New York: Anchor Books, 2003).

Muir, Edwin. Review of *The Hawk in the Rain*, by Ted Hughes, *New Statesman* (September 28, 1957).

Myers, Lucas. *Crow Steered Bergs Appeared: A Memoir of Ted Hughes and Sylvia Plath* (Sewanee, TN: Proctor's Hall Press, 2001).

Narbeshuber, Lisa. "The Poetics of Torture: The Spectacle of Sylvia Plath's Poetry," *Canadian Review of American Studies* 34.2 (2004), 185–203.

Nehring, Christina. "Domesticated Goddess," review of *Her Husband: Hughes and Plath—A Marriage*, by Diane Middlebrook, *Atlantic Monthly* (April 2004), 120–6.

Nietzsche, Friedrich. *The Gay Science*, trans. Walter Kaufmann (New York: Vintage Books, 1974).

—— *Thus Spoke Zarathustra*, The Portable Nietzsche, trans. Walter Kaufmann (New York: Penguin, 1982).

—— *Basic Writings of Nietzsche*, trans. and ed. Walter Kaufmann (New York: Modern Library, 2000).

Oates, Joyce Carol. "The Death Throes of Romanticism: The Poetry of Sylvia Plath," *Southern Review* 9.3 (1973), 501–22.

Ostriker, Alicia. *Stealing the Language: The Emergence of Women's Poetry in America* (Boston: Beacon Press, 1986).

—— "The Americanization of Sylvia," in Linda Wagner-Martin (ed.), *Sylvia Plath: The Critical Heritage* (Abingdon: Routledge, 1989), 97–109.

Paulin, Tom. "Protestant Guilt," *London Review of Books* (April 9, 1992).

Pearsall, Cornelia D. J. "The War Remains of Keith Douglas and Ted Hughes," in Tim Kendall (ed.), *The Oxford Handbook of British and Irish War Poetry* (Oxford: Oxford University Press, 2007), 524–41.

Peel, Robin. *Writing Back: Sylvia Plath and Cold War Politics* (London: Associated University Press, 2002).

—— "The Ideological Apprenticeship of Sylvia Plath," *Journal of Modern Literature* 27.4 (2004), 59–72.

—— "From Dogs to Crow: Ted Hughes and a 'world lost,' 1956–1970," *English* 55.212 (2006), 157–80.

Perloff, Marjorie. "The Two *Ariels*: The (Re)Making of the Sylvia Plath Canon," in Neil Fraistat (ed.), *Poems in Their Place: The Intertextuality and Order of Poetic Collections* (Chapel Hill: University of North Carolina Press, 1986), 308–33.

Plath, Sylvia. "Cambridge Letter," *Isis* (May 16, 1956), 9.

—— *The Colossus and Other Poems* (New York: Alfred A. Knopf, 1962).

—— *The Bell Jar* (London: Faber and Faber, 1963).

—— *Ariel* (New York: Harper and Row, 1965).

—— "Interview with Peter Orr," in Peter Orr (ed.), *The Poet Speaks: Interviews with Contemporary Poets* (New York: Barnes and Noble, 1966).

—— *Johnny Panic and the Bible of Dreams* (London: Faber and Faber, 1977).

—— *Letters Home*, ed. Aurelia Plath (London: Faber and Faber, 1978).

—— "Nine Letters to Lynne Lawner," *Antaeus* 28 (1978), 31–49.

—— *Collected Poems*, ed. Ted Hughes (London: Faber and Faber, 1981).

—— *The Unabridged Journals of Sylvia Plath, 1950–1962*, ed. Karen Kukil (London: Faber and Faber, 2000).

—— *Ariel: The Restored Edition* (New York: HarperCollins, 2004).

Pollak, Vivian R. "Moore, Plath, Hughes, and 'The Literary Life,'" *American Literary History* 17.1 (2005), 95–117.

Pollit, Katha. "Peering Into the Bell Jar," review of *Birthday Letters*, by Ted Hughes, *New York Times*, March 1, 1998).

Porter, David. "Beasts/Shamans/Baskin: The Contemporary Aesthetics of Ted Hughes," in Leonard Scigaj (ed.), *Critical Essays on Ted Hughes* (New York: G. K. Hall, 1992), 49–66.

Pound, Ezra. *Literary Essays of Ezra Pound*, ed. T. S. Eliot (London: Faber and Faber, 1954).

Press, John. "A Poet Arrives," *Sunday Times* (November 3, 1957).

Ramazani, Jahan. *Poetry of Mourning: The Modern English Elegy from Hardy to Heaney* (Chicago: University of Chicago Press, 1994).

Rawson, C. J. "Ted Hughes: A Reappraisal," *Essays in Criticism* 15.1 (1965), 77–94.

—— "Ted Hughes and Violence," *Essays in Criticism* 16.1 (1966), 124–9.

Rich, Adrienne. *On Lies, Secrets, and Silence: Selected Prose 1966–1978* (New York: Norton, 1979).

Riviere, Joan. "Womanliness as Masquerade," in Victor Burgin, James Donald, and Cora Kaplan (eds), *Formations of Fantasy* (London/New York: Methuen, 1986), 35–44.

Roberts, Neil. "The Common Text of Sylvia Plath and Ted Hughes," *Symbiosis* 7.1 (2003), 157–73.

—— *Ted Hughes: A Literary Life* (Basingstoke/New York: Palgrave Macmillan, 2006).

Robins, Corrine. "Four Young Poets," *Mademoiselle* (January 1959), 32–5.

Rose, Jacqueline. *The Haunting of Sylvia Plath* (London: Virago, 1991).

Rowland, Antony. *Holocaust Poetry* (Edinburgh: Edinburgh University Press, 2005).

Royle, Anthony. "Letter to the Editor: Sylvia Plath and the Depression Continuum," *Journal of the Royal Society of Medicine* 96 (2003), 471–2.

Sacks, Peter. *The English Elegy: Studies in the Genre from Spenser to Yeats* (Baltimore: Johns Hopkins University Press, 1987).

Sagar, Keith. *The Art of Ted Hughes* (Cambridge: Cambridge University Press, 1975).

—— "The Poetry Does Not Matter," in Leonard Scigaj (ed.), *Critical Essays on Ted Hughes* (New York: G. K. Hall, 1992), 99–108.

—— *The Laughter of Foxes: A Study of Ted Hughes* (Liverpool: Liverpool University Press, 2000).

Schoefield, Annie. "Hughes and the Movement," in Keith Sagar (ed.), *The Achievement of Ted Hughes* (Athens: University of Georgia Press, 1983), 22–36.

Schopenhauer, Arthur. *The World as Will and Representation*, trans. E. F. J. Payne, 2 vols (New York: Dover, 1969).

Scigaj, Leonard. *The Poetry of Ted Hughes: Form and Imagination* (Iowa City: University of Iowa Press, 1986).

Seymour, William Kean. "To Note and To Observe," *Poetry Review* (January 1958).

Showalter, Elaine. *A Literature of Their Own: British Women Novelists from Brontë to Lessing* (Princeton: Princeton University Press, 1977).

—— *The Female Malady: Women, Madness and English Culture, 1830–1980*, 2nd edn (London: Virago, 1987; 2001).

Silkin, Jon. "Ted Hughes and Violence," *Stand* 6 (1963).

Skelton, Robin. "Current Verses," *Manchester Guardian* (October 4, 1957).

Smith, Stan. "Wolf Masks: The Early Poetry of Ted Hughes," in Leonard Scigaj (ed.), *Critical Essays on Ted Hughes* (New York: G. K. Hall, 1992), 67–81.

Sontag, Susan. "Fascinating Fascism," review of *The Last of the Nuba*, by Leni Riefenstahl, and *SS Regalia*, by Jack Pia, *New York Review of Books* (February 6, 1975).

Stein, Gertrude. *Everybody's Autobiography* (New York: Vintage, 1973).

Steiner, George. *Language and Silence: Essays on Language, Literature, and the Inhuman*, 2nd edn (New Haven: Yale University Press, 1970; 1998).

—— "In Extremis," in Eric Homberger, William Janeway, and Simon Schama (eds), *The Cambridge Mind: Ninety Years of the Cambridge Review: 1879–1969* (London: Jonathan Cape, 1970), 303–7.

Stevenson, Anne. *Bitter Fame: A Life of Sylvia Plath*, 2nd edn (New York: Penguin, 1990; 1998).

Stillinger, Jack. *Multiple Authorship and the Myth of Solitary Genius* (New York: Oxford University Press, 1991).

Stone, Marjorie, and Judith Thompson (eds). *Literary Couplings: Writing Couples, Collaborators, and the Construction of Authorship* (Madison: University of Wisconsin Press, 2006).

Tanner, Michael. *Nietzsche: A Very Short Introduction* (Oxford: Oxford University Press, 2000).

Bibliography 251

Thurley, Geoffrey. *The Ironic Harvest: English Poetry in the Twentieth Century* (London: Arnold, 1974).

Tyler, Ralph. "A Good Time to be a Poet," *London/American* (April 27–May 3, 1961), 7.

Uroff, Margaret Dickie. *Sylvia Plath and Ted Hughes* (Urbana: University of Illinois Press, 1979).

Van Dyne, Susan. "Fueling the Phoenix Fire: The Manuscripts of Sylvia Plath's 'Lady Lazarus,'" in Harold Bloom (ed.), *Sylvia Plath* (New York: Chelsea House, 1989), 133–47.

—— *Revising Life: Sylvia Plath's Ariel Poems* (Chapel Hill: University of North Carolina Press, 1993).

Vendler, Helen. "An Intractable Metal," *New Yorker* (February 15, 1982), 124–38. Rpt. in Paul Alexander (ed.), *Ariel Ascending: Writings about Sylvia Plath* (New York: Harper and Row, 1985).

Vogel, Amber. "Not Elizabeth to His Raleigh: Laura Riding, Robert Graves, and the Origins of the White Goddess," in Marjorie Stone and Judith Thompson (eds), *Literary Couplings: Writing Couples, Collaborators, and the Construction of Authorship* (Madison: University of Wisconsin Press, 2006), 229–39.

Wagner, Erica. *Ariel's Gift: Ted Hughes, Sylvia Plath, and the Story of* Birthday Letters (London: Faber and Faber, 2000).

Wagner-Martin, Linda. *Sylvia Plath: A Biography* (New York: Simon and Schuster, 1987).

—— (ed.). *Sylvia Plath: The Critical Heritage* (Abingdon: Routledge, 1989).

Weisser, Susan Ostrov. "Introduction," in D. H. Lawrence, *Lady Chatterley's Lover* (New York: Barnes and Nobles, 2005).

Weissman, Gary. *Fantasies of Witnessing: Postwar Efforts to Experience the Holocaust* (Ithaca, NY: Cornell University Press, 2004).

Whittington-Egan, Richard. "Ted Hughes and Sylvia Plath—A Marriage Examined," review of *Her Husband—Hughes and Plath: A Marriage*, by Diane Middlebrook, *Contemporary Review* 286.1669 (2005), 117–19.

Wiesel, Elie. "A Plea for the Dead," in Lawrence Langer (ed.), *Art from the Ashes: A Holocaust Anthology* (New York: Oxford University Press, 1995).

Wineapple, Brenda. *White Heat: The Friendship of Emily Dickinson and Thomas Wentworth Higginson* (New York: Knopf, 2008).

Wood, James. "Muck Funnell," review of *Birthday Letters*, by Ted Hughes, *New Republic* (March 30, 1998), 30–3.

Wyatt-Brown, Bertram. "Ted, Sylvia, and St. Botolph's: A Cambridge Recollection," *Southern Review* 40.2 (2004), 352–69.

Young, James. *Writing and Rewriting the Holocaust: Narrative and the Consequences of Interpretation* (Bloomington: Indiana University Press, 1988).

Index

HUGHES, TED, general: (*cont.*)
"You Hated Spain" 98–9
"Your Paris" 99–100
Fiction and Drama:
"The Calm" 108, 149
"The Rain Horse" 161
"Snow" 49
"The Suitor" 205
The Wound 59, 143–5

Industrial Revolution 211

Jung, Carl 15, 125

Kafka, Franz 138
Kavanagh, Patrick 217
Kenner, Hugh 172
Krook, Dorothea 40

Laing, R. D., *The Divided Self* 11, 132, 134–7,
141–2, 152
Larkin, Philip 27
Lawrence, D. H. 7, 10, 13, 15–16, 18, 20–3,
27, 34, 38, 125, 133, 139–40, 148,
171, 191 n., 193, 218, 232
Lady Chatterley's Lover 20, 23, 34, 41–2
"Love on the Farm" 38, 43, 232
The Man Who Died 40, 41 n.
"Rabbit Snared in the Night" 38, 43, 232
The Rainbow 23–4, 27
Sons and Lovers 42
"When I Went to the Circus" 139
Women in Love 21, 22, 35, 37, 45, 193
Leavis, F. R. 16 n., 40, 75, 95, 148
Leeming, Owen 1, 5, 9, 19, 129
Lowell, Robert 4, 13, 79, 97, 169 n., 171–5,
179–85, 187; *see also* Sylvia Plath, and
influence of Robert Lowell; *see also* Ted
Hughes, and Robert Lowell

MacNeice, Louis 68
Merwin, W. S. 17 n., 35, 65, 97, 182
Moore, Marianne 17, 18, 118 n., 162, 178
Movement, the 16, 17, 25–6, 51, 95, 119,
126–7, 179, 184
Muldoon, Paul 240
Myers, Lucas 3, 12, 17, 24, 52, 55–6, 61,
88, 92–5, 97, 175, 182, 188 n., 203,
222

Nietzsche, Friedrich 10, 15, 20–5, 28–34,
36–7, 40, 42, 45–6, 123–4, 132–4,
137, 139–41, 148, 217; *see also* Sylvia
Plath, and influence of Friedrich
Nietzsche; *see also* Ted Hughes, and
influence of Friedrich Nietzsche

Owen, Wilfred 15, 50, 57

Plath, Aurelia 5, 33, 96, 99, 241
Plath, Otto 99, 127–8, 165–6, 231
PLATH, SYLVIA, general:
American identity 11, 15, 88–109, 113,
115, 151, 228
and Anglophilia 89–90
antipathy toward the Movement 16–20,
127
collaboration with Ted Hughes 1, 13, 17,
18, 49–50, 52, 66
and confessionalism 146–7, 178–85
as consumer 15, 79, 92, 94
"Daddy" controversy 146–7, 153, 190–1
desire for independence within a romantic
relationship 35–6, 68–9
desire for masculine freedom 33, 113–14
desire for strength 33, 45, 66
disaffection toward England 89–92, 104,
109
experience at Cambridge University 88–94,
127–8, 180
experience in Yorkshire 101–9, 116–17
and fascism 29, 132, 138, 142–4, 147–8,
151, 153
fear of "remaking" 68–9, 112–16
and feminism 90
and the femme fatale 131–4, 138, 142,
145–6, 166
and the Holocaust 135, 137–8, 141, 146–9,
206
honeymoon of 69–72
and Ted Hughes
anger toward 12, 130, 132–4, 142, 151–3
attempts to "remake" 54–6, 64–5
construction of 6, 14, 20, 42–6, 54, 62,
101, 107–8, 177
desire to keep writing from 69, 180
faith in Hughes's "genius" 66, 72
as Hughes's "protégé" 29
influence of 1, 3, 9, 10, 12–13, 18, 41–2,
50, 61, 122, 127–9, 131–4, 138–169,
205
jealousy of 5, 8, 9, 67
love for 66, 164
rivalry with 1, 8, 9, 11, 13–15, 18–19,
46, 64, 67–87, 113–18, 121, 134, 151,
153–62, 224–5
separation from 9, 130, 153–5, 163
influence of Keith Douglas 50–2
influence of T. S. Eliot 148–9
influence of Sigmund Freud 134–5, 224–5
influence of Robert Graves 41, 61, 133
influence of R. D. Laing's *The Divided
Self* 134–7, 141